AF607976

LECTOR LUDENS: THE REPRESENTATION OF GAMES AND PLAY IN CERVANTES

Lector Ludens: The Representation of Games and Play in Cervantes

MICHAEL SCHAM

UNIVERSITY OF TORONTO PRESS
Toronto Buffalo London

© University of Toronto Press 2014
Toronto Buffalo London
www.utppublishing.com

ISBN 978-1-4426-4864-7

Library and Archives Canada Cataloguing in Publication

Scham, Michael, 1969–, author
Lector ludens : the representation of games and play in Cervantes / Michael Scham.

Includes bibliographical references and index.
ISBN 978-1-4426-4864-7 (bound)

1. Cervantes Saavedra, Miguel de, 1547–1616 – Criticism and interpretation. 2. Cervantes Saavedra, Miguel de, 1547–1616. Don Quixote. 3. Cervantes Saavedra, Miguel de, 1547–1616. Novelas ejemplares. 4. Games in literature. 5. Play in literature. 6. Leisure in literature. 7. Pleasure in literature. I. Title. II. Title: Representation of games and play in Cervantes.

PQ6351.S33 2014 863'.3 C2014-902069-4

University of Toronto Press acknowledges the financial assistance to its publishing program of the Canada Council for the Arts and the Ontario Arts Council, an agency of the Government of Ontario.

University of Toronto Press acknowledges the financial support of the Government of Canada through the Canada Book Fund for its publishing activities.

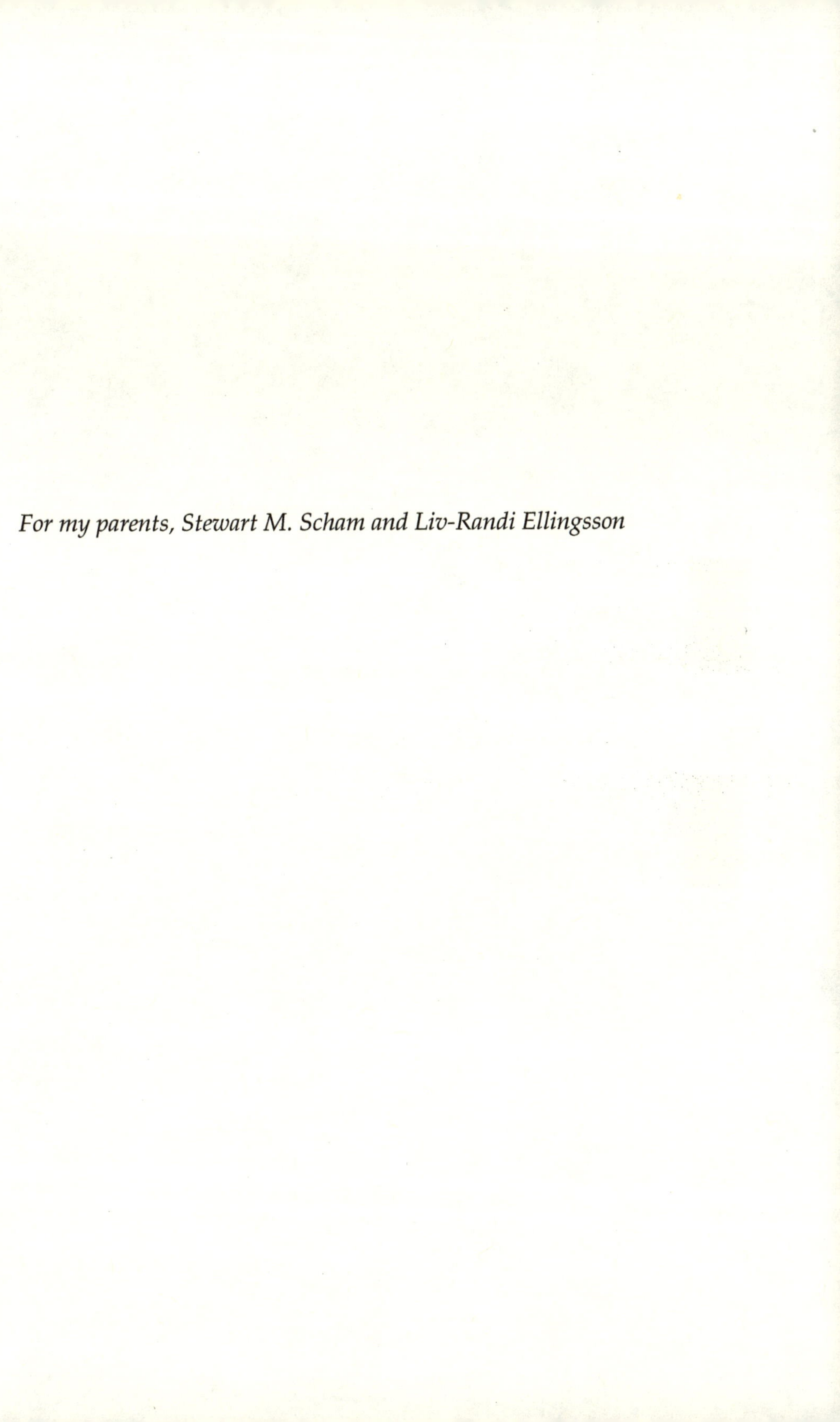

For my parents, Stewart M. Scham and Liv-Randi Ellingsson

Contents

Illustrations

Figures

Acknowledgments

My work on this book benefited from a number of people and institutions. I am especially grateful for the conversation and friendship of Alban Forcione over the years. Amiable correspondence and occasional meetings with William Clamurro, James Iffland (my first Cervantes mentor), and Luis Gómez Canseco have been vital in keeping me engaged. Encounters with Laura Bass in the Sala Cervantes of the Biblioteca Nacional invariably led to additional pertinent sources. Guillermo Morán helped with my palaeography in Ávila, and David Carvajal de la Vega's cheerful generosity at the Universidad de Valladolid and nearby archives was greatly appreciated. I am thankful for a cordial and encouraging group of colleagues at the University of St Thomas. Valentine Pakis provided some timely editing advice, although I prize him even more for our Friday night *agon* at the ping pong table. The ludic spirit of my friend and colleague Ashley Shams was of particular importance during the final stages of this project.

A Sabbatical Assistance Grant from the University of St Thomas for the 2007–8 academic year gave me the time and resources to research and write a substantial portion of the manuscript. A Research Grant from the Program for Cultural Cooperation between Spain's Ministry of Culture and US Universities (now *Hispanex*) facilitated additional work in the Biblioteca Nacional, Madrid, as well as in archives around Valladolid, in January of 2009. Earlier and much-amended versions of materials contained in this book have appeared in the following articles: "Concepts of Play in Literature of Golden Age Spain" (*Hispanófila* no. 135 [2002]); "*Don Quijote* and the Art of Laughing at Oneself" (*Cervantes* 29.1 [2009]); and "Dialogue and Exemplarity in Montaigne and Cervantes" (*Transitions: Journal of Franco-Iberian Studies* vol. 5 [Fall 2009]). My sincere gratitude goes as well to the anonymous readers of the manuscript.

Quotations from *Don Quijote* in Spanish are from the edition of Luis Andrés Murillo (Madrid: Castalia, 1978). Those from the *Novelas ejemplares* are from the Harry Sieber edition (Madrid: Cátedra, 1989). I use the English translation of *Don Quijote* by John Rutherford (Penguin, 2003). For the English passages of *El casamiento engañoso, El coloquio de los perros, El licenciado Vidriera, La gitanilla,* and *Rinconete y Cortadillo,* I use the translation of C.A. Jones (Penguin, 1972). All other translations are my own, unless indicated otherwise in the notes. I have attempted to reach a compromise with the cumbersome issue of original text and translations. Both Spanish and English versions of major primary works are included in the body of the text. This includes the works of Cervantes, and major archival sources from the Biblioteca Nacional in Madrid. For other sources, I include English translations in the main text, and the originals in notes.

LECTOR LUDENS

Introduction

If anyone tells me that it is degrading the Muses to use them only as a plaything and a pastime, he does not know, as I do, the value of pleasure, play, and pastime. I would almost say that any other aim is ridiculous.

(Montaigne, *Essays* III, 3, p. 629)

In addition to introducing a protagonist whose unbounded recreational reading begets an inspired lunacy, *Don Quijote* specifically addresses the reader ("desocupado lector") as an individual at leisure. In the prologue to his *Novelas ejemplares*, Cervantes invites readers to partake in his stories as players in a game: "Mi intento ha sido poner en la plaza de nuestra república una mesa de trucos, donde cada uno pueda llegar a entretenerse" ("My purpose has been to place in the square of our republic a billiards table where each can go to entertain himself"). In support of widely divergent interpretations, critics have held this billiards table up as an emblem of Cervantes's art. It has been compared to the "juego de bolos" – a bowling game – in *El coloquio de los perros*, as a play of arbitrary chance and indeterminacy; it has been taken as an expression of authorial trickiness and deceit, functioning as a companion image to the allegedly subversive reader described in the prologue to *Don Quijote* ("bajo mi manto, al rey mato" – "under my cloak I kill the king," 51); others have seen it as an expression of collaborative, meaningful interaction.[1] While such readings have yielded valuable insights, there has been a tendency to draw far-reaching conclusions regarding Cervantes's "mesa de trucos" without sufficient attention to the many specific games represented in his works, or to contemporary discussions of such games. The present study considers Cervantes's play references within the context of a substantial body of sixteenth and seventeenth-century writings on leisure.

The ludic space that so fascinated Cervantes was the subject of much controversy in contemporary Spain, as evidenced by a profusion of *provisiones* (warrants), *cédulas* (dipatches), *pleitos* (lawsuits) and *arbitrios* (petitions), as well as moral-theological tracts and humanistic writings on games and play (the *tractatus ludorum*). Debates about the permissibility of different games and pastimes centered on a variety of concerns, including the sex and social class of the participant, the venues in which the games were performed (as well as the time of day or night), the ratio of skill and chance involved, and leisure's relationship to the obligations of "purposive reality." Hunting, for example, was seen to provide both recreation and martial training for the nobility. Gambling was almost uniformly frowned upon, and reading fiction was deemed particularly perilous for women. Chess provided a fine mental exercise that reinforced an appreciation of hierarchy, and physical recreation was commonly viewed as salubrious for commoners.[2] As this cursory list suggests, the space of play varied greatly: from the rural *locus amoenus* of classical *otium* to the opulence of the urban court, from the open-air *plaza* to the hidden interior of the gambling den, from the tavern to the monastery courtyard, the *corral de comedias* to the parlour. In addition to structuring the experience in a unique way, each space involves a different sort of interaction, public or private, communal or solitary. The venues also suppose different kinds of spectators: approving and complicit onlookers, arbiters and watchful authorities, or audiences in collective awe, homogenized in mass response. Cervantes explored such variations with great curiosity, and he was well aware that offering his *Novelas ejemplares* as a game in the shared sunlight of "the plaza de nuestra república" was different from positing the reader of *Don Quijote* alone in private domesticity.

While the heart of our inquiry is Cervantes's Spain, we will also consider how the primary works in question were informed by classical writings, and how they in turn have contributed to the development of modern and postmodern concepts of play. In Spain, Alfonso X's interest in games that balance skill and chance (*Libro de los juegos*, 1280) and Jovellanos's emphasis on the civic benefits of leisure (*Memoria sobre las diversiones públicas*, 1790) provide an illuminating frame. Between these reference points, early modern Spain saw the culmination of play as a vital and diverse cultural phenomenon, and also saw intimations of the more restrictive role it was to have within Enlightenment utilitarianism. A number of the documents under consideration pertain to the colonies, and we will observe how the principles set forth in domestic debates (e.g., the rationale for pastimes appropriate to different social strata, and to the clergy within Spain) are extended to the new situation in the Americas. There are, among other things, discussions of how particular recreations affect indigenous people and Chinese workers in the Philippines, why women in the colonies should be prohibited from gaming venues, and why conquistadors may be allowed certain exemptions. What emerges is a diverse body of writings that often produced nuanced arguments for and against the pastimes in question. Despite the constrictive pressures exerted by the Counter-Reformation and the rise of absolutism, and the accompanying interests in limiting and controlling recreation, Spain did not lack advocates of play; and even some of the more censorious moralists reveal an appreciation of the very games they want to prohibit.[3] It therefore would be inaccurate to view Cervantes as a luminous exception to a dour and repressive norm. But Cervantes is unique in the comprehensiveness of his examination of the perils and profits of the individual at leisure.

Play theory comprises a vast field of different disciplines, including literary theory, philosophy, and the social and applied sciences.[4] While we will consider a number of modern theoretical writings on play, it bears emphasizing that the age of Cervantes, Montaigne and Shakespeare produced particularly rich and varied discussions of the topic. Countering the common notion that the consciousness of leisure arises alongside industrial capitalism, Peter Burke points out the emergence of historians of play in early modern Europe, and an interest in leisure from a range of disciplines and discourses, including educational, legal-political, moral-theological, and medical (142–46). My use of play theory ranges from the rather broad consideration of how literature was either justified or censured along with other leisure activities during the period, to analysing the literary work itself as a game, with conventions and "rules" that structure a particular type of experience for the reader. The connections between these two levels of analysis are clarified through attention to the games depicted within the works, and to how they are set forth as analogues to the reading activity (as in the aforementioned examples in the *Novelas ejemplares* and *Don Quijote*). Such an approach allows for the examination of significant formal and narratological questions: What sort of generic markers must be recognized for a successful reading? Is the reader expected to submit to the authority and control of the narrator, as in much didactic literature of the period, or is he or she encouraged to be a participant, creatively engaged in the act of reading?[5]

Since specific recreational activities (or even the possibility of having leisure) depended on one's social position, and since different literary genres were associated with different social strata, a focus on play contributes to our understanding of Cervantes's engagement with his literary horizon and the historical moment reflected and transposed therein: the picaresque with its card-players (e.g., *Rinconete y Cortadillo*), don Quijote's chivalric desire to participate in tournaments, wealthy youth dressing up in pastoral garb to play out dramas of love and escape from society, itinerant entertainers, and so forth. Cervantes's varied shepherds, knights and *pícaros* bear out Huizinga's identification of a high cultural play function in the pastoral and the chivalrous modes during the Renaissance, to which André Jolles added the picaresque.[6] Play theory also permits a rethinking of the peculiar semi-autonomy of the aesthetic space. As a game, the literary work functions according to its own conventions and logic, independent of the real world. But it is not solipsistic; it always refers back to the world, and our participation in play can condition our return to reality. Critiquing the work / play dichotomy characteristic of much Western thought, Norbert Elias argues that play's "reality" resides in its inherently social orientation:

> The theory of leisure set out here would remain incomprehensible if it were not clearly understood that individual leisure activities are social activities in highly differentiated no less than in simpler societies. Even if they take the form of a person's withdrawal from others, they are intrinsically directed either from others to that person, as is the case when he or she listens to a record or reads a book, or from that person to others – whether they are present in the flesh or not – as is the case when he or she writes poetry or plays the violin alone. They are, in short, communications received from or sent out by people in specific group configurations. (*Quest for Excitement* 104)

Cervantes frequently represents characters' transitions between the play sphere (e.g., puppet shows, story manuscripts, card decks) and the social world and, in the process, compels his readers to reflect upon their own transition upon closing the book. Along with the readerly game of recognizing and realizing genre, Cervantes tends to include a "metapoetic" game, a sustained negotiation – with an assortment of fictive readers and narrators – of the shifting rules and boundaries of our activity.[7]

I am particularly interested in examining Cervantine representations of play in the context of humanist and other contemporary writings dealing with recreation and individual development, self-knowledge and social interaction. Important ideas include: Erasmus's understanding of the educational value of play, and of the game as both escape from society and metaphor for participation in it; the "dignity of man" tradition emphasizing the individual's power of imaginative self-transformation (Pico, Vives); and Montaigne's sceptical critique of leisure and the imagination. A consideration of the courtier figure, from Castiglione's conception of civilizing play and social cohesion, to Gracián's vision of the strategically duplicitous individual within the agonistic court society of absolutist Spain, will help clarify the historical development of humanist thought on play. Cervantes, whose affinities with Renaissance humanism inform his perception of what Maravall (*La cultura del Barroco*) characterized as the conflictive, mass culture of Baroque Spain, exhibits elements of these varied outlooks throughout his works. His ideological profile is notoriously ambiguous. The possibility that Cervantes conceived of his *Novelas ejemplares* and *Don Quijote* as radically different works finds support in how leisure activities appear within the respective narratives. Some of his depictions of leisure would seem to authorize the official social hierarchy; others, to register the emergence of a mercantilist, secular mentality, or even liminal societies representing a challenge to official culture. Our survey of the contemporary non-literary writings on play will allow for a refinement of such familiar interpretations. But we will also consider how Cervantes advocates play as valuable apart from pragmatic and political concerns. The freedom play affords to contemplate varieties of experience denied by the limitations of mundane existence, and, not least, the pleasure such activities bring, are paramount concerns throughout his works.

1 Leisure and Recreation in Early Modern Spain

Theoretical Contexts

According to Huizinga's seminal definition, a game is an agreed-upon fiction, an experience created by a particular structure: "It is an activity which proceeds within certain limits of time and space, in a visible order, according to rules freely accepted, and outside the sphere of necessity or material utility" (132). The ordering demarcation of play, and its freedom from both obligation (to participate) and utility (to produce) are fundamental principles, and it will be instructive to see how they are adhered to or transgressed in the specific games considered below. Pointing out that Huizinga's notion of play focuses primarily on competition, Roger Caillois offered refinements of typology, setting forth four primary categories of play – *agon* (competition), *alea* (chance), *mimicry* (acting/simulation) and *ilinx* (vertigo) – along with six basic combinations of these categories: competition-chance, competition-simulation, competition-vertigo, chance-simulation, chance-vertigo, simulation-vertigo. Caillois described these combinations as existing in "contingent" and "fundamental" relationships, and understood play to take place within a continuum between the polarities of *paidia* (free-flowing, spontaneous play) and *ludus* (rule-bound). While bearing the risks of systematization, such categories are useful for examining the nature of the player's engagement in a particular game and how it may relate to the culture in which it takes place. As a form of rule-bound *agon,* for example, the tournaments in which don Quijote hopes to participate reflect an aristocratic ideal of martial prowess. The stasis of Durandarte's plight, haplessly awaiting rescue in the underworld of the Cueva de Montesinos, like a losing player hoping to be dealt a better hand, is aptly expressed in the repetitive *alea* of his famous "paciencia y barajar" ("shuffle the pack and deal again" [*Don Quijote* II, 23]). Cañizares's solitary, hallucinatory "unturas" ("anointings"), the observance of which is the culmination of Berganza's nightmare journey in *El coloquio de los perros*, is a sort of *ilinx*, a solipsistic fantasy that signals her radical detachment from human community.

Both Huizinga and Caillois speculate on the role of play in the development of culture and civilization. An underlying principle of such an approach is akin to sublimation: primal desires and fears are channelled creatively in the play-forms of a particular culture. In "El origen deportivo del estado," cited by Huizinga (55), Ortega y Gasset proposes an ethnography according to which civilization arises through rival groups vying for each other's women. Rather than a simple obeisance to biology, Ortega speculates that an inspired amorous impulse is at work, one that idealizes the distant women of the other group. However questionable Ortega's specific example may be, it is significant in its identification of an agonistic element in the rise of culture, and in its distinction between and sequencing of two fundamental forms of activity, play and work: "an original activity, creative and vital par excellence – which is spontaneous and disinterested – ; another activity which avails itself of and mechanizes the first and which is of a utilitarian character. Utility does not create, it does not invent, it only avails itself of and stabilizes what was created without it."[1] Ortega aligns the play impulse with the artistic, creative faculty, a "sublime inquietude" (642) yielding a surplus that is later put to use by the rational faculty. It is thus inaccurate, for example, simply to understand science as a displacement of myth. The imaginative play of myth, according to Ortega, proposes explanations and possibilities that science then attempts to "mechanize" and quantify.[2]

The trajectory suggested by Huizinga's account of civilization's rise has lead to charges of positivism, ethnocentrism, and an impoverished view of play, one that inevitably gives it a secondary role within a dichotomy between "play" and "seriousness."[3] Jacques Ehrmann maintains that "Caillois subscribes to the same conception of history as Huizinga, a history which would have meaning (direction), i.e., which would move from an original meaninglessness to present meaningfulness; a history in which the 'civilizing' process would have allowed men gradually to rid themselves of the illogicality of the 'earliest ages'; in a word, a history of the conquests of reason" (50).

The following passage from Caillois is a propos of what Ehrmann objects to:

> Any corruption of the principles of play means the abandonment of those precarious and doubtful conventions that it is always permissible, if not profitable, to deny, but the arduous adoption of which is a milestone in the development of civilization. If the principles of play in effect correspond to powerful instincts (competition, chance, simulation, vertigo), it is readily understood that they can be positively and creatively gratified only under ideal circumscribed conditions, which in every case prevail in the rules of play. Left to themselves, destructive and frantic as are all instincts, these basic impulses can hardly lead to any but disastrous consequences. Games discipline instincts and institutionalize them. (55)

Ehrmann rejects a notion of cultural ascendance based on allegedly Western values, for example rationality, productivity, hierarchy and law. His is a familiar and instructive scepticism, in some ways similar to Ortega's critique of the "mechanization" and "quantification" of primal creativity, and it serves as a caution against an unreflective acceptance of official values. It forms part of a broad polemic surrounding the notion of civilization itself. As Burke points out, Norbert Elias and Michel Foucault, much of whose work focused on early modern Europe, represent opposing views: Elias celebrates the refinements of "civilization," while Foucault objects to "discipline," the increasingly rule-bound, regimented nature of modern life (Burke 149–50). While the positive notion of "civilization" implies more sophisticated possibilities of individual expression and group interaction, "discipline" concentrates on the coercive effects of power, on the rise in sophisticated means of control. Without taking sides – although his conclusion seems to endorse Foucault – Burke makes the point that the rise in political and social organization in the early modern period was a catalyst for an awareness and definition of play: "As free time was increasingly organized, and institutionalized, people became more conscious of it as a separate domain, rather than as a pause between bouts of work. As work became less playful and working hours were more sharply defined, there was more need for the non-utilitarian activities we have come to call 'leisure'" (145–6).

As Burke suggests, the ambivalent idea of "civilization" may be considered in terms of a productive tension rather than a reductive polarity. For example, Freud's discussion of varieties of discontent that result from the necessary constraints placed on instinct by civilization is neither highly original nor nuanced, but it treats a seemingly inescapable quandary that arises whenever human communities form (see *Civilization and Its Discontents*). The following account of the "civilizing process" by Huizinga displays an awareness of this tenuous balance:

> As a civilization becomes more complex, more variegated and more overladen, and as the technique of production and social life itself become more finely organized, the old cultural soil is gradually smothered under a rank layer of ideas, systems of thought and knowledge, doctrines, rules and regulations, moralities and conventions which have all lost touch with play. Civilization, we then say, has grown more serious; it assigns only a secondary place to playing. (75)

Ehrmann overstates his case by claiming that in Caillois and Huizinga's writings, "Culture, *their* idea of culture, is at no time called into question by play. On the contrary, it is *given*: a fixed, stable, pre-existent element, serving as a frame of reference in the evaluation of play" (55). One might well ask who is dealing with "fixed, stable, pre-existent" notions here. Despite their limitations, the studies of Caillois and Huizinga do contain nuance and scepticism and self-reflection. Below, we will consider further how Huizinga assigns to play the crucial function of calling into question precisely that which is given, fixed, and stable.

While acknowledging Ehrmann's critique, Eleni Papargyriou proposes that a possible misunderstanding arises from Huizinga and Caillois effectively describing "games" (thus the insistence on a separation from purposive reality), and failing to adequately define "play." This would suggest that the shortcomings of Huizinga and Caillois are due more to the incompleteness of their approach rather than to a fundamental conceptual flaw.[4] Drawing upon Schiller, Gadamer, the developmental psychologist Jean Piaget, and the anthropologist Gregory Bateson, Papargyriou characterizes play as a fictional mode of engagement, a sort of willing suspension of disbelief in which the player at the same time affirms and negates the premise of the activity. In Caillois's *alea*, for example, the player simultaneously yields to arbitrary chance while acting as if it can be controlled or predicted; in *mimicry*, one assumes a new persona while also retaining one's original identity (Papargyriou 12–18). Prefacing her study of games in the modern Greek novel, Papargyriou elaborates on the shifting function and quality of play in literature: "The fact that in play two propositions are simultaneously equated and distinguished means the boundaries between play and reality are fragile and often at risk of breaking down. By the same token, modern and postmodern texts problematize the framing of reality: the act of deception involved in games contributes towards the understanding of modernist techniques, which transgress the stated limits of fictions" (18). B.W. Ife noted the same fundamental ambiguity in his study of Plato's insight into the mysterious enchantment of fiction. Rationally, one understands that a story is a fabrication; but on an aesthetic level, one is swept up into the illusion. Ife makes the important point that we may be unable to maintain the distinction between rational and aesthetic belief, and that the "voluntary *suspension* of disbelief" may in fact require less effort than the *regaining* of it: "An audience can decide to listen or a reader decide to read, but once they have agreed to play along with the author for the sake of argument they will quickly find it difficult to resist the enchantment of the tale" (59). It is only with works that intentionally interrupt the fictional illusion, thereby compelling readers to reflect rationally upon the artifice being presented to them – for example, in picaresque narratives, with the disjunctions between the experiencing and narrating protagonist – that Plato's critique is validly confronted.[5] Consistent with Ife's thesis on the "response" to Platonic objections by the likes of Quevedo, Alemán and Cervantes, Papargyriou traces an increasing activation of the reader in works that foreground their own artificiality. She also identifies a heightened *aleatory* component to reading postmodern narratives, which insist on unpredictability, and the possibility of multiple meanings (25). As a general account of the trajectory of aesthetics from "realism" to "modernism" and "postmodernism," this seems persuasive enough. But it is always tempting to substitute Cortázar and Robbe-Grillet, with their distinctions between passive, conventional readers, and active, unconventional ones, with the likes of Cervantes and Laurence Sterne, who in many ways were never outdone at such games. Borges, himself a master of postmodern play, understood that Cervantes's art has a particular capaciousness in this regard. His reflections in "Magias parciales en el *Quijote*" upon how Cervantes plays intricate games with artifice and literary conventions, set off against a prosaic realm of plausible reality, underscore Cervantes's awareness of the entire range of literary "belief."[6]

A focus on the relative autonomy of the artwork can help us understand its quality as a game ("ludus") as well as the experience and consciousness of play ("paidia") it offers. As Papargyriou suggests, an examination of the ambivalent attitude assumed by the player may resolve some of the objections Ehrmann and others voice to the "play" / "seriousness" dichotomy. On the one hand, the game is a realm of experience and meaning that is realized according to its own structure. Giamatti discussed how the separation of the game from reality affords the freedom to create new possibilities of thought or being: "The purpose of autotelic activity, whether called play or study or leisure or artistic activity, is to fulfil itself without regard to consequence" (38). About the "disinterested" quality of play, Huizinga wrote: "Not being 'ordinary' life it stands outside the immediate satisfaction of wants and appetites, indeed it interrupts the appetitive process" (9). Play is thus free in two senses: there is an absence of coercion to participate; and the game itself is actualized according to its own special logic and rules, that is, not beholden to those of "real life." Reflecting on the literary work as a game, Mihai Spariosu noted that "its effectiveness depends upon its being able to create a free, self-enclosed space or *neutral* play ground, where certain models for or alternatives to reality can be proposed, tested, adopted, and rejected at will" (*Dionysus* 27). Schiller, who asserted that we are most human when at play, discussed how such freedom allows the subject to mediate between the "sensuous" and the "formal drives," that is, between the appetite and the intellect. Such synthesis results in the superior perspective of the "play drive" – superior because it involves an integration of body and mind. Schiller dismisses the false dichotomy between play and seriousness:

> Does it not belie the rational concept as well as the dignity of beauty – which is, after all, her being considered as an instrument of culture – if we limit it to *mere play*? … But how can we speak of *mere* play, when we know that it is precisely play and play *alone*, which of all man's states and conditions is the one that makes him whole and unfolds both sides of his nature at once? (*Letters* 130)

This is an elaboration of the insight expressed some two hundred years earlier by Montaigne: "If anyone tells me that it is degrading the Muses to use them only as a plaything and a pastime, he does not know, as I do, the value of pleasure, play, and pastime. I would almost say that any other aim is ridiculous" (III, 3, 629). For both thinkers, play functions as a vital check to the ossification of an excessively rational and utilitarian outlook. They also remind us that, throughout the so-called Western tradition, there is a consciousness of the fluidity between playfulness and seriousness. It is true that a current of thought – extending from the early modern moralists through Enlightenment figures and the ethos of productivity associated with the Industrial Revolution – does explicitly relegate play to a secondary, supportive role to serious and useful endeavours. But there is also a counter-current that validates and desegregates play, from the Renaissance humanists to the various forms of modernism.

In addition to facilitating reflection upon the physical impulses and the ordering aspirations of the mind, the independence of the game from quotidian concerns allows for an understanding of the relationship between reality and the play sphere. The proposition is not paradoxical because the relationship between play and reality is, as noted above, ambivalent; the independence of the game is in fact a semi-autonomy. As Gadamer observed, play inevitably bears some relationship to purposive reality, however oblique:

> The player, sculptor, or viewer is never simply swept away into a strange world of magic, of intoxication, of dream; rather, it is always his own world, and he comes to belong to it more fully by recognizing himself more profoundly in it. There remains a continuity of meaning which links the work of art with the existing world and from which even the alienated consciousness of a cultured society never quite detaches itself. (133–4)

Huizinga was also aware of this continuity: "It is through playing that society expresses its interpretation of life and the world" (46). And such "interpretations" may or may not approve of the status quo. Games can, for example, reproduce or invert the existing social structure: one might think of Geertz's study of the Balinese cockfights as an example of the former, Bakhtin's account of carnivalesque festivities (*Rabelais and His World*) the latter. Caillois noted that "it is not possible to determine, without prior analysis, which [games] are in accordance with, confirm, or reinforce established values, and conversely, which contradict and flout them, thus representing compensations or safety valves for a given society" (66). Victor Turner observed of post-industrial societies that "the function of many games is to reinforce the mental paradigms we all carry in our heads which motivate us to carry out energetically the tasks our culture defines as belonging to the 'work' sphere" (58–9).[7] This would seem to confirm Ehrmann's critique of Western subordination of play to productive work. And so does the passage cited above by Caillois, since the notion of a "safety valve" implies that, once the disordering inclinations have been innocuously released, one can return to activities that reinforce "established values." Indeed, carnivalesque inversions, like other manifestations of festive culture, contained within prescribed days of the calendar, could also be said to serve the essentially conservative function of the safety valve.[8] But Turner also examines leisure activities that might form the basis for alternative communities, and thus pose a challenge to the status quo. Below we will consider Turner's concepts of the "liminal," the "liminoid," and different forms of "communitas," to examine the extent to which Cervantes's representations of play might articulate alternative modes of being, ones that implicitly critique contemporary arrangements. Vis-à-vis established literary genres, Cervantes's experiments with form and genre can be considered (to play on Huizinga's phrasing above) as "*counter*-interpretations of life and the world."

Cervantes wrote during a historical period that is often described in terms of rupture, crisis, and transition. We will see that his representations of play reflect and react to some of the momentous tensions of Counter-Reformation Spain, including what Huizinga, Caillois, and others traced as a development towards increasingly orderly types of play in more highly structured societies. Elias described as part of the "civilizing process" a diminishing tolerance for violent play and an increase in rules that would lower the potential for injuries, and he traces a key moment in the emergence of this sensibility to one of the central figures of the present study:

> The ruling of conduct and sentiment became stricter, more differentiated and all-embracing, but also more even, more temperate, banishing excesses of self-castigation as well as of self-indulgence. The change found its expression in a new term launched by Erasmus of Rotterdam and used in many other countries as a symbol of the new refinement of manners, the term "civility," which later gave rise to the verb "to civilize." (*Quest for Excitement* 21)

Caillois describes a development not only from uninhibited *paidia* to rule-bound *ludus*, but also from *mimicry* and *ilinx* to *agon* and *alea*, which mark the transition from spontaneous, "Dionysian" societies to rational ones: "In the first type there are simulation and vertigo or pantomime and ecstasy which assure the intensity and, as a consequence, the cohesion of social life. In the second type, the social nexus consists of compromise, of an implied reckoning between heredity, which is a kind of chance, and capacity, which presupposes evaluation and competition" (87).[9] Spariosu draws a distinction between societies that privilege games of chance and violent conflict, and those favouring rule-determined, non-violent (or *irenic*) forms of play (*Literature, Mimesis, and Play*). He terms the former "prerational" and associates them with an aristocratic mentality that privileges leisure; the latter he terms "rational," associated with a middle-class mentality, prioritizing work. Evidence of Elias's civilizing process, like Spariosu's rational play, can be seen in many of the early modern debates on leisure, although the process was by no means linear. As we will see, the conflictive atmosphere of Cervantes's Spain contained play expressing what Elias called both a civilizing as well as a "de-civilizing process" (46), a descent into violence, vertigo, and unchecked impulses.

Spariosu's studies of play concepts in philosophy suggest that, prior to Plato and Aristotle, play was understood less as sublimation than as a distilled expression of power. It is not until Classical Greek thought that play involves an element of mediation, as well as a sense of delimitation from "serious" endeavours:

> The major prerational play concepts include play as prerational agon, play as the arbitrary and violent conflict of physical forces or as a manifestation of ceaseless physical Becoming, play as chance-necessity, mimesis-play, play as an *as if* prerational mode of being, and play as unrestrained freedom. Among the major rational play concepts are play as nonviolent, rational agon, play as the rational order of Being, play as the rule-determined interaction of chance and necessity, play as mimesis-imitation, play as an *as if* rational mode of being, and play as rational or limited freedom. (*Dionysus Reborn* 12)

Spariosu points out how such notions manifest themselves in the educational, legal, and religious systems of given cultures and periods. In a recent study of play in Victorian literature and culture, Matthew Kaiser has offered further typological refinements in the form of seven "logics" of play: (1) "competition," similar to the *agon* of Caillois; (2) "self-creation," which accords with the rise of the concept of leisure as an antidote to mechanization brought on by work; (3) "subversion," a sort of Victorian carnivalesque; (4) "paideia," promoting the idea that people – especially children – can be socialized and otherwise taught through play; (5) "imaginary," the free play of the mind associated with nineteenth-century ideas on art and aesthetics; (6) "identity," a de-individuating process experienced in popular festivals; and (7) "fate," the realization that we are playthings of the cosmos, of chance (Kaiser 22–39). Predictably, Dickens is the richest and most ambivalent figure when it comes to registering, propagating, and questioning the "logics" of Victorian play. Other authors, according to Kaiser, pointedly contest the prevailing play logics that support the rise of middle-class privatization and the agonistic spirit of capitalism: Brontë's *Wuthering Heights*, for example, rejects the positivistic and utilitarian logic of paideia, emphasizing instead the sublime violence of the cosmos; Wilde acts as a sort of "spoilsport" who refuses to partake in the agonistic play of the mercantilist mentality, opting instead for a sort of Christian folly (Kaiser, chs. 3 and 5). It is significant that such authors propose a "counter-play" to the play modes they critique, for part of Kaiser's thesis is that the Victorian age is notable for its consciousness of the pervasiveness and inescapability of play – a quality that sets it apart from preceding cultures in which play was prevalent:

> Although Shakespeare's metaphor of the world as stage, we as actors, contains a prescient glimmer of our trope, it differs in a significant way. A stage implies the existence of an audience, an orchestra pit, a mezzanine, balconies, or in other words, an *outside*, a psychological and epistemological vantage from which to observe oneself, one's world, at play … *The World in Play* makes the case that this epistemic foothold offstage, this solid ground outside the game, dwindles and eventually disappears, in the minds of a growing number of people, by the early nineteenth century, swallowed by the totalizing concept of a world truly in play, by the modern conviction that we are trapped in the infinite regress of ludic representation, in a game that never ends, in the illusion's reflection. (4)

A preliminary consideration of Spariosu's notion of epochal shift, as well as some of the play categories outlined above, in light of three fundamental generic modes will help establish a framework for our later analysis of works by Cervantes. We will also see that the early modern period was perhaps more "prescient" than Kaiser realizes.[10]

Prerational and Rational Play in the Epic, the Picaresque, and the Quixotic

The epic *El cantar de mío Cid* broadly corresponds to a prerational ethos, depicting the violent *agon* of exalted, unrestrained heroism. The poem traces the roving warrior's loss and recuperation of honour amidst complex borders and factions, Christian and Muslim, with their accompanying internal tensions. But it is also a transitional work, registering a shift from the prerational to the rational. From the outset, there are elements that signal the emergence of a rational, proto-statist notion of law: although the Cid has been wrongfully exiled by King Alfonso, he remains a loyal subject, sending the king tributes from his numerous conquests. The Cid's ability to control his sense of personal grievance is most dramatically displayed in his reaction to the sadistic abuse suffered by his daughters at the hands of the Infantes de Carrión. Rather than setting the stage for a spectacular revenge along the lines of Odysseus's righteous slaughter of Penelope's dissolute, dice-playing suitors, the Cid seeks formal redress within the ordered judgment of the king's court.[11] A notable aspect of the trial scene is how it combines the modern aspects of rational, verbal argument before a jury with the emotionally satisfying spectacle of single combat. In this sense it is a transitional moment between Spariosu's prerational and rational, as well as between what Richard Posner describes as primitive justice based on revenge, associated with a "heroic code," and modern justice achieved through formalized law. Of law in a prerational society, Spariosu remarks, "Right is restored by violent means, according to the principle of blood revenge or retribution. The ethics of the victimizer prevails over that of the victim. Shame rather than guilt is the most effective social censor" (*Dionysus* 7). While the Infantes de Carrión subscribe to such a notion of law, the Cid masters his vengeful desire and individualistic impulses within the systematized justice of the trial. As Posner observes, "law channels rather than eliminates revenge – replaces it as system but not as feeling" (58).

The culminating trial scene of *El cantar de mío Cid* illustrates what Huizinga called "the relationship of the contest to the rise of a law-system" (76). Rather than avenging with his own sword his daughter's dishonour, the Cid participates in the orderly, "civilizing" process presided over by King Alfonso. The king sets the terms for the trial, which is to take place in Toledo: "Sean jueces de ello el conde don Enrique y el conde don Ramón y los demás que no son del bando. Meditad todos el caso, pues lo conocéis, y decidid lo que sea justicia, porque yo no mando hacer injusticias. Y mantengámonos en paz de una y otra parte" ("let the judges of this matter be counts don Enrique and don Ramón, and these other counts who are not in the Carrión faction. You who are learned in law, be attentive and consider carefully, find out what is just, for I would command no injustice. To one party and the other, I say, that today we are at peace," III, 137, p. 299).[12] We note the emphasis on the rational faculty ("meditad todos el caso"), justice and peace, as if the king were displacing the agonistic with an irenic culture. But when the judges agree to the first argument ("Eso está muy puesto en razón" – "This is all quite reasonable"), resulting in the return of the Cid's two swords, the hero's reaction reveals the thin line between law and revenge: "Todo el cuerpo se le alegra y parece que se le ríe el corazón. Tomándose entonces las barbas dice: 'Por estas barbas, que nadie ha mesado todavía, así iremos vengando a doña Elvira y doña Sol'" ("He felt a joy rise through his body, and he smiled cheerfully, raised his hand and stroked his beard: 'By this beard of mine, which no man has ever pulled, now we'll proceed to the vengeance of doña Elvira and doña Sol'" [III, 137, p. 303]). Posner's study helps contextualize the ethos of a work like *El cantar de mío Cid* within the development of law:

> Cultures in which revenge plays a significant role in the regulation of social interactions place great emphasis on honour. Shame, the reaction to being dishonoured, helps overcome fear and so makes it more likely that a victim will retaliate if attacked or abused. Out of the interplay of honour, shame, and revenge grow notions of exchange, balance, reciprocity, "keeping score" – notions later taken up by law, initially under the rubric of "corrective justice." (51)

What makes *El Cid* intriguing in light of law and play is its ambivalent quality, its subsuming the volatile interplay of honour, shame, and revenge within an ordered trial.

Noting that even modern law retains its ludic character on the linguistic plane, Huizinga writes that it is in the "archaic phase of this verbal battle" that "the agonistic factor is at its strongest and the ideal foundation of justice at its weakest. Here it is not the most meticulously deliberated juristic argument that tips the balance, but the most withering and excoriating invective" (84). The verbal *agon* between Garci Ordóñez and the Cid illustrates Huizinga's characterization perfectly:

> – De muy alta sangre son los infantes de Carrión, que ni para barraganas les servían las hijas del Cid …
>
> Entonces dijo el Campeador, llevándose la mano a las barbas.
>
> –Si ésta es larga, es porque fue criada con regalo: ¿qué tenéis vos, conde, que achacarle a mi barba? Desde que nació fue criada con regalo. Que nunca me la ha mesado hijo de mujer, moro ni cristiano, como yo a vos, conde, en aquel castillo de Cabra. Cuando tomé a Cabra, y también a vos por las barbas, no hubo rapaz que no mesara su pulgarada. La que yo os

arranqué todavía no se os empareja, que aquí la traigo alzada en mi bolsa. (III, 140, pp. 309–11)

["The infantes of Carrión are of such high birth that they ought not to want his daughters even for whores …

Then the Campeador put his hand up to his beard:

"(O)f course my beard is long, it took its own time growing pleasantly. What have you got going, count, to drag in my beard? Since it started to grow it's taken its own sweet time, and no son of woman has ever laid a hand on it, no one's ever dared pull it, Moor or Christian, as I pulled yours, Count, at the fortress at Cabra. When I took Cabra, I seized you by the beard, and there wasn't a kid there who didn't get his fistful. And the hunk that I tore out hasn't grown back yet, see? Here it is. I've carried it in my purse ever since!"]

Clearly not "meticulously deliberated juristic argument," the Cid's invective – complete with a stinging zeugma ("Cuando tomé a Cabra, y también a vos por las barbas") – nevertheless helps his case before the king and his court. As Posner noted, "[a] revenge society places a premium on rhetorical skill" (52).[13] The "reviling-match" (Huizinga 84) between the Cid and the Infantes centres on the classic tension between *obras* y *sangre*, the former party pointing out the cowardice and shameful acts of their adversaries, the Infantes gloating over their exalted lineage. Asur González illustrates how the "actions vs. blood" debate relates to Spariosu's characterization of prerational vs. rational values: "¡Oh, señores! ¿Cuándo se vio cosa semejante? ¿Quién diría que por parte de nuestro Cid habíamos de ganar nobleza? Váyase en hora mala al río de Ubierna a picar sus molinos y a cobrar (el precio de la molienda en) puñados, como suele hacerlo. ¿Quién casó su sangre con la de Carrión?" ("Ya, gentlemen, who's ever seen such crap as this? Since when are we taking our honors from mio Cid de Bivar? He ought to go back to the Ubierna River and hack away at his mills, and charge his percentage of grain, like he's used to! Who'd ever think of marrying people like that to Carrión?" [III, 148, p. 319]). The exaltation of noble lineage goes hand-in-hand with a disdain for work, as Asur González accuses the Cid of mercantile activities, participating in the management of mills. Despite his humble lineage, the end of the poem intermingles the Cid's bloodlines with those of the imperial monarchy.[14]

Consistent with the heroic ethos of the poem, as well as the transitional quality being foregrounded in the present analysis, the verbal agon is followed by the gratifying spectacle of physical combat. The terms of engagement – the time, space, weaponry, chain of authority and judgment – are carefully negotiated by the opposing parties and King Alfonso. An interesting tension between rational justice and heroic agon intensifies at this point of the trial. We noted how the verbal contest, ostensibly involving reasoned argument, contains a good measure of the more primal hostilities of exchanging insults. The culminating scenes of single combat diverge even further from a rational notion of justice. And yet there are repeated assurances that justice will be served, that the "fair play" of the combat will reveal the righteous party: "Los del Cid velaron las armas y rezaron. Ya pasa la noche, quiebran los albores, muchos buenos y ricos hombres se han congregado con el deseo de presenciar aquella lid. Y sobre todo está el rey don Alfonso, para cuidar de que se imponga el derecho, no la injusticia" ("The Cid's champions sit vigil by their arms, the night's cut up into pieces and the day comes. Many rich men have gathered at the site to see a fight that will give them pleasure and furthermore and above all else, of course, King Alfonso to see justice done, and no treachery permitted" [III, 150, p. 331]). From the perspective of the framework proposed by René Girard in *Violence and the Sacred*, the trial scene in *El Cid* fluctuates along the continuum of revenge attenuation, from sacrificial rites to modern law.[15] The ludic quality of the trial is enhanced by the fact that it is also a public spectacle (of course, a number of high-profile court cases in our own time affirm that the distinction between the trial as an affirmation of order and justice and as a "spectator sport" is a tenuous one). Still, what we are calling the "rational" aspects of the trial continue to assert themselves, for example in the desire to establish unambiguously the facts of the battle: "El rey les ha designado jueces de campo para que declaren lo que sea justo, y no disputen entre sí sobre si sucedió esto o aquello" ("The king appoints judges to pronounce what is right and what not, and no one is to argue with their 'yes' or their 'no,'" [III, 150, p. 333]).

Another transitional aspect of the *Cantar de mío Cid* is the way the hero, initially ranging the borderlands of the Iberian Peninsula with his band of loyal men and bent on avenging the dishonour suffered by his family, ultimately subsumes his concerns within the incipient national narrative. As Posner notes, such a development is a key factor in the transition from societies based on revenge to those based on law: "a revenge culture breeds intense loyalty within the extended family. But powerful loyalties within small groups retard the formation of larger loyalties, to the tribe, the *polis*, or the nation. This seems to have been Plato's objection, in the *Republic*, to the portrayal of Achilles in the *Iliad*" (52–3). The Cid never disavows his allegiance to King Alfonso, and his final "legal" victory culminates in his family's bond to the nation: "Los de Navarra y Aragón hicieron sus pláticas, tuvieron junta con el rey don Alfonso, y al fin doña Elvira y doña Sol se casaron … que ya sus hijas son señoras de Aragón y Navarra" ("The infantes of Navarre and Aragón renew their suits, and all are met together with Alfonso de León. They solemnize the marriage of doña Elvira and doña Sol … for now his daughters are queens of Aragón and Navarre" [III, 152, p. 343]).

In addition to exhibiting a development from a prerational to a rational society in its depiction of legal contest, *El cantar de mío Cid* portrays a play spirit that is both strikingly "early modern," anticipating the strategic deceptions of the *pícaro*, and as old as the wiliness of Odysseus. When the smiling Cid deceives Raquel and Vidas with the treasure chests full of sand, he demonstrates a virtue noted by Huizinga in numerous mythological traditions: "the act of fraudulently outwitting somebody else has itself become a subject for competition, a new play-theme, as it were" (Huizinga 52). Spariosu elaborates on this ethos in the Homeric epic, signalling its pertinence to our present context:

> Odysseus, for example, is praised as being *aristos* in counsel because of his ability to bring about, through skilful manipulation or cunning (*metis*), his own party's success in war or peace. Throughout Homeric society – and this is true of the early medieval heroic world as well – power represents itself in the form of (predominantly violent) agonistic play. This means not only that competition has a crucial function in Homeric life, but also that the Greek hero sees his relationship to other heroes and to the gods, as well as to existence in general, in terms of a huge power game. (*Dionysus* 13)

Consistent with the larger trajectory of *El cantar de mío Cid* as a work that expresses an incipient rational outlook against a prerational, agonistic backdrop, the Cid justifies his trickery and appeals to a higher authority: "Llévenles las arcas de noche, no lo vea nadie. Sólo lo vea y lo juzgue el Criador, con todos los santos; Él sabe que no puedo más, que lo hago forzado" ("They should come to get it at night so that the Christians don't see. Let the Lord and all his saints besides witness I do this unwillingly, there's nothing else I can do" [I, 7, p. 59]). The fact that the hero deceives the culturally "other," stereotypically greedy Jews, also helps rationalize his actions, and blunt the implications of existence as a "huge power game": his recourse to cheating is a rare exception, and his victims, "haciendo cuentas de sus ganancias" ("counting over what they have earned in profits" [I, 9, p. 59]), deserve what they get. It is not until the advent of the picaresque genre that the potentially destabilizing play of the dedicated cheat is fully expressed within Spain.

We noted above how Asur González's insult of the Cid's humble background is meant to maintain the distinction between the privileged leisure class and lowly labourers and the world of commerce ("a picar sus molinos y a cobrar"), and how the Cid's triumph does not ultimately pose a serious challenge to such a world view: the individualistic hero submits to royal authority, and his bloodlines are ennobled by his daughters' unions. Three centuries later, the picaresque plays on the same distinction to which Asur González appeals. Commenting on how *pícaros* reflected the values of the nobility whose ranks they would threaten, Peter Dunn makes the following observation:

> The segmentation of time into units of value permits the traditional elitist opposition *negotium/otium* to escape from the favoured precincts and to become generalized and, in so doing, to assume new forms and meanings. Leisure is no longer the privilege of rank but may be bought with money, and it is all the same whether the money be earned or stolen. (*Spanish Picaresque Fiction* 301)

As Dunn's comments suggest, the picaresque contains a combination of Caillois's *agon* and *mimicry*. The pícaros' *mimicry* is that of the impostor, as they try to pass themselves off as members of the privileged class. Quevedo's *Buscón* represents the most ferocious repudiation of such an endeavour, as Pablos's attempts to present himself as a man of leisure, courting women in the privileged precincts of recreation in Madrid, are cruelly exposed and punished (*La vida del Buscón* III, 6–7). The picaresque *agon* is not the productive competition of work, but rather the predatory conflict of swindle and violence. Michel Cavillac's socio-economic study of *Guzmán de Alfarache* considers how Alemán represents the stifling of an incipient mercantilism in Spain, in which *otium*, instead of a creative cultural space, comprises an avoidance of productive *negotium*. The narrating Guzmán repeatedly sermonizes against the vice of idleness, echoing the tone of contemporary moralists: "Es la ociosidad campo franco de perdición, arado con que siembran malos pensamientos, semilla de cizaña, escardadera que entresaca las buenas costumbres, hoz que siega las buenas obras, trillo que trilla las honras, carro que acarrea maldades y silo en que se recogen todos los vicios" ("Idleness is an open field for perdition, a plough with which evil thoughts are sown, seed of discord, a weed-puller who extracts good customs, a sickle that mows good works, a thresher that threshes honours, a cart that hauls evils and a silo in which all vices are gathered" [I, ii, 6]).

When Guzmán-protagonist dupes the merchant, don Juan Osorio, in Milan, the hollowness of the merchant class and decadence of the nobility are both apparent: "me hizo grande contradición y dificultoso de creer que hombres nobles, hijos de padres tales, permitan dejarse llevar tan arrastrados de sus pasiones, que, olvidado el respeto debido a su nobleza, contra toda caridad y buena policía, sin precisa necesidad hagan bajezas, quitando a otros la hacienda y honra" ("it seemed to me very contradictory and difficult to believe that noblemen, sons of such men, allow themselves to be so dragged by their passions that, forgotten the respect due to their nobility, against all charity and good custom, without any particular need they commit base deeds, taking property and honour from others" [II, ii, 5]). Guzmán's swindle involves a complicated planting of evidence and falsifying of the merchant's books. However it is not a case of an earnest, productive businessman being cheated by a pícaro: "Conformidad teníamos ambos en engañar; mas eran muy diferentes mis trazas que él debía de tener pensadas" ("We made a compact of deception; but my designs were very different from what he anticipated" [II, ii, 6]). Given the presumed disrepute of the victim, the trick partially resembles the Cid's deception of Raquel and Vides, also involving the feigned transfer of valuables. And when the conflict escalates, a sort of public trial takes place, before a constable and bystanders on the street. If the Cid's victory involved besting his opponent with sharp insults, Guzmán deploys a different kind of rhetorical ability: "Y con una cólera encendida, que parecía echar fuego por todo el rostro, dije" ("And with inflamed ire, so my face seemed all afire, I said"); "largué los pliegues a la boca, lanzando por ella espuma, y a grandes gritos dije" ("I parted my lips, spewing foam from my mouth, and amidst great yelling said"); "Hacía unos estremos como un loco furioso, de manera que creyeron ser sin duda verdad cuanto decía"

("I made excesses like a furious lunatic, so that they believed without a doubt all I said" [II, ii, 6]). His theatrical display recalls elements of the collusion between the constable and pardoner in *Lazarillo de Tormes* (ch. 6), and, along with the planting of evidence in the merchant's drawers, he wins over popular and legal opinion alike. Of course, in contrast to the Cid's legal *agon*, Guzmán's victory comprises a travesty of the values he would purport to affirm – not the heroic values of the epic, but the productive values of mercantilism: "de allí en adelante quedé con crédito y hacienda" ("from then on I had credit and property" [II, ii, 6]). His "crédito" is based on a deception, and his "hacienda" will not be husbanded prudently, but rather used to support his picaresque leisure.

Recent "materialist" approaches to *Don Quijote* focus on a shift from medieval, aristocratic ideals to a gradual accommodation of modernity, with its legalistic structures, technological advances, and relationships based on monetary exchange. David Quint efficiently illustrates this trend, and his account of the trajectory of *Don Quijote* calls to mind Spariosu's distinction between aristocratic vs. middle-class mentalities:

> In Part One a Don Quijote who sets out to revive chivalry finds himself imprisoned by a modern world of money and law … In Part Two, a Don Quijote who seems to have adapted some of the more peaceable and moderate traits of that world's middle class finds himself imprisoned by his old chivalric delusions, fed back to him by the Duke and Duchess … This regressive movement of Part Two thus has a historical correlative. Cervantes's novel discovers a new social transformation whose values compete with those of an older feudal-aristocratic order. The Duke and Duchess, representatives of an aristocracy whose power is still entrenched and socially dominant, drag *Don Quijote* back toward the past. Their class may exert a similar drag on Spanish society and culture as a whole. (*Cervantes's Novel of Modern Times* 133)

We will consider below how specific recreational activities depicted in the novel – the hunt, rustic contests, cards and chess – relate to such socio-economic conditions, as well as to broader epistemological questions.

Spariosu argues that *Don Quijote* illustrates the importance of keeping play and reality separate, a lesson Alonso Quijano learns on his deathbed as he renounces the folly of his chivalric enterprise. However Spariosu goes somewhat beyond the "hard school" tradition of

Cervantes criticism, since his premise is that *everything* is play: "aesthetic fictions" (games, literature) are different from "practical fictions" (philosophy, history, science) only because Western power structures speciously legitimize the latter as true. *Don Quijote* therefore dispels naiveté by emphasizing the fictionality of literary discourse, the artificiality of artistic convention. But this is only a semi-scepticism, and, as such, actually contributes to a larger deception:

> This differentiation is sanctioned, for example, in English by the common usage of the word "fiction" which is the generic name for many aesthetic fictions, while practical fictions bear such respectable names as philosophy, science, religion, history, etc. Thus by telling the truth Cervantes reinforces a lie, but this lie is for him a necessary one: confusion between play and action will inevitably result in aestheticism, de-simulation, perspectivism, and ontological vertigo. (*Wreath* 85)

According to this line of reasoning – which is similar to Ehrmann's objections to the cultural "givens" taken for granted by Huizinga and Caillois – Cervantes may not *intentionally* conspire to keep his readers subordinate to the powers that be; rather, he is simply unprepared to contemplate the constructed nature of all truth. As a consequence, Cervantes's readers are partially passive – empowered as literary critics, yet ideologically indoctrinated. Martínez-Bonati also maintains that Cervantes's playful subversions lack "metaphysical transcendence. They are not anxious games of an autonomized imagination or a reason without firm ground under its feet. These encounters of irreconcilable systems of interpreting experience produce a relativization not of the sense of reality but of the conceptual and artistic codes, of the forms with which we want to articulate the consciousness of reality" (121). As my chapter on humour in *Don Quijote* asserts, Cervantes did not in fact maintain such a clear barrier between practical and aesthetic fictions, and his questioning of conceptual and artistic codes could, indeed, have destabilizing implications – if not politically, then epistemologically.

Maravall maintains that everything was indeed perceived as play in Baroque Spain, and that those in power availed themselves of such a worldview – indeed, cultivated it – in order to subjugate the urban masses. According to Maravall, artists who created particularly self-referential plays, paintings and narratives (e.g., Calderón, Velázquez, Cervantes) did not merely enhance the aesthetic sophistication of the public; such works created the "ontological vertigo" Spariosu writes of, a profound sense of disorientation:

> If reality is theatrical, if the spectators find themselves submerged in the great theater of the world, what they contemplate on the stage is a theater to the second degree. This provides an obvious image of the plot of the scene being lived, but the introduction of the three-leveled complication also lessens the distances between them and softens them; by this means, the psyche is effectively prepared for accepting the phenomenal character of reality. (*Culture of the Baroque* 200)

According to Maravall, "confusion between play and action" (to refer again to Spariosu's commentary above) is precisely what reigned in the period. The fluid relationship between art and experience was consistent with a sense that life itself was a game. But such a consciousness actually effects the opposite of the instability and decentring of authority described by Spariosu:

> But the widespread practices, especially in art, of "deceiving the eye" had no pretence of making us believe that what we saw prepared by an artist's skilful manipulation was the true reality of things, but of moving us to accept that the world we took to be real was no less apparent. By means of these procedures, the politician as much as the moralist and the artist judged it easier to obtain acceptance for or submission to the Church, the monarchy, the social order (with its distinctions of regimented groups), the power of the rich, and those other discriminations supporting the stability of the system. In other words, they showed people that in relations with the world one must adhere to a game ruled by knowledge and prudence; they told them that, regardless, this world, however apparent it may be, is what confronts one and what must be dealt with; and they reminded them that, precisely because of its condition as illusory appearance, one must wholly enter into the game in terms of whatever becomes present to us. (*Culture of the Baroque* 198)

Like Spariosu, Maravall adheres to a somewhat reductive polarity: the play element in a particular culture will either contribute to the authorization or the subversion of the dominant power structures. Maravall's model describes the intensification of a play ethos in Baroque Spain as part of a strategy to contain and neutralize the tumultuous changes throughout Europe: the novelty of Lope's theatre undermines

Aristotle's authority, but solidifies that of the monarchy; instead of contributing to a rise in mercantilist activity and scientific progress, technological innovations are deployed to amuse the public in the form of mechanical playthings and spectacles (*Culture of the Baroque*, ch. 9).[16] The peculiar emergence that Maravall traces of a new consciousness of individuality, of the importance of an active and strategic posture before the play of the world, does not correspond with a new rise in freedom. It is, rather, the result of experiencing the social sphere as *agon*, as an inhospitable realm of competition between isolated "monads" (*Culture of the Baroque*, ch. 6). Given such conditions, the citizenry is effectively awed into submission by the extravagant displays – in theatre, pageants, festivities – of an absolutist monarchy: "In wonder, the spectators asked themselves what would be beyond the power of whoever did all this to achieve what was apparently such a small thing, for a few instances of pleasure" (242). Perhaps the fireworks described by Maravall in the final chapter of his study best represent the apotheosis of Baroque play as *ilinx*, of a vertiginous humbling of the spectator before a State that has displaced nature as a source of the sublime.

But lest we ourselves succumb to the massive spectacle of modern theorizing, we shall now turn to the rich and varied primary sources.

"No vivo para jugar, sino juego para poder vivir": The Space and Function of *Eutrapelia*

Aristotle's concept of beneficial play in moderation, resuscitated by Aquinas, had broad currency in early modern Spain. The citation above, from the prologue of Juan García Canalejas's *Libro del juego de las damas* (1650), encapsulates the principles of *eutrapelia*: excess is to be avoided ("no vivo para jugar" – "I do not live to play"); but rather than a frivolous luxury, play is indispensible ("juego para poder vivir" – "I play to be able to live"). In this section we will examine the many factors that contribute to determining the mean in recreation, such as venue, company, and striking a balance between clowning and boorishness. There is also the complicated matter of ends and means, the extent to which recreation and its attendant pleasures were justifiable on their own terms, or only so far as they served some other, ostensibly more serious, purpose. The Spanish thinkers consistently reveal their indebtedness to Aristotelian-Thomist tradition, and a Christian moral framework informs their notions of pleasure and profit. But there are also secular elements to the discussions, particularly regarding assertions of the value of play for social cohesion as well as for physical and psychological health.[17]

Aristotle calibrates the recreational mean by distinguishing between the humorless *agroikos* and the excessively frivolous and vulgar *bomolochos* (*Ethics* IV). The *eutrapelos* possesses the intellectual agility and tact to be witty in an appropriate manner. Acceptable parameters for playful banter depend on context and the disposition of those involved: "Might one then define the person good at joking as saying what is not inappropriate to a generous spirit, or as not causing pain to one who hears it or even causing merriment [in the one made fun of]? Or is this sort of thing not even definable? For different things are hateful and pleasant to different people" (*Ethics* 1128a25). Castiglione, whose courtier would possess a distinctly Renaissance strain of the judgment of Aristotle's *eutrapelos*, amusingly comments on some of the factors that must be taken into account:

> [T]he Spaniards are instinctively witty. But there are many among them, and of other races too, who let their loquacity run away with them and become insipid and inept, because they pay no regard to the kind of people with whom they are talking, to the place where they happen to be, or to the rules of sobriety and modesty that they ought to observe. (152)

The focus on such issues as company ("kind of people"), venue ("place"), and conventions ("rules") recalls Aquinas, who, as Olson observes, "cites Cicero and Ambrose to point out that the 'delectatio' offered by amusement must not be indecent, must not dissipate all 'gravitas anime,' and must be ordered according to the proper circumstances – time, place, person" (98).[18] And with regard to company, Castiglione is consonant with Aristotle's repeated assertion that the responsibility for maintaining decorum lies with the *listener* as well as the teller of the jokes: "And a property that belongs to the mean active condition is adroitness, and it is a characteristic of one who is adroit to say and listen to things of a sort that are fitting for someone decent and of a generous spirit" (*Ethics* 1128a17); "So also are the things someone will listen to, for what one puts up with hearing, it seems one also does" (1128a12).

A brief consideration of the trajectory of the courtier, taking as our points of reference Castilgione's *cortegiano* and Gracián's *discreto*, illustrates some of the shifting views on propriety and the *eutrapelos*. Despite marked differences in purpose and vision, Castiglione and Gracián clearly draw upon similar sources in their discussions of propriety and joking. One important background figure is Epictetus, whose somewhat severe attitude towards levity ("Let not your laughter be much, nor on many occasions, nor excessive") includes an emphasis on the audience's (or interlocutor's) responsibility not to encourage excessive joking (*The Manual*, Sect. 33). Where Castiglione is epicurean in sensibility, Gracián is much more stoic in his prescription of austerity and self-control. Moreover, each figure reflects different visions of individual and community. Gracián, whose *Discreto* seems explicitly to reject Castiglione's project, recalls the austere outlook of Mateo Alemán: "Nunca se ha de dar materia de risa ni a un niño, cuanto menos a los varones cuerdos y juiciosos; y hay muchos que parece que ponen todo su cuidado en dar qué reír, y que estudian cómo dar entretenimiento a las hablillas" ("One should never provide laughable subject matter to a child, and even less to rational and judicious men; it seems there are many who put all their effort into causing laughter, and who study how to make entertaining gossip" [*El Discreto* 103]).[19] Gracián's *discreto* is more sombre and restrained than Castiglione's courtier: "ni los varones sabios se hallan entre el cortesano bullicio" ("wise men do not find themselves amidst the courtly clamor" [51]). But Gracián does attempt to delineate a sort of *eutrapelia*, however muted. In the chapter titled "No estar siempre de burlas" ("Refrain from constantly speaking in jest" [ch. 9]), he also cites Cicero and echoes Aquinas's emphasis on time, place, and person: "no hay mayor desaire que el continuo donaire. Su rato han de tener las burlas; todos los demás las veras … Hase de hacer distinción de tiempos, y mucho más de personas" ("there is no greater gracelessness than continuous banter. Jokes should have their moment; all the rest must go to truths … One must make distinctions of time, and much more of people" [77]). Like Tasso, Gracián's view of courtly interaction is more tactical and Machiavellian than Castiglione's portrait of flirtation and showcasing gentlemanly virtues.[20] In the context of exercising and maintaining power, joking becomes perilous: "En hombres de gran puesto se censuran más y, aunque los hace en algún modo gratos al vulgo, por la llaneza, pone a peligro el decoro con la felicidad, que como ellos no la guardan a los otros, ocasionan el recíproco atrevimiento" ("Men of high station receive greater scrutiny and, although levity makes them in some ways more pleasing to commoners, for its plainness, if they do not refrain from it, others will be emboldened to respond in kind" [78]). As absolutism increases its hold, there is less tolerance for unpredictable and potentially unruly play.

Renaissance commentators and practitioners of *eutrapelia* displayed a range of opinions regarding the permissibility of playing for its own sake or as a means to something more valuable. The tensions with regard to ends and means are part of a broad cultural-historical progression, spanning the notion of Greek *schole*, in which humanity's fullest intellectual, social and spiritual potential is achieved in leisure, to modern materialism which views leisure as a useful space of recovery, facilitating a productive return to work.[21] As we shall see, Spanish *ocio* was an ambivalent term, sometimes signifying beneficial *recreación*, but perhaps more often – like the adjective *ocioso* – denoting idleness and wasted time. But even *ocio* in the positive sense of leisurely recreation often came with certain imperatives attached – that play should contribute to increased piety, virtue, or productivity. A certain amount of ambiguity exists in Aristotle himself, who seems to suggest that the relaxation achieved through *eutrapelia* serves more "serious" ends:

> But to play in order that one might be serious, as Anacharsis says, seems to be right, since play seems like relaxation, and since people are incapable of laboring continuously, they need relaxation. So relaxation is not the end, since it comes about for the sake of being-at-work. And the happy life seems to be in accord with virtue, and this involves seriousness and does not consist in play. And we speak of serious things as better than those that bring laughter and involve play, and say that the activity of the better part or of the better person is always the more serious, and the activity of what is better is more powerful and more conducive to happiness from the start. (*Ethics* 1176b32ff)

Care must be taken, however, not to give Aristotle's concept an overly utilitarian hue. "Play" in the above passage comes from one of the seminal words and concepts of the ludic vocabulary, *paidia*. While such play does, according to Aristotle, allow a return to seriousness and excellence (*spoudazein*), the "relaxation," from *anapausis* (to "cease" and regain strength), is itself therapeutic. As the passage above stipulates, the relaxation effected by play is a means to resume "activity." But this word, *energeia*, does not mean productive work, but rather the active use of one's faculties. Aristotle places great value on pleasure (*hēdonē*), although he distinguishes different orders: "Sight surpasses touch in purity, and hearing and smell surpass taste, and their pleasures differ in a similar way; and the pleasures that have to do with thinking surpass these, and those of each sort have differences one from another" (*Ethics* 1176a). For Aristotle, the most serious activity is also that which affords the greatest pleasure, and it is intrinsically valuable, not a means to something else: "So if … the being-at-work of the intellect seems to excel in seriousness, and to be contemplative and aim at no end beyond itself, and to have its own pleasure (which increases its activity), so that what is as self-sufficient, leisured, and unwearied as possible for a human being, and all the other things that are attributed to a blessed person, show themselves as the things that result from this way of being-at-work, then this would be the complete happiness of a human being" (1177b20).[22] Play involves activation of the higher faculties, putting them, so to speak, "to work."

The ambiguity regarding ends and means is evident in the differing views on Cervantine *eutrapelia*. Jones and Wardropper, both of whom focus on Aquinas's revival of Aristotle, arrive at significantly different characterizations. Wardropper emphasizes the didactic, moral quality of the *Novelas ejemplares*, and includes the following comment in his discussion of the *Summa Theologica*: "whoever seeks pleasures must always remember that the purpose of play is the return to seriousness."[23] For Wardropper, the return to seriousness involves resuming work and piety morally fortified by leisure ("con un propósito moral fortalecido" 169), in no small measure due to the positive and negative examples of conduct that have been modelled in the entertainment. Jones, who maintains that Cervantes's aesthetic recreation is morally neutral, claims that "the *Summa* makes no reference to utility."[24] The following passage from Aquinas is to the point:

> The activity of playing looked at specifically in itself is not ordained to a further end, yet the pleasure we take therein serves as recreation and rest for the soul, and accordingly when this be well-tempered, application to play is lawful. Hence Cicero says, *It is indeed useful to turn to sport and fun, but as it is to turn to sleep and other solaces, that is, when we have discharged our obligations in grave and serious matters.* (2a2ae. 168, 2)

Like Aristotle, Aquinas finds play "useful" to the extent that – to return to our opening citation by García Canalejas – it allows us to live. The emblematic image of such recreation is the "relaxing of the bow-string." In Cassian's account, a philosopher in hunter's garb, sceptical at the sight of John the Evangelist petting a partridge, is asked by John why he does not keep his bow constantly strung: "'That is not supposed to be done. Constant bending would relax its tensile strength, and it would be weakened and ruined' … 'Nor,' said the blessed John, 'should this small and brief recreation of our mind offend you, young man. If by a certain relaxation it did not occasionally lighten and loosen its taut tension, it would not be able to harken to the power of the spirit when necessity demanded, since it would be weakened by its unrelenting exertion'" (24.21, p. 842).[25]

It is significant that, in his discussion of enjoyment (*fruitio*), Aquinas maintains that pleasure can be an intrinsic good: "They are called fruits because they are to be sought for their own sake, not indeed because they are not subordinate to happiness, but because they hold in themselves what is pleasing to us" (1a2ae, 11, art. 3). Also following Aristotle, Aquinas distinguishes between sensual (appetitive) and cognitive (intellective) enjoyment, and for him the highest pleasure combines both (1a2ae, 11, art.2). As Rahner puts it, with Aquinas *eutrapelia* is "a virtue of Greek *humanitas*, baptized in Christ" (91). The effects of such syncretism are a tempering of the ascetic strains of medieval Christianity (Rahner 95), and an attenuation of conventional Aristotelian-Horatian demands regarding the utility of literature – that is, viewing it as a means rather than an end (Jones 28). Our consideration of literature as play is significant in part because, although often presented in terms of *eutrapelia* and through the metaphor of the game, which would imply a lower-order leisure activity according to Aristotle, the reader's experience is in fact more akin to contemplation, the highest ideal of leisure. In other words, Cervantes's *mesa de trucos* may suggest what Aristotle characterizes as a "childish" game, providing only the momentary relaxation that allows for a more productive return to work. But when Peralta declares, at the end of *El coloquio de los perros*, that "he recreado los [ojos] del entendimiento" ("I have refreshed the eyes of the understanding"), he signals the true import of Cervantes's play.

Many of the Spanish commentators insisted on a dichotomy between pleasurable play and serious, productive work, and allowed the former as a means to increase the yield of the latter. Some of the writings on the proper uses of *ocio*, however, involve both play and contemplation, sensual as well as intellectual pleasures. Some even endorse such pleasures as intrinsically good. The Dominican Pedro de Covarrubias relates the need for play to the "mixed" condition of humans, whose physical, animal nature cannot completely be separated from the spirit: "La definicion del juego es que es dicho o hecho en el qual se procura deletacion de las virtudes animales. Siguese de necessidad que para relevar y recrear el espiritu es necessario en la vida humana juego, deporte, passatiempo" ("The definition of play is a saying or action in which the corporeal virtues procure pleasure. It follows by necessity that in order to relieve and refresh the spirit, play, sport, and pastime are necessary in human life" [fol. 6]). Ascribing such "animal" attributes to Christ, however, could prove risky; the humanist Francisco Sánchez de las Brozas ("el

Brocense") endured an Inquisitorial trial for, among other things, claiming that the Christ child played ball games: "El mesmo dijo que los reyes magos no habían venido a adorar a nuestro Señor luego que nació, sino de ahí a dos años, que andaría jugando a la chueca con los otros muchachos" ("The same said that the three kings had not come to adore our Lord just after his birth, but rather two years later, and that he was at the time playing ball with the other children" [Tovar y Pinta Llorente 33]). Rather than a gloomy, post-lapsarian severity, Covarrubias's view of humanity's middle ground between *feritas* and *divinitas* reflects a positive disposition towards pleasure in moderation. It is an attitude that falls between the licentious carnivalesque, with its disordering celebration of the "lower stratum," and sombre, flesh-denying asceticism. Montaigne – again anticipating Schiller – would describe a similarly hybrid human nature: "But I, being of a mixed constitution, and coarse, am unable to cling so completely to this single and simple object as to keep myself from grossly pursuing the present pleasures of the general human law – intellectually sensual, sensually intellectual" (III, 13, p. 850). Covarrubias also voices a strong suspicion of those who are unable to take pleasure in music: "los que de graves o muy religiosos huyen de otros juegos deven holgar eneste que conviene no menos a angeles que a hombres. Y si tampoco deste huelgan señal es efficaz que son mal compuestos y peor condicionados y de aquellos me guarde dios" ("those who, on account of being grave and religious, flee from other games should take enjoyment in that which is appropriate no less to angels than to men. And if they cannot even take enjoyment in this [i.e. music], it is a sure sign that they are poorly composed and even more poorly conditioned, and may god protect me from such people" [fols. 17r–18]). There seems to be something inhuman about rejecting recreation altogether. Shakespeare memorably has Lorenzo express a similar sentiment in *The Merchant of Venice*: "The man that hath no music in himself, / Nor is moved with concord of sweet sounds, / Is fit for treasons, stratagems, and spoils; / The motions of his spirit are dull as night, / And his affections dark as Erebus. / Let no such man be trusted. Mark the music" (5. 1. 92–7).

The Jesuit Pedro de Guzmán, contemporary of Cervantes, includes in his definition of *eutrapelia* an appealing scepticism towards the *agroikos* as well as the *bomolochos*: "que puede aver vicio en la demasiada austeridad, y aborrecimiento al juego, y entretenimiento, aunque no tan grave, como en el vicio de la chocarreria" ("there can be vice in excessive austerity, and abhorrence of play and entertainment, although not as serious a vice as that of buffoonery," fol. 409). This idea comes from

Aristotle via Aquinas: "since play is for repose and delight, and these are not to be sought for their own sake as objective ends in themselves, but for the sake of the acts they complement, as Aristotle points out, too little playing is less wrong than too much" (*Summa* 2a2ae. 168, 4). It is interesting that Guzmán should emphasize that abstinence from play is also a vice, rather than a stern virtue. According to Guzmán, man's physiognomy indicates a divine prioritization of *negotium* over *otium*: "los instrumentos que Dios nuestro Señor dio al hombre en su mismo principio y formacion, los braços, ombros, manos, dedos, la forma y estatura del cuerpo, la postura de los sentidos, las fuerças que en un tan pequeño cuerpo puso, nos estan diziendo, que no le crió para estarse ocioso, y mano sobre mano, sino para el trabajo" ("the instruments God our Lord gave to man at his beginning and formation, arms, shoulders, hands, fingers, the physical form and stature, the bearing of the senses, the powers that he put in such a small body, tell us that he did not raise him to be idle, hands folded together, but rather to work" [5–6]). In Eden these qualities were put to pleasant use: "no queria el Señor al hombre ocioso, y asi para darle ocupacion contra el ocio, le entregó el jardin del Parayso; para que le labrasse y guardasse" ("the Lord did not want man to be idle, and so in order to give him occupation against idleness, he gave him the garden of Paradise, so that he could cultivate and care for it" [5]). For fallen humanity, the imperative is more onerous: "En el sudor de tu rostro te sustentarás" ("By the sweat of your brow you will eat" [17]). This decree from the Book of Genesis resonates through many discussions of play, from early modern to the present. In an appeal to disabuse him of his chivalric ideas, the practical Tomé Cecial, disguised as a squire, quotes it to a tired and hungry Sancho Panza (*Don Quijote* II, 13); a modern *pícaro* makes more ironic use of it in Roberto Arlt's *El juguete rabioso*: "¡Ah!, cierto es que estaba cansado … ¿mas no está escrito: 'ganarás el pan con el sudor de tu frente'?" ("Ah! of course he was tired … but isn't it written: 'you will win your bread by the sweat of your brow'?" [83]). The cover page to the 1614 edition of Guzmán's *Bienes del honesto trabajo y daños de la ociosidad* includes emblems of industry – shears, measuring devices, hammers, as well as the contrasting images of a sleeping man and toiling ants and bees – that flank a central image of man in nature, equipped with tools, below the inscription "Homo nascitur ad laborem" ("Man is born unto labour" [see Figure 1]). Lucretius had also characterized humanity's plight on earth as one of laborious struggle – not, as with Guzmán, because of a fall from grace, but because of an absence of the divine

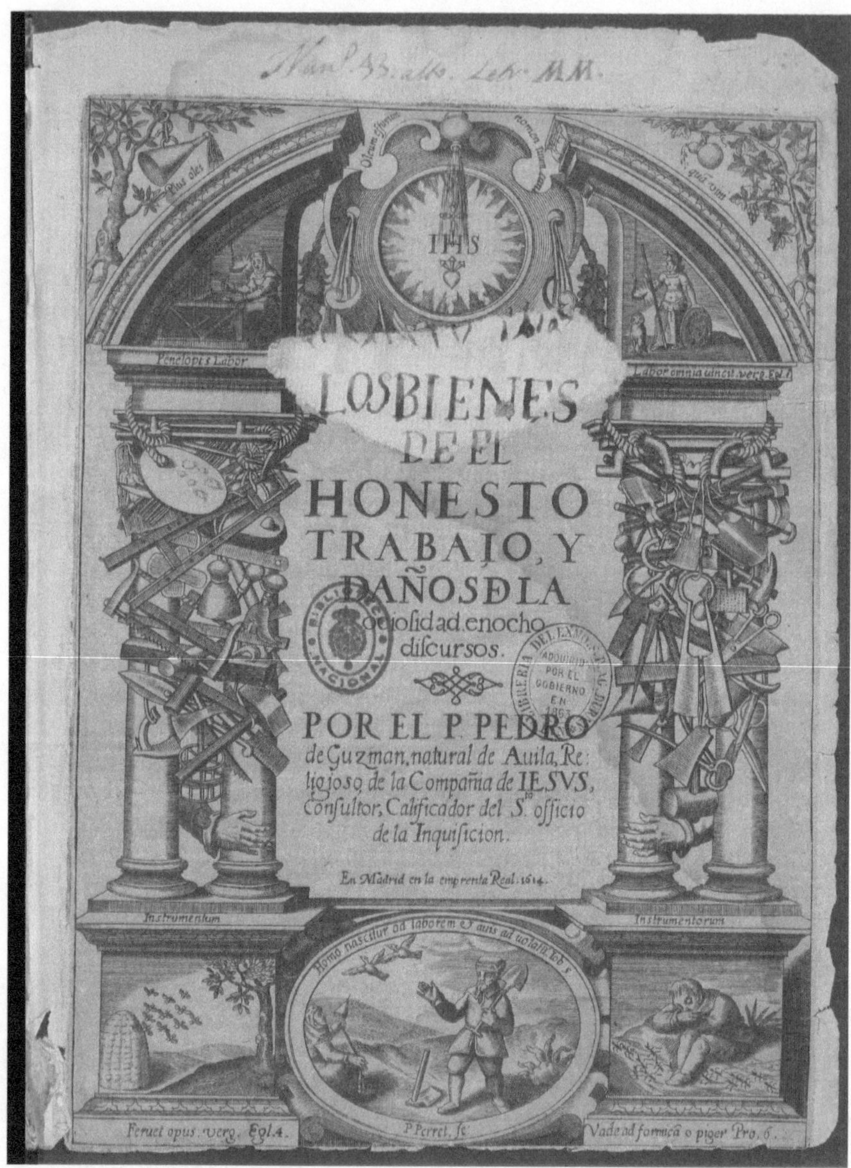
LOS BIENES
DE EL
HONESTO
TRABAJO, Y
DAÑOS DE LA
ociosidad en ocho
discursos.

POR EL P. PEDRO
de Guzman, natural de Auila, Religioso de la Compañia de IESVS,
Consultor, Calificador del S.to officio
de la Inquisicion.

En Madrid en la emprenta Real. 1614.

Figure 1 Cover illustration from Pedro de Guzmán's *Bienes del honesto trabajo y daños de la ociosidad*, Madrid, 1614 (Biblioteca Nacional, Madrid R/7707).

("the universe was not created for our sake / By powers divine, since as it stands it is so deeply flawed" [V, l. 198–9]). It is the inhospitable indifference of the world that necessitates toil:

> If with our labouring we did not urge the land to birth
> By turning over fertile clumps of clay with the plough's share,
> And breaking the land, crops could not rise into the liquid air
> On their own. Meanwhile even plants that cost the sweat of our brow,
> Although in leaf across the land and all in flower now,
> Either the sun will scorch them, sending too much heat below,
> Or sudden cloudbursts and the icy hoarfrost lay them low,
> Or they are hammered by a storm when violent whirlwinds blow.
> (*The Nature of Things* V, l. 209–17)

For Lucretius, the Ovidean "Golden Age," during which nature freely gave her fruits to an idle humanity – a view so amenable to Christian providential design – never existed.

Pedro de Guzmán proceeds with an account of the first fallen man, naked and without provisions in a dangerous world. But rather than a meditation on a helpless and repugnant creature, Guzmán extols human creativity:

> Pero he yo considerado muchas vezes con admiracion la ingeniosa traça, y sabiduria del Señor, para ocupar al hombre, que le necessita por una parte a buscar el sustento, el vestido, la habitacion, y las demas cosas necessarias a la vida, y por otra ofrece a sus artificiosas manos, y le pone en ellas los materiales donde ha de sacar estas cosas, toscos e informes, como son las canteras y montes de donde se corta la piedra y madera para los edificios, las venas de tierra arcilosa para los vasos de barro, de que en muchos usos suele servirse, los minerales de oro, plata y hierro, y de otros metales, para adornarse, o armarse, las lanas y pieles de los animales, y las yervas de do se tuerce el lino y cañamo para vestirse y cubrirse, ocupandole toda la vida en la disposicion, composicion y labor destas cosas, añadiendole instrumentos, y potencias de sentidos, imaginacion, ingenio, o industria, los mas a proposito que se podian imaginar. (fols. 8–9)

> [But I have considered many times with admiration the ingenious design, and wisdom of the Lord, to occupy man, who on the one hand is given the need to seek sustenance, clothing, shelter, and other life necessities; and

> on the other is offered skilful hands, and receives in them the materials with which he can find these necessities, crude and unformed, as are the quarries and mountains from which the stone and wood are cut for buildings, the clayey veins of land for earthen vessels, which have many uses, the minerals of gold, silver and iron, and of other metals, in order to adorn himself, or arm himself, the furs and skins of animals, and the plants from which linen and hemp are wound in order to dress and cover himself, giving him lifelong occupation in the disposition, composition and labour of these things, giving him in addition instruments, strength of senses, imagination, ingenuity, or industry, the most efficacious imaginable.]

It is significant that this approving description should also include the non-utilitarian ("para adornarse" – "to adorn himself"), as well as an emphasis on imagination, industriousness, and that most suggestive attribute, *ingenio*.[26] Near the end of his lengthy and frequently subtle disquisition on play, Guzmán describes how some exalted figures found recreation: "Inocencio VIII en podar arboles … El Emperador Maximiliano segundo, y su hermano el Archiduque Carlos labravan en oro, y plata, sincelavan, y pintavan" ("Innocent VIII in pruning trees … The Emperor Maximilian the Second, and his brother the Archduke Charles worked gold, and silver, carved, and painted").

The same creative attributes that set man apart from beasts are exercised in play, and Guzmán's explanation of why it is done reveals a deceptively profound aspect of *eutrapelia*: "Y a otros muchos Reyes, y Principes, y Emperadores, y (lo que es mas) a santissimos, y doctissimos varones, antiguos y modernos, no les parecia indigno de su grandeza, o de su modestia, y santidad, *humanarse un poco* en semejantes recreaciones, para condecender con la flaqueza de la humana fragilidad, y naturaleça" ("And many Kings, and Princes, and Emperors, and (what is more) most saintly and learned men, ancient and modern, did not deem it below their greatness, or their modesty and saintliness, *to humanize themselves a bit* in such recreations, to yield to human weakness and fragility, and nature" [fol. 420, my italics]). Play allows for an expression of exalted qualities (creativity, imagination, skill), while at the same time it humbles, permitting an indulgence in childlike curiosity and exuberance. We will return to this fruitful ambivalence.

The social and cognitive aspects of recreation emphasized in the Aristotelian-Thomist tradition are also present in the Spanish writings. Pedro de Guzmán associates play with both friendship and conversation: "*Juego*, o entretenimiento, *es necessario para la conversacion humana*, dize el Angelico Dotor Santo Thomas; y adonde dize, *conversacion*, luego que lo lei, entendi que dezia *conservacion*. Y cierto es assi, que a penas se pueda conservar la vida de otra manera" ("*Play*, or entertainment, *is necessary for human conversation*, says the Angelic Doctor Saint Thomas; and where he says, *conversation*, when I read it, I understood it to say *conservation*. And it certainly is so, that one can hardly conserve life by other means" [fol. 407]). As Aristotle said of friendship: "it is a certain kind of virtue, or goes with virtue, and is also most necessary for life" (*Ethics* 1155a2); and "friendship seems to hold cities together, and lawmakers seem to take it more seriously than justice" (1155a23). Aristotle also underlines the importance of the company one keeps, a concern that would be voiced in Spanish complaints against gambling dens:

> And whatever *being* consists in for any sort of people – whatever it is for the sake of which they choose to be alive – this is what they want to be engaged in with their friends. This is why some friends drink together, others play dice together, and still others engage in athletic exercise together and go hunting together, or engage in philosophy together, each sort spending their days together in whatever it is, out of all the things in life, that they are most contented by; for since they want to share their lives with their friends, they do those things and share those things that they believe living together consists in. (*Ethics* 1172a1)

People do not come together simply for protection and pooling of resources. Human nature is sociable, and community provides the context for creating both meaning and pleasure.

In his *Libro de los daños que resultan del juego* (1599), Adrian de Castro emphasized the connection between private and public, friendship and social cohesion, and notes the corrosive effect of excessive play:

> Tambien se pierde la amistad, y conversacion de los amigos que es menester tiempo para grangearlos, porque por virtud del trato y comunicacion se grangean. Es tal el amistad que dize della San Chrysostomo, que es muro y fortaleza de la republica necessaria para la conservacion de la paz, util para la vida publica, provechosa para la domestica, rica para nuestra pobreza, alegre para nuestra tristeza, medicina para nuestras enfermedades, deleytosa para la vida humana. (fols. 134r–135)

> [One also loses the friendship and conversation of friends, who take time to win over, because by virtue of intercourse and communication they are earned. Such is friendship that Saint Chrysostom says of it, that it is a wall

> and fortress of the republic necessary for the conservation of peace, useful for public life, beneficial for domestic life, wealth for our poverty, glee for our sadness, medicine for our maladies, pleasurable for human life.]

Proper recreation with the right company, then, has a far greater function than simply "relaxing the bow-string." It provides a space in which individuals convene and model different types of social interaction. As the Spanish commentators recognize, the dynamic is complex: on the one hand, the right type of leisure activity can have a normative function, inculcating virtuous qualities in those who participate; on the other hand, a game may be played well or poorly, and people often reveal their true characters through play. As Pedro de Covarrubias notes, the intense involvement of play can overwhelm normal social inhibitions: "conviene a saber en el juego somos incautos porque en el estudio y beodez del nos declaramos quales somos. Alli se abren nuestros pechos y muestran los vicios secretos" ("it is advisable to know that in play we are incautious because in its study and inebriation we reveal who we are. There we open our hearts and show our secret vices" [49]). Despite their admonitory tone, such comments hint at the potential for play also to reveal positive aspects of identity normally suppressed within the strictures of everyday life.

Two brief twentieth-century examples illustrate the notion of realizing the ideal through play. Although they are both somewhat comic, they reveal deep connections with the intellectual traditions that inform our early modern debates. In Thomas Mann's "A Man and His Dog," the narrator's canine companion displays his essence during their recreational outings to his "hunting-ground." It is there that the "auto-telos" of play reigns, and where the dog breaks free from his prosaic and servile role in the domestic sphere: "The tracking out, the driving up, the chasing – these are ends in themselves to the sporting spirit, and are plainly so to him, as anybody would see who watched him at his brilliant performance. How beautiful he becomes, how consummate, how ideal! Like a clumsy peasant lad, who will look perfect and statuesque as a huntsman among his native rocks. All that is best in Bashan, all that is genuine and fine, comes out and reaches its flower at these times" (*Death in Venice and Seven Other Stories* 267). Although Montaigne was sceptical of "that cousinage between man and the animals," he recognizes the same impulse that forms the seed of Mann's story: "I am not afraid to admit that my nature is so tender, so childish, that I cannot well refuse my dog the play he offers me or asks of me outside the proper time" (*Essays* II, 11, p. 318). Nabokov's socially awkward and ungainly Pnin undergoes a similar metamorphosis to Mann's canine protagonist when he plays croquet:

> As soon as the pegs were driven in and the game started, the man was transfigured. From his habitual, slow, ponderous, rather rigid self, he changed into a terrifically mobile, scampering, mute, sly-visaged hunchback. It seemed to be always his turn to play. Holding his mallet very low and daintily swinging it between his parted spindly legs (he had created a minor sensation by changing into Bermuda shorts expressly for the game), Pnin foreshadowed every stroke with nimble aim-taking oscillations of the mallet head, then gave the ball an accurate tap, and forthwith, still hunched, and with the ball still rolling, walked rapidly to the spot where he had planned for it to stop. With geometrical gusto, he ran it through hoops, evoking cries of admiration from the onlookers. (*Pnin* 130)[27]

We will do well to keep in mind the likes of Bashan and Pnin when we later consider the ludic transformations of humans and dogs alike in *Don Quijote, El coloquio de los perros* and *La ilustre fregona.*

The venue of *eutrapelia* informs the activity by limiting movement and imposing a certain order, and in so doing also affirms its separation from real life. As we will discuss in some detail later, much attention was given to how different spaces – interior / exterior, private / communal – determined the nature of the activity. With its roots in classical *otium, eutrapelia* was frequently discussed in association with the *locus amoenus,* the Arcadian ideal of nature as a space of sanctuary and renewal. A representative example appears in Luque Faxardo's *Fiel desengaño contra la ociosidad y los juegos,* as the space of the dialogue is demarcated from the urban sphere:

> Bien entretiene el alameda con la gallardía de sus antiguas colunas, el primor de sus fuentes, hermosura y orden de su arboleda, álamos, paraisos y naranjos, cuya variedad junta deleita; quédese allá para los agridulces discretos de nuestro tiempo, que quieren campo y ciudad sin distinción de puestos. Todo tiene su sazón y punto, y en tanto será bueno o mejor un sitio, cuanto no le ofusquen y escurezcan otros. Este lugar está regalado y apacible, suave olor de azahar a uno y a otro lado, la ciudad a las espaldas con su atropellado ruido, sin hacer aquí el de las aguas alguno que nos impida, antes la buena consonancia de tal silencio despierta y da aliento a nuestra conversación, que fío será apacible. (bk. I, ch. 3)

> [Pleasing is the boulevard with the gallantry of its ancient columns, the finery of its fountains, the beauty and order of its woods, poplars, chinaberry and orange trees, whose variety gives pleasure; away with the bittersweet sages of our time, who want city and country without distinction. Everything has its time and place, and the better a place is, the less it is obfuscated and overshadowed by others. This place is comfortable and pleasant, the soft scent of orange blossoms here and there, its back turned to the city with its clamorous noise, the water here making no sounds that may impede us; rather, the fine consonance of such silence awakens and gives breath to our conversation, which I trust will be pleasant.]

In part, Luque Faxardo offers a pastoral, Guevaraesque praise of country over city. The erudite Laureano must persuade Florino, a penitent gambler with urban sensibilities: "A quien deja la [conversación] del barrio, siendo su gusto el naipe ... bien poco satisfacen o alegran las del campo" ("Whoever leaves the conversation of the *barrio*, cards being his pleasure ... finds little satisfaction or pleasure in country conversations" [61]). Laureano wants to turn Florino from the degenerate gambling dens ("casas de conversación"), and engage in the authentic conversation of dialogue. Laureano does not reject the city, but rather places an emphasis on limit and separation ("Todo tiene su sazón y punto"), the city associated with work, the country with regenerating leisure. It is also worth emphasizing that Luque Faxardo does not present a paradisiacal, innocent and untouched realm of nature. The image of the *alameda* represents an integration of artifice and nature, the man-made elements (colunas) and the shaping of the natural elements (fuentes, arboleda) creating variety within order.

We will continue our discussion of classical conceptions of leisure and their legacy in early modern humanism below. For now, a consideration of a different space will shed light on the other side of a fundamental polarity: the private versus the public individual. Pedro de Covarrubias's endorsement of solitary leisure offers an interesting alternative to social play. The privileging of contemplation over games recalls the Aristotelian hierarchy of pleasures:

> A las frias escusas de los cavalleros que juegan, los unos diziendo que de otra manera estarian solos. Los otros diziendo que no tienen que hazer ni en que passar tiempo: respondo brevemente. A los primeros digo que no ay solo salvo el mal acompañado, ni es penosa la soledad salvo al nescio que no tiene materia para contemplar y al malo que no puede sufrir compañia de si mesmo: ca por esso va buscando con que se distraera y alexara

de si porque no puede estar consigo. El virtuoso sabio entonces esta mas acompañado: quando esta mas solo. (fols. 56r–57).

[To the lame excuses of gambling gentlemen, the ones saying that otherwise they would be lonely, the others saying that they have nothing to do nor with which to pass the time, I respond briefly. To the first I say that nobody is lonely except for the one who is poorly accompanied, nor is solitude burdensome except for the fool lacking in material to contemplate and for the wretch who cannot stand his own company, and who therefore goes looking for what will distract him and distance him from himself, because he is unable to be with himself. It follows that the virtuous sage is most accompanied when most alone.]

In addition to promoting a traditional "examination of conscience" ("rebusca los escondrijos de su conciencia: mira lo que hay de emendar y lo que ay de mejorar" – "he searches the hidden corners of his conscience, and looks at what must be corrected and what must be improved"), Covarrubias invokes the scholarly *topos* of the company of good books: "que mejor compañia que la de los libros en los quales estan presentes los claros varones passados: las nobles hazañas: los virtuosos exemplos" ("what better company than that of books in which are present the illustrious men of the past, the noble feats, the virtuous examples" [57]). A sense of "conversación" is recuperated when the reader actively engages with another mind. As we will consider below, some of the greatest examples of such leisure are the ruminations of Montaigne and Robert Burton, whose every page bears the presence of their dearest classical authors. But even if they represent an approximation to the divine, the solitary pleasures of the intellect are partial. Genuine *eutrapelia* does not exclude humanity's corporeal and social nature.

Humanist Models of Play

The ambiguities outlined above in the classical sources reappear as early as Alfonso X, who is notable for his endorsement – and theological justification – of enjoyment and levity: "Por que toda manera de alegría quiso Dios que hobiesen los homnes en sí naturalmente por que pudiesen sofrir las cueitas e los trabaios cuando les viniesen, por end los homnes buscaron muchas maneras por que esta alegria pudiesen haber cumplidamientre" ("Because God wanted men to have naturally for themselves all manner of happiness in order to bear the troubles and hardships that befall them, therefore men dutifully sought out many ways by which they could have this happiness" [204]). In his comments on some advantages of board games, Alfonso X promotes numerous types of play:

> E como quiere que todos estos iuegos son muy buenos cadaunos en el tiempo e en el logar o convienen, pero porque estos iuegos que se facen seyendo son cutianos e se facen tan bien de noche como de día, e porque las mugeres que non cabalgan e estan encerradas han a usar desto, e otrosi los homnes son vieios e flacos, o los que han sabor de haber sus placeres apartadamientre por que non reciban en ellos enoio nin pesar, o los que son en poder ageno asi como en prision o en cativerio o que van sobre el mar; e comunalmientre todos aquellos que han fuerte tiempo, porque non pueden cabalgar nin ir a caza ni a otra parte, e han por fuerza de fincar en las casas e buscar algunas maneras de iuegos con que hayan placer e se concortenn e no esten baldios. (204)

> [And since all these games are very good each one in the appropriate time and space, but because these games that are played seated are common and are played as well at night as by day, and because women who do not ride horseback and are enclosed should avail themselves of it, and also men who are old and weak, or those who prefer to take their pleasures apart from others in order to avoid anger and sorrow, or those who are under external restraint such as prison or captivity or who travel the sea; and commonly all of those who have come upon hard times, because they cannot ride a horse nor hunt nor go elsewhere, and who are obliged to stay indoors and look for some manner of games with which they find pleasure and comfort themselves and avoid idleness.]

The passage is remarkable for its sensibility to the space and circumstances of recreation, including the player's sex and social estate. Alfonso X anticipates nearly all the concerns that would occupy later commentators. He also reminds us that some medieval minds were at least as enlightened as early modern ones.

Some seventy years later, Boccaccio echoes Alfonso X when he offers his tales as a therapeutic distraction for love-sick ladies, whose recreational options are more limited than those of men:

> [T]hey remain most of the time enclosed in the confines of their bedrooms where they sit in almost complete idleness ... If men are afflicted with

> melancholy or heavy thoughts, they have many ways of alleviating or forgetting them, for if they wish, they can go out and hear and see many things; they can go hawking, hunting, or fishing; they can ride, gamble, or attend to their trades ... As support and comfort for those ladies in love (to those others who are not I leave the needle, spindle, and wool winder), I intend to tell one hundred stories, or fables, or parables, or histories, or whatever you wish to call them... (Author's Preface)

Adopting the terminology of Olson and Mazzotta, we can say that play in Boccaccio is "hygienic" in two principal ways: it offers a salutary outlet for the love-malady; and the group of storytellers escapes death as plague ravages Florence. To recall our discussion of Aristotle's *eutrapelia*, it is also notable that Boccaccio also offers an apology for literature's lack of practical value. As Mazzotta argues, "The 'uselessness' of literature will turn out to be ... literature's profound value, with its power to challenge, even as it is fascinated with, the utilitarian, 'real' values that have currency in the social world" (74). In other words, the *process* of storytelling itself, of suspending disbelief and exercising the imagination in a fictional realm, may be more important than the *product*, the meaning or applicability of a story. The implications of such an outlook, not least with regard to the tradition of exemplarity, would be developed by writers like Montaigne and Cervantes.

A consideration of three *tractatus ludorum* from varied perspectives – one medical, one historical/antiquarian, one theological – will illustrate the broad interest in games and play in early modern Spain, as well as a common thread of humanist concerns.

Therapeutic Exercise: Cristóbal Méndez, Rodrigo Caro, and Fray Alonso Remon

> "[E]sta medicina del exercicio es movimiento voluntario: y lo podeys hazer quanto quisieredes: y como quisieredes: y donde quisieredes" (140)

> ["[T]his medicine of exercise is voluntary movement, and you may do it as much as you like, and how you like, and where you like"]

Cristóbal Méndez's *Libro del ejercicio corporal y de sus provechos* (1553) stands out among early modern European works on leisure activities and health (and its central concern with the ill effects of sedentary living is prescient). In contrast to other *tractatus ludorum*, Méndez mostly foregoes moral justification or censure. His attention to "humour" theory, to the several faculties – memory, cogitation, fantasy, imagination – and to the interdependence of mental and physical processes are in the galenic tradition, and familiar to any reader of Huarte de San Juan's *Examen de ingenios* (1594). Of special interest to the present study is an aspect only touched upon by the later and more famous tract: what sorts of games and activities can beneficially affect the complex human organism. Méndez considers men, women, infants and the aged, the agile and the handicapped. The positive effects of exertion include the infant's cry, making faces during adolescence, and heated arguments in adulthood. And while he deems walking the most beneficial and generally accessible form of recreation, his inquiry extends to ball games, cards, backgammon and chess.

Given Méndez's psychosomatic convictions, he repeatedly emphasizes the need to exercise the physical organs in order to maintain the cognitive faculties:

> De manera que el que tiene costumbre de mucha especulacion: assi de pinturas o edificios notables: en que aya alguna mora en juzgallas: aqui se exercita (como dixe) el organo en passar por el: y sentido comun en considerallas. Y por esso en oyr musicas bien ordenadas con bozes muy suaves: a señoras: y oyr lectiones a predicadores muy sabios: y muy subtiles: y declarar cosas muy obscuras: se exercita mucho esta virtud: y es muy grande la utilidad y provecho que se toma del tal exercicio. y no vienen a ser los hombres ynabiles en semejantes cosas: sino en no tener uso en aquesto: y no trabajar en emplearse en la consideracion y expeculacion de lo dicho. (117–18)

> [So that he who is accustomed to much speculation, for example of paintings or notable buildings, in which there is some effort in judging them, here (as I said) the organ through which it passes is exercised, as is the common sense in considering them. And because of this by listening to well-ordered songs with pleasing voices, to women, and listening to lessons by wise and astute preachers … this faculty is much exercised, and great is the utility and profit taken from such exercise. And men do not become incapable in such things, except by not making use of this, and not working on occupying themselves with the consideration and speculation of that stated above.]

Since the *sentido comun* is the faculty concerned with comprehending and judging the external world, the physical organs require frequent use and training so as to enable a clear mediation between phenomena and the mind. But Méndez is not advocating continual "work" of the organs in his caution against sedentary idleness. Maintenance of the organs may also be done at leisure, for example while listening to music with pleasing voices. Nuns even benefit from producing such music: "Las señoras monjas por tener coro y cantar: les ayuda mucho para exercicio" ("Nuns by having choirs and singing get much helpful exercise" [130]). Méndez then describes the importance of exercising the other mental faculties: memory, fantasy (capacity for invention) and imagination (for giving order to what the fantasy proposes). All of these capacities can be honed in games, including chess and cards (see Méndez II, chs. 6–7). In one of the many amusing anecdotes that illustrate his science, Méndez recounts a conversation with a gentleman whose son is proficient at games: "es el mejor jugador de todos juegos: que aveys visto: y por cierto que me huelgo mucho dello: y yo le dixe: en verdad señor que de buena virtud alabays a vuestro hijo: y de gran cosa os holgays: que sepa. Y deziame: este señor para qualquier negocio lo halle muy adelante" ("he is the best player of all games that you have seen, and I am certainly very pleased by it, and I told him, in truth, sir, know that you praise your son with good reason, and you are happy about a great thing. And I said to myself, this man is well-prepared for any sort of business" [123]). For Méndez, the benefits of play do not derive simply from the opportunity to recuperate from strenuous work; in play, one can develop skills, both physical and cognitive, that are transferable to important "real life" endeavours.[28]

Like Alfonso X, Méndez is concerned with the value of recreation and play for different estates, ages and genders. His prescription for the landed gentry suggests an alternative to the excessive indoor reading that addles Cervantes's famous man of leisure: "Los hombres desocupados que tienen haziendas en el campo: pueden muy bien muchos dias del campo exercitarse y tomar plazer: con lo que a otros da trabajo: y ganan su vida" ("Idle men who own property in the country can very well and for many days take exercise and enjoyment from the land, with what for others gives work and a livelihood" [125]). The fact that physical work represents a contrast to the nobleman's normal activities converts what would be work for others (the peasantry) into leisure. It also reflects again Méndez's emphasis on a "holistic approach" to health, the importance of exercising the body as well as the mind. His description of recreational labour also expresses the principles of pleasing variety and freedom of choice – elements ostensibly absent for the labouring peasant:

> Que mejor cosa seria que tener hecha su hachuela: o calaboço hechizo: y aun su podadera a proposito: y limpiar sus olivos y arboles: o cortar si tienen sus frutales: el ramo seco: o alguna estaca demasiada: y si fuere menester tomar un açadon y cavar el pie del peral: durazno: o mançano: o ciruelo: Esto tomandolo a su tiempo: y con mucho plazer y voluntad libre: que son las condiciones del exercicio: traen todos los provechos que del se siguen. (125)

> [What better thing could there be than to have ready the hatchet and even the pruning shears for this purpose, and clean your olive trees, or to cut, if you have, fruit trees, the barren limb, or an extra branch, and, if necessary, take up a spade and dig at the base of a pear, peach, apple or cherry tree. And this taking one's time, and with much pleasure and free will, which are the conditions of the endeavour, brings all the benefits that come of it.]

Work is thus transformed into play, fulfilling Huizinga's conditions of limits of time and space, absence of coercion, and, in the case of the nobleman, taking place "outside the sphere of necessity or material utility" (Huizinga 132). The pleasure taken in moulding the physical environment with the pruning sheers and the spade anticipates Pedro de Guzmán's approval of a pope finding leisure in pruning ("Inocencio VIII en podar arboles," cited above), as well as Cervantes's association of landscape gardening with *eutrapelia*: "Para este efeto se plantan las alamedas, se buscan las fuentes, se allanan las cuestas y se cultivan, con curiosidad, los jardines" ("For this effect poplar groves are planted, springs sought out, hills are smoothed down and gardens curiously cultivated," *Novelas ejemplares* Prólogo). As we will see, even the peasant Sancho Panza appreciates the therapeutic diversion that such physical labour can provide: "pues mientras estoy cavando no me acuerdo de mi oíslo, digo, de mi Teresa Panza, a quien quiero más que a las pestañas de mis ojos" ("because while I'm digging I haven't got a thought for my better half, by which I mean my Teresa Panza, and I love her more than these lashes over my eyes" [II, 70, p. 569]).[29]

Méndez recommends a similar regimen of physical exertion for sedentary students, "llenos de sarna … quanto bien trayga lo que es traboso: tomado con voluntad y por plazer" ("full of scabies … how beneficial is that which is arduous, undertaken willingly and for pleasure" [126–7]). With regard to women, Méndez recognizes, like Boccaccio before him, the deprivations particular to their sex: "Notorio esta que las mugeres por no hazer exercicio: vienen a incurrir en grandes enfermedades … y principalmente las señoras que tienen ociosidad" ("It is well known that women, for lack of exercise, come down with great illnesses … and principally the ladies who have leisure," 128). Noting that women of the lower classes do receive physical exercise through their daily tasks, Méndez limits his commentary to noblewomen and nuns. The former take salubrious exercise in overseeing the servants throughout the house, and Méndez stipulates that women should not shrink from the opportunity to argue vigorously with servants – they might even fabricate reasons to do so: "y aun tambien con reñir los descuydos de las moças: que nunca faltan: y aun con fingir que los haya: porque les es muy provechoso tomar yra y dar bozes (como tenemos dicho) les sera su exercicio: y traera gran salud" ("and even with arguing over the carelessness of the servant girls, which are never lacking, and even feigning that there has been [carelessness], because it is very beneficial to get angry and raise one's voice (as we have said) it will be their exercise, and bring them great health" [129]). He then recommends the conventional domestic exercises of needlework and weaving, which also provide positive examples to the girls of the house ("como para dar exemplo a las hijas si las hay: como a las moças o donzellas desocupadas" – "by way of giving an example to any daughters, as to the unoccupied servant girls and maidens"). Walking again proves the most accessible and beneficial form of recreation, and it is an activity that women may adapt to their own restrictive spaces: "porque yo siento: que aya señora: que no puede mandar cerrar la puerta de su quarto: y por una sala de aquellas passearse dos horas antes de comer: yo juro: que aunque sus señorias se passan: y biven sin hazer lo que digo: que biviran mas: y con vida sin trabajo" ("because I am sorry if there isn't a woman who cannot order the door to her room closed, and in one of those rooms stroll around for two hours prior to eating. I vow that although the ladies stroll about … that they will live more, and have an unburdened life" [130]). One imagines that Carrizales, in *El celoso extremeño*, might have been more successful in preventing the disruptive curiosity of his young wife had Leonora been prescribed this particular pastime in her captive domesticity. Of course, Cervantes is interested in the destructive nature of the captivity itself, despite the array of pleasing, if infantilizing, recreations the old man allows his wife (*El celoso extremeño*).

For skilled labourers, Méndez gives the curious advice that they make interludes of play out of their own work: "y seria que antes de comer: o cenar: por su plazer: y no con voluntad subjecta trabajassen el tiempo que les pareciesse: hasta que toma en cansancio: y sudassen un rato" ("and this would involve, prior to lunch or dinner, at their own pleasure, and not subject to another's will, that they work however long they like, until weariness sets in and they perspire a bit" [132]). In this manner, workers "gastan se muchas superfluydades: y alcançan lo que se sigue del exercicio ordenado" ("they expend many superfluities and attain what follows from ordered exercise" [133]). To the galenic principle of purging excess humours through vigorous activity (the benefits of which we would probably recognize today as the stimulation of endorphins), Méndez adds a psychologically acute insight into the nature of recreation: what separates work from play is not so much the activity itself, but whether or not it is taken up freely, and temporally delimited. Elements of Méndez's proposal can be found some three hundred years later in the famous mowing scene of *Ana Karenina*. The nobleman Levin, who reflects to himself that "I need physical movement, otherwise my character definitely deteriorates" (248), joins his peasants for a day in the fields, after which he exclaims to his brother: "I want to enrich medical science with a new term: *Arbeitskur*" (257). Like Sancho Panza, Levin describes a happy obliviousness while immersed in the rhythm of his scythe-strokes: "it's such cheerful and at the same time such hard work, that one has no time to think" (248); "more and more often those moments of unconsciousness came, when it was possible for him not to think of what he was doing" (252). In his idealized image of country labour, Tolstoy depicts the serfs themselves displaying a ludic quality in their work: the muzhik Titus, who "walked straight ahead without bending, as if playing with his scythe" (249); and the old man, "swinging his arms while walking, as if in play" (252). Méndez would not have been surprised.[30]

Summarizing the virtues of walking, Méndez underscores how it can be combined with other pleasurable activities – seeing, listening, conversing, contemplating – which brings him back to his psychosomatic understanding of the human being:

> Que mas quereys que todas las potencias animales (como tengo dicho) en esto se exercitan: y vea lo cada uno de lo que tenemos mostrado: en lo que

> se oye y vee el sentido comun: y en lo que podeys ymaginar y fantasear la ymaginativa y fantasia. Y en lo que quisieredes pensar: la memoria y cogitativa todo esto passeando os lo podeys hazer. No digo juntamente: sino quando lo uno o lo otro: que bien se entiende. De modo que en el tal exercicio todo plazer se puede alcançar. (139)
>
> [What more could you want than that all of the physical capacities (as I have said) in this are exercised, and may each see from what we have shown: the common sense in that which is heard and seen, the faculties of the imagination and fantasy in what you can imagine and fantasize about. And of what you might want to think, memory and cognition, all of this you may do while strolling. I do not mean all at once, but one at a time, which is well understood. So that in such exercise one can achieve all manner of pleasure.]

In addition to his Aristotelian association of pleasure with activation of the intellectual faculties, Méndez's medical interest in the physical and mental effects of various recreations places him within a growing tradition of early modern humanists. As Frances Gage has shown in a study of Italian treatises on gardens and picture galleries (with French and English illustrations as well), there was an intense interest in the connections among physical movement, the cultivation of the intellect, and overall health, and in which recreational activities most effectively achieve such ends: "Physicians and laymen alike attributed the health of the body to the operations of the soul, which governed physical and mental processes, including the nourishment and movement of the body and the acquisition and preservation of knowledge through the senses" (Gage 1183). The key thinkers discussed by Gage, including Girolamo Mercuriale, Giocondo Baluda, Thomas Elyot, and Robert Burton, are all anticipated by Méndez.

If Méndez is more concerned with the physiological – rather than the moral and social – effects of play, the Andalusian priest Rodrigo Caro offers, in his *Días geniales o lúdricos* (1626), an expansive history of games from the perspective of the fervent antiquarian. Caro's study serves partly to reveal the origins of many pastimes in contemporary Spain, including ball games, throwing the bar ("tirar la barra" [I, 116]), theatre, story-telling, dancing, and even practical jokes ("burlas graciosas," II, 213); but he is also motivated by a humanist desire to unearth as much classical Greek and Roman culture as possible. Caro possessed two copies of Lucretius's *De Rerum Natura* (Greenblatt, *The Swerve* 250), and one can detect aspects of the Roman's thought in his writings. As we will see below, Lucretian ideas such as the interdependence of body and spirit, and the Epicurean interest in the promotion of good health through pleasing activities, are present in many of the figures under consideration.[31]

It should come as no surprise that the primary justifications for play Caro finds in the classical world are similar to those frequently voiced in early modern Spain:

> Conocieron los antiguos ser necesarios los juegos, y más entre la gente lozana y briosa en la mocedad; y así, para apartarlos de vicios que acarrea la curiosidad, ordenaron juegos que, juntamente con entretener y alegrar, dispongan la naturaleza a la agilidad y fuerza para las ocasiones de veras y para conservar la salud. (I, 140)
>
> [The ancients knew games to be necessary, and more so amongst fresh and energetic youth; and so, to keep them away from the vices caused by curiosity, they organized games that, along with entertaining and delighting, dispose nature to agility and strength for earnest occasions and to preserve health.]

From the moral prophylaxis of preventing idleness and curiosity to the approval of entertainment and pleasure, from honing skills for the real world to improving health, Caro identifies in Greek and Roman thought on play most of the considerations discussed in contemporary Spanish writings. A separate chapter treats the importance of moderation in play (I, 142–8). When describing a Roman inscription referring to an official whose task it was to monitor schools, Caro points to the connection between play and learning: "porque *ludus* en la lengua latina significa la escuela maternal en que algo se aprende; pero *lusus* significa los juegos de esta edad. De manera que este oficio era para ordenar y reformar los tales juegos, con que está bastantemente encarecido el cuidado de aquella gran república en la educación de los muchachos" ("because *ludus* in the Latin tongue means the maternal school in which something is learned; but *lusus* means the games of this age [i.e. youth]. So that this occupation was to organize and reform such games, which substantially increases the value of care that great republic places in the education of children" [I, 133]). We will consider below how Erasmus and Vives were also very interested in the role of play in childhood education.

Perhaps the greatest contemporary relevance of *Días geniales o lúdricos* has to do with its genre. Caro's antiquarian knowledge is disseminated through the conversation between don Diego and don Pedro, who, along with their comic coachman, Melchor, visit don Fernando at his country estate. That this treatise on play takes the form of a Renaissance dialogue creates an extra ludic layer, resulting in a sort of play (or games) within a play.[32] The emphasis on friendship between the interlocutors, the deceptive insignificance of their endeavour ("estas niñerías" – "these trifles" [II, 9]) and the venue of the undertaking signal that the dialogue itself is a form of recreation: "¡Qué de memorias alegres nos reduce este agradable sitio! En ninguna manera permite vagar la imaginación a cosas tristes, porque la hermosura de este jardín, desenfado del patio, y todo el edificio y sitio de esta heredad entretiene los ojos y ocupa su hermosura el entendimiento" ("To what happy memories this pleasant place returns us! In no way does it permit our imaginations to stray to sad things, because the beauty of this garden, the unaffectedness of the patio, and all the architecture and space of this estate entertains the eyes and engages with its beauty the understanding" [I, 106]). The praise of the rejuvenating country house underlines the relevance of the dialogue's classical subject matter, since the *locus amoenus* exists on the outskirts of seventeenth-century Seville. The venue also indicates the parallels between the dialogue and the games discussed therein – the diversion from quotidian concerns, and therapeutic engagement of body and mind. Perhaps Caro was inspired by one of his copies of Lucretius, which contains the following image of rural recreation:

> And often a party of them sprawled on the soft carpet of grass
> Beside the riverbank, in the shade of a lofty tree, would pass
> The time refreshing their bodies at no great cost. And with more reason
> When fair weather smiled upon them, and it was the season
> That prinked out all the greenery with flowers. That was the time
> Of joking, and of conversation, and sweet laughter's chime,
> For that was when the Rustic Muse was at the height of her powers.
>
> (*The Nature of Things* bk. V, ll. 1392–8)

Agustín del Campo observed "Rodrigo Caro's love of this quiet existence, half rural and half urban, part solitary and part sociable, as much turned towards antiquity as facing the present, intermixed with outlandish news and local happenings."[33] The liminality of the dialogue in

Días geniales o lúdricos, and of the author's bearing, reinforce the underlying notion of the in-between realm of play: its semi-autonomy from purposive reality, and earnestness amidst the levity.

The final dialogue concludes with don Fernando returning to his reservations over the frivolity of the subject matter, and thus of the activity to which the men have dedicated much time: "¡Quién pensara que después de tres días que ha que tratamos de estas niñerías no estuviesen ya vuestras mercedes cansados o enfadados!" ("Who would have thought that after these three days we've been discussing these trifles Your Graces would not already be tired or annoyed!" II, 9). We are again reminded of Campuzano's self-deprecating remarks regarding Cervantes's greatest dialogue: "esos sueños o disparates, que no tienen otra cosa de bueno si no es el poderlos dejar cuando enfaden" ("these dreams or absurdities, whose only virtue is that you can leave them off when they annoy you" [*El casamiento engañoso* 295]). Like Caro, Cervantes ultimately justifies the activity amidst associations with the *locus amoenus* and the health of the body and mind: "Yo alcanzo el artificio del *Coloquio* y la invención, y basta. Vámanos al Espolón a recrear los ojos del cuerpo, pues ya he recreado los del entendimiento" ("I appreciate the art and invention of the colloquy, and let that suffice. Let's go to the Espolón and refresh the eyes of our body, for we've already refreshed those of the understanding" [*El coloquio de los perros* 359]). Rodrigo Caro, like Cervantes, vindicates his scientific-literary creation in the terms of *eutrapelia* and in the tradition of *serio ludere*:

> Justo es que respire y se alegre para cobrar nuevos alientos; y siendo esto, no sólo voluntario, sino forzoso, muy acertada diversión y entretenimiento buscó vuestra merced en los juegos de los muchachos, porque ¿qué mejor entretenerse que en aquello que en primer lugar merece este nombre? ¿Qué más inculpable diversión que en los sencillos juegos de la niñez?
>
> No sólo juzgo que vuestra merced se ha entretenido docta y discretamente, pero que merece alabanza y agradecimiento de la posteridad. (II, 258–9)

> [It is right that one relax and be cheerful in order to regain one's strength; and this being the case, not only voluntary, but necessary, and very proper diversion and entertainment did Your Grace seek out in children's games, because what better entertainment than in that which originally deserves this name? What more harmless diversion than in simple childhood games?

> I not only judge that Your Grace has entertained himself in a learned and discreet manner, but that he deserves the praise and gratitude of posterity.]

The supposedly puerile escapism of the grown men is shown to be quite substantial indeed.

By comparison with the scientific and literary sophistication of Caro and Méndez, Fray Alonso Remon, in his *Entretenimientos y juegos honestos, y recreaciones christianas* (1623), would seem to consider play from a conventionally moralistic perspective. Promoting *eutrapelia* of the Aristotelian-Thomist tradition, Remon contends that play should nurture virtues and avoid vice, and a premium is placed on exemplarity. In contrast to Alfonso X and Boccaccio's relatively sympathetic views regarding the enclosure of women, he bemoans contemporary feminine freedoms, and argues for their strict subordination within traditional hierarchy: the cultivation of flowers and herbs, drawing, and the lessons of "buenos libros" – presumably of devotion – should be recreation enough for women. But despite his ostensible piety, Remon's account is comprehensive, suggesting appropriate leisure activities for the noble and the humble, the lay and ecclesiastical, the four ages, both sexes, those who rule, judge, and make laws, and soldiers. And he seems particularly attuned to the complementarity of body and mind, as when he calls for play that involves "contrarias acciones," that is, leisure activities that contrast with one's habitual occupations:

> [S]i el que se sale a recrear tiene por principal oficio estar siempre estudiando, o escriviendo, y siempre sentado trabajando el espiritu, sin que trabaje el cuerpo: la recreacion que tomare ha de ser de tal manera, que haga algun exercicio el cuerpo, y descanse el espiritu, y ansi en las personas de negocios, y papeles, y estudiosos, será conveniente que busquen entretenimientos, y recreaciones en que se haga algun exercicio corporal. (fol. 60)

> [[I]f he who goes for recreation has as primary occupation constant studies, or writing, and is always seated exerting his spirit, without exerting the body, the recreation that he takes should be such that the body does some sort of exercise, and that the spirit rests; and also so with people engaged in business, and paperwork, and studious people, it will be suitable that they find entertainments and recreations by which some corporal exercise is performed.]

Such attention to the particularities of experience, and the possibility of tailoring leisure for maximum benefit, recalls Méndez's medicinal insights, and places Remon in the hygienic tradition.

Human Divinity and Depravity: Vives, Erasmus, Montaigne

As our survey of the authors above suggests, the spectrum of Renaissance humanism is broad – not least due to the richness of the medieval precursors. An interesting polarity exists, for example, between the optimistic "dignity of man" school of Pico, and what we might call the sceptical "humility of man" outlook, most eloquently represented by Montaigne. The "dignity" tradition affirms humankind's powers of self-transformation, the ability to master chance through skilful exercise of the will, and the primacy of reason and the creative imagination. Art improves upon nature, and human civilization, along with the virtuosic performances of the individuals who comprise it, represents a triumph of artifice, an exercise of godlike faculties and freedom. As Kristeller noted, it involves human beings declaring themselves independent of any fixed position in the traditional hierarchy of the cosmos (*Renaissance Thought* 129–39). By contrast, the "humility" tradition emphasizes human limitations and the subordination of individual agency to chance. It recognizes the disordering, destructive potential of the imagination, is sceptical of the power of reason, and aware of the tenuousness of community. The balance is tipped away from *divinitas*, in a downward focus on *feritas*, our kinship with beasts. As Friedrich discussed, an emphasis on man's proximity to animals was a conventional way of depicting humanity's fall from grace and need of redemption; but with Montaigne, it can signal a modest conformity with benevolent nature: "The *miseria hominis* for which he decides is not wretchedness, rather, it is a gray but serviceable soberness."[34] For Pascal, on the other hand, humankind's dignity consists in embracing its abject nature: "Man's greatness lies in his capacity to recognize his wretchedness" (*Pensées* VII, 146, p. 36). A progression can be traced from a Renaissance notion of equilibrium between artifice and nature, and optimism regarding the coherence of human individuality and community, to a more conflicted Baroque view of polarization, instability and scepticism.[35] This is a rather crude generalization, and there are points of overlap. In Cervantes we find elements of both currents, partly because of chronology – Cervantes's life spanning a period of transition in early modern civilization – and partly due to the capaciousness of his sensibilities. As we shall see, such divergent visions correspond to different conceptions of play, with varying combinations of Caillois's *agon*, *ilinx*, *alea* and *mimesis*. The structured competition of chess, for example, involves a skilful realization of a role within rigid hierarchy; improvisational *mimesis*, on the other hand, represents potentially liberating self-invention.

Vives's *A Fable About Man* follows Pico's exaltation of god-like humanity: "There indeed was a mind full of wisdom, prudence, knowledge, reason, so fertile that by itself it brought forth extraordinary things. Its inventions are: towns and houses, the use of herbs, stones and metals, the designations and names of all things, which foremost among his other inventions have especially caused wise men to wonder" (*A Fable* 392). The emphasis on human ingenuity is similar to Pedro de Guzmán's account of the first post-lapsarian man, who creates things and order out of the unrefined clutter of raw materials (cited above). So impressed are the gods in Vives's *Fable* that they invite man to join them as a spectator to their games and plays, and to feast with them at the banquet. Someone who would approvingly write of humans "surpassing the nature of man and relying entirely upon a very wise mind" (389) is in important ways quite far from Montaigne and Erasmus. But this is Vives at his most exuberant. Elsewhere he prioritizes natural objects over artificial ones, asserting that man finds greater pleasure in the *lugar ameno* than in the contemplation of art, and concluding with the somewhat paradoxical reasoning that "que somos seres naturales, nos interesan más las obras de la Naturaleza que las del artificio humano" ("since we are natural beings, works of Nature interest us more than those of human artifice" [*Obras completas* 1279]). As his well-known invective against popular literary works demonstrates, Vives was not an enthusiastic advocate of the free imagination.[36] And his stark demarcation of the body and spirit contrasts with the synthesizing views discussed above: "Los placeres del cuerpo y los del alma se repelen mutuamente. Los que se han dado a los placeres corporales no perciben los que tienen su asiento en el alma, y al revés. Combátense entre sí con gran saña, según sea su excelencia y vileza y no toleran suerte alguna de comunicación" ("The pleasures of the body and those of the soul repel each other. Those who have given themselves over to corporal pleasures do not perceive the ones seated in the soul, and vice versa. They fight amongst themselves viciously, according to their respective excellence and vileness, and they tolerate no form of communication" [*Obras completas* 1279]). Rather than the complementary relationship between body and soul expressed in the writings of Méndez and Remon, and the resulting promotion of games that activate both faculties, Vives would seem to give a rigid interpretation of Aristotle's hierarchy of pleasures. But we shall see that his meditations on play and childhood education do not, in fact, reflect such a regimented view.

Vives's concern with education and civic harmony are on display in another passage of the *Fable*, after man has just finished transforming himself into "a thousand wild beasts": "the curtain was drawn back and he returned a man, prudent, just, faithful, human, kindly, and friendly, who went about the cities with the others, held the authority and obeyed in turn, cared for public interest and welfare, and was finally in every way a political and social being" (389). His writings on games contain these same ethical concerns. Vives's *Diálogos* were meant as a Latin primer for schoolboys, and his belief in the educational value of games for children is evident throughout. Youth's malleability, its susceptibility to edifying and corrupting influences, was a major concern in Plato's *Dialogues*, an important source for the writers presently under consideration (see, for example, "Euthyphro"). In the dialogue, "Las leyes del juego" ("The laws of play"), Vives sets forth a model of play that examines fundamental concerns of chance and human agency, authority and group interaction, utility and pleasure. One of the characters, Centellas, has just returned from France and reports on his trip to his companions Borja and Cabanillas, as they stroll through the streets and plazas of Valencia. The conversation of the three friends includes much praise of the beauty and order of their own city, and it is their arrival before the governor's house and the tribunals of law and commerce that inspires an exposition of "the rules of play" ("Ningún sitio mejor que esta plaza y esta Audiencia para hablar de leyes" – "No better place than this town square and this Tribunal for talking about laws" [148]). *Eutrapelia* finds expression in the first rule: "los juegos se inventaron para recreo del ánimo fatigado de las cosas serias" ("games were invented for recreation of the spirit fatigued by serious things" [149]). According to Vives, the relationship between play and work is complementary, not oppositional, and his articulation of play in a community setting suggests the importance of recreation in the very process of socialization. Vives's play involves the body as well as the mind, and while *alea* is present, his game emphasizes the individual's ability to control chance and create a structure opposed to natural disorder: "Se ha de procurar, mientras lo permitan la salud y el tiempo, que el juego, a par de diversión, sea ejercicio del cuerpo. Y también que no sea el juego de tal calidad que dependa todo de la suerte, sino que la experiencia y el saber corrijan los malos azares de la fortuna" ("One must see to it, while health and time permit, that the game, while diverting, also provide exercise for the body. And also that it not be of such a quality that it depend completely on chance, but rather that experience and knowledge be able to correct the arbitrary ills of fortune" [149]). The community of players affirms order and respects authority, facilitating harmonious interaction: "Recuerda que los que miran son como los jueces del juego, y cede a su dictamen sin dar señales de que no te parece bien. De esta suerte el juego es recreo, y también grata y generosa educación de un mancebo hidalgo" ("Remember that those who watch are as the judges of the game, and cede to their rulings without showing signs that you disagree. This way the game is recreation, and also enjoyable and generous education for a young nobleman" [150]). Vives's celebration of free will over arbitrary fortune optimistically expresses a belief in the development of individual virtue and capabilities within a social context. As we will see, Montaigne shared a similar conviction regarding the importance of games in both refining and revealing the character of children: "it must be noted that children's games are not games, and must be judged in children like their more serious actions" (I, 23, p. 79). The presence of Vives's onlookers, acting as judges ("jueces"), would thus be important for Montaigne's young players as well.

To refer back to the trajectory outlined earlier in this study, continuities can be traced from Alfonso X and Vives through Cervantes's "mesa de trucos" (*Novelas ejemplares*), to Jovellanos's advocacy of games "de útil ejercicio como trucos y billar" ("of useful exercise, such as billiards" [*Memoria sobre las diversiones públicas* 196]). They all draw upon similar aspects of the classical and Christian ideas on *eutrapelia* discussed in the previous section. Vives's emphasis on mastering chance and adverse fortune with skill recalls Alfonso X's description of "tablas," or backgammon: "que por el iuego de ellas que el qui las sopiere bien iogar, que aunque la suerte de los dados le sea contraria, que por su cordura podrá iogar con las tablas de manera que esquivará el daño que puede venir por la ventura de los dados" ("that in the playing of them he who knows how to play them well, although the dice may be unfavourable, by dint of good sense will be able to play backgammon in a way that will avoid the harm that can come from the fortuity of dice" [206]). But within such continuities, one can detect progressively restrictive views on leisure, an increasingly subordinate role vis-à-vis work and productive activity.[37] The optimism in Vives's conception of the game as an expression of social cohesion, of the possibility that the sensibilities cultivated in play could translate to collaborative action in the public sphere, would for later humanists become increasingly difficult to sustain.

Like Vives, Erasmus composed dialogues on games, and there are many concordances: the importance of establishing a suitable structure – of time, space, and rules – within which the activity takes place, the emphasis on fair play and deference to authority, the combining of skill and chance, the belief in physical and intellectual benefits of play in moderation, the game as metaphor for society. In Erasmus, however, in addition to the moral seriousness there is a greater emphasis on the pleasure of play. "Knucklebones," which describes a primitive variant of dice, comically concludes with a depiction of Charles and Quirinus getting ready to play: "*Quir.* Go ahead. But it's best to shut the doors, so our cook won't see us playing like children ... *Char.* Ho there, boy, shut and bolt the door, to keep some spectator from popping in without notice. Then we can play to our heart's content" (*Colloquies* 441). Rather than displaying exemplary leisure to an appreciative public, the men are acting foolishly; but Erasmus seems to endorse the childlike enjoyment they derive from the inconsequential game. A similar approval of innocent adult play can be found in Montaigne: "And among so many admirable actions of Scipio, the grandfather, a personage worthy of the reputation of celestial descent, there is nothing that lends him more charm than to see him playing nonchalantly and childishly at picking up and selecting shells and running potato races by the sea with Laelius" (III, 13, p. 851). As Caro concluded in his dialogue, "¿Qué más inculpable diversión que en los sencillos juegos de la niñez?" ("What more harmless diversion than in simple childhood games?" [*Días geniales* II, 259]).

Erasmus's "The Epicurean" advocates temperate indulgence of the senses, reminding the reader to cultivate the pleasures of the body as well as those of the mind. These values are most fully developed in "The Godly Feast," which contains many of the principles observed in our discussion of *eutrapelia*. The *locus amoenus* where the friends convene – the country house and gardens of Eusebius, a "well-cultivated place" – represents a synthesis of natural beauty and variety with human order and artifice. Indeed, the idea of striking an appropriate balance between nature and artifice underpins the entire colloquy. Erasmus's familiar critique of religious ceremony (expressed here moderately regarding Catholicism, virulently against Jews) is to a large degree a warning against placing excessive value on artifice. Man should, in piety, in choosing vocations, and in other endeavours, listen to "Nature," which, Eusebius says, "is not silent but talks to us all the time, on every hand, and teaches the observant man many things if she finds him attentive and receptive" (*Colloquies* 48). But there is also emphasis on pleasure, which is increased by supplementing nature with artifice:

> *Timothy*. Oh! These must be the Epicurean gardens I see.
> *Eusebius*. The entire place is intended for pleasure – honest pleasure, that is: to feast the eyes, refresh the nostrils, restore the soul. (51)

There are numerous other references to attending to body and mind, including Timothy's later observation that "When the whole man is refreshed, this is abundant refreshment indeed" (62). Faced with such imagery and clear thematic exposition, few readers of Cervantes would fail to recall the curiously cultivated garden in the prologue of the *Novelas ejemplares*, along with its profound resonance at the collection's finale: "Yo alcanzo el artificio del *Coloquio* y la invención, y basta. Vámanos al Espolón a recrear los ojos del cuerpo, pues ya he recreado los del entendimiento" ("I appreciate the art and invention of the colloquy, and let that suffice. Let's go to the Espolón and refresh the eyes of our body, for we've already refreshed those of the understanding"). Erasmus's country house and gardens form a supreme recreational space, and the leisure ideal expressed therein involves not the "bawdy stories" and "dirty songs" of the *bomolochos*, but "profitable conversation" (56); not dice, but the visual "wonders of my palace" (76). The primary loci are the garden, the banquet table, and finally the library, which contains classical and Christian texts. A key background work – for Cervantes as well as Erasmus – is Boccaccio's *Decameron*, where a "country mansion" is the venue for conversation and storytelling, "with a beautiful large inner courtyard with open colonnades, halls, and bedrooms, all of them beautiful in themselves and decorated with cheerful and interesting paintings; it was surrounded by meadows and marvelous gardens, with wells of fresh water and cellars full of most precious wines" ("The Author's Introduction"). While many of Boccaccio's tales would certainly be deemed "bawdy stories" by Erasmus, it is interesting that the community of the *Decameron* also explicitly favours their conversation over the "games and chessboards" present at the estate. The agonistic nature of such games runs contrary to their purpose, which is to generate pleasure for participants and spectators alike.[38] The pleasure, in turn, is instrumental in sustaining a homogenous if fragile community, against a backdrop of urban calamity.

As noted, the play sphere is a sort of "parenthetical space,"[39] sectioned off from the concerns of everyday life – or, in the case of the *Decameron*, from the horrors of a disastrous epidemic; but it also relates back to that reality, sometimes in unsettling ways. Erasmus gives an entertaining commentary on the tenuous relationship between game and reality in "Exorcism," in which some friends plan an elaborate ceremony to make sport of a superstitious priest: "[A] spot was chosen in the field adjoining the brier patch from which the voice was heard, and a circle, large enough to hold the numerous crucifixes and the various signs, marked off. All of this was executed with the proper ritual" (233). For the gullible Faunus, the space represents a transcendent order of highest consequence, a forum in which good might vanquish evil; for the tricksters, it provides the mechanism of a practical joke, or *burla* (as we shall see, the *Cabeza encantada* episode in *Don Quijote* II, 62, also ostensibly by means of "occult arts," contains a similar dynamic of amazing the gullible, entertaining initiates, and illustrating how fiction accesses truth). But play and prosaic reality converge unexpectedly, as the "devil" gets a bit carried away with his game:

> Polus, who played the devil, rushed forward as if he were going to break into the circle. When Faunus opposed this with exorcisms and sprinkled a lot of holy water on him, the devil finally cried that he cared not a straw for all that. "You've had dealings with a girl," he said. "You're mine by rights." Polus said this as a joke but evidently chanced to hit upon the truth, for the exorcist was silenced by this utterance and withdrew to the center of the circle and whispered something or other to the priest. Observing this, Polus fell back to avoid hearing what was unlawful to hear. (235)

The game does not serve a clearly didactic function in disabusing Faunus of his superstition. Rather, after he has become dangerously obsessed with his newfound power and potential riches, the friends contrive a letter from the possessed spirit, saying that he has been freed, and exhorting the priest to "live a happy life." While the colloquy is a satire on superstition, dubious ceremony and fraudulent documents, the effects on the primary "player," Faunus, are ambiguous in a typically Erasmian manner:

> *Thomas*. This wasn't freeing a man from insanity but changing the brand of insanity!
> *Anselm*. Very true, except that now he's mad in a more pleasant way. (237)

We will presently consider the concept of "pleasant madness."

In his hastily-composed defence of the "usefulness of the colloquies," Erasmus justifies the entertaining quality of his writings as integral to their didactic value, in what amounts to a concise exposition of *serio ludere*: "Socrates brought philosophy down from heaven to earth; I have brought it even into games, informal conversations, and drinking parties. For the very amusements of Christians ought to have a philosophical flavor" (630). He sees the game as an educational tool for youth, a sort of middle ground between the dry intellectualism of formal book learning and the perils of real life: "Young people learn these things better from this little book, I believe, than from experience, the teacher of fools ... Aristotle's *Ethics* is not suited to boys, the theology of Scotus still less ... But to implant from the start a taste for excellence in young minds *is* urgent. Moreover, I'm not sure anything is learned better than what is learned as a game. To confer benefit through a trick is surely deception of the most innocent sort" (625).[40] As mentioned above, this is very similar to the pedagogy Rodrigo Caro described in antiquity: "Los latinos a la escuela donde aprenden los muchachos llamaron *ludus*, y al maestro, *ludi magister*, para significar que habían de aprender jugando y jugar aprendiendo" ("The Latins called the school where the children learned *ludus*, and they called the teacher, *ludi magister*, to signify that they were to learn playing and play learning" [I, 143]). Erasmus's conception of his writings as a sort of game, or "trick," recalls one of the basic meanings of *tropelía* as a virtuosic deception – one that, as we also shall see with Cervantes, may be used to gain knowledge. It is the very "messiness" of reading Erasmus, the stumbling upon paradox and the puzzling in ironic humour, that gives his works greater dimension than conventional moral-philosophical tracts, and that activates a fuller engagement with his texts, one that involves a strong affective as well as intellectual component. And his justification of the colloquies notwithstanding, Erasmus does not confine the value of *serio ludere* to schoolboys. Unlike with the severe Gracián, who would advocate a development from the youthful "inclinación a cosas poco graves" ("inclination toward frivolous things") to the unmitigated seriousness of "la madurez," maturity (see "El hombre en su punto," in *El Discreto*), retaining a youthful playfulness throughout life is an essential element of Erasmus's philosophy.

The Praise of Folly is the fullest articulation of what we can call Erasmus's "ludic vision," and it is a radical, destabilizing work. In addition to conventional targets such as popular superstition, the stoics, and scholastics, Folly and her army of Democrituses laugh at Plato and Aristotle and the very foundations of the "dignity of man" tradition. The haze of philosophical abstractions and rational systematizing is dispelled by the heat of physical, emotional, inconsistent humanity. Rather than being invited to sit alongside the deities, as in the fables of Pico and Vives, man provides the gods with a ridiculous spectacle to be enjoyed at their leisure: "[W]hen they're well liquored up with nectar and unfit for serious business, then they adjourn to a convenient promontory of heaven and sit there with faces bent downward to see what humans are up to ... Lord almighty, what a theatre is this, what a wild storm of follies!" (49). Man is deposed from the throne he hopes to occupy near the gods, and placed firmly back on earth, more appropriately to follow his animal nature. "Cities," "empires," "legal and religious systems," "political and religious structures" – all artifice and ingenuity fall within Folly's realm: "in fact, human life as a whole is nothing but a kind of fool's game" (27). But from this thorough subversion of some of the most cherished Renaissance ideals arises a different sort of optimism, one founded on doubt and delusion, and that only partially depends on the work's closing Christian vision for its vitality.

Folly appealingly represents social interaction itself as a form of play. The individual's acceptance of rules and conventions, despite their imperfections, is a mark of the humility and compromise necessary for social cohesion. For without certain agreed-upon fictions, society cannot function:

> As wisdom out of place is the height of the ridiculous, so prudence perversely misapplied is the height of imprudence. The perverse man fails to adjust his actions to the present state of things, he disdains the give-and-take of the intellectual marketplace, he won't even acknowledge the common rule of the barroom, drink up or get out – *all of which amounts to demanding that the play should no longer be a play*. On the other hand, the truly prudent man reflects that since he is mortal himself, he shouldn't

> want to be wiser than befits a mortal, but should cast his lot in with the rest of the human race and blunder along in good company. (29, my italics)

It bears emphasizing again that the game of life advocated by Folly is frequently the opposite of a cerebral exercise. While the above passage refers to prudence, reflection, and the intellectual marketplace, the dominant images are affective and corporal: play, drinking, and blundering along in good company. And while an intellectual understanding of limits is important for social interaction, Folly repeatedly suggests that pleasure plays an even greater role. "For what is this life, should it even be called life at all, if you remove pleasure from it?" (13); "but absurdities like these are what binds society together in mutual pleasure" (21). Fundamental to the wisdom of Erasmus's paradoxical praise is that happiness and community are achieved in part through rational reflection, but perhaps even more through felicitous delusion.

As mentioned, Montaigne is in some ways farthest in spirit from the "dignity of man" school and the optimism expressed in the early humanism of the likes of Pico and Castiglione.[41] Montaigne's belief in the radical subjectivity of experience, the primacy of chance in determining events, humankind's proximity to the animal realm, and his mistrust of the disordering potential of the imagination imbue his writings with a profound scepticism, not to say an underlying pessimism. From humanity's seat alongside the gods in Vives and Pico, to its serving as a comic spectacle in Erasmus, Montaigne delivers a further demotion: "The gods play pelota with us and drive us about in every way" (III, 9, p. 733). Since we can never confidently predict the outcome of our actions, an emblematic game for Montaigne is dice, presided over by fickle Fortune (e.g., II, 12, pp. 434–5). Rather than revering it as a divine faculty, Montaigne regards the imagination with considerable ambivalence: "Who does not know how imperceptibly near is madness to the lusty flights of a free mind and the effects of supreme and extraordinary virtue? Plato says that melancholy minds are the most teachable and excellent: likewise there are none with so much propensity to madness" (II, 12, p. 363). While Montaigne's rejection of "the Lancelots of the Lake, the Amadises … and such books of rubbish" (I, 26, p. 130) is based more on aesthetic than moral grounds, like Vives he is wary of the effects of stimulating the imagination:

> People are right to give the tightest possible barriers to the human mind. In study, as in everything else, its steps must be counted and regulated for

> it; the limits of the chase must be artificially determined for it. They bridle and bind it with religions, laws, customs, science, precepts, mortal and immortal punishments and rewards; and still we see that by its whirling and its incohesiveness it escapes all these bonds. (II, 12, p. 419)

A favourable view of structure and convention pervades the *Essays*, but not because Montaigne feels that rules and customs have an absolute value. He sees them rather as artificial restraints that are necessary to give form and provisional meaning to existence – and without which chaos and conflict would reign. His discussion of the "legitimate fictions" of science, law, and philosophy (II, 12, p. 401) calls to mind Spariosu's comments regarding the dubious distinction between "aesthetic" and "practical fictions" (see above, "Theoretical Contexts"). Montaigne implies that religion, too, is largely comprised of the "false and borrowed beauty" of human invention (particularly interesting is his discussion of anthropomorphic conceptions of God, II, 12, pp. 396–401). It is therefore fitting that Montaigne should repeatedly discuss games and playing, in literal as well as broadly metaphorical terms.

Like Vives, Montaigne promotes the civic benefits of pleasurable activities:

> Good governments take care to assemble the citizens and bring them together for sports and amusements as well as for the serious functions of piety; sociability and friendliness are thereby increased. And besides, they could not be granted more orderly pastimes than those that take place in the presence of everyone and right in the sight of the magistrate. And I should think it reasonable that the magistrate and the prince, at their own expense, should sometimes give the people this treat, out of a sort of paternal goodness and affection; and that in populous cities there should be places intended and arranged for these spectacles – a diversion from worse and hidden doings. (I, 26, p. 131)

With its promotion of the harmonizing effects of orderly recreation in the public sphere, bestowed upon a grateful citizenry by benevolent authorities, this is a rather conservative, and potentially authoritarian, view of leisure. The palliative function of public play, offering an outlet that may prevent "worse and hidden doings," is similar to Castillo's advocacy of public physical recreation for commoners ("exercicios en que las fuerças se abivan y los miembros se sueltan y ponen ligeros: no dentro de casa escondidos con los naypes y dados de dia y de noche" – "activities by which strength is enlivened and the limbs are loosened and made agile: not indoors hidden with cards and dice day and night" [*Tratado muy útil*, no pagination]), and anticipates Jovellanos's prescription for a placated working class. But just as Cervantes's conventional depiction of orderly *eutrapelia* in the "plaza de nuestra república" (*Novelas ejemplares*) is complicated by the image of the private and potentially subversive individual at leisure in the prologue of *Don Quijote* (not to mention by the stories themselves), Montaigne's notions of play are nuanced, and of civic, epistemological, and metaphysical import.

Like Erasmus and Vives, Montaigne advocates the educational value of play for children, and his is a particularly ample and integrated view:

> Even games and exercises will be a good part of his study: running, wrestling, music, dancing, hunting, handling horses and weapons. I want his outward behavior and social grace and his physical adaptability to be fashioned at the same time with his soul. It is not a soul that is being trained, not a body, but a man; these parts must not be separated. (I, 26, p. 122)

Montaigne's emphasis on the development of "social grace" calls to mind the tact and judgment required of Aristotle's *eutrapelos*, as well as Castiglione's ideal of *sprezzatura*. As Erasmus praises instructive and enjoyable "tricks," Montaigne affirms the pedagogical superiority of play over conventional study because of the fuller engagement of the faculties, and the pleasure it generates: "[T]here is nothing like arousing the appetite and affection; otherwise all you make out of them [students] is asses loaded with books" (I, 26, p. 131). While Montaigne acknowledges that we are "fashioned" by education and culture, he is always aware that such conformity must be balanced with individual aptitudes and dispositions: "There is no one who, if he listens to himself, does not discover in himself a pattern all his own, a ruling pattern, which struggles against education and against the tempest of the passions that oppose it" (III, 2, p. 615). The perception of such individual patterns is much like the listening to "Nature" urged by Erasmus in "The Godly Feast" (see above pp. 60–1). Interestingly, it is in private life and in play where this authenticity reveals itself. In his rejection of chess as a game that requires excessive time and attention, Montaigne nevertheless observes how self-knowledge can be facilitated in play: "what ample opportunity it here gives everyone to know himself, and to judge himself rightly" (I, 50, p. 220). The emphasis on knowing oneself and developing judgment, and the complicated relationship between public and private self, point to some important particularities of Montaigne's notion of play. His model of pedagogy can be seen to shift from the preparation of productive citizens to the cultivation of an individual consciousness.[42]

Montaigne's description of studying Greek with his father emphasizes again a pedagogical virtue of play, while also suggesting an underlying principle of the *Essays*: "We volleyed our conjugations back and forth, like those who learn arithmetic and geometry by such games as checkers and chess. For among other things he had been advised to teach me to enjoy knowledge and duty by my own free will and desire, and to educate my mind in all gentleness and freedom, without rigor and constraint" (I, 26, p. 129). Gadamer, who also believed that self-knowledge arose through play, had this to say about its dynamic quality: "The movement to-and-fro obviously belongs so essentially to the game that there is an ultimate sense in which you cannot have a game by yourself. In order for there to be a game, there always has to be, not necessarily literally another player, but something else with which the player plays and which automatically responds to his move with a countermove" (105–6). A remarkable aspect of Montaigne's thought is that it comprises a sort of game with himself, but without the solipsism that such an activity might suggest. On the contrary, the ludic inclination of his mind results in a more expansive, comprehensive manner of thinking: "Many times (as I sometimes do deliberately), having undertaken as exercise and sport to maintain an opinion contrary to my own, my mind, applying itself and turning in that direction, attaches me to it so firmly that I can no longer find the reason for my former opinion, and I abandon it" (II, 12, p. 426). The dialogic principle in Montaigne's writing functions at various levels: in the to-and-fro motion of his own thoughts; in his interaction with the great minds whose writings he cites so liberally; and, finally, with the reader of his essays. The play metaphor reappears when he discusses our reception of his words: "Speech belongs half to the speaker, half to the listener. The latter must prepare to receive it according to the motion it takes. As among tennis players, the receiver moves and makes ready according to the motion of the striker and the nature of the stroke" (III, 13, p. 834). Our solitary reading of Montaigne is in fact a sort of conversation, and he encourages in us the agility he himself demonstrates.

As noted above, Montaigne does not hold that the measure of autonomy possible in human existence is predicated on rejecting the constraints of social convention, however arbitrary and foolish they appear: "it seems to me that all peculiar and out-of-the-way fashions come rather from folly and ambitious affectation than from true reason, and that the wise man should withdraw his soul within, out of the crowd, and keep it in freedom and power to judge things freely; but as for externals, he should wholly follow the accepted fashions and forms" (I, 23, p. 86). Montaigne articulates an ambivalence similar to that of Erasmus, an irony at the heart of the ludic vision. It does not demand full disclosure or total consistency of the individual subject, and even encourages a degree of mechanical conventionality. The lack of purity to Montaigne's defence of duplicity and Erasmus's proposal that we "blunder along" is liberating, for it involves a non-utopian acceptance of ambiguity and imperfection.

Erasmus and Montaigne delicately negotiate a tension that has persisted throughout the centuries. It is worth recalling, for example, Maravall's passive subject of the absolutist state, who has no choice but to play by the rules imposed by those in power ("one must wholly enter into the game in terms of whatever becomes present to us" [*Culture of the Baroque* 198]). This notion is quite similar to Pascal's view of positive law and custom, which is that both are based on power and deception: "Custom is the whole of equity for the sole reason that it is accepted. That is the mystical basis of its authority. Whoever tries to trace this authority back to its origins, destroys it. Nothing is faultier than laws which put right faults. Whoever obeys them because they are just is obeying a justice he merely imagines, but not the essence of law. It is self-contained, it is the law and nothing more" (IV, 94, p. 24). Like Dostoevsky's "Grand Inquisitor" (*The Brothers Karamozov* II, bk. 5, ch. 5), Pascal maintains that the political subject "must not be allowed to be aware of the truth about the usurpation" (IV, 94, p. 25), that is, that law is not the issue of reason but of force. The "absurd man" of Albert Camus, on the other hand, is closer to Montaigne. Camus's "man with his mind made up to take up his bet and to observe strictly what he takes to be the rules of the game" (*The Myth of Sisyphus* 62) embraces life and structure despite its potential meaninglessness, and represents an appealing variation on "existence as play." He endorses the measure of community and pleasure we can experience in life. As Henri Peyre observes, Camus was in spirit closer to Lucretius than to Pascal: "But he added to Lucretius's resigned pessimism the modern concept of men's solidarity" (67). Pascal, who could not abide Montaigne's embrace of humanity despite its flaws, embodies the extremity of the *desengaño* position that all such pleasure and play are pernicious distractions from the sombre truth of our wretchedness and mortality.

The frequent earthiness and corporeality of Montaigne's references and metaphors – the focus on food and drink, sex, bodily processes of all sorts – embraces physical existence ("nature") in its limitations as well as its pleasures. Montaigne famously elaborates upon the art of existing in "Of Experience":

> Greatness of soul is not so much pressing upward and forward as knowing how to set oneself in order and circumscribe oneself. It regards as great whatever is adequate, and shows its elevation by liking moderate things better than eminent ones. There is nothing so beautiful and legitimate as to play the man well and properly, no knowledge so hard to acquire as the knowledge of how to live this life well and naturally; and the most barbarous of our maladies is to despise our being. (III, 13, p. 852)

There is of course a paradox in all of this. Montaigne's non-pedantic, unassuming ideal is predicated on tremendous erudition and book-learning; his "natural" man is fundamentally theatrical.[43] Endowed with imagination and an active, mediating intelligence, humans cannot simply *be*; we "play the man," which means balancing freedom and constraint, the intellect and the senses, individuality and conformism, in a productive tension that makes a sense of self and human community possible. We will return to Montaigne's sense of play when examining dialogue and exemplarity in Cervantes.

Play Types in Golden Age Spain

> El ocio no es hacer nada, porque éste es ocio de muertos, sino hacer algo que deleite o que no fatigue. En el ocio, en no haciendo algo bueno, es preciso caer en algo malo, que aunque ello no sea malo por su naturaleza, lo es porque embaraza para hacer algo bueno. Y así, es menester elegir buen ocio. (Zabaleta 387)

> [Leisure is not doing nothing, because this is dead leisure, but rather doing something that pleases and does not fatigue. In leisure, by not doing something good, one perforce falls into something bad, for even though it is not bad by nature, it is bad because it impedes doing something good. And so, it is necessary to choose good leisure.]

The dour moralism and entertaining *costumbrismo* of Juan de Zabaleta's *El día de la fiesta por la mañana* depicts and censures a wide range of leisure activities and social strata. Zabaleta is representative of many contemporary writers in that his demands that leisure activities serve some end – in many cases, a pious one – are coupled with a recognition of pleasure's value. Discussing licit forms of recreation for the first estate, Diego de Castillo invokes the traditional association of *eutrapelia* with the nobility, which needs to "relax its bowstring" in order to alleviate fatigue: "que todo hombre deve a las vezes entre sus cuydados bolver plazer y alegria: porque muchas vezes la cosa que una vez no huelga no puede mucho durar: como la vallesta que estoviesse contino armada" ("everyone should occasionally intermix serious concerns with pleasure and happiness: because often the thing that does not rest cannot last long: like the permanently armed crossbow" [n.p.]). Castillo reminds the nobles that their primary occupation is to "play" with "mozos turcos y infieles" ("young Turks and infidels"), that is, to vanquish the enemy at arms. The agonistic character of many games reflects a Manichean vision of good pitted against evil. But such traditional categories and distinctions were breaking down. As many satirists and *arbitristas* noted, the nobility was increasingly becoming an idle class, whose leisure had more to do with escaping boredom than refining their valour and martial skills. Such thinking shares a kinship with the stern theology of Pascal, who contended that humans are uniquely susceptible to boredom, and that games (billiards, hunting, cards) distract from the very things they ought to be contemplating: mortality, sinfulness, God.[44] Machiavelli, for his part, critiques the "ambitious idleness" of Christians, in evidence when they consider the authors of antiquity, "as from not having a true knowledge of histories, through not getting from reading them that sense nor tasting the flavour that they have in themselves. From this it arises that the infinite number [of Christians] who read them [the ancients] take pleasure in hearing of the variety of accidents contained in them without thinking of imitating them" (*Discourses on Livy*, Preface). A symptom of Christian "idleness" is superficial reading skills, seeking diversion instead of relevance.

There was also an awareness during the period that "free time" was a substantial realm of experience for a growing portion of the citizenry, and a keen interest in distinguishing between good and bad uses of it. In a "Consulta" ("Opinion") directed in 1598 to Felipe II by Don Pedro de Castro, Archbishop of Seville, theatre is cited as a poor use of time that compromises all social ranks, from noblemen to *doncellas* (maidens) and servants. Castro attributes the decadence of an idle populace to theatregoing, and laments the implications for national productivity and security: "From representations and comedies follow another very grave injury, and that is that people give themselves over to idleness and enjoyment and delight and divert themselves from the militia with the lewd dances that every day the players invent and with parties and banquets and meals the people of Spain become soft and effeminate and useless for affairs of work and war."[45] Spain's principal enemies – "el Turco, o, Xarife, o Rey de Inglaterra" ("the Turk, the Moor, or the King of England") – could not have invented a more efficient weapon than "estos faranduleros" ("these theatre troupes" [fol. 6]). And even though Castro cites Aquinas in acknowledging that such recreations are not intrinsically evil, he concludes that the required reforms of theatre would be too great, and the social risks too high (fol. 10). As Zabaleta pointed out (above), since time is limited, even the pursuit of a benign activity is suspect, for it precludes a more virtuous one. In the paradoxical formulation of Fray Pedro de Guzmán, one should aspire to the ideal of "ocio con negocio" ("leisure with business," Discurso VI). Juan García Canalejas makes a similar claim for the chess-like "juego de las Damas": "no es ocio, sino un entretenido negocio" ("it is not leisure, but an entertaining business" [*Libro del juego de las Damas*, 1650, "Al lector"]). On the one hand, we might consider the sense of *negocio* as an activation of the higher faculties during leisure, as Aristotle advocated (see above pp. 31–3). On the other hand, the emphasis on profitable use of time reflects an emerging ethos of productivity. As we will see below, such a view melded with theological currents, and can be seen as a precursor to notions such as the Protestant work ethic.[46]

Anticipating Caillois by several centuries, Pedro de Guzmán offers a typology of play, dividing games into physical and mental activities, those based on chance and those on skill: "Unos juegos consisten en ingenio, otros en fuerças corporales, otros en ambas cosas, otros en sola suerte, y ventura" ("Some games consist of wit, others of physical strength, others of both, others of only luck, and fortune" [195]). He then refines these categories by describing the motivations and effects of different pastimes. There are the cruel spectacles of bullfights, which only satisfy the inhumane inclinations of participant and spectator: "ay unos juegos que solo se ordenan a un vano entretenimiento y curiosidad, asi de los que los juegan, como de los que miran" ("there are some games only directed at vain entertainment and curiosity, both of those who play and those who watch" [195]). There are also the prurient entertainments of the theatre, masques and dances, and the inversions of carnivalesque revelry, "donde los criados se hazian amos, y los amos servian a los criados, y todo andava revuelto, y trocado, con suma licencia y libertad" ("where servants became masters, and the masters served the servants, and everything was mixed up and transformed, with extreme license and freedom" [195]). Among these morally suspect games he discusses gambling, which inspires avarice: "Otros juegos, fuera de la curiosidad y vano entretenimiento, cruel, o poco honesto, tienen tambien una vil ganancia, y provecho temporal; como los juegos de dados, naypes, tablas, trucos, axedreces, juegos de pelota" ("Other games, apart from curiosity and idle entertainment, [are] cruel, or indecent, also include vile profit, and temporal gain; like games of dice, cards, backgammon, billiards, chess, and ball games" [196]). Significantly, he grants that the last three in the list – the billiards, chess, and ball games – may also comprise licit recreation for body and mind (we will discuss this further, below). Of particular interest is Guzmán's inclusion, along with the charged moral vocabulary to approve of or condemn ("de provecho" vs "deshonesto," "cruel," "vano"), of types of play that can be neutral: "Otros juegos hay indiferentes" ("Other games are indifferent" [196]). The categorization of certain games as "indifferent" reflects a fascinating forbearance on the part of authorities who seemed more comfortable in the business of censure or advocacy.[47] The forbearance surely stems in part from theological tradition, starting with the Desert Fathers. In his discussion of fasting, Cassian invoked Ecclesiastes to emphasize that the value of many activities depends on various factors: "It has therefore been determined that none of these things is a permanent good, except when it is carried out at the right time and in correct fashion. Thus, the very things that turn out well now, since they were done at the right time, are found to be disadvantageous and harmful if they are tried at an inopportune or inappropriate moment" (21.12, p. 728). Nevertheless, it is telling that when Guzmán deploys the term, he includes an accompanying qualification: "aunque se pueden ordenar a buen fin"; "y puedense ordenar a buen fin" ("even though they can be directed to a good end"; "and they can be directed to a good end" [196, 197]). It seems the neutral realm of leisure, the "uselessness" extolled from classical Greece to defenders of the modern liberal arts curriculum, was too ambiguous. Lest such activities lead the players astray, Guzmán corralled them with purposeful goals. Physical competitions (wrestling, races, gymnastics), for example, could hone skills necessary for military and seafaring endeavours (196). And he is careful to stipulate that the activities recognize one of the basic tenets of *eutrapelia*: "Las sortijas, y mascaras, quando no se mezclan cosas deshonestas, ni torpes, las caças, asi las de fieras, como las de cetreria, y volateria, entran tambien en esta cuenta, usadas con moderacion" ("Ring-jousting, and masques, when they do not combine things dishonest or lewd, the hunt, of beasts as well as foul, and falconry, also form part of this category, when practiced in moderation" [197–8]). With excess, even licit forms of recreation deteriorate.

In addition to the concern with promoting beneficial activities and discouraging corrupting ones, that is, with how different games influence behaviour and sensibilities in different ways, there existed the belief that individuals reveal their true nature in play. As Pedro de Covarrubias observed: "en el juego somos incautos porque en el estudio y beodez del nos declaramos cuales somos" ("in play we are incautious because in our immersion and drunkenness with it we reveal ourselves" [49]). The "drunkenness" (beodez) of play is ambivalent: it can sweep the participant into a realm of fantasy, thereby distancing the player from reality; but it can also allow truths to emerge. In the pages that follow, we will examine how the ideas discussed in the preceding sections on *eutrapelia* and humanist play inform discussions of particular leisure activities. While the advocates of *eutrapelia* typically assumed the leisure in question was that of the male nobility or clergy, we will see that the same principles were also applied to play for commoners and women, and even, as the documents pertaining to the Colonies reveal, to more distant "others."

Chess

The foundational Spanish commentary on chess by Alfonso X (*Libro de ajedrez*) underlines the dignity of a game predicated on intelligence and agency. As one of the three figures in his introductory parable argues, "más valie seso que ventura. Ca el que vivie por el seso, facie sus cosas ordenadamientre e aun que perdiese, que no habie y culpa, pues que facie lo que le convinie" ("brains are worth more than fortune. For he who lives by brains, does things in an orderly way and even though he lose, there is no fault, for he does what is fitting" [205]). Within the ordered realm of the chess board, the players act according to reason. The victory goes not only to the player with the highest aptitude, but to the one who applies himself most diligently: "el que mayor seso hobiese e estudiase apercebudo podrie vencer all otro" ("whoever possesses the highest intelligence and studies most perceptively may defeat the other" [205]). Chess would appear to be the highest form of rule-bound *agon*. Nabokov would explore the limits of this notion in *The Luzhin Defense*, in which the protagonist's developing insanity is linked to his attempt to control the game completely, to rule out any impingement of chance or irrationality. As Karshan discusses, Luzhin's attempt to "systematise" impulse is presented by Nabokov as a perversion of play (Karshan 90–106).

Early modern accounts of chess generally follow Alfonso X, although with an increasing focus on its metaphorical value. In contrast to his moralizing condemnation of gambling, and despite his reservations about *juegos de industria* (games of diligence), Luque Faxardo views chess as a game that teaches those with power the importance of benevolent rule (bk. I, ch. 6). Sánchez de la Plata offers an almost identical description of chess's virtues, attributing its origins to Xerxes, "el qual queriendo refrenar la crueldad, y braveza de un tyrano, por exemplo deste juego le demostro que muy poco vale la Magestad del Rey sin fuerças, y poca seguridad tiene sin ayuda de los hombres, porque a la verdad por este juego de axedrez se demuestra a la clara que el rey sera vencido, sino tiene mucha vigilancia, y si de los suyos no es defendido" ("who wanting to reign in the cruelty and fury of a tyrant, by example of this game showed him that the Majesty of the King is little worth without forces, and he has little security without the help of the men, because truthfully by this game of chess it is clearly shown that the king will be defeated, if he is not very vigilant, and if he is not defended by his own men" [fol. 167]). These are important differences from the "neutral" recreation of pleasant diversions (*indiferentes*), not to mention from the tyranny that gambling could provoke in the nobility (see below). Chess possesses a didactic quality as a sort of participatory metaphor: the player acts within a reproduction of the feudal order to which he belongs, gaining an appreciation of the reciprocal relationships that must be respected to sustain the ordered system. Alfonso X's repetition of "a semejanza de" when describing the chess pieces signals this sense of analogy (206–9). Chess thus bears an aesthetic as well as functional relationship to the real world. As Luque Faxardo puts it, "De semejante ejercicio, pues, salían los antiguos enseñados para las ocasiones de veras" ("From such exercise, then, the ancients emerged prepared for real-life events" [bk. I, ch. 5]). In a discussion that underscores questions of gender, social estate, martial strategy, and right rule, Pedro de Covarrubias expounds upon the game's benefits: "es juego de ingenio y de industria provechoso no solo para huyr el tedioso y triste ocio: mas tambien para contemplar lo que significa y tomar aviso. Es de notar en el la gravedad del rey como esta acompañado / con quanto peso se mueve: no como iracundo / apassionado / o vindicativo. Como se presenta sabiduria con clemencia" ("it is a game of skill and diligence profitable not only to flee tedious and sad leisure: but also to contemplate what it means to take counsel. One should note the dignity with which the king is accompanied, with what gravity he moves, not like one irascible, passionate and vindictive. How wisdom with clemency is presented" [Cap. IV fol. 11]). Canalejas endorses in comparable terms "el juego de las Damas," which represents a "viva imagen de la guerra" ("a vivid image of war"), a game of skill and strategy that avoids the vices of gambling: "pues en él se exercita el discurso, no se desmanda la lengua al juramento, ni la hazienda a la perdición, ni el animo a la impaciencia; no es efecto de la ventura como otros, sino del saber" ("because in it speech is exercised, the tongue is not given over to wayward oaths, nor is property to perdition, nor the spirit to impatience; it is not, like other games, the result of fortune, but rather knowledge" [*Libro del juego de las Damas*, "Al lector"]).

It hardly needs to be emphasized that the relationship between chess and the existing social structure was highly complementary, the former reflecting and reinforcing the latter. Chess was an elitist game, reserved for the first two estates. Castillo, for example, mentions it as a licit form of recreation for the nobility and the priestly class, but not for the *medianos y menores* (those of middling and lower conditions); moreover, for the prelates and clerics he has specific instructions regarding how it should be played: "sea unos con otros: no entre legos ni con ellos; no en la yglesia mas un una casa en secreto" ("may it be amongst themselves: not amongst the laity nor with them; not in the church but rather in a house in secret" [n.p.]). The participants must be of the same social class and the game should occur in a private, hidden place – as opposed to the open, public sphere in which the third estate was to take its recreation. On the other hand, the ephemeral quality of such play, and the tumbling of all the pieces into the same sack at game's end, presented an effective lesson in humility to those in power. As Canalejas explains in his *Libro del juego de Damas*, "y aun el varon entendido saca el precioso desengaño de su semejanza con las cosas de este mundo, viendo que las pieças que ahora puestas en el tablero valen algo, y se estiman, unas son Damas, y otras peones, recogidas luego en su saquillo, y amortajadas en él, son iguales sin distinction alguna, acabándose con la burla aquella su momentanea estimacion" ("and even the learned man gains the precious disillusionment from its similitude with things of this world, seeing that the pieces now placed on the board are worth something, and esteemed, some are Dames, and others peons, thereafter gathered up into their sack, and shrouded therein, are equal, without any distinction, putting an end to their fleeting esteem" ["Al lector"]). As we will see below, such conventional allegorization did not escape Cervantes's playful irony.

The very complexity of chess contributed to its elite status and, as Étienvre notes, limited its usefulness as a sustained aesthetic metaphor: "It seems almost impossible to construct an entire metaphorical narration based on a chess game, barring a stylistic exploit."[48] This same quality gave chess a questionable status as recreation, as Pedro de Covarrubias concludes:

> Y porque ocupa mucho tiempo no deven usar del / los muy ocupados porque no dexen lo necessario por lo escusado. Este passateimpo / no es sino para los muy ociosos ingenios por redimirlos de malos pensamientos o para los congoxados que dessean desasir la mente de algun gran cuydado que les da pena y trabajo. (Cap. IV, fol. 13)

> [And since it takes much time those who are very busy should not partake of it, so that they do not abandon the necessary for the frivolous. This pastime is only for the very idle minds, in order to redeem them from bad thoughts, or for the anguished who want to detach the mind from some great care that gives them pain and trouble.]

We see again the awareness of different classes of players, for whom particular games may prove especially dangerous or beneficial. In one of the novel's many analogues to don Quijote's excessive reading, don Gaiferos neglects his own chivalric duties while immersed in a game of *tablas*, an early form of chess (*Don Quijote* II, 26). Montaigne also bemoans the excessive application required of chess: "I hate it and avoid it, because it is not enough a game, and too serious an amusement; I am ashamed to devote to it the attention that would suffice to accomplish something good" (I, 50, p. 220). Such excess is reinforced by the comically violent denouement of Castiglione's account of the monkey playing chess with the gentleman who, upon finding himself in checkmate, "flew into a rage (as people who lose at chess invariably do), took up the King (which, being of Portuguese make, was very big), and gave the monkey a great blow on the head" (165). The gentleman attacking the monkey illustrates what Montaigne, like Covarrubias, understood ("what ample opportunity it here gives everyone to know himself, and to judge himself rightly" [I, 50]). The stress of competition and the game's complexity make the player's true disposition and limitations apparent.

While chess was generally promoted for the positive qualities outlined above, its image and function did not remain completely uniform from the Reconquista through the Counter Reformation. Étienvre describes a significant shift in its metaphorical import: "'Moralized chess' certainly dates back to the Middle Ages, but back then the game was represented, for example in Jacobus de Cessolis, as an image of society. It was not until the Renaissance that the metaphor of chess as paragon of strategy was established."[49] If the order, hierarchy, and reciprocal obligations emphasized above make it an *imagen de la sociedad* that promotes the virtues of such a society and encourages collaboration among its citizens, chess as a *parangón de estrategia* would seem to privilege the astute individual. Amidst the destabilization of the old feudal hierarchy as a manifestation of cosmic order, there is a heightened emphasis on the chess player's skilful manipulation of an intricate field of play in order to gain advantage over an opponent.[50] As noted, the relationship between individual agency and group cohesion is a central concern of those who discuss the social implications of play. If increased emphasis on strategy and excessive time demands could make chess a suspect form of recreation, it should come as no surprise that games involving gambling were commonly condemned as threats to social cohesion.

"La embriaguez del mal ejemplo": Games of Chance, from Cards and Dice to Books

From literary and pictorial representations to moral-political writings of the period, cards and dice are almost invariably associated with greed, mendacity, heresy, and other vices. Many are the imprecations against gamblers who neglect work and church, stay up all night, abuse their families, blaspheme, curse, deceive, and physically attack one another, often ending up in financial ruin. Among other classical references, Suárez de Figueroa cites the degeneracy of Penelope's idle, dice-playing suitors in the *Odyssey* (fol. 255); the Roman soldiers dicing for Christ's tunic is also a common reference (e.g., Guzmán, 393). Adrián de Castro laments the error of calling gaming houses "casas de conversación" (houses of conversation) as the activities taking place therein are the opposite of social recreation: *murmuración* (slander) instead of *conversación*, deception in place of communication, conflict over cohesion, vulgarities instead of discrete witticisms (ch. 33). Zabaleta illustrates these principles in his satirical portrait of "La casa de juego," which begins by noting that "Naturalmente cruel es todo animal" ("Every animal is naturally cruel" [II, ch. 3, p. 339]). But gambling man is emblematic of fallen humanity which, according to traditional moral vocabulary – and contrary to the Aristotelian ideal – frequently sinks below the bestial: "Sólo un animal hay en el mundo que, sin odio ni ira, quiere destruir al animal de su semejanza: éste es el hombre tahúr, y éste es el más cruel de todos los animales" ("There is only one animal in the world which, without hatred or ire, will destroy its ilk: this is gambling man, and this is the cruellest of all animals" [340]).[51] In similar fashion, after invoking the topos of *homo homini lupus*, Luque Faxardo notes: "Basta decir: el hombre contra el hombre, es hombre" ("Suffice it to say: man against man, is man" [II, ch. 15]).[52] Such are the destructive inclinations unleashed by suspect play.

While cards and games that incorporate dice appear to contain the ideal blend of chance and human agency promoted by Alfonso X and later by Vives, the *agon* combined with prospects for material gain distort the ingenuity and inventiveness celebrated in other contexts. Economic interest compromises the game's autonomy, blurring the distinction between play and work. Luque Faxardo laments various consequences: the poor see in gambling a means of social mobility (bk. I, ch. 18), and the nobility, whose role is to administer justice, becomes tyrannical (bk. II, ch. 18); the power of card-playing even threatens royal authority, since a gambling-obsessed citizenry ignores the king's rule (bk. III, ch. 15). Such games present opportunities to cause mischief in a particularly human manner, as players constantly devise new ways to outsmart their opponents, often with a veiled and ruthless disregard for the rules. Luque Faxardo and others point out that "cuanto uno es más honrado, tanto es más fácil de engañar" ("the more honourable one is, the easier to deceive" [bk. III, ch. 16]). Compliance with rules signals gullibility, an attribute of the victim in a predatory world. It is easy to see why such games are so often depicted among the dupes and confidence men of picaresque narratives, as well as in the genre paintings of Caravaggio, La Tour, ter Brugghen, and others. Ter Brugghen's *The Gamblers* (see Figure 2), like many of the *tractacus ludorum*, emphasizes a number of aspects that make the play degenerate: the money strewn about the table, the spectacles symbolizing moral short-sightedness, the dice emblematizing blind chance, the accusation of cheating, and the menace of the scabbard jutting into the centre of the composition.[53]

Figure 2 Hendrick ter Brugghen, *The Gamblers*, 1623 (oil on canvas). Minneapolis Institute of Arts, MN, USA / The William Hood Dunwoody Fund / The Bridgeman Art Library.

There is a grand tradition of representing card players in the visual arts, from Holbein the Younger's *Death and the Devil Come for the Card Player* (Scharffenberg's lithograph from the year of Cervantes's birth, 1547), to Balthus's twentieth-century depictions of adolescents at play. The Holbein image comprises perhaps the most explicit moral and theological censure of such play, as the conventional "Totentanz" death figure, who comes to collect his souls just as the gambler in the foreground sweeps the coins towards himself, must compete for the condemned man with the Devil himself (see Figure 3). For a theatrical comparison, we might think of the spectacular final scene of Tirso's *El burlador de Sevilla*, when don Juan's wager ("¡Qué largo me lo fiáis!") is finally called, and the statue drags him down to hell. A recent exhibition of Cezanne's "Card Players" illustrates how thoroughly early modern debates about the game anticipate the concerns of the nineteenth-century. For example,

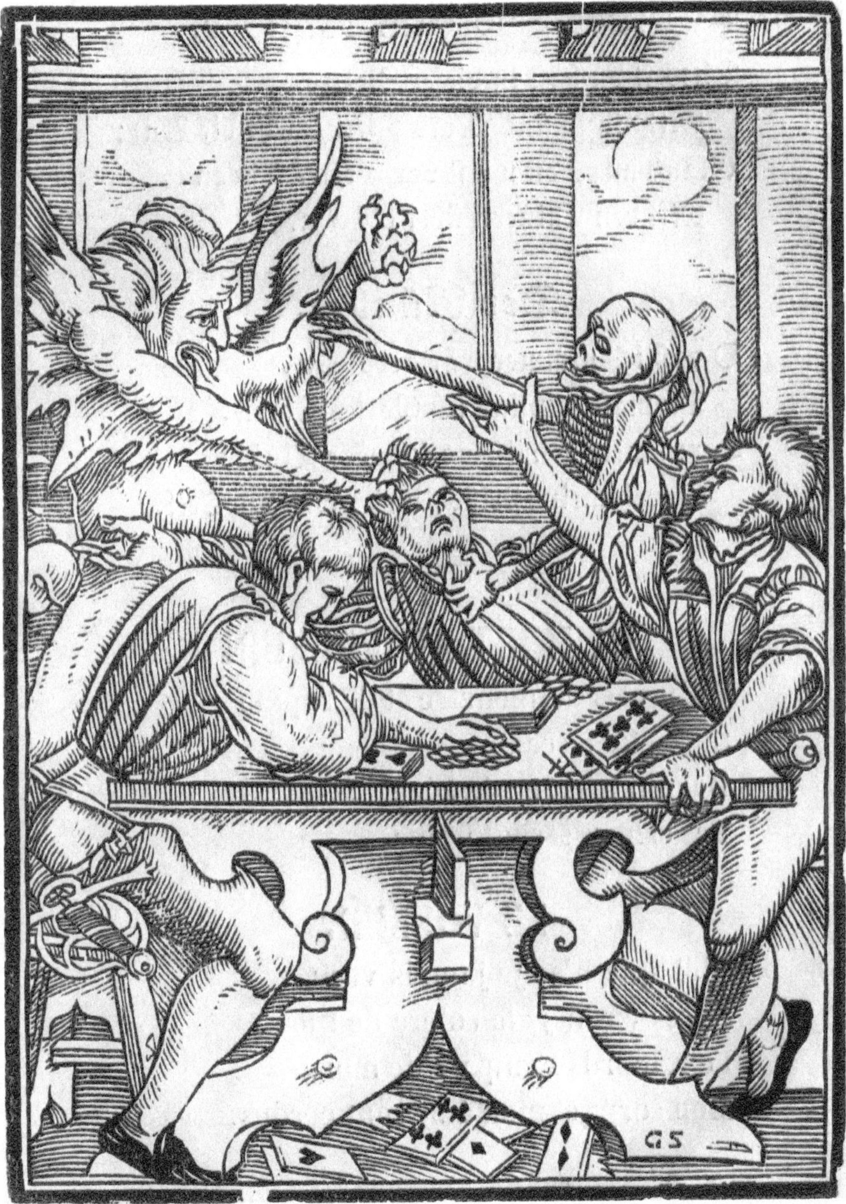

Figure 3 After Hans Holbein the Younger, 1547. Georg Scharffenberg, *Death and the Devil come for the Gambler*, 1843 (lithograph), from "Der Todten Tanz", published Basel, 1843 (litho). Private Collection / Ken Welsh / The Bridgeman Art Library.

the contrasting visions of rural life as wholesome, authentic and productive, or sordidly bestial and avaricious, frequently hinged on the way peasant recreation was depicted. Zola's debased view in *The Earth* is in line with genre paintings associating peasant card playing with gambling, inebriation, idleness and relationships destroyed by greed and lust. But there was also a counter-tradition, depicting the players in rustic civility, good humour, and – work implements set aside, and taking nourishment of bread and wine – relaxation from the stresses of labour. Some representations evoke Christ at Emmaus, others the philosophical contemplation of the symposium or *salon*.[54] In Cézanne's masterpiece, the five men are immersed in a sort of ancient ritual, but one of ambiguous social import: as Meyer Schapiro commented, although seated around the same table, they seem to be playing "collective solitaire" (Ireson and Wright 26; see Figure 4). According to

Figure 4 Cézanne, *The Card Players*, 1890 (oil on canvas). The Barnes Foundation, Philadelphia, Pennsylvania, USA / The Bridgeman Art Library.

Borges, a similar element of ritual and suspension of time occurs in the Argentine card game of trucos, during which a primal identity is affirmed: "Each player, in essence, does no more than re-play remote hands. His play is a repetition of past games, which is to say, moments of past livings. Generations of now-invisible criollos are as buried alive in him: they are him, we can affirm without metaphor."[55] While most of Cervantes's depictions of card-playing hew to the moralizing tradition, we will see that his *naipes* can also have broader metaphorical significance.

Luque Faxardo's advocacy of games of pure chance might represent a solution to some of the problems outlined above:

> [L]a diferencia consiste en suerte o en industria: los de suertes y fortuna, según su principal fin, que es recrear, más lícitos son que los de industria, pues en éstos puede haber notable ventaja, porque como aquí gana el hombre conforme lo que sabe, forzosamente ha de ganar al menos diestro; lo qual es muy diferente en los de suertes si, como deben, van los jugadores sujetos a la fortuna. (bk. I, ch. 5)
>
> [[T]he difference consists of luck or ability: those of chance and fortune, according to their principal end, which is recreation, are more licit than those of ability, since in the latter there may be distinct advantage, because as in these one wins in accordance to what one knows, necessarily he will defeat the one of lesser talent; which is very different from those of chance if, as they should, the players proceed subject to chance.]

Because games of dice are chance-determined, they are inherently more egalitarian and, according to Luque Faxardo, more purely recreational than games of knowledge and skill. On the other hand, Pedro de Covarrubias bases one of his objections on the very fact that there is no challenge, no need of skill, and therefore any simpleton can play: "para hazer lo que es de fortuna qualquiera rudo y grosero sabe: quien no sabe arrojar unos dados sobre una mesa" ("any coarse and vulgar person can do fortune's bidding: who does not know how to cast some dice upon a table" [fol. 37r]). An interesting counterargument is Montaigne's rejection of fencing, preferring instead the duel in its primitive form. Rather than advantages gained by cultivated skill and cunning, one should depend "entirely on fortune and assurance" (II, 27, p. 527).[56]

The very category of "juegos de azar" (games of chance) evokes one of the period's most fraught concepts. Reflected in the judgments of *alea* are the various notions of *fortuna*: from a mysterious manifestation of divine will, to an indifferent natural process, to a malign force.[57] For Renaissance humanists concerned with providence and free will, and the presence or absence of arbitrary chance and contingency in the universe, *alea* was of central importance. Are human beings capable of controlling chance and thus determining the outcome of their lives, as the "dignity of man" school would have it? If, by contrast, we are subject to chance, is it because of our depraved, post-Lapsarian condition, in which chance is actually the inscrutable will of God, and is the only option to have absolute faith in providence and relinquish the hubris of self-determination? Stoicism notably suggests the futility of controlling the erratic flow of phenomena, from which the wise individual withdraws in resignation. On the other hand, a universe in which chance prevails might, according to an atomistic and Epicurean view, prove liberating: good and ill fortune do not represent divine punishment or reward, but rather indifferent occurrences, before which the natural reaction is to cultivate and enjoy the pleasures of good luck, and exercise forbearance amidst misfortune. Lucretius set forth the greatest image of randomness in the creation of the universe itself, as arbitrary swerves in the rushing atoms combine to create all manner of forms, both beneficial and hurtful to human beings (*The Nature of Things*, especially bk. II). And Lucretius's Epicureanism is a major influence behind what Lyons calls "Montaigne's triumphant scepticism," which Descartes sought to offset by subduing the role of chance in the universe (159). Pascal's famous "wager," in which he applies probability theory to salvation, exhorts humankind to relinquish its vanity and partake of the cosmic coin toss, for the abject human intellect is hopelessly far from grasping divine will:

> At the far end of this infinite distance a game is being played and the coin will come down heads or tails. How will you wager? Reason cannot make you choose one way or the other, reason cannot make you defend either of the two choices ... And thus, as you are forced to gamble, you have to have discarded reason if you cling on to your life, rather than risk it for the infinite prize which is just as likely to happen as the loss of nothingness. (153; 154–5)

Borges pointed out that Pascal's notion of the universe is very similar to that of Lucretius: "Pascal's world is that of Lucretius (and also Spencer's), but the infinitude that captivated the Roman frightens the Frenchman. Although it is true that the latter seeks God and the former intends to free us from fear of the gods."[58] In metaphysical terms, Pascal's insistence on predestination would reject games of skill, in which human agency could influence the outcome (damnation or salvation); a true believer must simply submit to a lottery.[59] Milton's "golden scales," in which the outcome of the impending battle can be read in the constellations, conflates a sense of *fortuna* with divine will. Gabriel elucidates: "Satan, I know thy strength, and thou know'st mine, / Neither our own but giv'n; what folly then / To boast what Arms can do, since thine no more / Than Heav'n permits, nor mine, though doubl'd now / To trample thee as mire: for proof look up, / And read thy Lot in yon celestial Sign / Where thou art weigh'd, and shown how light, how weak, / If thou resist" (bk. IV, l. 1006–13). Seeing that his "lot" is unfavourable, Satan flees.

As this summary indicates, the issue of chance was at the centre of the period's momentous tensions, both between the Christian and Classical traditions, and within Christianity, as Martin Luther and his followers vehemently rejected attempts to harmonize human dignity and agency with the dictates of a supreme and infallible deity.[60] From a political perspective, we recall Spariosu's characterization of a society that favours the control of chance and affirmation of human agency as "rational." Caillois made a similar assertion regarding the ludic element in political modernization: "Democracy arises amidst agon and alea, merit and chance" (109–14). Consistent with his civilizing notion of play, Caillois held that games of pure chance are morally suspect because they do not "develop aptitudes" (56). The recent controversy over the US Congress's "Unlawful Internet Gambling Enforcement Act" (2006), which prohibited online poker on the grounds that its "dominant factor" is chance rather than skill, reveals that the moral suspicion of *alea* still exists. Levitt, Miles, and Rosenfield argue that the government's standard of "dominant factor" is flawed, and that in poker, skill in fact outweighs chance. Their broader critique of the prohibition is particularly interesting, since it calls into question the extent to which we are aware of – and able to tolerate – the element of chance in other areas of life experience: "In applying the test ['dominant factor'], some courts (at least once, even the same court) have reached conflicting conclusions about the legality of particular games. Also, the test cannot distinguish activities commonly understood to be gambling from … those that are not, including athletic competitions and widely accepted business practices such as insurance underwriting and derivatives contracting" (5). Levitt et al. suggest that the government's ostensible concern with the moral hazard of gambling and *alea* are in tension with its desire to control the substantial revenue streams generated by such activity. This is essentially the same quandary faced by the early modern Spanish authorities – both on the Peninsula and in the Colonies – who railed against the ravages of gambling, yet profited from controlling the sales of the card decks, or *barajas*. As Deleito y Piñuela noted, the various attempts, from Carlos V to Felipe IV, to distinguish between licit and illicit games, and to curb the abuses of the latter, were hampered by the State's economic interest, since it controlled the sale of card decks: "The sanctions against gaming could not be very efficient when it constituted a monopoly of the State, which, under such auspices, was making up to 50,000 *ducados* annually."[61] As part of his program of "Enlightenment" infrastructure, educational and economic reforms, Carlos III was still trying to prohibit certain games of chance, especially those involving wagers (Ansón Calvo et al. 717–18).

The ambivalence in the period towards games of chance is registered in Sebastián de Covarrubias's definition of "Suerte": "*Latine sors*, algunas vezes sinifica ventura buena y mala. Echar suertes y sortear a quien le cabe la suerte. Algunas vezes es lícito, y otras no" ("*Latine sors*, sometimes means good fortune and sometimes ill. To cast dice and raffle to see who is lucky. Sometimes it is licit, sometimes it isn't"). Adrian de Castro expresses the common view of the goddess fortune as a personification of God's adversary: "los tablajes no son otra cosa sino altares donde se haze sacrificio al demonio, que entonces era adorado en nombre de fortuna" ("the gambling dens are nothing but altars where sacrifice is made to the devil, who was then adored in fortune's name" [11–12]). Pedro de Covarrubias also gives heretical overtones to such play: "las locuras de los jugadores son peores que ydolatras negando la obediencia a dios y dandola a los dados o naypes" ("the insanity of gamblers is worse than the idolatrous, denying obedience to god and giving it to dice and cards" [fol. 52r]). Pedro de Guzmán makes a similar observation: "Los naypes son otro libro, aunque descuadernado, adonde los ociosos tambien estudian. Esta es su Biblia, donde se sacan sus figuras, y puntos, y no de oracion" ("Cards are another book, although unbound, where the idle also study. This is their Bible, where they derive their figures, and principles, and not of prayer" [fol. 396]). In the Goliardic tradition, such a travesty of religious observance could be found in the *Officium lusorum*, or "Gamblers' Mass" of *Carmina Burana*: "Let us all mourn Decius, / lamenting the holy day, / for the sorrow of all gamblers: / at whose nakedness the Decii rejoice /

and praise the son of Bacchus."[62] On the other hand, the Augustinian Friar Gaspar de los Reyes allegorized the card game triunfo and other popular recreations according to Catholic theology in his *Tesoro de concetos divinos* (1613).[63]

Although Guzmán writes metaphorically in the passage above, there did in fact exist books that comprised games of chance – and they elicited the ambivalent reactions described by Sebastián de Covarrubias. The popular *Libro de las suertes* (Anonymous, sixteenth century), which makes an appearance in Lope's *Arcadia*, involves a complex sequence of chance and choices: players select from a series of questions (often pertaining to sentimental and career affairs) at the outset; they then cast dice or choose among options represented by different planets, cities, or nymphs, which eventually lead to one of the many possible "oracles" relating to the initial question, in the form of a proverb (e.g., "Bien sabes que no puedes ser casado, / y que estás para clérigo guardado" – "You well know that you cannot marry, / and that you are meant for the clergy" [303]). Such book-games illustrate the period's broader conceptions of reading, and of literary/poetic language itself, as a highly ludic enterprise. Skilful reading, as well as the artful use of language, takes on the quality of contest and spectacle (we will return to such considerations below). Gerónimo de Pinar's earlier *Juego trobado* involved more interpretation and literary prowess than *El libro de las suertes*, while still containing the elements of chance. According to Jacobo Sanz Hermida's description, "the mechanism of the game would consist of interpreting the couplet that has corresponded to each 'dame' or 'lady' – after casting the dice and choosing the card from the deck that previously was to have been configured with the four chances – by means of the sum of the symbolic values that underlie the four elements, in order to end up discovering qualities of the masculine personage that is hidden behind them. It therefore consisted of a game of pairs in which each dame would seek the man who most closely approximated the conventions of courtly love."[64] The *Juego trobado* was specifically designed as recreation for Isabela la Católica and the women in her court, and thus involved a relatively high degree of female agency: "the appearance of the masculine sex has its reason for being as part of the inner mechanism of this diversion, but not as an active participant in it. Thus, this game is presented as a courtly diversion in which the queen and her retinue could display their symbolic erudition and their knowledge of songs and ballads."[65] In her discussion of *Gonzaga II*, McClure shows how Tasso also conceived of parlour games and courtly performances as venues in which women could develop and display their *ingegno* and prudence, thereby promoting skills that had political currency. Tasso's notion of play therefore supported a more radical sense of female agency than the *Juego trobado* which, with its focus on the courtly love, reinforced conventional gender roles.

Given the emphasis on skilful interpretation and the pertinence of the outcome to the life of the player, we can see how such book-games (the *Juego trobado* and the *Libro de las suertes*) are related to a work like *El conde Lucanor*. Although ostensibly involved in a highly literary experience (as emphasized in Juan Manuel's stylistic boasting in the prologue), the reader of *El conde Lucanor* is in a similar position to the player in the book-game: he or she can seek a particular dilemma, related to sentimental, professional, or spiritual life, based on Lucanor's opening question to his advisor, Patronio. After the aesthetic experience of the story, the final couplets and authorial approval of the narrative's meaning provide an "answer," or solution to the initial conundrum – one that is applicable to the life of the reader. An important distinction is that these latter examples, which emphasize readerly skill, have presumably eliminated the element of chance. We can look to a work like Cortázar's *Rayuela* for a return to the type of play offered by *El libro de las suertes*. The "narrative" of a game like *El libro de las suertes*, in which different choices of nymphs and cities send the player jumping back and forth to pages containing further options, anticipates Cortázar's twentieth-century novel structured on a game. The relationship between playing cards and dice and reading imaginative fiction was intuited well before postmodernists would make the game of chance an emblem of the book and the universe.[66]

Despite the sonnet proclaiming *El libro de las suertes* a harmless parlour game ("con buena o mala suerte esté contento, / porque con él se parten bien las peras, / advirtiendo que burlas, burlas son" – "be content with good or bad luck, / because with it the pears are divided well, / making known that jests remain jests" ["Clave para entender la obra," 143]), divining the future even in play proved too disquieting for many players and ecclesiastic authorities. As Navarro Durán notes in her introduction to the Valencia edition (1528), "if they were consulted according to a determined ritual, they could satisfy the religious feeling that accompanies curiosity."[67] The indulging of curiosity, and the delimiting of individual freedom (expressed in the hopeful questions posed by the players) within the astrological components and oracle's foreknowledge brought the game perilously close to unresolved theological and scientific debates. It is significant that Rodrigo Caro notes that the ancients created games not only to preserve health but to *distract* from curiosity (II, 140). Like its predecessor, Lorenzo Spirito's *Libro delle sorti*, *El libro de las suertes* was banned by the Spanish Inquisition (Sanz Hermida 604, note 39). Cervantes's own *cabeza encantada* is asked questions very similar to those in the *Libro de suertes* (on spousal love, on children), and raises similar suspicions: "[don Antonio] temiendo no llegase a los oídos de las despiertas centinelas de nuestra Fe, habiendo declarado el caso a los señores inquisidores, le mandaron que lo deshiciese y no pasase adelante, porque el vulgo ignorante no escandalizase" ("he was afraid that it might reach the ears of the watchful sentinels of our faith, so he told the inquisitors about it himself and they ordered him to dismantle it and never to use it again, to prevent the ignorant from being scandalized" [*Don Quijote* II, 62, p. 517]). The combination of curiosity and superstition is too potent, converting the "play" into something more serious, and menacing.

Naturally, many players did not believe the arbitrariness that games of *alea* were meant to embody, that is, they felt the outcomes signified something. Caillois observed how the search for meaning compromises the games of chance: "With superstition, the corruption of *alea* is born. It is indeed tempting for one who submits to fate to try to predict the outcome, or at least influence it in his behaviour. The player finds special significance in all kinds of phenomenon, encounters, and omens, which he imagines to be forebodings of good or bad luck" (ch. 4). Castillo bemoans how many gamblers became *agoreros* (soothsayers), believing they could somehow control the arbitrary distribution of the cards (ch. III, "El tercero estado de medianos y menores"), and Pedro de Covarrubias provides the following illustration:

> Diziendo que el dia que han de jugar que no les han de hablar sus mugeres: que lo tienen por aguero: aguardan de no jugar ciertos dias y no por devocion mas por abusion diziendo que ay en aquellos dias ciertas horas menguadas. Otros riñen quando les hablan mudando los dados y los naypes: diziendo que han de ganar con unos mas que con otros siendo differentes quitanse la capa y la espada diziendo que aquello les haze perder: mudan el tablero buelven la silla al reves besan los naypes porque les sean propicios: si pierden alçando con la mano derecha alçan con la ezquierda no quieren mirar sus cartas hasta que los otros ayan visto las suyas: si echan azares en las primeras suertes creen que en las postreras tienen cierta la ganancia: si al principio echan las mejores esperan de buen comienço

alegre fin. Encomiendanse al demonio creyendo que por pagarles en este mundo les sera favorable. (fols. 50r–51)

[Saying that on the day they gamble their wives cannot speak to them, which they treat as an omen. They refrain from playing on certain days, and not out of devotion but rather superstition, saying that there are during those days certain adverse hours. Others argue when they are spoken to while changing the dice or cards, saying that they will win more with some than with others; they remove their cloak and sword saying that they [cloak and sword] make them lose. They change tables and turn the seat backwards, they kiss the cards so that they will be favourable. If they lose reaching with the right hand they reach with the left, and they will not look at their cards until the others have seen theirs. If their first throws of the dice are fortunate they think it secures their latter winnings, anticipating from a good start a happy finish. They commend themselves to the devil, believing that he will be favourable to them by paying them in this world.]

Covarrubias comically portrays the mind's overheated attempt to find patterns, and to grasp the mechanisms of cause and effect. The oft-repeated accusations in lawsuits against gamblers who are seen playing *de día y noche* (day and night) and *a deshoras* (at odd hours) bespeak something more than material greed.[68] The addictive quality of games of chance is in large measure due to their ability to captivate the hopeful imagination. As one of the more famous exiles from the Iberian Peninsula would note, the hope and fear created by vicissitudes of fortune create ideal conditions for superstition. Spinoza maintained that such mental aberrations – including "reverence of misguided religion" – would not occur in a rational (or extremely lucky) world: "Men would never be superstitious, if they could govern all their circumstances by set rules, or if they were always favoured by fortune: but being frequently driven into straits where rules are useless, and being often kept fluctuating pitiably between hope and fear by the uncertainty of fortune's greedily coveted favours, they are consequently, for the most part, very prone to credulity (3)." In his *Tractatus Theologicus-Politicus*, Spinoza longs for a rational society while vividly describing the present state, a thoroughly "prerational" one. It is not surprising that his critique of religions that capitalize on fear and confusion should recall Maravall's account of the "directed culture" of the Baroque: "Immense pains have therefore been taken to counteract this evil [i.e., revolutions] by investing religion, whether true or false, with such pomp and ceremony, that it may rise superior to every shock, and be always observed with studious reverence by the people" (Spinoza 5).

Anticipating the criticism of such sceptics, Castillo draws a distinction between the sanctioned rituals of Christianity and those of the gambler, whose ceremonies are *no por devocion mas por abusion* (not out of devotion but superstition). Erasmus, Montaigne and Cervantes were well aware of the potential for clouding these issues (and we will see similar ambiguities emerge in discussions of card-playing in the *Indias*, below). In comments that have obvious implications for recreational reading, Montaigne summarizes the human dilemma: "And if it is true that he alone of all the animals has this freedom of imagination and this unruliness in thought that represents to him what is, what is not, what he wants, the false and the true, it is an advantage that is sold to him very dear, and in which he has little cause to glory, for from it springs the principal source of the ills that oppress him: sin, disease, irresolution, confusion, despair" (II, 12, p. 336). Montaigne's list of ills efficiently summarizes the portraits of gamers found in Covarrubias, Zabaleta, Castillo, and other early modern *tractatus ludorum*.

The ineluctable human inclination to attempt to organize and interpret chance can be observed as early as the fourth century BCE, with the cult of Tyche.[69] As one might expect, Borges took the implications of such an inclination to their vertiginous peak. In "La lotería en Babilonia," in which a society organizes itself on the basis of a lottery, Borges presents an extreme, Kafkaesque version of the *Libro de las suertes*:

> Imaginemos un primer sorteo, que dicta la muerte de un hombre. Para su cumplimiento se procede a un otro sorteo, que propone (digamos) nueve ejecutores posibles. De esos ejecutores, cuatro pueden iniciar un tercer sorteo que dirá el nombre del verdugo, dos pueden reemplazar la orden adversa por una orden feliz (el encuentro de un tesoro, digamos), otro exacerbará la muerte (es decir le hará infame o la enriquecerá de torturas), otros pueden negarse a cumplirla… Tal es el esquema simbólico. En la realidad el *número de sorteos es infinito*. Ninguna decisión es final, todas se ramifican en otras. (77)

> [Let us imagine a first drawing, which dictates a man's death. To fulfil it one proceeds to another drawing, which proposes (for instance) nine possible executioners. Of those executioners, four may initiate a third drawing that will reveal the name of the hangman, two may replace the adverse

> sentence with a happy one (the discovery of a treasure, for instance), another will exacerbate the death (that is, make it horrific or enrich it with tortures), others may refuse to carry it out... Such is the symbolic outline. In reality the *number of drawings is infinite.* No decision is final, all of them branch into others.]

Inscrutable though it may be, the lottery facilitates what Girard described as the original acts of coercion necessary for establishing a social order: "The sacred nature of Chance is reflected in the practice of the lottery. In some sacrificial rites the choice of victim by means of a lottery serves to underline the relationship between Chance and generative violence" (Girard 314).

The mere acceptance of blind chance – to the extent that it could actually be achieved – was also theologically problematic in early modern Spain, not easily reconciled with providential design. In this light it is interesting to consider Adrian de Castro's warning against exposing one's wealth to chance. If the gamblers understood the dubious nature of the undertaking, "nunca perderian, porque nunca se inclinarian a cosa tan dudosa como es la suerte; antes procurarian conservar lo poco, o mucho que Dios fue servido de darles, sin procurar alcançar mas por tan ilicito camino, y tan dudosa via como es el juego, cuya ganancia llaman los Theologos, Ganancia torpe" ("they would never lose, because they would never be inclined to something so uncertain as chance; rather they would try to conserve the little or much that God saw fit to give them, without attempting to achieve more by such illicit means, and such an uncertain path as gambling, the winnings of which the Theologians call vile gains" [fol. 33]). If the Fall brought vicissitudes of fortune into the world in the first place, it is also postlapsarian man who is obliged to make his living *con el sudor de su rostro*, to avoid spending his time *sin provecho* (unprofitably), and to husband his resources well. In addition to coinciding with contemporary theological currents of a mercantilist bent, such views anticipate Enlightenment linking of piety and productive work. As Jovellanos put it: "El hombre, condenado por la Providencia al trabajo, nace ignorante y débil. Sin luces, sin fuerzas, no sabe dónde dirigir sus deseos, dónde aplicar sus brazos. Fue necesario el transcurso de muchos siglos y la reunión de una muchedumbre de observaciones para juntar una escasa suma de conocimientos útiles a la dirección del trabajo, y a estas pocas verdades debió el mundo la primera multiplicación de sus habitantes" ("Man, condemned by Providence to labour, is born ignorant and weak. Without illumination, without strength, he does not know where to direct his desires, where to employ his arms. It required the passage of many centuries and the collecting of copious observations in order to join a meagre sum of knowledge useful for directing labour, and to these few truths the world owes the first proliferation of its inhabitants" ["Elogio a Carlos III," 184]). Gambling with dice is inimical both to the nascent bourgeoisie mentality and associated theological currents. As we observed above, *Guzmán de Alfarache* characterizes society not only by its travesty of the values of honest work, but also by its degradation of the significance of one's property: "Que todo lo quita quien la hacienda quita, pues no es uno estimado en más de lo que tiene más" ("Whoever takes away property takes all, since one is esteemed only in accordance with possessions" [II, ii, 5]). As noted above in reference to Cavillac's study, Alemán depicts the very mercantilist mentality impeded by an idle nobility and an opportunistic criminal class – the last two, as Dunn pointed out, not always easily distinguished from one another. The thieving Guzmán offers the following recommendation for useful, efficient labour: "Que meter costa en lo que ha de ser de poco provecho es locura. Los empleos hanse de hacer conforme a las ganancias. Que ponerse un hombre a querer alambicar su entendimiento muchas noches en lo que apenas tendrá para cenar una no conviene" ("To invest much in what yields little gain is insanity. Occupations must be undertaken according to their gains. It is unseemly for a man to want to distil his intelligence for many nights in something that will scarcely provide dinner for one" [II, ii, 5]).

That gambling with cards and dice typically took place in enclosed spaces compounded the potential harm.[70] Pedro de Guzmán gave the venue an air of cultish mystery: "pues fuera de sus astucias, fullerias, y trampas se cierran como raposas en secretas cuevas, y retretes para que nadie les estorve el jugar" ("and apart from their cunning, cheating, and tricks they enclose themselves like foxes in secret caves, and small chambers so that nobody may impede their play" [fol. 399]). Part of his remedy was to bring the activity out into the open: "naypes, dados … que se suelen exercitar a puertas cerradas … pretendemos sacar a plaça, y en publico lo que la ociosidad particular ha inventado y … lo que la ociosidad comun ha introduzido" ("cards, dice … that are habitually played behind doors … we intend to bring out to the square, and in public what individual idleness has invented and … what common idleness has introduced" [fol. 193]). Not only was gambling often a nocturnal activity, but the reviled *casas de conversación* tended to be subterranean, accessible by descending a staircase (García Santo-Tomás 150, 157). This presented concerns regarding commoners, who needed to be monitored lest their play degenerate. For the higher estates, the privacy of play was often considered desirable, since it helped protect their image as social exemplars. In a study of the diocese of León, José Sánchez Herrero cites a number of synods documenting improper venues for clerical play:

> The priests played frequently for mere entertainment dice, backgammon, cards, amongst themselves and with other honest laity, in their houses … or in other places. But they also probably played, despite it being prohibited them, publicly, before the laity and with them in gambling houses, at "dishonest and prohibited" games, "as are dice, or card games … or other prohibited games in their houses, nor should they go to play in houses where such boards were assembled," gambling "cash," not for mere entertainment, but to achieve gains.[71]

In a recent study of canon and common law discourse in *Don Quijote*, Susan Byrne cites early modern synods bemoaning gambling within churches (Byrne 55). A criminal suit from 1564 in the town of Villalpando, Castilla, documents even more damning accusations arising from gambling among laymen and friars: "About: accusing them of injurious words to some friars from the convent of San Francisco, from beyond the walls of said town, when they were playing by the milestone of the pine grove of the same (calling them common licentious heretics, that they carried girls to the pine grove, that they forced the women, and other things)." The marginal venue of the gambling – on the outskirts of town ("al mojón en el pinar") – is associated with the greater crime of rape.[72]

The concern with the way space informs social interaction, and with the importance of the company one keeps while playing, was also evident in Castillo's instructions on how prelates and clerics should play chess: "sea unos con otros: no entre legos ni con ellos; no en la yglesia mas en una casa en secreto" ("may it be with each other: not amongst the laity nor with them; not at church, but in a house, in secret" [n.p.]). The allowance for certain estates to play games that are prohibited for others, and that must consequently be played in secret, reflects an interesting complexity. As mentioned above, games like cards and dice were often catgorized as *indiferentes*, neither intrinsically bad nor good. Whether or not they provide licit or corrupting recreation depends on the judgment and disposition of the players. But exemplarity has little use for what is *indiferente*, or ethically neutral. It requires either models of ideal behaviour to be imitated, or the inverse, an unambiguous admonition (*escarmiento*). In his discussion of card games and the *tractatus ludorum*, Enrique García Santo-Tomás points out how the reformers believed they could "domesticate chance" and limit the damage of monetary exchange by controlling the space, duration, and company of card-players. The result would be an aristocratic pastime that could solidify class identity and restore the degraded ideal of *conversación*: "If done properly, the transfer of capital can become an exercise in style much like the *sprezzatura* of the good conversationalist" (159). Deleito y Piñuela gave an account of the range of activities taking place in "conversation houses," suggesting its potential for the refined interactions envisioned by the reformers: "People of quality would congregate in them, to converse and spend time in various entertainments. They chatted gracefully, lavishing upon each other ingenious subtleties, holding contests of intricate riddles, awarding prizes to those who solved them, and various objects were raffled or sold, such as small bags, stockings, gloves, trinkets, more or less valuable ornaments, and even comestibles and drinks."[73] But if the genteel *agon* of wits, the exchange of accessories and partaking of food and drink would seem to subdue the threat of gambling within a larger, socially cultivated context, Deleito y Piñuela observed what Adrián de Castro and others were quick to point out: "But gambling was the soul of such get-togethers, although it was carried out with certain decorum. The word 'conversation' tended to be a euphemism, which concealed that vice."[74]

In addition to the players of such games, the spectators are also subject to degradation. If the onlookers in Vives's model of play represent a harmonizing authority to whom the players respectfully defer, Zabaleta describes the *mirones* receiving the players' scorn: "De los que juegan, el que pierde los tiene por azar y el que gana por enfado" ("Of those who play, the one who loses takes them for misfortune and the winner for annoyance" [341]). The losers suspect the spectators, attributing to them their poor fortune; the winners resent having to pay them the customary tips. Pedro de Covarrubias argues that spectators of a prohibited game are complicit: "Es de notar que no tan solamente son prohibidos estos juegos mas aun de verlos ... El error que no es resistido y corregido parece ser aprovado" ("It should be noted that not only the playing but even the watching of these games is prohibited ... The error that is not resisted and corrected appears to be approved" [fol. 52]). Zabaleta allows for the possibility of gambling houses for purely recreational purposes, "los que van a entretenerse, no a jugar sino a parlar, no a la inclinación sino al divertimiento" ("those who go to entertain themselves, not to gamble but to converse, not on account of their proclivity but rather for diversion" [346]). But even such participants succumb to the poisonous atmosphere: "Allí el ejemplo malo le ofusca el entendimiento. Ve a unos decir mal de otros, y él también dice mal de alguno. Con la embriaguez del mal ejemplo, ve porfiar y porfía" ("There the bad example obfuscates the understanding. One sees some speak ill of others, and he also speaks ill of someone. In the inebriation of the bad example, he sees quarrelling and then quarrels" [346]). To the drunkenness ("beodez") of the players swept up in their game (see previous section) is added the inebriation of the spectator, who is influenced by observing errant behaviour. Such objections overlook the possibility that those involved might be able to sustain an analytical distance amidst all the fun, to mediate the activity with conscious reflection – a possibility that fascinated and perplexed Cervantes.

Mateo Alemán presented one of the more profound reflections on the peculiar effects of play on the spectator. Beyond the conventional concern with the influence of negative behavioural examples, Alemán explored the nature of vicariousness itself. As Guzmán de Alfarache observes a card game taking place at an inn, his initial motives seem benign, what the writers above might call *indiferente*: "viendo lo que pasaba, quise por entretenimiento llegarme acerca" ("seeing what was afoot, I wanted, for entertainment, to approach" [II, ii, 3]). But Guzmán experiences a troubling sense of identification with what he watches:

> Ellos no tenían pena y a mí me la daba, sin qué ni para qué más de por sólo mirarle sus naipes, las veces que dejaba de ganar o perdía. ¡Oh estraña naturaleza nuestra, no más mía que general en todos! Que sin ser aquellos mis conocidos, ni alguno dellos, ni haberlos otra vez visto, pues aquella fue la primera, por haber estado preso aquellos días, y sin haberlos nunca tratado, me alegraba cuando ganaba el de mi parte. (II, ii, 3)

> [They felt not sorrows although I did, without any more cause than by merely looking at their cards, the times that one stopped winning or was losing. Oh our strange nature, not only mine but common to all! That without their being acquaintances of mine, not even one of them, nor having seen them before, since that was the first time, having been in jail those days, and without having ever interacted with them, I became happy when the one I sided with was winning.]

While Guzmán means to illustrate with this example the vice of excessive curiosity regarding the affairs of others ("Cuánta ignorancia es echarse sobre sus hombros cargos ajenos, que ni en sí tienen sustancia ni pueden ser de provecho" – "How ignorant to take upon oneself the concerns of others, which in themselves are neither of consequence nor profitable" [II, ii, 3]), one could say he also illustrates an aspect of the human capacity for empathy. We are unable to watch others without becoming emotionally involved: "Si gustas de ver jugar, mira desapasionadamente si puedes; mas no podrás, que eres como yo y harás lo mismo" ("If you enjoying watching gambling, watch dispassionately if you can; but you won't be able to, since you are like me and will do the same" [II, ii, 3]). Of course, he is right to emphasize the potentially corrosive effects of such identification, so often apparent in the fanaticism of sports fans.[75] The identification of the spectator with the player, as Guzmán stresses, involves him in the polarization of the contest: the desire for his own party to win is accompanied by a fervent hope that the other party – equally unknown to him – lose.

Alemán's satirical novel insists on the unremitting agonism of human nature, a disposition that manifests itself in spectator and player alike. For this reason, like the more severe moralists considered in this study, Guzmán is sceptical about the possibility of moderate, recreational play:

> Que no llamo yo jugar a quien lo tomase por juego una vez o seis o diez en el año, de cosa que no diese cuidado ni pusiese codicia, mas de por sólo gusto. No embargante que tengo por imposible sentarse uno a jugar sin codicia de ganar, aunque sea un alfiler, y lo juegue con su mujer o su hijo.
>
> Que, cuando no se juega interés de dinero, juégase a lo menos opinión del entendimiento y saber, y así nadie quiere que otro lo venza. (II, ii, 3).

> [I don't call gambling what one takes for play one time, or six or ten in a year, in a way that would not give cares, nor inspire greed, but rather for mere enjoyment. Nevertheless I consider it impossible to sit down and play without covetousness to win, even though it be a needle, and one be playing with his wife or son.
>
> Even when money isn't at stake, one still plays for esteem of intelligence and knowledge, and so nobody wants to be vanquished by the other.]

The corruption of card games comes not only from greed, from the prospects of material gain. The ambition to affirm superiority over one's opponent, and to guard one's reputation for superior skill, would seem to preclude, in Alemán's world, the possibility of genuine *eutrapelia*.

Dostoevsky's *The Gambler* (1867) offers a distilled illustration of the durability of such concerns, and how some of the cultural implications of *alea* may be developed. The author himself had first-hand experience with gambling addiction, and appreciated as much as Covarrubias and Alemán that, while greed may be an aspect of the compulsion to continue playing, human beings tend to create an elaborate web of significance around arbitrary events, giving the shuffled deck, rolled dice, or roulette wheel the force of narrative. As he approaches a climactic night of gambling, Alexei reflects upon the meanings with which he has endowed the game:

> Yes, there are times when the wildest idea, the most obviously impossible scheme, becomes so strongly implanted in one's mind that one begins to regard it as something quite realizable. Moreover, if that thought is combined with a powerful and passionate desire, at certain moments it will loom as something fateful, inevitable, predestined, as something that cannot fail to happen. Perhaps this feeling is due to a combination of premonition, enormous strength of will, and intoxication with one's own fantasy, or perhaps something else – I don't know. But that night something wonderful that I'll never forget happened to me. And although what happened can easily be accounted for by simple arithmetic, nevertheless it struck me as a miracle. For how could I have felt so sure about it for such a long time? It is true, I had thought of it not as a chance that, among others, might (and therefore also might not) happen, but as necessity that simply couldn't fail to happen. (142–3)

The mundane fact – which Alexei repeatedly acknowledges – that the game is completely arbitrary, beholden to no other law than that of statistics, does not prevent him from seeing transcendent forces at work. Like Georg Simmel's hero, he approaches chance as if it were necessity. But the transcendence evaporates as his heroism at the roulette table does not lead to a triumphant union with his love object, Paulina. The end of the novel finds him grimly dedicated to his game, which has become his sole point of reference, the only system through which he finds validation. Rather than affirming meaning about the world around him (and his place in it), the game of chance deteriorates into confining solipsism. Alexei's powerful imagination is, as Montaigne would say, "an advantage that is sold to him very dear" (II, 12, p. 236).

Prior to the final implosion in *The Gambler*, Dostoevsky gives vivid expression to the other possibilities of *alea* outlined above. Alexei's observation regarding the play of the nobility as opposed to that of the "mob" illustrates Santo-Tomás's argument that the proper conduct of play among the upper classes – the exercise in *sprezzatura* – can solidify group identity and values:

> If he wins, he may, for instance, burst into loud laughter or make some amusing comment to a neighbor, or he can stake the whole thing again and even double it; but he may only do so out of curiosity, just to experiment with probabilities, and never for the sake of a plebeian preoccupation with gain. In brief, a gentleman must view all the gaming tables, all roulette and *trente et quarante* as merely a sport organized exclusively for his enjoyment. He is not even allowed to suspect the lures and traps on which gambling is based ... A true gentleman must remain unruffled even if he loses his whole fortune. Money must be so much less important than good manners that it isn't worth bothering about. (30–1)

Of course, Dostoevsky exudes scorn upon these gentlemanly values, exposing the delusion and hypocrisy involved: "So it becomes permissible for him [the gentleman] to mingle with the crowd as long as he convinces himself that he is only a spectator and in no way part of it" (31). Like Zabaleta, Dostoevsky knows that everyone – players and spectators alike – is complicit; and not unlike the Spanish moralist, he takes a certain pleasure in the "grotesque spectacle" (108). In characteristic form, Dostoevsky also turns one of the classic evils of gambling – that it is a desecration of the ideal of prudent husbanding of resources – into a critique of the very culture espousing such values. As Alexei provocatively comments to his smug French and outraged German interlocutors, "in the course of history, the ability to accumulate capital had come almost to head the list of virtues required by a man reared in Western civilization ... it still remains to be seen which is more repulsive – Russian haphazardness or German accumulation of wealth through honest labour" (42). Dostoevksy's denizen of the gambling dens is akin to his "underground man," lashing out at the official values of the Enlightenment while wallowing in his own self-destructive proclivities. To the eminently rational ethos of German work and ordered accumulation, he proposes a reversion to a more "primitive" state: his manner of approaching the roulette table is in fact a fine illustration of "play as chance-necessity," which Spariosu identified as a characteristic of the prerational (*Dionysus Reborn* 12). And the spiritual implications of Dostoevsky's critique call to mind Pascal's plea to abandon rationality and materialism, and submit to the wager. Goncharov's indolent Oblomov similarly represents an alternative to his industrious friend, Stoltz, of German extraction (*Oblomov*).

It should by now be clear that the concerns surrounding games such as cards and dice were often the same as those voiced by literary theorists and censors: the preoccupation with the human inclination to imitate, and consequent susceptibility to behavioural models; the realization that the spectators comprise a vital part of the total dynamic, not only being influenced by but also affecting the play; the observation that the stimulated imagination can become irrational and obsessive; the awareness that such dangers are greater if the activity takes place in a private space, and, conversely, may be mitigated in a group or public setting. All of these considerations will be present in our consideration of Cervantes's narrative art.

Physical Activity and Competition

The conditions of physical recreation curtail many of the problems with the games discussed above. The activities tend to take place outdoors, with daylight dispelling the aura of covert privacy associated with cards and dice. Paul Bril's canvas *Landscape with Men Playing "Mail a la Chicane"* (1624) offers a contrast to the suspect activities depicted in the paintings of card players (see above pp. 79–81). Representing an early form of golf, Bril associates play with the recuperative space of the *locus amoenus*, in which civilization and nature harmonize. As in the ludic ideal proposed in some of the literary works under consideration, the participants compete in tranquil sociability (see Figure 5). Castillo recommends for commoners "exercicios en que las fuerças se abivan y los miembros se sueltan y ponen ligeros: no dentro de casa escondidos con los naypes y dados de dia y de noche" ("activities by which strength is enlivened and the limbs are loosened and made agile: not indoors hidden with cards and dice day and night" [n.p.]). Physical exertion also imposes a natural limit on the activities, attenuating the excesses of gambling. Not only are physical recreations well-suited to the daily endeavours of peasants (a rustic corollary to how the tournament would complement the nobility's principle charge); the skills developed in such play are a sign of individual virtue. It is, as we will see below, one of the ways in which Basilio demonstrates his suitability to Quiteria (*Don Quijote* II, 19); and the noble Andrés exhibits his quality on the many occasions that present themselves while the gypsies rove the countryside: "En todas las aldeas y lugares que pasaban había desafíos de pelota, de esgrima, de correr, de saltar, de tirar la barra y de otros ejercicios de fuerza, mañana y ligereza, y de todos salían vencedores Andrés y Clemente" ("In all the villages and places they passed through there were contests of ball, of fencing, of running, of jumping, of throwing the bar and other activities of strength, skill and agility, and in all Andrés and Clemente emerged victorious" [*La gitanilla* 117]). This is the same sort of unaffected participation Castiglione's Pallavicino describes: "[M]any of our young gentlemen are to be found, on

Figure 5 Paul Bril, *Landscape with Men Playing "Mail a la Chicane,"* 1624 (oil on canvas). Minneapolis Institute of Arts, MN, USA / The William Hood Dunwoody Fund / The Bridgeman Art Library.

holidays, dancing all day in the open air with the peasants, and taking part with them in sports such as throwing the bar, wrestling, running and jumping. And I'm sure there's no harm in this, for the contest is not one of nobility but of strength and agility, regarding which ordinary villagers are often just as good as nobles; and I think this kind of familiar behaviour has a certain charming open-mindedness about it" (117). It was such "open-mindedness" that Levin would exhibit during his "recreational work" and drinking with the peasants (*Ana Karenina*, see above p. 50).

Despite the potentially harmful effects of *agon*, Pedro de Covarrubias, like Luque Faxardo (bk. I, ch. 2), argues that tournaments are less-deserving of prohibition than games of chance:

> Digo que la causa es: porque en los torneos ay cansacio [sic] que fatiga y macera la carne y la retraye y aparta de la luxuria y entorpecimiento y deprende arte y industria militar. De manera que concurre exercicio de ingenio y de fuerças: y assi no se ponen totalmente a caso de fortuna por lo qual si el tornear no fuesse prohibido por la yglesia hecho con buena intencion y templadamente sin provable peligro: seria licito especialmente por redundar en provecho de la republica y por esto el derecho civil no le prohibe. (fol. 48)

> [I say that the cause is: because in tournaments there is exhaustion that fatigues and softens the flesh and removes and distracts it from lust and lewdness and teaches military art and diligence. So that the exercise of wit and strength are combined: and in this way one is not subject completely to fortune, such that if participating in tournaments were not prohibited by the church, done with good intentions and in moderation without probable danger, it would be licit, especially as it benefits the republic, and for this reason civil law does not prohibit it.]

Skill masters chance, exertion cultivates the body, and the acquired abilities are useful to society. As we have noted, the "utility" also extends to the ideological function of affirming class, national, and religious identity. The agonistic and martial imagery in Castillo's account of *eutrapelia*, for example, reminds the nobility that their leisure is meant to refresh them for renewed opposition to *mozos turcos y infieles* ("infidel Turkish youths"). Barbara Fuchs has noted how "Moorish dress was regularly adopted for ceremonial occasions such as the *juegos de cañas* – a jousting game of Moorish origins – or mock battles that celebrate victories over Moorish enemies. In these cases, ethnic cross-dressing and the performance of ersatz Moorishness contribute to the construction of a 'fictive ethnicity' for Spain that as a nation has overcome Islam by fetishizing its visible manifestations in the context of ceremonial performances" (6).[76]

Acknowledging the opposition to tournaments by ecclesiastical authorities, Pedro de Covarrubias stipulates that they be conducted in moderation, and that measures be taken to reduce the likelihood of bodily harm. Modern accusations regarding the cruel sensibilities of the age overlook the consistent efforts to implement humane standards of recreation. Pedro de Guzmán, for example, speculates on the possibility of making bullfights less dangerous, asserting that "si uno quiere aventurar o desperdiciar su vida, lo deve el buen governador estorvar, y quitar al loco y atrevido de las manos el instrumento de su daño" ("if one wants to risk or waste one's life, a good governor should prevent it, and remove from the crazy and rash individual's hands the instrument of his undoing" [260–1]). Cristóbal Pérez de Herrera proposed to Felipe II a series of reforms that would make bullfighting safer, including a reduction in the number of events, prohibiting the participation of unauthorized fighters, blunting of the bulls' horns, and improving medical facilities for the injured. Herrera's recommendation of alternative forms of agonistic entertainment confirms the utilitarian and ideological functions of play considered above:

> Y mas aviendo, como ay otras muchas suertes de fiestas y regozijos en que poderse entretener las gentes, que con ser para este efecto, tambien servirian de exercitarse en armas, y habilitarse para ocasiones de guerra, como son jugar cañas y tornear a caballo y a pie, justar, y jugar la sortija, y hazer mascaras y zuyzas, combatiendo castillos entre Moros y Christianos, como se acostumbra hazer, luchar y correr palios, y trepar por arboles ensevados a ganar premios quien lo sepa hazer seguramente, y esgrimir, y otros exercicios y regozijos a este modo, muy facil seria passar en muchas fiestas con esto, sin que forçosamente ayan de ser los plazeres tragedias, con acabar en muertes y sucessos tristes, y quando ayan de ser acompañadas con toros se haga por alguno de los modos que se diran, o otro a proposito, que sea sin perjuyzio de tan gran numero de almas y vidas, y de mayor passatiempo y gusto para todos. (15)
>
> [And there being, since there are many other types of festivities and celebrations in which the people may enjoy themselves, which by being for

> this effect, they would also serve to train themselves in arms, and get themselves into shape for times of war, as are cane jousting, tournaments on horseback and on foot, jousting, ring-jousting, making masks and Swiss arms, fighting castles between Moors and Christians as is custom, wrestling and racing for silk cloths, climbing greased trees for prizes for those who know how to do so most assuredly, and fencing, and other activities and celebrations of this type, it would be very easy to stay with such festivities as this, without necessarily taking pleasure in tragedies, by ending in death and sad events, and when they must be accompanied with bulls may it be done in one of the following ways, or another such, in which it be without the peril to so many souls and lives, and of greater pastime and enjoyment for all.]

Deforneaux describes the prevailing "prerational" ethos of bullfighting in early modern Spain: "If a toreador was 'affronted' by a bull, either because a dart had not been properly planted or the bull had jostled his horse and perhaps knocked him out of the saddle, the toreador was honour bound to kill the bull with a thrust of the sword. This he could do either mounted or on foot, but nobody was allowed to go to his aid" (134). Herrera's plea for a departure from what he sees as the primitive and heathen delight in suffering ("de ser los plazeres tragedias") is further evidence of a "civilizing" sensibility. His proposed modifications of the bullfights are very similar to the reforms Elias describes in late medieval football and boxing, all designed to reduce the physical hazard of the activities. Such pastimes, through containment within humane rules, undergo a process Elias calls "sportization" (21–2). Of course, as virtually no physical activity is completely free of risk, even in the seventeenth century questions of liability and litigation impinged on the play sphere. There was, for example, a curious lawsuit on behalf of a woman who, strolling through the *locus amoenus* of an orchard, was struck and injured by a boy playing *bolos*. Fortunately, she recovered.[77]

Along with martial training for the nobility, and easily-monitored outdoor recreation for the third estate, physical activity was recommended for early youth. Consistent with Vives and Montaigne, and anticipating modern ideas on *paidia*, the Augustinian Friar Marco Antonio de Camos wrote on the importance of play in the development of children, particularly as an outlet for the restless energy of adolescence ("los bullicios de la adolescencia"). Of prime importance, he argued, was to prevent idleness by keeping children busy, "agora con bolos, ora a la pelota, sacandoles al campo: ya, quando de más edad, en hazerles correr cavallos, en el exercicio de las armas, en la caça: que esto les haze muy rezios y sufridores. Esto digo para los que su estado no consiente se ocupen en exercicios viles y baxos" ("now with billiards, now with ballgames, taking them out to the country: now, when older, in having them race horses, in the exercise of arms, in the hunt, for this makes them strong and resilient. This I say for those whose estate prevents them from occupying themselves in vile and vulgar activities" [fol. 93]).[78] An interesting variation on the "education of children" motif is Ercilla's description of how the Araucanians instiled their martial ethos through recreational activities from an early age:

En lo que usan los niños en teniendo
habilidad y fuerza provechosa,
es que un trecho seguido han de ir corriendo
por una áspera cuesta pedregosa,
y al puesto y fin del curso revolviendo,
le dan al vencedor alguna cosa:
vienen a ser tan sueltos y alentados
que alcanzan por aliento los venados.

Y desde la niñez al ejercicio
los apremian por fuerza y los incitan,
y en bélico estudio y duro oficio,
entrando en más edad, los ejercitan;
si alguno de flaqueza da un indicio,
del uso militar lo inhabilitan,
y el que sale en armas señalado
conforme a su valor le dan el grado. (*La Araucana*, Canto I, 15–16)

[When they are of propitious ability and strength, children are made to run without rest up a rough and rocky hill, and upon their return the victor is given some prize: they become so flexible and tenacious that they have wind enough to run down deer.

And from childhood they compel them by force and incite them, and in bellicose study and hard tasks, as they age, they train them; and if one gives signs of weakness, they incapacitate him for military use, and to whomever shows skill in arms, they give him the rank according to his worth.]

Hunting was perhaps the favourite physical recreation of early modern Spain, and it carried an impressive array of associations, benefits and potential hazards. Like Pedro de Guzmán (432), Castillo extolls the virtues of hunting for nobles:

> Demas desto diximos que los grandes pueden usar la caça de qualquier manera que sea: la razon es porque ayuda mucho a quitar los pensamientos y la saña que lo que es mas necessario a los grandes que a otros hombres: y allende desto da salud: y aun que en la caça se toma trabajo si es con mesura haze comer y dormir bien, que es la mayor parte de la vida del hombre: y el plazer que enella se rescibe es otrosi grande alegria: en apoderarse de las aves y de las bestias bravas: hazer que los obedezcan. (n.p.)
>
> [In addition to this we said that the great may partake of the hunt in many ways. The reason is that it helps them much to banish preoccupations and ire, which the great are in more need of than are other men. And beyond this it gives health. And although in the hunt one exerts oneself, if it is done in moderation it makes one eat and sleep well, which is the greater part of the life of man. And the pleasure taken therein is a great happiness, in exercising dominion over birds and mighty beasts, to bring them to obeisance.]

Castillo synthesizes a broad range of contemporary thought on leisure. Since nobles bear a greater degree of social responsibility, they are more in need of recreation than others. And class identity is an extension of universal hierarchy, as the hunt reaffirms man's primacy over the animal world. In addition, it is excellent training for war, a primary charge of the nobility. Castillo also invokes the hygienic justification of play, as he discusses the alleviation provided by physical exertion, which sharpens the appetite and facilitates sounds sleep, thereby benefitting both body and mind.

There were, however, those who took issue with such claims. As we saw above, Boccaccio pointed out that the hunt was a gender-specific recreation, to the disadvantage of women ("If men are afflicted by melancholy or heavy thoughts … they can go hawking, hunting, or fishing"). Pedro de Covarrubias noted that, the moderating effects of physical exertion notwithstanding, hunting did lead to excess: "Que cosa es veros el madrugar: y dar priessa como arrebato de enemigos arrojaros por rios, lagunas, espesuras, malezas: con musica infernal de vuestros disonantes gritos" ("What a thing to see you rise early, and rush as if ambushing enemies, throw yourselves into rivers, lagoons, thickets, undergrowth, with infernal music of your dissonant shouts" [fol. 35]). The moderation, harmonious tones and *locus amoenus* associated with *eutrapelia* are trampled in zealous pursuit of the quarry. In part, the excess seems to be caused by the awakening of a predatory instinct, inciting man's bestial nature. But Covarrubias observes that something very "human" is also at play: "Que cosa es veros bolver a la noche como quien ha hecho algo muy ufanos con una pluma en la cabeça: porque mejor buele el seso repetiendo lo que passo: qual de los paxaros volo mejor, qual tiene estragada la cola: si ha gastado lo que comio" ("What a thing to see you return at night as one who has accomplished something, all proud and your head adorned with a feather. Because the mind better takes flight repeating what happened, which birds flew best, which had its tail destroyed, if he has spent what he ate" [fol. 35]). Beyond admonishing pride, Covarrubias observes the workings of the stimulated mind: like the birds, the imagination takes flight ("buele el seso"), and it is suggested that the repetition of lived experience in the mind's eye, and relating it to others in the form of a story, is perhaps more pleasurable than the experience itself. And this is not wholly due to the opportunity it affords to boast; an appreciation of the details and nuances of the day is part of the fun. The hunt is frequently employed as a metaphor for the amorous pursuit, and Celestina's encouragement of Pármeno's friendship with Sempronio also cites the pleasures of recounting conquests: "El deleite es con los amigos en las cosas sensuales y especial en recontar las cosas de amores y comunicarlas" ("Pleasure amongst friends is in sensual matters and especially in recounting affairs of love and communicating them" [71]). The wise old procuress understood what Elias identified as an inherently social aspect to the pleasures of leisure, the human inclination to communicate them to others: "que los bienes, si no son comunicados, no son bienes" ("that goods, if they are not communicated, are not goods" [Rojas 64]). Covarrubias, however, does not intend to marvel at our propensity to transpose experience into art, but rather to warn against what he considers a frivolous pursuit.

Zabaleta, who penned a colourful satire of *el cazador*, attributes part of the hunting inclination to human cruelty, and comically questions how well man does in fact establish dominion over beast, given the health effects of such fanatical behaviour: "Para mí tengo que han muerto más cazadores las perdices, los conejos y las palomas, que los cazadores han muerto palomas, conejos y perdices" ("In my estimation the partridges, rabbits and pigeons have killed more hunters, than hunters have killed pigeons, rabbits and partridges" [241]). Skipping mass in favour of the hunt is likened to heathen sacrifices (243), which recalls the *idolatría* of gamblers (see above p. 86). And Zabaleta's comments regarding the industriousness of the hunter are noteworthy: "Madrugar para trabajar es señal de corazón solícito. Ganar día para ganar es discretísima arte para vivir. Madrugar para holgarse es no entender de holguras" ("To rise early in order to work is the sign of a solicitous heart. To gain daylight in order to profit is a most wise art for living. To rise early to be idle is to not understand enjoyment" [242]). We will revisit aspects of these debates when we consider a particular "gran madrugador y amigo de la caza" ("an early riser and a keen huntsman" [*Don Quijote* I, 1]). For the present, it suffices to recognize that, in their critique of the hunt, figures like Covarrubias and Zabaleta are consonant with humanists who abhor the cruelty and excess of this aristocratic pastime. And, as Zabaleta demonstrates, the critique of decadent aristocracy is sometimes connected to a promotion of the incipient mercantilist values of productivity and work.

Mimesis

Plato famously derides mimesis when he says of imitation that it "is only a kind of play or sport," one that stimulates the lower, affective faculties, and the products of which are neither true nor useful (*The Republic* X). Addressing Plato's objection to the affective nature of aesthetic engagement, El Pinciano agrees that emotional arousal is pernicious in an ideal state; he suggests, however, that it may have a positive – that is, didactic – function in the imperfect real world: "supuesto lo qual, dize muy bien que en esta República, a do los moradores son tan buenos y es necessario que lo sean, no son menester poetas que turben y mientan para quietar y deleytar los ánimos de los hombres, ni por tales medios traellos a la enseñança y virtud" ("supposing which, he is right to say that in this Republic, where the denizens are so good and it is necessary that they be so, poets are not needed who disturb and lie in order to pacify and delight the spirits of men, nor by these means to bring them edification and virtue" [II]). Ife, who calls El Pinciano "Plato's best Spanish representative" (20), points out that the attempt to refute Plato on the grounds that literature is capable of presenting virtuous examples ("traellos a la enseñança y virtud") is flawed, for Plato's objections extended to the very way in which literature functions, that is, the deceptive use of language and creation of an illusory, alternate reality.[79]

El Pinciano understands that literature possesses a unique power, and that its exemplary function ("la enseñança") is perhaps secondary. Unlike Plato, he claims for fiction's enchantment a potentially salutary effect, one that is less precise than the purported ethical gain from the presentation of good examples. Approximating Aristotle's notion of catharsis – which represents a more robust response to Plato than the verisimilitude touted by so many neo-Aristotelians – El Pinciano maintains that art can have a therapeutic operation on the spirits ("para quietar y deleytar los ánimos de los hombres" – "to calm and delight the spirits of men"). In the Eighth Epistle we are reminded that, like tragedy, comedy has a purgative capability: "comedia es imitación activa hecha para limpiar el ánimo de las passiones por medio del deleyte y la risa" ("comedy is active imitation done to purge the spirits of passions by means of delight and laughter"). And while this cleansing of passions does seem related to the cognitive content of the play (the happy ending in which virtue prevails, and folly and vice are condemned), El Pinciano's extended discussion of ways to cause laughter suggests that the comic effect is desirable for its own sake. El Pinciano's reference to the tranquillity and entertainment that laughter provides, like the justifications of *eutrapelia*, point up the need for recreation in an imperfect world, in which the limits of people's ability to conform to the rigors of reason and solemnity are frequently strained. These arguments do not definitively refute Plato's objections to art, and the corrupting potential of the attractive and artificial world it creates will always be a source of debate. (The "willing suspension of disbelief" is still a mysterious phenomenon). But in spite of an inability to justify it fully on theoretical grounds, literary theorists and authors of the Golden Age were prepared to risk the dangers involved in artistic representation; for they were, like so many readers, unwilling to do without. As El Pinciano observes, "es tan grande la autoridad de Homero en el mundo, que el mundo todo se riera de Platón si de Homero se apartara, quanto más si le desterrara" ("the authority of Homer in the world is so great, that the world would laugh at Plato should he distance himself from Homer, and even more should he exile him" [II]).

Pedro de Covarrubias provides a representative summary of concerns regarding mimicry in his enumeration of twelve objections against masques (*máscaras* Cap. 16). Citing classical and scriptural authorities, he expresses the period's ambivalence towards illusion, the fundamental mendacity and artifice of representation. Platonic at base (imitation displaces truth), the arguments extend to the social and theological. Nobles who put on masks sin against decorum, undermining their dignity. And maskers inhabit a nocturnal world of distortion and subterfuge: "los mascarados son como los malhechores de noche: porque assi como la noche es capa de peccadores y cobierta: assi lo es la mascara para dezir sin verguença y hazer toda vileza" ("maskers are like evildoers of the night: because just as the night is the cloak and cover of sinners, so is the mask for speaking shamelessly and doing all manner of vileness" [fol. 39]). Such representation is associated with the devious shape-changing of the devil, and with a desecration of man's natural, God-given form: "macular y falsear el gesto y bulto natural del hombre en el qual resplandesce la celestial hermosura y se señala mas el anima ymagen de dios es cosa tan mal hecha que aun las leyes civiles no consienten se le haga esta injuria" ("to blot and falsify the natural aspect and form of man, in which celestial beauty shines, and the spirit most reveals the image of god, is such an awful act that even civil laws prohibit this affront" [fol. 30]). In this view, the *máscara* does not correspond to the protean potential of the "dignity of man" tradition discussed above, but rather to a monstrous deformation. Instead of the freedom to realize an ideal, it provides the license to transgress.

In his creative speculation on the playing of Abraham's sons, Pedro de Guzmán extends the principle of insidious deception to the very definition of play: "Un docto y moderno escritor dize que alli *ludere* significa *illudere*, hazer escarnio y burla, y por esta burla que hazia Ismael de Isaac fue desterrado de la casa de su Padre" ("A learned and modern writer says that there *ludere* means *illudere*, to ridicule and make fun of, and for that trick that Ishmael played on Isaac he was exiled from the house of his Father" [fol. 400]). Most games involve at least an element of mimicry, since a role is adopted in the very act of observing rules, in entering the play realm. This is what Papargyriou and others identify as the fundamentally fictional mode of engagement in play (see above pp. 11–12). Elias noted how the mimetic component of sports, the simulation of conflict in order to arouse emotions in a socially acceptable, controlled manner, is instrumental to their cathartic function.[80] In his commentary on the "spoil-sport," who refuses to mimic, and the "cheat," Huizinga examines the same etymological point as Guzmán:

> The player who trespasses against the rules or ignores them is a "spoil-sport." The spoil-sport is not the same as the false player, the cheat; for the latter pretends to be playing the game and, on the face of it, still acknowledges the magic circle. It is curious to note how much more lenient society

> is to the cheat than to the spoil-sport. This is because the spoil-sport shatters the play-world itself. By withdrawing from the game he reveals the relativity and fragility of the play-world in which he had temporarily shut himself with others. He robs the play of its *illusion* – a pregnant word which means literally "in play" (from *inlusio, iludere* or *inludere*). Therefore he must be cast out, for he threatens the existence of the play-community. (11)

While a moralist in the platonic mould such as Covarrubias would view mimicry and illusion as creating a dangerous distancing from truth, Huizinga's comments remind us of a potentially constructive social and cognitive function. The positive function has to do with what Erasmus and, centuries later, Caillois, recognize as the element of mimetic play that makes society possible: "Any corruption of the principles of play means the abandonment of those precarious and doubtful conventions that it is always permissible, if not profitable, to deny, but the arduous adoption of which is a milestone in the development of civilization" (Caillois 55).

Some of literary history's great spoilsports point up civilization's need for citizens to validate its conventions – or, as Erasmus would say, its ambivalently foolish illusions. Goncharov's consummate idler, Oblomov, Melville's passively resistant Bartleby, and Camus's impassive Meursault all pose grave challenges to the mimetic, participatory premises of their societies. Shakespeare's charismatically inebriated Bernardine, a candidate for capital punishment in the Duke's prison, adds the compelling case of a refusal to endorse the theatrical gravity of a legal decree: "Friar, not I. I have been drinking hard all night, and I will have more time to prepare me, or they shall beat out my brains with billets. I will not consent to die this day, that's certain" (*Measure for Measure*, IV, iii, l. 56–9). Bloom notes the radically subversive implications of exposing such institutions as theatre: "The superb Bernardine will not play by the rules of Vincentio's Vienna, and is equally unaffected both by its mortality and its mercy" (*Shakespeare and the Invention* 376). We might contrast this with the Cid's collaboration with the king's "legal theatre," which helps to contain the raw violence of revenge, and to legitimize the incipient state (see above pp. 18–21). Affirming the broad reach of Huizinga's insights, David Surman discusses how cheats in present-day cyber games can actually create status, innovation, and a deeper appreciation of the play structure: "Cheating creates an opportunity to play with design, think about it, and tinker around. By effectively unbalancing a game, we can move behind the screen to consider games through their limits" (77). As Papargyriou noted, the ludic quality of many "postmodern" literary works lies in their tendency to question the limits of fiction, to "problematize the framing of reality" (18). We have already considered elements of the humanist tradition (Pico, Castiglione, Erasmus) that embraced the positive potential of mimetic artifice, the protean ability to imitate and create identities. We will further discuss the aesthetic, social and metaphysical implications of this issue in our consideration of don Quijote and Sancho's mimetic play, and in Cervantes's engagement with the picaresque, the genre *por excelencia* of cheats and spoilsports.

Ilinx

From the mass vertigo of the awesome spectacle to individual derangement and loss of identity, *ilinx* presents intriguing possibilities and challenges:

> Various physical activities also provoke these sensations, such as the tightrope, falling or being projected into space, rapid rotation, sliding, speeding, and acceleration of vertilinear movement, separately or in combination with gyrating movement. In parallel fashion, there is a vertigo of a moral order, a transport that suddenly seizes the individual. This vertigo is readily linked to the desire for disorder and destruction, a drive which is normally repressed. (Caillois 24)

There are numerous literary examples of *ilinx* (both physical and moral) in the period under consideration, including Cañizares's hallucinogenic *unturas* mentioned above (*El coloquio de los perros*), Gracián's tightrope acrobat (*El Criticón*), "eros-thanatos" imagery and snowballing scenes of violent farce. They are nearly all antithetical to the civilizing ideal of ordered play. As Spariosu argued, a society can derive meaning and values from ordered competition and the balancing of chance and agency (rational), or violent *agon* and arbitrary *alea* (prerational). But vertigo would seem destabilizing even to a prerational society. Girard's discussion of *The Bacchae* and Dionysian culture emphasizes the allure of vertigo and the importance of overcoming it: "*Dionysus is the god of decisive mob action.* Once stated, it should be easy to see why such a god is called for and why he is revered. He claims legitimacy not from his ability to disturb the peace but from his ability to restore the peace he has himself disturbed – thereby justifying, a posteriori, having disturbed it in the first place" (134).

Pedro de Guzmán describes the familiar trajectory from the discipline and utility of Greek games to the decadent ostentation of the Romans (Cap. 11). Greek industriousness and virtue is partly attributed to the rigors of warfare, whereas Roman vice is born of peace and tranquillity: "Cesó el temor, entróse con la paz la seguridad, y tras ella la ociosidad, y con ella infinitos males, y daños" ("Fear ceased, peace and security began, and after it idleness, and with that infinite evils, and harms" [fol. 216]).[81] A Greek wrestler, for example, follows a regimen that excludes activities associated with *ilinx*: "mucho ha de sufrir, y hazer; padecer calor, y frio, abstenerse de Venus, y vino, que es la ley que da Platon a los luchadores" ("much must he endure, and do; suffer heat, and cold, and abstain from Venus, and wine, which is the rule that Plato gives to wrestlers" [fol. 200]). Nero's Rome, on the other hand, dedicated tremendous resources and technological innovation – aqueducts, mechanical devices, fireworks – to create spectacles that imitated and displaced the cosmos: artificial lakes and forests with fish and beasts, rains concocted of wine mist (fol. 210), fires and spheres and explosions rivalling natural astronomical and meteorological phenomena (fols. 212–13). Although the superlatives used to describe all of this ("hermoso estanque," "hermosisimo bosque con altisimos verdes arboles") express an admiration for the variety and creativity of the spectacles, Guzmán ascribes to them an insidious function: "Pero lo que mas encarece la grandeza destos espectaculos, y la fuerça que tenian para tirar los coraçones, y sentidos para si, es lo que el mismo [Tertuliano] dize de los Christianos de aquel tiempo: *Mas hallarás que se apartan desta secta,* y Christiana Religion, *por no privarse de los gustos destos espectaculos, que por no carecer de la vida*" ("But what most elevates the greatness of these spectacles, and the force they had to compel the hearts and senses, is what he himself [Tertullian] says of the Christians of that time: *You will find that they will stray from this sect*, and Christian Religion, *more in order not to deprive themselves of the pleasures of these spectacles, than not to be deprived of life*" [fol. 202]). It is appropriate that his description of the manipulation of the senses and the will ("tirar los coraçones, y sentidos") should anticipate Maravall's accounts of the effects of mass spectacle in Baroque Spain, for Guzmán is using the example of Roman decadence to condemn the excesses he sees in his own country. As Sánchez Herrero notes in his study of the diocese of León, even men of the cloth were susceptible to such decadence: "the very inclination of the clerics to vagabondage; to literature, recitation or charlatanry; to sleights of hand, acrobatics and mimicry; to dance."[82] Rather than the lascivious gyrating of the zarabanda, Guzmán recommends

> las honestas danças y saraos, como los que suelen hazerse en las casas reales, las ingeniosas invenciones, particularmente los del fuego, de que ay mas curiosidad entre los Christianos, quiçá por la excelencia de su polvora, y otros materiales a proposito para esto, los juegos de manos, Eutropelias, destreças en maromas, o en bueltas sobre el suelo, esgrimas, y todo exercicio militar, no con espadas blancas por el peligro, son algunas de las recreaciones, que licitamente se podian tomar. (fol. 437)
>
> [honest dances and soirées, like those commonly put on in royal houses, ingenious inventions, particularly those of fire, of which there is more curiosity amongst Christians, perhaps because of the excellency of their powder, and other materials to this purpose, sleights of hand, Eutropelias, feats on tight-ropes, or in somersaults on the ground, fencing, and all military exercises, not with swords because of the danger, are some of the licit recreations that could be taken.]

The distinctions are not always clear between political motivations (of distracting and controlling a mass audience) and more benign ones, such as the therapeutic pleasure of a diverting spectacle. As Guzmán notes, even "espectaculos de fieras ... se podian renovar, perficionar y usar sin daño de nadie, y con alegría de los miradores" ("spectacles with beasts ... could be renovated, perfected and used without harm to anyone, and with joy for the spectators" [fol. 437]).

As noted above, the pursuit of *ilinx* often carries erotic associations, a perpetual threat to civilizing order. Even the sublimation of the sensual drive in the service of piety, as with the ecstasy of mysticism, could, due to the intensity and individuality of the experience, be viewed as destabilizing. But it is the pursuit of vertigo in what Caillois calls "illicit sex relations" (27) that presents the greatest social challenge. Vives describes how even relatively innocent situations can devolve: "Los hay que no tienen capacidad para tanto y atollan en la molicie, en los juegos, en el ocio infecundo y embrutecedor, o con fácil pie se deslizan en los placeres e ilusiones de los sentidos hasta sumirse en aquella abyecta brutalidad, que se lleva arrebatada el alma en el vértigo de los deseos desenfrenados" ("There are those who do not have the capacity for so much and become mired in softness, in games, in infertile and dulling idleness, and with a light foot they slide into the pleasures and illusions of the senses until they submerge themselves in abject brutality, that carries off the captivated soul in the vertigo of unchecked desire" ["Tratado del alma" II, Cap. 9]). A *seranilla* in Lope's *El villano en su rincón* depicts such a progression, associating the hunt with the illicit amorous pursuit:

A caza va el caballero
por los montes de París,
la rienda en la mano izquierda,
y en la derecha el neblí.
Pensando va en su señora,
que no la ha visto al partir,
porque como era casada,
estaba su esposo allí.
Como va pensando en ella,
olvidado se ha de sí. (II, v)

[The gentleman goes hunting through the hills of Paris, the reins in his left hand, and the falcon in his right. Thinking of his lady he goes, as he did not see her at his departure, because since she was married, her husband was there. As he goes thinking of her, he has forgotten himself.]

Forcione's study of Lope's play discusses Tello as a manifestation of the repressed sensual drive, and includes the following summary of the above poem as an expression of *ilinx*: "The *seranilla* itself, with the characteristic concentrated dream imagery of folksong, presents a vision of hunting; violent sexual desire; betrayal; loss of self-control and direction; a search for shelter amid a dark, labyrinthine landscape; a forbidden world of transgressive eros; and a loss of identity in the complete surrender to desire" (*Majesty and Humanity* 62). Rather than the nocturnal mystic ascent of the spirit, as in San Juan's "Noche oscura," there is a bestial descent into a lower order.

Vives's image of the errant step ("con fácil pie se deslizan") reveals the principally negative associations of *ilinx*, and its presence as a counter-example in the literature of *desengaño*. Góngora's sonnet, "De un caminante enfermo," provides an illustration:

Descaminado, enfermo, peregrino
en tenebrosa noche, con pie incierto
la confusión pisando del desierto,
voces en vano dio, pasos sin tino.

[Led astray, sick, the pilgrim, in gloomy night, with uncertain foot traipsing the confusion of the desert, gave useless shouts, aimless steps.]

Once again, carnal desire, night, disorientation, and disease are associated with Caillois's "vertigo of a moral order." A more generalized illustration of the abyss faced by all, of a vertigo that we should but often fail to experience, is found near the end of *El Criticón*, as Gracián's pilgrims witness a high-wire act in a public square in Rome: "Assí fue, que a poco rato vieron salir bailando y brincando sobre una maroma un monstruo que en la ligereza parecía un pájaro y en la temeridad un loco. Estaban los que le miraban tan pasmados cuanto él intrépido; ellos temblando de verle, y él bailando porque le viessen" (So it was, that soon they saw dancing and leaping on a tightrope a monster who in nimbleness resembled a bird and in temerity a lunatic. Those who watched were as stunned as he was fearless; they trembling at seeing him, and he dancing at being seen" [764]). Gracián's grotesque spectacle is not so much an uncovering of a moral vertigo as an expression of the metaphysical condition of all humanity, including the awestruck spectators who mistakenly believe they are witnessing something extraordinary: "todos los mortales somos volatines arriesgados sobre el delgado hilo de una frágil vida" ("we mortals are all daring acrobats upon the thin thread of a fragile life" [765]). *Ilinx* is in fact the ordinary condition of a rootless humanity.[83]

The desire of a *desengaño* writer like Gracián to create a sense of vertigo in the reader (and one can think of the entire tradition of *el mundo al revés*) corresponds to an awareness of how tenuous the underpinnings of civilized order really are. As a consequence, one should not assume a false sense of stability, permanence, or hubris; our own personal abyss (mortality) or the chaos of a predatory world, lie just below the elaborately-adorned surface. In his comic and disturbing memoir on death, Julian Barnes muses on one of Montaigne's twentieth-century descendants: "[H]adn't Camus said that the proper response to life's meaninglessness was to invent the rules for the game, as we had done with football?" (19). Of Caillois's four basic play types, *ilinx* most closely approaches the function of Huizinga's spoilsport: it negates the structuring, signifying roles of *agon*, *mimesis*, and even *alea*. It is therefore not surprising that most early modern thinkers would look for ways to contain the *ilinx* impulse in order to mitigate its threat to society. And yet the emergence of the private, individual reader during the period contributed to the potential for *ilinx*. The interior space with which such a reader is associated, and, in the absence of a homogenizing crowd or a clear didactic structure, the losing of one's bearings that may result, clearly preoccupied and fascinated Cervantes.

Regulating Play in the *Indias*

A brief excursus on play in the American colonies will help to illustrate a number of the principles discussed above, and provide context for our later discussion of literary representations of play. As evidenced in numerous dispatches and warrants ("cédulas," "provisiones"), petitions ("arbitrios") and letters from viceroys to the crown, there was much concern with weighing the economic and social benefits against the subversive potential of cards and dice and other forms of gambling. A main justification for allowing them was the substantial revenue generated from licensing and selling the card-decks, which was designated to fortifications, housing, and assorted charities. A royal warrant ("Real Cédula") from 1622 allowed for theatrical representations and an early form of croquet ("juego de barras"), under the conditions that proceedings went not to personal gain but to the charitable work of the hospital of Zacatecas.[84] Another, from 1607, permitted *fiestas* and jousting games ("juegos de cañas") in port cities of the colonies, provided the naval commanders not force the ship owners to contribute funds for such recreations: "none of the said generals may oblige them to put on said festivities nor to make any distributions of funds for them above what they voluntarily would like to make."[85]

In addition to recreation and economic benefit, the Spanish authorities recognized that, for some of their subjects, play also had a spiritual function. The concern in the seventeenth century with regulating the play of the Chinese workers, or *sangleyes*, in the Philippines is particularly interesting, since they occupied an ambiguous position between the Spaniards and the *indios*. In records pertaining to the proceeds from sangley gambling, it is evident that the Spanish authorities, recognizing the great economic benefits of the Chinese presence, were at pains to strike a balance between placating and constraining the sangleyes. The venue of their habitation and play is significant: "in the merchant neighbourhood that they call Parian, on the outskirts of this city."[86] It is a space both marginal, outside the walls of Manila, and central, an important locus of commerce. The ambivalence of the Spanish authorities is clear in the following remarks on the time and space of sangley play:

> These Chinese have as a custom during the festivities of their moon during the month of February to play five days on some boards at evens and odds on the ground upon a mat. There in their land they play for fifteen

> days which are those of the waxing moon and here all the governors preceding me (having consulted the opinions of many theologians as I have which one may do in good conscience) have given them the ten additional days to play as long as they are behind closed doors.[87]

Most authorities stressed that five days of play be officially permitted, with the tacit allowance of the additional ten that comprised their *Pascua*. Beyond the typical problems accompanying gambling (vagrancy, robbery, etc.), the profound cultural significance of such games marked the presence of a liminal community, with its associated threats to official culture. As a result, there were concerns that Christians who participated in them would flag in their faith, *indios* might become less docile, and the productivity of black slaves would wain.[88] As Andrew Wilson observed, "Not even the Spanish were blind to the fact that the Chinese possessed attractive alternatives to Catholicism and European culture. Both church and state were concerned that the evangelical mission in the Philippines would be hindered if the natives were exposed to Chinese belief systems" (39). Although Wilson's study is primarily concerned with late Colonial Manila, the documents cited above show that these belief systems were already intricately related to their play in the early modern period.

There is an intriguing ambivalence in the fact that the sangley games were frequently tolerated as theologically licit ("having consulted the opinios of many theologians"), while it was also asserted that the playing during the February lunar cycle was a "supersticion de gentiles."[89] As in Cézanne's famous canvass, the age-old ritual of dealing the cards is respected as an affirmation of cultural identity. But the recognition of the cultural and religious significance of the play is accompanied by its dismissal as ignorance and superstition. Card playing is thus acknowledged as a legitimate ritual within the sangley culture, even as this culture and its beliefs are denigrated. According to the judgments of the authorities, these activities fall somewhere in between the comically absurd credulity of Pedro de Covarrubias's gamblers and the excesses of Catholic ceremony often criticized by humanists of the Erasmian mould.

Cervantes's *Los baños de Argel* provides an interesting perspective on this dynamic, with the Spaniards cast as the cultural other in North Africa. The Muslim authorities grant the Christians time for recreation in the garden, even as productive work is emphasized. The Warden exclaims, "¡Hola! ¡Al trabajo, cristianos! … Que trabajen todos quiero, /

ya pápaz, ya caballero" ("Hey! Get to work, Christians! ... I want everyone, priest or nobleman, to work" [Act I]).[90] But, like the Spanish authorities vis-à-vis the Chinese labourers in the Philippines, the Muslims allow the captives their religious recreations:

Guardián.
Por diez escudos no daré mi parte.
Sentaos, y no dejéis entrar alguno,
si no pagan dos ásperos muy buenos.

Moro.
La Pascua de Natal, como ellos llaman,
veinticinco ducados se llegaron.

Guardián.
Los españoles, por su parte, hacen
una brava comedia. (Act III)

[**Warden.**
I won't give up my share for ten escudos. Sit down, and don't let anyone in unless they pay two full ásperos.

Moor.
On Christmas, as they call it, it came to twenty-five ducats.

Warden.
The Spaniards, for their part, are putting on a great play.]

The Moors' concession to the Spaniards contains a similar ambivalence to that of the colonial authorities discussed above. It suggests a measure of religious tolerance, but it is also motivated by economic interest. In addition to the revenue from entrance fees to the theatrical productions referenced in the preceeding passage, the Moors counted on a higher ransom payment if their captives remained steadfast in their faith. Their masses, processions, and theatrical productions contributed to their sustained "value" (see Fuchs and Ilika, note 1, p. 67).

A "Real Provisión" from 1529 relating to the conquistadors in Mexico contains a curious justification of otherwise dubious play: "because it is advisable that in order to find themselves always together during altercations, and there being cause to keep watch in the towns where they resided, it was permitted that they play cards at night and bowling during the day, so that they might always be together, because not being so, in addition to the reasons above many deaths of Christians were caused, and horse thieving and other things."[91] It is practical to allow the conquistadors these games since it keeps them awake and together, so that they may better defend the people and goods of *Nueva España*. In the opening scene of Moorish invasion in *Los baños de Argel*, Cervantes illustrates the alternative: "Ya vienen las escalas prevenidas, / y están las atalayas hasta agora / con borrachera y sueño entretenidas" ("The ladders are ready now, and so far the sentries are distracted with drink or sleep" [Act I]). Deleito y Piñuela noted that Spanish soldiers had long been granted gambling privileges, even as the authorities recognized and attempted to contain the dangers of doing so.[92] Such allowances notwithstanding, cards were generally frowned upon for the colonists. The "casas de juego" seemed equally prevalent and pernicious in the Americas as on the Peninsula, and with as much social reach: nobles and commoners, laity and clergy, men and women. A prohibition by the government in Mexico (1583) maintained that women were susceptible not only to the typical problems associated with cards and dice, but also to the salacious atmosphere of the venues ("other greater excesses in offense of god our lord"), necessitating comprehensive bans: "Nor should the said married, or single, or widowed women be allowed to play."[93] Exceptions might include women playing in moderation with other women, or, as a 1597 prohibition stipulates, with "some degrees of relations, like sons and daughters with their fathers, husbands with wives, brothers with sisters."[94] For the most part, however, *casas de juego* and *tablageros* were considered grave dangers, and the authorities recommended strict penalties. We will return to this in our consideration of Sancho Panza's controversial suggestions for reform in Barataria (*Don Quijote* II, 49).

Since a fundamental interest in the American endeavour was economic, it should come as no surprise that many communications express concern with the effect of games on *mercaderes*. The following royal dispatch ("Real Cédula") from 1538 is pertinent:

> [M]any damages have been caused and continue to be caused to the citizens and inhabitants of those parts, especially the merchants and traders, apparently by the very disordered gambling that occurs there, which, seen by our council of the Indies, wanting by whatever means possible to prevent these problems, it was agreed that it should be ordered directly

> through you, and I approved and therefore command that you order that no cards or dice be taken to any part of our said Indies.[95]

Another similar prohibition, by the viceroy of Mexico in 1539, includes a reference to the space of such play: "one of the principal things that in this country destroys the people, especially the merchants, is gambling, on account of being disordered … and of playing in secret and interpolating in said games oaths and other frauds."[96] In addition to the concern with the enclosed, private venue of such activity, and the frequently foul language, the repeated fear over the *disorder* caused would suggest that we are in an incipient stage of what Spariosu termed rational society, and that gambling was a threat to the mercantilist ethos of order, productivity and the protection of property (*hazienda*). As we saw, a countervailing concern was the substantial profits collected by the crown through regulation and sale of the card decks. Such economic interest motivates Diego de Espina, in a "Memorial" from 1638, to extend the play period for the Chinese workers: "The days of said easter having ended, as the said sangleyes remain hooked, they come to request another new license from some governors for ten days, and they grant them it because they pay for it four or five thousand pesos; and in said extended period they do not release additional card decks to said authorities."[97] In the workers' addiction to the game there is an opportunity for profit. As noted above, the same ambivalence – arising from a concern with gambling's degradation of the players, along with a desire to capitalize on large revenue streams – can be seen in present-day arguments over online gambling. The debates surrounding play in the *Indias* get to the heart of the unresolved tensions within the colonial enterprise between economic exploitation and moral and spiritual edification of the new subjects. Although it is beyond the scope of this study, a fuller investigation into the ambivalent Spanish attitudes towards such play would be rewarding.

2 Solitary, Collaborative, and Complicit Play in *Don Quijote*

Near the end of their wanderings, don Quijote and Sancho are brought back to the ducal palaces for a final entertainment, this time to rescue an Altisidora laid low by her unrequited love for the knight. There are many resonances from earlier episodes, but they are for the most part distorted and moribund, signalling the nearly complete deterioration of don Quijote's imaginative enterprise. The game imagery of don Quijote's descent into the Cueva de Montesinos expressed a resignation that did not close off all hope for redemption: "y cuando así no sea, paciencia y barajar" ("if not, shuffle the pack and deal again" [II, 23]). But when asked by Sancho about her underworld journey, Altisidora gives the following account of purgatorial play:

> La verdad es que llegué a la puerta [of hell], adonde estaban jugando hasta una docena de diablos a la pelota, todos en calza y en jubón, con valonas guarnecidas con puntas de randas flamencas, y con unas vueltas de lo mismo, que les servían de puños, con cuatro dedos de brazo de fuera, porque pareciesen las manos más largas; en las cuales tenían unas palas de fuego; y lo que más me admiró fue que les servían, en lugar de pelotas, libros, al parecer, llenos de viento y de borra, cosa maravillosa y nueva; pero esto no me admiró tanto como el ver que, siendo natural de los jugadores el alegrarse los gananciosos y entristecerse los que pierden, allí en aquel juego todos gruñían, todos regañaban y todos se maldecían. (II, 70, p. 566)

> [The fact is that I reached the gate, where about a dozen devils were playing pelota, all stripped down to doublet and hose, with broad, floppy collars trimmed in Flanders lace, and ruffles of the same material serving as cuffs, and displaying four inches of arm to add length to their hands, in

which they were holding rackets of fire; and what most amazed me was that instead of balls they were serving books, full of wind and stuffing, an extraordinary, unheard-of thing. But this didn't astonish me as much as seeing that, although it's natural for the winners at games to be happy and the losers to be glum, in that game they were all grumbling, quarrelling and cursing each other.]

This conflation of the book and the game is the opposite of the *mesa de trucos* in the prologue to the *Novelas ejemplares*. Rather than a pleasurable public game contributing to a harmonious social order, the infernal play breeds suffering and discord among winners and losers alike.

In Part I, some books escaped the flames because they were recognized as legitimate forms of recreation, and others were redeemed by chance: the curate noticed a copy of *Tirante el Blanco* that had fallen from a bundle destined for the bonfire (I, 6); the narrator happened upon a basket of papers in the streets of Toledo, allowing him to make the manuscript whole (I, 9). In Altisidora's vision, all books, old and new, disintegrate at first volley by the blazing rackets ("al primer voleo no quedaba pelota en pie, ni de provecho para servir otra vez; y así, menudeaban libros nuevos y viejos, que era una maravilla" – "there wasn't one ball that could withstand the first volley or was in any condition to be served again, and so books old and new came in quick succession, an extraordinary sight" [II, 70, p. 566]). And when a smash by one of the devils reveals the entrails of a particular book, clemency is farthest from Cervantes's mind:

"Mirad qué libro es ése." Y el diablo le respondió: – "Ésta es la segunda parte de la historia de don Quijote de la Mancha, no compuesta por Cide Hamete, su primer autor, sino por un aragonés, que él dice ser natural de Tordesillas." –"Quitádmele de ahí," respondió el otro diablo, "y metedle en los abismos del infierno: no le vean más mis ojos." "¿Tan malo es?," respondió el otro. "Tan malo," replicó el primero, "que si de propósito yo mismo me pusiera a hacerle peor, no acertara." (566)

["Go and see what book that is." And the other devil replied: "It's the second part of the history of Don Quixote de la Mancha, not written by Cide Hamete, its first author, but by some Aragonese person who says he comes from Tordesillas." "Remove it," replied the other devil, "and consign it to the depths of hell; I never want to see it again." "Is it as bad as all that?" the other one asked. "It's so bad," replied the first devil, "that if I'd tried my very hardest to write a worse one the task would have been beyond me."]

If the demonic dialogue judging books functions as a distorted echo of the curate and the barber as they conducted a somewhat nuanced survey of don Quijote's library (I, 6), the comparative constructions subvert another of the many narratives happened upon in the course of the novel: " – ¿Tan bueno es? –dijo don Quijote. –Es tan bueno –respondió Ginés – , que mal año para *Lazarillo de Tormes* y para todos cuantos de aquel género se han escrito o escribieren. Lo que le sé decir a voacé es que trata de verdades, y que son verdades tan lindas y tan donosas, que no pueden haber mentiras que se le igualen" ("Is it as good as all that?" said Don Quixote. "It's so good," replied Ginés, "that I wouldn't give a fig for *Lazarillo de Tormes* and all the others of that kind that have been or ever will be written. What I can tell you is that it deals with facts, and that they're such fine and funny facts that no lies could ever match them" [I, 22, pp. 271–2]). While Ginés, in referring to "todos cuantos de aquel género," delivers a furtive blow to one of Cervantes's competitors (Mateo Alemán), the tennis-playing devil expresses overt indignation at Avellaneda. Cervantes excoriates the lies of inferior (and counterfeit) art, and the tennis ball and stuffed book images reinforces his opening salvo against Avellaneda in the form of the anally-inflated dog (II, Prólogo). Contaminated by the worldly concerns of artistic piracy, illusion has lost its regenerative power. What remains is the *agon* of artistic creation, the struggle to affirm originality and authenticity in the face of rival writers.[1]

Cervantes holds up the apocryphal *Don Quijote*, devoid of interest and bloated with air and pretence, as the opposite of the modest book don Quijote happened upon a few scenes earlier, at the print-shop in Barcelona: " – *Le bagatele* –dijo el autor – es como si en castellano dijésemos *los juguetes*; y aunque este libro es en el nombre humilde, contiene y encierra en sí cosas buenas y sustanciales" ("*Le Bagatelle*," said the author, "means something like *Trifles*; and although the book has a humble title, it contains excellent material of real substance" [II, 62, p. 518]). Like the prologue game in the *Novelas ejemplares*, this book of "little games" represents Cervantes's ideal of beneficial recreation. The inconsequential appearance belies an underlying virtue; the childlike activity is in fact substantial.[2] Such recreation links the aesthetic experience of play with the ethical import of *serio ludere* and the *silenus* figure. As I have been arguing, Cervantes's frequent comparisons of imaginative literature to other forms of play are imbued with this humanist tradition. But before pursuing this more optimistic thread, we must further examine why the end of his masterpiece contains such a bleak portrayal of literary play.

In a major revision of Stephen Gilman's characterization of Avellaneda's *Don Quijote* as an ascetic Counter-Reformation work, James Iffland emphasizes the aristocratic ethos of the apocryphal continuation. Vis-à-vis the ambivalent, carnivalesque, and potentially subversive humour of Cervantes, Avellaneda's reception amounts to a "fiesta confiscada" ("confiscated festivity") in which the destabilizing implications of roaming knight and squire, whose festive delusions resonate at numerous levels of society, are sanitized and contained. Avellaneda relegates the popular, contagious folly of don Quijote and Sancho to a laughable object, at a safe remove from the laughing upper classes (see Iffland, *De fiestas*, especially I, ch. 4, and II, chs. 1 and 2). That is to say, Avellaneda does what Cervantes's Duke and Duchess attempt – but ultimately fail – to do.

The Altisidora scene considered above comes close on the heels of don Quijote's defeat on the Barcelona waterfront, and Sancho, having renounced the hubris of his governorship, lies in a cot next to his master. The regenerative power of sleep is denied as the Duke and Duchess are incapable of foregoing an opportunity to play another joke on their guests, drawing the following comment by Cide Hamete: "que tiene para sí ser tan locos los burladores como los burlados, y que no estaban los duques a dos dedos de parecer tontos, pues tanto ahínco ponían en burlarse de dos tontos" ("he considers that the perpetrators of the hoax were as mad as the victims, and that the Duke and Duchess, going to such lengths to make fun of two fools, were within a hairsbreadth of looking like fools themselves" [II, 70, pp. 564–5]). Following her account of the demonic tennis game, Altisidora herself breaks the illusion, don Quijote's declaration of fidelity to Dulcinea having touched her pride: "¿Pensáis por ventura, don vencido y don molido a palos, que yo me he muerto por vos? Todo lo que habéis visto esta noche ha sido fingido; que no soy yo mujer que por semejantes camellos había de dejar que me doliese un negro de la uña, cuanto más morirme" ("You aren't by any chance imagining, are you, you defeated and cudgelled wretch, that I died because of you? Everything you saw last night was a sham – I'm not a woman to let so much as my little finger ache for an old camel like you, let alone die for one" [567]). As Cide Hamete noted, the ducal jokes have become a bit tired, and not much is at stake in Altisidora's admission. It simply further denigrates the laughable objects. But Sancho's response is a bit more interesting, as it seems to subvert a more substantial fiction: "Eso creo yo muy bien … ; que esto de morirse los enamorados es cosa de risa: bien lo pueden ellos decir; pero hacer, créalo Judas" ("I can believe that all right … All this stuff about people dying of love is a joke. They might well say it, but as for doing it – they'd better try pulling another one" [II, 70, p. 567]). Similar scepticism was absent in Part I, amidst the dramatic lamentations before Grisóstomo's corpse (I, 14). The characters found Grisóstomo's amorous despair entirely plausible; at issue was the assignment of blame. The Altisidora episode contains an additional deflationary pastoral allusion when a poet walks in, and don Quijote inquires about a point of literary decorum: "¿qué tienen que ver las estancias de Garcilaso con la muerte desta señora?" ("What have Garcilaso's stanzas to do with this lady's death?" [568]). The poet's response furthers the critical tenor of the episode: "que ya entre los intonsos poetas de nuestra edad se usa que cada uno escriba como quisiere, y hurte de quien quisiere, venga o no venga a pelo de su intento, y ya no hay necedad que canten o escriban que no se atribuya a la licencia poética" ("it's normal nowadays for novice poets to write however they please and steal from whomever they like, whether it's to the point or not, and there isn't an absurdity they sing or write that isn't put down to poetic licence" [568]). If Cervantes's original image of the free individual reader is clouded by the excess of Alonso Quijano, the 1605 prologue's affirmation of poetic license and the unfettered artist have also come in for some serious qualification.

The ensuing conversation between don Quijote and Sancho and the ducal pair seems to advocate productive work as an antidote to frivolous play, indicating a further turning away from imaginative literature. Don Quijote sensibly recommends that Altisidora busy herself with occupations appropriate to her gender, for this will distract her over-heated imagination: "[Q]ue todo el mal desta doncella nace de la ociosidad, cuyo remedio es la ocupación honesta y continua … que ocupada en menear los palillos, no se menearán en su imaginación la imagen o imágenes de lo que bien quiere" ("All this maiden's problems are born of idleness, the remedy for which is honest and constant occupation … because so long as she is busy with her bobbins, the image or images of her desires will not be busy in her mind" [568]). Sancho enthusiastically concurs, and adds an illustration from his own frame of reference: "que las doncellas ocupadas más ponen sus pensamientos en acabar sus tareas que en pensar en sus amores. Por mí lo digo, pues mientras estoy cavando no me acuerdo de mi oíslo, digo, de mi Teresa Panza, a quien quiero más que a las pestañas de mis ojos" ("busy girls think more about finishing the job in hand than about their boyfriends. I'm speaking from experience, too, because while I'm digging I haven't got a thought for my better half, by which I mean my Teresa Panza, and I love her more than these lashes over my eyes" [569]). Sancho's declaration would seem to resonate with the finale to *Candide*: "All I know … is that we must cultivate our garden" (93). Freud cites Voltaire's conclusion not as en example of squarely facing the reality principle, but as an example of one of the three basic "palliative measures" devised by civilization – "deflections, which cause us to make light of our misery" (*Civilization and Its Discontents* 22). In the context of the men's counsel to Altisidora, Sancho's example of digging in the fields, like needlework for women, does indeed function as a sort of "deflection," a distraction from tedium or suffering. The emphasis is therefore not so much on the productivity of such endeavours as on their therapeutic effect, as Méndez – and later Tolstoy – observed (see above pp. 45–51). In other words, it fulfils a purpose similar to that of play. But does Cervantes anticipate Voltaire in suggesting that existence itself may be unbearable without palliative distractions?

Don Quijote and Sancho's abandonment of home in pursuit of love and adventure elicits repeated calls to return to domestic order. Drawing on Deleuze and Guattari's discussion of nomadism, Iffland maintains that the movement of Cervantes's protagonists represents a threat to the state: "Because channelled, intentional mobility need not have negative connotations, while aleatory wandering or vagabondage certainly do, even when not concerning a lunatic."[3] Chance-determined itineraries, the interruption of commerce (the Toledan merchants) and of the king's justice (the *galeotes*), and of religious processions all make don Quijote's errantry inimical to the ordered traffic of the Spanish state, which would prefer that those citizens not involved in such sanctioned activities remain *sosegados*, tranquilly in their place: "Nor should we ignore that it is the priest Pero Pérez who most insists on bringing him back home, and that he ultimately does so accompanied by agents of royal authority. That is to say, the two faces of political sovereignty, Mitra and Varuna, cooperate in the re-territorialisation of the warrior, who is effectively defined as crazy, deformed, usurper (he exercises an authority that does not belong to him)."[4] Don Quijote's final resistance to domestication, this time to his niece and housekeeper's sober entreaty, is notable:

> Mire señor, tome mi consejo; que no se lo doy sobre estar harta de pan y vino, sino en ayunas, y sobre cincuenta años que tengo de edad: estése en

> su casa, atienda a su hacienda, confiese a menudo, favorezca a los pobres, y sobre mi ánima si mal le fuere.
>
> – Callad, hijas –les respondió don Quijote – ; que yo sé bien lo que me cumple. Llevadme al lecho, que me parece que no estoy muy bueno, y tened por cierto que, ahora sea caballero andante, o pastor por andar, no dejaré siempre de acudir a lo que hubiéredes menester, como lo veréis por la obra. (II, 73, p. 585)
>
> [Look, sir, take my advice, which I'm not giving you on a belly full of bread and wine but on an empty stomach and fifty years of experience – stay at home, look after your property, go often to confession, give alms to the poor, and on my conscience be it if I'm wrong.
>
> "Hush, my daughters," Don Quixote replied, "I know what's good for me. Take me to my bed now, because I don't feel very well, and rest assured that, whether an actual knight errant or a would-be-shepherd, I shall never fail to provide for your needs, as you will see for yourselves."]

If the prologue to the *Novelas ejemplares* argues for the importance of including *otium* alongside *negotium* and *templum*, the housekeeper reminds don Quijote that he has tipped the balance much too far in the other direction (as have, also, the Duke and Duchess). It is time for him to attend to his property, and to piety. And this is what he ends up doing: the inheritance is distributed, last rites performed, and Avellaneda and knight-errantry novels and even the anticipated pastoral are left behind.

The question looming over the finale is whether this *desenlace* represents the successful "re-territorialisation" of don Quijote within the official space and values of his society. The critical energies emanating from the final scene are not so much meant to invalidate literary recreation as to hold up Cervantes's own game as the ideal. Herein lies the paradoxical logic of the entire sequence. Cervantes debunks inferior literature and pastimes in order to authenticate his own; he kills off don Quijote in order to preserve him. Iffland argues that the structure and logic of the episodes from Parts I and II would lead us to expect a continuation of don Quijote's adventures, not his death: "our hero, conceived from the deeply-rooted mechanisms of popular festive culture, rises automatically from each of his falls (even though it is true that he does it with less energy in the last stage of his career). To have him die is not only a worthy response the insane asylum of Toledo, but it also erects a more or less insurmountable obstacle to future falsifications."[5] As Torrente Ballester appealingly puts it: "Don Quijote is what has flown from yesterday's nests. The nest is Quijano himself, who has become empty by his own will, to die simply. The bird –don Quijote – will continue flying."[6] Motivations of artistic ego aside, Cervantes's endorsement of play is all the more persuasive for his awareness of its potential dangers. In the pages that follow, we will consider a number of ways in which he articulates such critiques and endorsements, along with his persistent willingness to take the very risks he warns about.

Cervantes and the Ambivalent Freedom of Play

> – Ya os he dicho, amigo –replicó el cura – , que esto se hace para entretener nuestros ociosos pensamientos; y así como se consiente en las repúblicas bien concertadas que haya juegos de ajedrez, de pelota y de trucos, para entretener a algunos que ni tienen, ni deben, ni pueden trabajar, así se consiente imprimir y que haya tales libros creyendo, como es verdad, que no ha de haber alguno tan ignorante que tenga por historia verdadera ninguna destos libros.
>
> (*Don Quijote* I, 32, p. 397)

> ["I have already told you, my friend," replied the priest, "that this is only done to while away our idle moments; and just as in well-ordered societies such games as chess, tennis and billiards are permitted for the amusement of those who do not, should not and cannot work, so permission is also granted for the publication of such books, in the justified belief that there can't be anybody so ignorant as to read them as if they were true histories."]

The curate's response to the semi-quixotic innkeeper, for whom the authority of the printed word inspires belief in the historical existence of chivalric heroes, anticipates the prologue to the *Novelas ejemplares* in presenting the act of reading as a game. While the context of the above discussion, centring on the diversion afforded to the fieldworkers by knight-errantry novels ("el efecto que vos decís de entretener el tiempo, como lo entretienen leyéndolos vuestros segadores" – "the purpose you've just mentioned, passing the time of day as your reapers do when they sit listening to it" [397]), evokes the traditional opposition of work and leisure, the curate's analogy of games to reading suggests a range of leisure classes. It also recalls Alfonso X's desire to accommodate, with board games, the needs of women, captives, the aged and the infirm. As in the rest of Europe, the nobility was the principal leisure class in early modern Spain, comprising "those who should not and cannot work."[7] But Cervantes was also interested in what was, due to socio-economic shifts in the period, an expanding spectrum of games and players. The noblemen, maidens, wedding-revellers, peasants and *pícaros* who populate his pages are associated with a variety of different recreational activities, and his literary *eutrapelia* is particularly comprehensive. Cervantes offers his games to a readership far more varied than the conventional division of the *lector vulgo* and *lector culto*.

As we turn our attention to Cervantes, it is important to recall the distinctions between multiple levels of play (see chapter 1), and how they interrelate. *Don Quijote*, for example, contains representations of specific games and leisure activities such as cards, dice, chess, and hunting. At a slightly more abstract level, there is the *mimesis* performed by various characters, including don Quijote's imitation of the chivalric, and Marcela and Grisóstomo's of the pastoral. It is more abstract, because the *mimesis* is, for the characters, serious, or purposive. Their ostensible goal is not recreation – although, as we will discuss, the issue as to whether or not they are aware of "playing" is complicated. These first two types of play take place within the plot, that is, they are activities engaged in by the characters. A well-known feature of Cervantes's novel is the preponderance of narrative voices (Cide Hamete Benengeli, translator, primary narrator, characters), which dramatizes the very process of artistic creation. This "meta-plot," chronicling the adventure of storytelling, complements the main plot of the adventures of knight and squire. Of particular interest to the present study is how play images and dynamics are present throughout, on the diegetic as well as the mimetic levels. Étienvre has discussed how the specific play references in Cervantes relate to his larger narrative designs: "Original and explicit at the same time, Cervantine play avails itself of games – and particularly the most vulgar of all, cards – as a common language that becomes, under his pen, language of creation. And this language, like any other language or, rather, language in general, does not serve Cervantes to represent reality, but to disrupt it: with cards from the deck, he shuffles subjects."[8] Torrente Ballester argued that the novel's frequent shifting between the descriptive ("informativo") and the evaluative ("valorativo") is a narrative game that creates a productive cognitive tension in the reader, who must judge the characters by mediating between the two modes of narration: "the *Quijote* is told 'playing', the 'game is its own mode of being told'. The correlation, then, between narratable material and narrative technique is appropriate. Is there anything more logical than to playfully tell the story of a game?"[9] As Torrente Ballester and Étienvre indicate, our recreation as readers actualizes all the other games – a point made explicit by Cervantes in the *mesa de trucos* image in the prologue of the *Novelas ejemplares*. While these levels, then, operate at different degrees of abstraction, Cervantes often reminds us that they exist in a continuum, in mutually illuminating relationships. And the author's playful act of creation invites an equally ludic response in the reader.[10]

In addition to the levels outlined above, we will keep in mind the parameters and functions of the play. The most conventional is framed in the language of *eutrapelia*, and is associated with holiday, festivity, and other "parenthetical" spaces, delineated against a backdrop of serious endeavour to which the participants will return. Instances of such play include the wedding games during the Bodas de Camacho (DQ II, 19–21), the hunting of don Diego de Miranda (II, 16), and fieldworkers recuperating from their labours by listening to knight-errantry stories (I, 32). There is also play that Cervantes presents as a sort of rite of passage, a *mocedades* or developmental life stage – the picaresque adventure of the two boys in *La ilustre fregona*, or in *Rinconete y Cortadillo*, for example. For Andrés in *La gitanilla*, his *mimesis* of gypsy life tests his commitment to Preciosa. Finally, there is what we might call "play as a mode of existence," in which the activity transcends conventional limits of time and space, with no apparent demarcation from the character's purposive reality. Don Quijote is the most obvious example, but there are others, such as the Duke and Duchess (II), and the "shepherd" Marcela (I, 12–14). An example of the mutual illumination referred to above can be found in the Maese Pedro episode, from the primary game represented, Don Gaiferos's *tablas*, to the puppet show itself, to don Quijote's knight-errantry (II, 26). The presumed *eutrapelia* of Gaiferos's chess game has led to excess: "Jugando está a las tablas Don Gaiferos, / que ya de Melisendra está olvidado" ("And Don Gaiferos is at the tables, / He has not a thought for Melisendra now" [II, 26, p. 240]). As indicated by Sancho's assertion that his occupation in the fields makes him forget his own wife (II, 71), there is a fine line between salubrious distraction from cares and harmful evasion of responsibility. Roused by his irate father-in-law, Gaiferos violently curtails the recreation ("arroja, impaciente de la cólera, lejos de sí el tablero y las tablas y pide apriesa las armas" – "in his rage hurling the backgammon board far from him and calling for his arms and armour" [240]), prefiguring what don Quijote does with the entire representation.[11] Gaifero's destruction of the game represents a correct resumption of his chivalric responsibilities, drawn from the prestigious ballad tradition; don Quijote's devastation of the puppets indicates his failure to appreciate the fictional space as play.

Such a focus is meant to bring out some of the ways in which Cervantes's consummate understanding of literary tradition is brought to bear on contemporary social and cultural realities. André Jolles's discussion of three main forms of *mimesis* in Renaissance court culture – as noted above – provides relevant context, corresponding to the literary genres most extensively cultivated by Cervantes: the pastoral, the chivalric, and the picaresque. Of course, Cervantes almost never writes purely within a particular mode. He tends rather to examine the sometimes contradictory premises within each genre, as well as how such representation measures up against reality. He also continuously reflects upon why people find themselves compelled to participate in these different realms of experience – or "regions of the imagination," to use Martínez-Bonati's phrase – and what the implications are of doing so. The variety of the source material, ranging from popular to high culture, adds to the reading challenge. Does Cervantes represent aristocratic pastimes ironically? Do his appropriations of folkloric figures release the potentially subversive power of popular culture, or contain and sanitize it? Whichever the case, the readers of episodes such as Maese Pedro's puppet show find themselves, by extension, meditating upon the implications of their own leisure activity.[12]

The prologues provide key characterizations of the type of game Cervantes sets forth, and of the implications of being an individual at leisure. As many have insightfully discussed, the prologue to Part One of *Don Quijote* posits a strikingly independent, private reader, implying an unprecedented freedom of interpretation as well as a potentially subversive citizen:

> [T]ienes tu alma en tu cuerpo y tu libre albedrío como el más pintado, y estás en tu casa, donde eres señor della, como el rey de sus alcabalas, y sabes lo que comúnmente se dice, que debajo de mi manto, al rey mato. Todo lo cual te esenta y hace libre de todo respeto y obligación, y así, puedes decir de la historia todo aquello que te pareciere, sin temor que te calunien por el mal ni te premien por el bien que dijeres della.

> [[Y]ou have your own soul in your own body, and your own free will like anybody else, and you are sitting in your own home, where you are the lord and master just as much as the king of his taxes, and you know that common saying, "Under my cloak a fig for the king." All of which exempts and frees you from every respect and obligation, and so you can say whatever you like about this history, without any fear of being attacked for a hostile judgement or rewarded for a favourable one.]

It is not only the *reception* of the work that takes place in a private, solitary venue; the work itself, engendered by the author's "estéril y mal cultivado ingenio" ("barren and ill-cultivated mind") is "lleno de pensamientos varios y nunca imaginados de otro alguno, bien como quien se engendró en una cárcel, donde toda incomodidad tiene su asiento y donde todo triste ruido hace su habitación" ("full of extravagant fancies that nobody has ever imagined – a child born, after all, in prison, where every discomfort has its seat and every dismal sound its habitation" [Prólogo]). Far away is the *locus amoenus*, with its fecund greenery and harmoniously murmuring brooks and singing birds. This heady association of solitude with authenticity and freedom is both celebratory and sinister. The interior spaces signify confinement and isolation, but also inventiveness unbridled by artistic tradition and social mores. The shifting images – prison cell / home – suggest the tenuous balance between originality and freedom on the one hand, and on the other, solipsism, lunacy, and social menace. The reader is invited to celebrate with the author the fruits of independent creativity; don Quijote tips the balance in the other direction, although not unambiguously.[13]

The prologue to the *Novelas ejemplares* apparently signals a completely different – and more conventional – conception of leisure:

> Heles dado el nombre de ejemplares, y si bien lo miras, no hay ninguna de quien no se pueda sacar algún ejemplo provechoso; y si no fuera por no alargar este sujeto, quizá te mostrara el sabroso y honesto fruto que se podría sacar así de todas juntas como de cada una de por sí. Mi intento ha sido poner en la plaza de nuestra república una mesa de trucos donde cada uno pueda llegar a entretenerse, sin daño de barras; digo, sin daño del alma ni del cuerpo, porque los ejercicios honestos y agradables antes aprovechan que dañan.

> [I have given them the name "exemplary," and, if you look at it carefully, there is not one from which some profitable example might not be gained;

and were it not to avoid drawing out this subject, maybe I'd show you the tasty and honest fruit that could be gained from all of them together as well as each one individually. My intent has been to place in the *plaza* of our republic a billiards table where each may come for entertainment, without peril to soul or body, because honest and pleasant exercises give benefit rather than harm.]

The billiards table in the *plaza* characterizes reading as an overtly sociable form of recreation, one that has its place within the well-ordered life of a productive citizen: "Sí que no siempre se está en los templos ... no siempre se asiste a los negocios ... Horas hay de recreación, donde el afligido espíritu descanse" ("For one is not always in the temples ... one cannot always attend to business ... There are hours for recreation, where the afflicted spirit may rest"). This pleasant and beneficial activity expresses the classical ideal of *eutrapelia,* alleviating the concerns of work and worship, and allowing the individual to resume them with renewed vigour. Cervantes presents another interesting variant on the "relaxed bowstring" in *Los baños de Argel,* when the Christian captives are granted recreation in the garden of Agimorato:

Allí podremos a solas
danzar, cantar y tañer
y hacer nuestras cabriolas:
que el mar no suele tener
siempre alteradas sus olas.
Demos vado a la pasión
cuanto más, que es la intención
del cadí que nos holguemos,
y que los viernes tomemos
honesta recreación. (Act II, italics mine)

[There we can dance, caper about, sing and play our instruments undisturbed: for the sea is not always rough. Let us give our cares a rest, especially as the Cadí wants us to take our ease and enjoy honest sport on Fridays.]

The sea itself enjoys moments of repose, and even the Muslim Cadí recognizes the virtue of *eutrapelia.* Of course, the question arises as to whether such play is mere revitalizing (and temporary) escape, or whether – and how – the recreation might affect the individual's perception of the reality to which he or she returns. As we shall discuss below, in the case of *Los baños de Argel*, the play both revitalizes the captives for work, and helps sustain their Christian identity.

We noted above how Fray Alonso Remon's *Entretenimientos y juegos honestos, y recreaciones christianas* (1623) expresses an appreciation for a wide range of leisure activities, and their moral, social and physical benefits (and dangers). Coincidentally, Remon treats three major forms of play in the same sequence in which they appear in the above-cited passage from *Don Quijote*: "se consiente en las repúblicas bien concertadas que haya juegos de ajedrez, de pelota y de trucos," ("in well-ordered societies games of chess, tennis and billiards are permitted" [I, 32; see Remon, fols. 56–7]). He has this to say about the game at the centre of the *Novelas ejemplares*: "El juego de los trucos tiene grande gala, y participa de todo, de alegre recreación, y razonable ejercicio, y mejor que la pelota, para los grandes señores" ("The game of billiards has much to recommend it, and involves everything, joyful recreation, and reasonable exercise, and better than tennis, for grandees" [fol. 57]). The game of *trucos* provides a pleasurable respite that includes a modest amount of physical engagement – without the levels of exertion required in tennis, which can render them indecorous for the nobility. For this it receives high praise from Remon as a *juego honesto* with broad appeal.

Nerlich sets forth one of the more radical interpretations of the "mesa de trucos" in the *Novelas ejemplares*, associating it with the "juego de bolos" in *El coloquio de los perros*. This game, according to Nerlich, emblematizes what Berganza's interlocutor – our primary surrogate within the story – learns from the narrative: "The 'discreción' acquired by Cipión in the dialogue with Berganza consists of the acknowledgment of chance as the ordering principle for the practice of life and the production of discourses, for thinking, speaking, and writing: the natural order of things is founded on the 'game of ninepins'" (292). It is indeed tempting to see such ball games (billiards and bowling) as metaphors for a random universe, and Nerlich – who productively compares Cervantes's reflections on language and meaning to Montaigne's interest in digression and chance – missed an opportunity by not citing Lucretius's cosmic account of atoms: "[T]his world is the product of Nature, the happenstance / Of the seeds of things colliding into each other by pure chance / In every possible way, no aim in view, at random, blind, / Till sooner or later certain atoms suddenly combined / So that they lay the warp to weave the cloth of mighty things" (*The Nature of Things* bk. II,

l. 1058–62). However, Nerlich somewhat overstates his case by insisting on blindness and the absurd in Cervantes's tale, which he reads as a "completely secularized passion play" (307), and whose image of the "juego de bolos" initiates a "descent into secular hell" that culminates in Samuel Beckett (321). The contention that the game imagery in Cervantes's story affirms "the role of chance in the social practice of human beings" (Nerlich 291) does not square with the definition of "juego de los trucos" given by the *Diccionario de Autoridades*: "juego de destreza, y habilidad, que se executa en una mesa dispuesta a este fin" ("game of skill, and ability, that is carried out on a table arranged for this end"). And rather than to the comically absurd universe of Beckett, one might look ahead to Cortázar, who presents *Rayuela* as a game ("hopscotch"), with numerous play-references within: "al margen de las conductas sociales, podría sospecharse una interacción de otra naturaleza, un billar que algunos individuos suscitan o padecen, un drama sin Edipos, sin Rastignacs, sin Fedras, drama *impersonal* en la medida que la conciencia y las pasiones de los personajes no se ven comprometidas más que a posteriori" ("at the margin of social mores, one could imagine interaction of another sort, a billiards that some individuals come up with or endure, a drama without Oedipuses, without Rastignacs, without Phaedras, an *impersonal* drama to the extent that the conscience and passions of the characters do not find themselves involved unless it is a posteriori" [ch. 62, p. 377]). What Cortázar explicitly promotes – the association of unconventional poetics with alternative possibilities of social arrangements – is what many critics argue is implied in the play imagery of Cervantes.

Pointing out the possible subversiveness of the word for billiards (*trucos*), Mary Gaylord suggests that Cervantes may be proposing a game of "tricks," an examination of real-world problems in his purportedly escapist play. The etymological link of *eutrapelia* to "tropelía," meaning prestidigitation or some other sort of deception, should certainly put the reader on guard. The "trick" may also refer to Cervantes's aesthetic innovations, although Gaylord insists on linkage: "What we may separate in analysis – the novellas' fictional reference and their literary-theoretical concerns – comes in one package. Genres mixed, codes travestied, structures twisted almost beyond recognition – these are the formal corollaries of transgressive itineraries, identities in question, values in flux in the represented world" (116). In her study of how Cervantes problematizes conventional notions of gender, race, and national identity, Fuchs made a similar contention: "The billiards table, with its seemingly random permutations and combinations, is located squarely in the middle of the commonwealth, as though to encourage the reader to think through the larger implications of textual bumps and jolts and other authorial tricks" (ix). Wardropper had identified a less transgressive quality in Cervantine *tropelía*: "There is in them no authentic conversion – not of social rank, nor of personality, nor of biological species. What happens in them is the removal of illusions."[14] Colin Thompson also suggests that the prologue's conventional claim of exemplarity may be a "joke on the reader" (265), who is in fact obliged to reflect upon his or her own complicity in the vices represented in the tales. And William Clamurro argues that the game is not as innocent as its presentation claims, and that Cervantes turns us into "picaresque readers," who learn to "read with an ear tuned to the contradictions and dissonances that issue forth from the interaction of dramatized example and surrounding social and cultural conflicts" (5). Clamurro, Thompson, Fuchs and Gaylord all elucidate aspects of *serio ludere*, and remind us that the playful and pleasurable aspects of the work are inseparable from the ethical components. In his analysis of literary play in Nabokov and the *ludus ingenii* of Erasmus and other humanists, Karshan describes the "game of wits" as follows: "Its essence is an intricate play of ironies which alternate between praising and satirizing folly; works in the genre typically have at their centre images of real games, which serve as emblems for this game of irony and parody" (198). It is not unusual for otherwise excellent studies of the roots of play in modern authors to overlook Cervantes's central place in the tradition.[15]

The pleasure of reading may somewhat dilute the social and philosophical import (for there would be no recreation, no rest for the "aflijido espíritu" if it were pure seriousness); but the enjoyment of the tales is also an effective inducement to ethical reflection. Characterizing the reader's enjoyment – the interpretative challenge of making sense of laughter in Cervantes – is itself a tricky task. While Gaylord suggests Cervantes cultivates the "scornful" and "bitter" laughter of the satirist, Thompson sees the moderate and light-hearted humour of the *eutrapelos*. We will consider the quality of Cervantine humour in more depth below (see "Play and Laughter in *Don Quijote*"). Despite the traditional characterization of play in the *Novelas ejemplares*, Cervantes clearly revises the Horatian dictum of *delectare et prodesse*, validating the pleasures and profits of reading in novel ways.

As these preliminary observations suggest, a fundamental concern in Cervantine representations of play is the varying relationship between freedom and constraint, individual desires and social cohesion, the game and purposive reality. At one extreme, unbridled, subjective will, however pleasurable, is inimical to an ordered coexistence; at the other, an excessively rigid structure tyrannizes the individual. Somewhere in between is the ideal of human community, and also Cervantes's ideal reader. A recurring idea is that our partaking of the world of the imagination is frequently the opposite of a private indulgence in solitude and subjectivity. The reader is often shown to be rescued from solitude in the very act of reading. Some of Cervantes's *words* – e.g., in the prologue to *Don Quijote* – seem to call for a radically subjective reader. But his *actions* as a novelist – the myriad representations of levels of reading competence, of successful and unsuccessful narratives – emphasize the importance of self-reflection, dialogue, negotiation and cooperation, that is, a constant mediation of subjectivity. A brief survey of many pairs of Cervantine characters reminds us that one of the surest antidotes to solipsism is good company and conversation. Such interaction is often cognitively imprecise and inconclusive; but it is also not chaos, chance, blindness and indeterminacy. The *ilinx* of the hallucinating witch, Cañizares, the *alea* of the shuffled cards in Durandarte's cave, and the joyless *agon* of the devils with their flaming books are exceptional cases – the nightmare visions of isolation and meaninglessness that Cervantes's protagonists contemplate before returning to what is, if not always a triumphant vision of total cohesion, at least a modest compromise, the consolation of human company and sympathetic imaginations.

The tensions outlined above, which point to the social implications of literary recreation, have been accounted for in different ways. Some critics have appealed to variations of the "two Cervantes" theory (originated by Castro), broadly assigning *Don Quijote* to Cervantes's vitalistic, contrarian, progressive tendencies; the *Novelas* – with a few notable exceptions – to his conformist, traditionalist writing. Others, accepting as a premise the thorough modernity of *Don Quijote*, assimilate the *Novelas ejemplares* to the epistemological and "novelistic" concerns of *Don Quijote*.[16] At stake in such shifts of emphasis are matters including the nature of Cervantes's comedy, whether our laughter is meant to be conventionally satirical (a corrective *laughing at*) or ambivalent (an empathetic *laughing with*); and his exemplarity, the relationship between fixed structures (genres, precepts) and the disorder of lived experience. The relevance of play to both comedy and exemplarity will be explored in separate chapters, below. To refer back to the critical polarities mentioned above, we will see that the radical implications of Cervantes's "modern" writings are almost always tempered by convention or recourse to a notion of good sense and common humanity; and his seemingly conservative or romance works dependably contain some mischievously destabilizing elements and perspectives.

Players and Games in *Don Quijote*

A major pastoral interlude in *Don Quijote* (I, 11–15) illustrates a number of the considerations discussed above. It follows an episode highlighting two fundamental levels of play contained in the novel: don Quijote has defeated the Basque, and the narrator, in an instance of what Torrente Ballester called "contar jugando," has walked through the streets of Toledo in search of the remaining manuscript. In other words, we have the play of don Quijote's chivalric adventure, and that of the reading process itself, as the narrative interruption foregrounds the nature of our interaction with the text. Continuities between the reader's situation and that of the characters are suggested throughout, not least in the ensuing examination of subjective individualism and community, of solipsism and subjugation. Sancho, whose participation in the chivalric mimesis makes him don Quijote's collaborator, becomes an increasingly pivotal figure. As Bloom observed, "an element in Sancho desires the order of play, uneasy as the rest of Sancho is with some of the consequences of Quixotic play" (*The Western Canon* 134). The ambivalence of Sancho's participation in don Quijote's play gives the entire sequence an additional layer of nuance and commentary.

The goatherds inhabit a relatively realistic mode of representation as they go about their prosaic business in the woods. Their offer of rustic hospitality to the bedraggled travellers, however, provides a set-piece for don Quijote, who seizes the opportunity to impress upon Sancho one of the many virtues of their relationship, and invites his squire to dine at his side: "porque de la caballería andante se puede decir lo mesmo que del amor se dice: que todas las cosas iguala" ("for of knight-errantry may be said what is said of love, that it makes all things equal" [I, 11, p. 154]). Of course, what comes to the fore is the artificiality of his chivalric enterprise – and, in the scenes that follow, the complicated nature of love. Sancho's resistance to the invitation comprises one of the major dramatizations of the prologue's solitary, free, and authentic individual: "mucho mejor me sabe lo que como en mi rincón sin melindres ni respetos, aunque sea pan y cebolla, que los gallipavos de otras mesas donde me sea forzoso mascar despacio, beber poco, limpiarme a menudo, no estornudar ni toser si me viene en gana, ni hacer otras cosas que la soledad y libertad traen consigo" ("what I eat in my own little corner without any fuss or bother, even if it is only bread and onions, tastes much better to me than all the fine turkeys on other tables where I'd have to chew slowly, drink hardly a drop, wipe my mouth all the time, never sneeze or cough if I felt like it, or do all those other things that being by yourself and free and easy lets you do" [I, 11, p. 154]). The parallel here between Sancho commencing a meal and the *desocupado lector* beginning to read bears emphasis. Cervantes tells us in the prologue that we are at liberty ("libre de todo respecto y obligación") and may therefore read as we see fit, just as Sancho would like to eat. When Sancho rejects his master's company, there is something affirmative about the anti-ceremonial ethos, and his position is all the more sympathetic when don Quijote physically compels him into his role: "Y asiéndole por el brazo, le forzó a que junto dél se sentase" ("And seizing Sancho by the arm he forced him to squat by his side" [155]). Don Quijote's enforced community is contrived – as artificial as the Golden Age communal spirit he proceeds to describe, and which neither Sancho nor the goatherds, in their comparative authenticity, appreciate.

The connection between the characters and the reader is further reinforced by the static image of narrator and narratee during the Golden Age speech. In contrast to the activation of judgment and imagination in the solitary domestic reader of the prologue, to whom the author cedes a good deal of authority, the goatherds and Sancho sit in passive befuddlement as don Quijote's pontifications outlast their meal: "sin respondelle palabra, embobados y suspensos, le estuvieron escuchando" ("who listened without uttering a word, bemused and bewildered" [157]). It would, however, be inaccurate to read the scene as an unqualified endorsement of Sancho's individualistic impulse (or the "realism" of the goatherds), just as we must not overplay the radical nature of the prologue's private reader. From the prologue on, Cervantes's reader is in fact not alone, but engaged in an extensive collaboration with the author. And despite Sancho's resistance to don Quijote's authoritarian request, he does partake of the goatherd's company, enjoying the wineskin and applying their hosts' herbal remedy to his master's ear. It is also important to recall that although the very literary Golden Age discourse is meaningless to the goatherds, the ear salve effectively recuperates one of its basic themes: "Y tomando algunas hojas de romero, de mucho que por allí había, las mascó y las mezcló con un poco de sal, y aplicándoselas a la oreja, se la vendó muy bien, asegurándole que no había menester otra medicina, y así fue la verdad" ("And the shepherd picked a few leaves of the rosemary that was growing there in great plenty, chewed them and mixed them with a little salt, applied them to the wound and bandaged it tightly, assuring Don Quixote that no other remedy would be necessary; which proved true" [161]). The simplicity of the mixture, derived from the abundant natural surroundings, is sufficient. Just as lawyers were not needed in the mythical Golden Age, the dreaded doctor is superfluous among the goatherds.

The treatment of literature and nature, society and freedom, becomes increasingly subtle throughout the episode. If the mimesis of don Quijote's chivalric play is predictably deflated in the previous scene, fulfilling once again the statement of purpose in the prologue ("deshacer la autoridad y cabida que en el mundo y en el vulgo tienen los libros de caballerías" – "to destroy the authority and influence that books of chivalry enjoy in the world and among the general public" [Prólogo]), the encounter with Marcela and Grisóstomo presents mimetic play of a still-prestigious genre: the pastoral. A compelling aspect of the Marcela and Grisóstomo episode is that each protagonist engages in pastoral mimesis for different, conflicting reasons. Cervantes creates a sort of *agon* within the *mimesis*, as the opposing claims of the characters draw upon different aspects of the genre. Grisóstomo and his friends represent the "erotic pastoral" tradition, predicated on expression and fulfilment of amorous desires. Marcela, on the other hand, plays out a "pastoral of the self," proclaiming her independence from disruptive emotions and her desire to lead a simple life of rural independence.[17] Cervantes is not simply pointing out the complex traditions upon which the pastoral draws. In addition to the escapist or creatively expressive possibilities of play, he illustrates the potentially destructive consequences of accepting without reflection culturally sanctioned forms of recreation.

As a "mode of existence," the play of the Marcela and Grisóstomo group is motivated by the desire to fulfil certain ideals or objectives, and the mimetic character of the activity is underlined by their contrast with the goatherds of the previous scene. Grisóstomo and his friend undergo a sudden transformation of identity: "Cuando los del lugar vieron tan de improviso vestidos de pastores a los dos escolares, quedaron admirados, y no podían adivinar la causa que les había movido a hacer aquella tan estraña mudanza" ("When the people in the village saw the two scholars suddenly dressed as shepherds they were amazed, and couldn't work out what had led them to make such an odd change" [I, 12, p. 163]). It is revealed that the cause is the love malady, and Grisóstomo's strategy catches on: "[N]o os sabré buenamente decir cuántos ricos mancebos, hidalgos y labradores han tomado el traje de Grisóstomo y la [Marcela] andan requebrando por esos campos" ("I couldn't tell you how many rich youths, hidalgos and farmers dressed up just like Grisóstomo, and wandered about the fields wooing her" [165]). But it is only Grisóstomo who, driven to suicide by his suffering, sees to completion the extreme logic of the disdained lover.[18] A celebrated aspect of the episode is how thoroughly Marcela refutes the claims and accusations of the male mourners, who adhere to the "erotic pastoral" of Grisóstomo:

> [T]engo libre condición y no gusto de sujetarme; ni quiero ni aborrezco a nadie. No engaño a éste, ni solicito aquél; ni burlo con uno, ni me entretengo con el otro. La conversación honesta de las zagalas destas aldeas y el cuidado de mis cabras me entretiene. Tienen mis deseos por término estas montañas, y si de aquí salen, es a contemplar la hermosura del cielo, pasos con que camina el alma a su morada primera. (II, 14, pp. 187–8)
>
> [I live in freedom and I don't like to be constrained; I neither love nor hate anybody. I neither deceive this man nor run after that; I neither toy with one, nor amuse myself with another. The innocent company of the village shepherdesses and the care of my goats keep me happy. These mountains mark the limits of my desires, and if they do extend any farther, it is only for the contemplation of the beauty of the heavens, the way along which the soul travels back to its first abode.]

In Marcela, Cervantes suggests how, given prevailing social conditions, the pastoral is particularly suited to female recreation, and her *conversación honesta* recalls a primary recreational ideal of the humanists.[19] Marcela's elaborate account of the state of nature as an aesthetically, morally, and spiritually superior realm echoes don Quijote's speech on the *edad dorada*, which depicted the seed of the current conflict: "Las doncellas y la honestidad andaban, como tengo dicho, por dondequiera, sola y señora, sin temor que la ajena desenvoltura y lascivo intento le menoscabasen, y su perdición nacía de su gusto y propria voluntad" ("Maidens and modesty roamed, as I have said, wherever they wished, alone and mistresses of themselves, without fear of harm from others' intemperance and lewd designs: their ruin was born of their own will and desire" [I, 11, p. 157]). Don Quijote's words grant the freedom and solitude aspired to by Marcela, but they also assume a natural erotic inclination, of which Grisóstomo imagined himself the deserving beneficiary.

Sancho anticipated all this when he affirmed his own *libre condición* before don Quijote's invitation to sit beside him. The destabilizing fact is that absolute freedom includes – as we noted above with Oblomov, Bernardine, Bartleby, Meursault – the choice *not* to participate, to reject community altogether. As Forcione observes:

> The scene pits Grisóstomo's implicit belief in the ["erotic pastoral"] ideal against Marcela's advocacy of a conception of freedom which is latent in the pastoral *desamorada's* refusal to love but which, in its complex elaboration in the *Quixote*, tragically contradicts "Arcadian innocent freedom," unmasks the Golden Age dream as escapist fantasy, and insinuates into the reductive imaginary world of pastoral the kind of complexity and ambiguity that surround moral choice by anyone involved in the realities of society and history. ("Marcela and Grisóstomo" 57)

Marcela's pastoral play is arguably more radical than any other type of mimesis in *Don Quijote*. In leaving her uncle's household and the social context of her town, and rejecting the amorous utopia proposed by the male *pastores*, Marcela's "conversación honesta de las zagalas destas aldeas y el cuidado de mis cabras" ("innocent company of the village shepherdesses and the care of my goats") suggests, to take Turner's concept of serious play, an alternative social arrangement:

> Communitas ... may be said to exist more in contrast than in active opposition to social structure, as an alternative and more "liberated" way of being socially human, a way both of being detached from social structure – and hence potentially of periodically *evaluating* its performance – and also of a "distanced" or "marginal" person's being more attached to *other* disengaged persons – and hence, sometimes of evaluating a social structure's historical performance in common with them. (50–1)

Marcela's feminine play community certainly represents an opposition to, and "evaluation" of, the masculine pastoral vision. Does it also do so vis-à-vis the social structure of Cervantes's Spain? There are other proto-feminist episodes that would support such a reading, for example the escaped girl interrogated during Sancho's *ronda* (II, 49). We will return to her below, along with other varieties of *communitas*, including

Ricote and his multinational group of pilgrims, the gypsies in *La gitanilla*, and Monipodio's society of thieves in *Rinconete y Cortadillo*.

There is, then, a discernible thread connecting the comically unrefined *soledad y libertad* aspired to by Sancho, the provocative independence of Marcela, and the prologue's image of the solitary and free reader. If Marcela and Grisóstomo's play turns our attention, as Forcione observes, to "the realities of society and history," Cervantes's "meta-plot" continuously awakens us to the complexities and ambiguities of reading. Despite being informed of the sole purpose of the book ("to destroy the authority and influence that books of chivalry enjoy in the world"), the reader realizes that the pastoral undergoes scrutiny and critique comparable to that of the chivalric romance. In fact, don Quijote's *locuras* are, in light of Grisóstomo, fairly benign. His judgment in favour of imitating Amadís over Orlando, for example, bespeaks a humane and self-consciously playful bearing (I, 25). It is also worth noting his ludic figures of speech when responding to Sancho's anxious inquiry: "'¿Y es de muy gran peligro esa hazaña' ... 'No' – respondió el de la Triste Figura – , 'puesto que de tal manera podía correr el dado, que echásemos azar en lugar de encuentro'" ("'And is this deed a very risky one?' ... 'No', replied the Knight of the Sorry Face, 'although the dice could roll in such a way that we score a double one rather than a double six'" [I, 25, p. 303]). But at the same time as discrepancies between each genre and reality are laid bare, as well as the potential harm that can result from conflating fiction and reality, the reader increasingly appreciates how Cervantes examines certain themes (freedom, love, nature) through the optics of different representational modes – what I refer to as "modulation." Cervantes thus provides multiple illustrations of the way games can refer back to purposive reality.

In the aftermath of the Marcela and Grisóstomo episode Cervantes gives an additional turn to the established themes. Despite don Quijote's endorsement of Marcela's position, he, like the other men, is unable to heed her words, and attempts to follow the eloquent beauty into the woods. After a fruitless search, the *locus amoenus* exercises its own siren call on the adventurers: "vinieron a parar a un prado lleno de fresca yerba, junto del cual corría un arroyo apacible y fresco; tanto, que convidó y forzó a pasar allí las horas de la siesta" ("they reached a meadow of fresh grass, with a cool, tranquil stream running alongside, which invited and indeed compelled them to spend the hours of early afternoon there" [I, 15, p. 190]). This is a curious echo of don Quijote's "invitation" to Sancho, with the same gradation from generous offer to compulsion ("convidó y forzó"). Of course, the forcefulness is a playful manner to emphasize its fresh appeal on a hot summer afternoon – nobody is being grasped by the arm and forced to sit.[20] Don Quijote and Sancho dig in to their saddlebags, and the repast is described as an enticing alternative to the chivalric arrangement don Quijote attempted to impose during the goatherd's banquet: "y, sin cerimonia alguna, en buena paz y compañía, amo y mozo comieron lo que en ellas hallaron" ("and, without ceremony, in peace and good fellowship, master and servant ate what they found in them" [190]). The narrator ironically references a discrepancy of status between the two ("amo y mozo") – one based on their role-playing adventure – while describing don Quijote and Sancho in a pleasant interlude of unaffected companionship. But discord again sullies Arcadia, this time in the form of Rocinante's out-of-character randiness upon catching wind of the Galician mares. His doomed amorous pursuit presents a final reverberation from Marcela and Grisóstomo, bringing "the dismantling procedure to its final point" (Forcione, "Marcela and Grisóstomo" 62), and resulting in yet another scene of chaos and farcical violence. Even Sancho's ass succumbs to the "demasiada libertad de aquel día" ("day's excess of liberty" [II, 15, p. 197]). A mischievous deflation, to be sure, but not a gratuitous one, as the bestial counterpoint to human behaviour will be extended in the Maritornes and muleteer episode in the following chapter. As Iffland emphasizes, such counterpoint exemplifies the carnivalesque cycle of uncrowning and fluctuations between the human and animal realms (*De fiestas*, see especially ch. 1). And the sequencing recalls the transition from the prologue – affirming a free reader – to the first chapter, which depicts the possible consequences of such freedom in the form of Alonso Quijano's dementia-inducing excess.

As the clobbered don Quijote and Sancho discuss the indignity of their situation, the parameters of chivalric mimesis are again foregrounded. Don Quijote first explains that the poor outcome was the result of not following the rules of chivalry: "Mas yo me tengo la culpa de todo; que no había de poner mano a la espada contra hombres que no fuesen armados caballeros como yo; y así, creo que, en pena de haber pasado las leyes de la caballería, ha permitido el dios de las batallas que se me diese este castigo" ("But I am to blame for it all, for I should not have drawn my sword against men who are not knights, as I am; and so I believe that, as a penalty for having broken the laws of chivalry, the god of battles has allowed me to be punished in this way" [192]). Then, contradicting the logic of his initial rationalization, he declares that such suffering would be unbearable were it not part and parcel of their profession:

> Y si no fuese porque imagino..., ¿qué digo imagino?, sé muy cierto, que todas estas incomodidades son muy anejas al ejercicio de las armas, aquí me dejaría morir de puro enojo.
>
> A esto replicó su escudero:
>
> – Señor, ya que estas desgracias son de la cosecha de la caballería, dígame vuestra merced si suceden muy a menudo, o si tienen sus tiempos limitados en que acaecen[.] (II, 15, p. 194)
>
> ["And if it were not that I imagine ... no, I do not imagine: I know for a certain fact – that all these discomforts are inseparable from the exercise of arms, I should be ready to die of sheer rage, here and now."
>
> To this his squire replied:
>
> "Sir, seeing as how all these disasters are as you might say the harvest of chivalry, I'd be grateful if you'd tell me whether they happen very often, or just at certain set times[.]"]

Sancho's question regarding the boundaries ("sus tiempos limitados") of this type of experience underlines the ludic nature of his identity as don Quijote's squire, recalling Huizinga's basic condition of "certain limits of time and space" (132). As Sancho's sense of the parameters of their activity becomes less clear and the hardships accumulate, he increasingly entertains the idea of returning to his domestic life and labour. Don Quijote, for his part, shows himself to be at the height of his ludic energies ("¿qué digo imagino?, sé muy cierto"); his certitude reflects the vitality of his creative powers at this early point in his wanderings. The oft-repeated "imaginar" is a key word, meaning "to deduce," "to surmise," but also "to create." It is through his imagination that don Quijote sustains his chivalric play, creatively divining patterns in the seemingly chaotic and mundane experience. As we shall see below, his inability to "imagine" in a late episode signals his imminent demise.

Don Quijote's "rulebook," of course, is the substantial body of chivalric texts he has read and committed to memory. And it is to this authority he appeals when, in the bathetic aftermath of the *batanes* adventure, he feels the need to calibrate his relationship with Sancho anew:

> [Q]ue en cuantos libros de caballerías que he leído, que son infinitos, jamás he hallado que ningún escudero hablase tanto con su señor como tú

con el tuyo. Y en verdad que lo tengo a gran falta, tuya y mía: tuya, en que me estimas en poco; mía, en que yo no me dejo estimar en más ... De todo lo que he dicho has de inferir, Sancho, que es menester hacer diferencia de amo a mozo, de señor a criado y de caballero a escudero. (I, 20, p. 250)

[[I]n all the books of chivalry I have read, an infinity of them, I have never come across any squire who talked to his master as much as you do to yours. And in truth I consider it a great fault in both you and me; in you, because you show me scant respect; in me, because I do not make you respect me more ... From all that I have said you should infer, Sancho, that a distance must be kept between master and man, between lord and lackey, between knight and squire.]

Irritated by Sancho's mockery, don Quijote rescinds his pastoral-inspired gestures and words of common humanity: in addition to emphatically reaffirming hierarchy, his insistence on possessive pronouns ("tuya y mía") contradicts his Golden Age oratory ("ignoraban estas dos palabras de *tuyo y mío*" – "men living in those times did not know those two words *yours* and *mine*" [I, 11, p. 154]). But it is the cause of their discord that reveals an essential aspect of their play. Having discovered the mundane origins of the terrifying nocturnal noises, the sudden deflation of suspense results in one of the most endearingly unaffected exchanges between the two adventurers:

Miróle Sancho, y vio que tenía la cabeza inclinada sobre el pecho, con muestras de estar corrido. Miró también don Quijote a Sancho, y viole que tenía los carrillos hinchados, y la boca llena de risa, con evidentes señales de querer reventar con ella, y no pudo su melanconía tanto con él, que a la vista de Sancho pudiese dejar de reírse; y como vio Sancho que su amo había comenzado, soltó la presa de manera que tuvo necesidad de apretarse las ijadas con los puños, por no reventar riendo. Cuatro veces sosegó, y otras tantas volvió a su risa, con el mismo ímpetu que primero ... (I, 20, p. 248)

[Sancho looked up at Don Quixote and saw that his head was sunk on his breast in manifest mortification. Don Quixote looked down at Sancho and saw that his cheeks were puffed up and his mouth was filled with mirth, about to explode with it; and the knight's dejection was not so great that it could prevent him from laughing at the sight of Sancho, and when Sancho saw that his master had begun to laugh, he released his own captive so suddenly that he had to press his fists to his sides so as not to explode.

> Four times he calmed down, and four times he started laughing again, every bit as hard as the first time …]

These paroxysms are a counterpart to the scatological manifestations of fear the night before, and the locus of adventure is once again Sancho's body.[21] The full mouth recalls his deflationary munching on the very acorns that inspired don Quijote's Golden Age speech. But this time, rather than a mouth stuffed with food, or a belly bursting with excrement, it is laughter that fills Sancho and that cannot be held back. It is a force of the spirit as much as one of the body, and even our grave knight is susceptible, his accustomed melancholy temporarily dispelled. There is a moment of authentic companionship between the two as don Quijote's laughter gives Sancho license to release his merriment fully. But the bond is fleeting, as Sancho cannot refrain from imitating his master's chivalric register during the previous night's suspense: "que yo nací, por querer del cielo, en esta nuestra edad de hierro" ("that I was born, by the will of heaven, in this iron age of ours" [248]). This quickly turns don Quijote's laughter to an equally irrepressible ire, which he unleashes on Sancho's back. From a play perspective, the scene is significant because it reveals the two attempting to adjust and maintain the equilibrium of their game amidst unexpected, chance occurrences: the plausible expectation of adventure with the sound of the fulling mills in the night; the comic liberation from fear, which nevertheless creates the potential for excessive license (Sancho acknowledges as much: "confieso que he andado algo risueño en demasía" – "I will admit I was a bit free with my giggles" [249]). As Huizinga observed: "The play-mood is *labile* in its very nature. At any moment 'ordinary life' may reassert its rights either by an impact from without, which interrupts the game, or by an offence against the rules, or else from within, by a collapse of the play spirit, a sobering, a disenchantment" (21). If don Gaiferos's absorption in chess is interrupted from "an impact from without," don Quijote and Sancho must repeatedly renegotiate the rules, and deal with multiple "soberings and disenchantments." In Part II, as well as in the *Novelas ejemplares*, we will see more complex instances of Cervantes's interest in the destabilizing impingement of chance and other "contaminants" in the structured realm of play. As Cervantes understands, such adjustments and renegotiations reveal a central ambiguity: the player knows that he is playing, yet takes the game seriously.

Inspired by Goethe's description of the childlike quality of artistic creation, Torrente Ballester offers some illuminating context to don

Quijote and Sancho's definition and refining of roles, as well as to the knight's pique at his squire's mocking:

> The child without a toy, the one who finds himself obligated to invent one in a veritable operation of *bricolage*, acts like don Quijote: the slightest and most distant resemblance serves him to transmute the real and to so create the world in which he can play. He points to the chair and decrees: This is a boat, and I am the captain. And, while the game lasts, the chair is boat and the child is captain, and although the child knows that it has to do with a convention – whence the ironic ingredient of every child who invents his toy – he is irritated when somebody does not accept the agreed-upon and denies the condition of boat to the chair, and captain to the child.[22]

The child's act of creating an imaginary world based on association and similitudes, and then entering into this world with an attitude of both earnestness and irony, is an apt comparison. Caillois also noted the serious play of children, the conscious creation of metaphor: "the basic intention is not that of deceiving the spectators. The child who is playing train may well refuse to kiss his father while saying to him that one does not embrace locomotives, but he is not trying to persuade his father that he is a real locomotive" (21). We can say that the child recognizes what Ife called the distinction between rational and aesthetic belief (*Reading and Fiction* ch. 3). Examining the mimetic quality of the protagonist's knight-errantry, Torrente Ballester maintains that don Quijote is not a lunatic, but is rather consciously adopting a role. This brings us back to Papargyriou's point about the fundamental ambiguity of play: "The fact that in play two propositions are simultaneously equated and distinguished means the boundaries between play and reality are fragile and often at risk of breaking down" (18). Torrente Ballester's interpretation works better for some sequences than for others, since Cervantes is not absolutely consistent in his characterization. But, as should be clear from the scene commentaries above, it seems a fruitful approach, especially given the pervasiveness of mimetic play throughout the work. As we shall see below, it is particularly illuminating for Part II, in which the "real world" becomes intensely theatrical, and during which Sancho Panza becomes the central ludic figure.

Before considering the play elements of Part II, some remarks on the comic nature of *Don Quijote* are in order. The seriousness with which don Quijote approaches his play would seem to exclude a comic self-awareness on his part, and suggest that he is meant as the object of laughter – our own, and that of other characters. And this is frequently the case. Don Quijote's anger after the *batanes* is occasioned not so much by Sancho's *laughter* (the knight himself laughed), as by the squire's joking about the contrast between don Quijote's heroic register and the prosaic reality of the noise: " – Sosiéguese vuestra merced; que por Dios que me burlo. –Pues, porque os burláis, no me burlo yo –respondió don Quijote" ("'Calm down, do, sir, please – I swear to God I was only joking.' 'You may be joking, sir, but I am not,' retorted Don Quixote" [1, 20, p. 249]). Sancho means that his joke is good-natured kidding, that he is not making light of his master as much as the peculiar situation in which they find themselves. Rather than the laughter of parody, which would signify don Quijote's inadequacy as a knight, Sancho suggests the logic of travesty (it is reality that does not measure up).[23] Don Quijote's claim of seriousness ("no me burlo yo") is meant to underline the fact that his valour was real, even if the circumstances turned out to be innocuous. He does, in fact, acknowledge the humorous quality of what has happened: "No niego yo –respondió don Quijote – que lo que nos ha sucedido no sea cosa digna de risa; pero no es digna de contarse; que no son todas las personas tan discretas que sepan poner en su punto las cosas" ("I do not deny," replied Don Quixote, "that what has happened to us is worth laughing at; but it is not worth telling, because not all people are intelligent enough to see things in the right perspective" [249]). The interesting distinction between something being worthy to laugh at but not to recount is ironic, since eliciting laughter is one of Cervantes's most cherished narrative achievements. But don Quijote's comments point to another fundamental concern of his author: reading competence, which involves discernment and subtlety ("que no son todas las personas tan discretas que sepan poner en su punto las cosas"). Are we reading in a vulgar manner if we simply laugh at don Quijote? Is there, as don Quijote seems to suggest, a particular context within which such laughable moments must be placed? This is the focus of the next section.

Play and Laughter in *Don Quijote*

Our own peculiar condition is that we are as fit to be laughed at as able to laugh.
– Montaigne, "Of Democritus and Heraclitus" (I, 50)

Nabokov's complaints over its "cruel and crude" humour notwithstanding, readers have responded to and identified a tremendous comic range in *Don Quijote*. As Nerlich remarked, "In the case of Cervantes …

we can say, as a hermeneutical minimum, that every understanding that omits laughter must be essentially wrong" (250). Anthony Close makes a similar point: "one cannot treat the comicality of Cervantes's fiction as simply an obvious and superficial layer, detachable from the more thought-provoking layers that lie beneath. It pervades and conditions the whole work, and if we neglect it, our understanding of the work is basically flawed" (*Cervantes and the Comic Mind* 7). Close's expansive study of humour and shifting cultural norms in early modern Spain is also constrictive, since he wants to temper the anachronistic exaggerations of critics who insist upon *Don Quijote* as the first modern novel, with all of the perspectivism, socio-political engagement, indeterminacy and metaphysical angst that such a label might imply.[24] Anyone who has sustained exposure to academic writing, and possesses a sense of humour, is likely to acknowledge the virtue of Close's argument. Much interesting speculation exists regarding what, precisely, we are laughing at in *Don Quijote*: a decadent nobility, a Spain that refuses to relinquish antiquated chivalric and pastoral ideals, the hubris and injustices of imperialism, repressed sexual inclinations. But occasionally we go astray, sometimes hilariously, when applying our interpretive sophistication to Cervantes's jokes – especially when they involve caricature, solecisms, and timely flatulence issuing from ample buttocks.

Azorín suggested that the comedy of a given culture provides the most accurate indication of its level of civilization: "The chapter of eutrapelia, of spiritual diversion, is extremely important in the history of human development; making the history of irony and humour, we would also have made that of human sensibility, and, as a consequence, that of progress, of civilization."[25] The distance Azorín perceives between the reactions of the modern reader and Cervantes's contemporaries to don Quijote's many beatings would indicate that we have progressed considerably: "Today there would be nobody of average sensibility – not even of extreme – who would be able to smile at these things. To the contrary: they would make us sad. Sensibility has been evolving."[26] Implicit in the judgments of Azorín and Nabokov is that one's enjoyment of cruel humour corresponds to cruelty in real life. But one might also say, along with Bakhtin, that such an "evolution" of sensibility is in the form of a progressive narrowing that seems to accompany heightened seriousness: a limitation of the play element, a blindness to the ambivalence of gaiety and derision that is contained in much of this bodily humour.[27] With regard to its potential destructiveness, much of the responsibility lies in the readers' ability to unquixotically sustain a consciousness of the boundaries between art and life. It is significant that Elias, whose "civilizing process" would seem very similar to Azorín's progress of the "sensibilidad humana," identifies in laughter, as in play, a crucial liberation from the seriousness demanded by civilization: "It [laughter] indicates quite graphically the fact of provision by means of biological institutions of ways and means of counterbalancing the strains and stresses of impulse-control" (*Quest for Excitement* 61). The following pages will suggest that perhaps it is a good thing that our sensibilities have not evolved as much as Azorín maintains.

Cervantes himself repeatedly pokes fun at various forms of pedantry, from the minutiae of hair-splitting scholarship to the over-determined formulas of theory. We have, for example, the *primo humanista* in Part II, always seeking grist for his superfluous books (II, 22–4).[28] After the farcical adventure of the Carro de la Muerte (II, 11) don Quijote pontificates on theatre as metaphor, only to have Sancho point out that his analysis is not exactly ground-breaking:

> [L]o mesmo ... acontece en la comedia y trato deste mundo, donde unos hacen los emperadores, otros los pontífices, y, finalmente, todas cuantas figuras se pueden introducir en una comedia; pero en llegando al fin, que es cuando se acaba la vida, a todos les quita la muerte las ropas que los diferenciaban, y quedan iguales en la sepultura.
>
> – Brava comparación –dijo Sancho – , aunque no tan nueva, que yo no la haya oído muchas y diversas veces ... (II, 12, p. 121)

> ["[T]he same happens ... in the play of this life, in which some act as emperors, others as popes and, in short, all the characters that there can be in a play; but when it is over, in other words when life ends, death strips them all of the costumes that had distinguished between them, and they are all equals in the grave."
>
> "That's a fine comparison," said Sancho, "only not so very original that I haven't heard it about a hundred times before ..."]

The impulse to allegorize is checked.[29] In such anti-pedantic moments Cervantes forms part of a rich comic tradition, from antiquity through Erasmus and Montaigne. There is an irony to this gentle ridicule, since the complex structure of Cervantes's novel compels us to interpret even while it illustrates the perils of interpretation. But Cervantes is also interested in the physical pleasure of a good laugh, or, as the narrator presages in one episode, at least a chuckle or monkey grin (II, 44). When, in the streets of Toledo, the curious narrator asks a *morisco* to translate some of the papers he has happened upon, the novel's ethos emerges: "En fin, la suerte me deparó uno, que, diciéndole mi deseo y poniéndole el libro en las manos, le abrió por medio, y leyendo un poco en él, se comenzó a reír" ("In short, chance provided me with a man who, when I told him what I wanted and put the book in his hands, opened it in the middle and after reading a little began to laugh" [I, 9, p. 142]). Amidst our ingenious explanations regarding the function of humour in *Don Quijote*, we do well to keep in mind that Cervantes, like Boccaccio, Castiglione, Huarte, El Pinciano and others, believed in the therapeutic effects of laughter. Such effects are at least partly based on a link between physical, affective and cognitive functions.[30]

At the risk of exposing myself to Cervantes's ridicule as another sophistic scholar, I will venture to analyse some rather subtle aspects of the humour in *Don Quijote*. As indicated above, a good deal of the comedy corresponds to the hygienic tradition, the conviction that the pleasure of laughter and play are conducive to physical and mental health. Much of the laughter is indeed generated by satirical humour, which finds resolution in the ultimate control of the narrator and the superior knowledge of the reader vis-à-vis the characters, with a clear separation between the former as laughing subjects, the latter, laughable objects. But in other instances there is a lack of clear resolution and restoration of order, a lingering disorientation. Such humour contains a suggestive scepticism – if not exactly the "prismatic" relativism rejected by Close, at least the awareness that rational and insane responses to the world differ more in degree than kind. A focus on epistemological aspects of Cervantes's humour reveals a range of contemporary knowledge systems mischievously drawn into the comic vortex. I do not intend to argue that Cervantes was necessarily a "subversive artist," overtly opposing the official values and epistemology of his time. Rather, as is typical with genuine humourists, when the comic logic of a particular situation ranges into sacrosanct terrain, Cervantes is sometimes willing to let it run its course. The result can be confusion as to precisely what we are laughing *at*. Laughing *with* Cervantes, we realize how, complicit in sustaining illusions, we are in certain ways not so different from don Quijote. In other words, we become aware of the nature of our own play as readers.

Laughing At, Laughing With

Before proceeding, some clarification of terminology is in order. Adrienne Martín's distinction between "humour" and "satire" in Cervantes helps illustrate a type of laughter I wish to emphasize: "While satirists refuse to forgive or to see in themselves the 'vices' they castigate and instead remain at a critical distance, humourists use ironical distance to allow them to include themselves in the collective object of their humour. This is one of *Don Quixote*'s most important lessons to the reader: the recognition that all of us are to an extent quixotic or pancine" (165). In his finely titled study, *The Irresponsible Self*, James Wood articulates what he calls a "comedy of correction," a *laughing at* that corresponds to a stable, theological, Aristotelian world-view, and which is "pre-novelistic." This he contrasts with a more lenient "comedy of forgiveness," a *laughing with* characteristic of an unstable and secular vision, and the domain of the novel (3–19). While Wood associates the full development of the novelistic "comedy of forgiveness" with late nineteenth- and early twentieth-century innovations in form and character, he identifies a few "transitional" works that contain both types of humour, *The Praise of Folly* and *Don Quijote* among them.[31] Like Pirandello's notion of "the feeling of the opposite" (and Martín's distinction of humour from satire), Wood's comedy of forgiveness involves an element of compassion, a breaking down of the derisive opposition between the laughing subject and comic object. A trace of pathos arises along with a broadening of our knowledge: we sense there is more to the laughable character than we originally judged. An example of such characterization, as Martín points out (171), is the unexpected dimension taken on by Maritornes, who initially appears as a comic type, the grotesque prostitute. The effect is even more notable when Maritornes extends humane charity to Sancho after he is laid low by the *bálsamo* (I, 17). Ranging from Bergson's laughter as a social corrective to Bakhtin's collective laughter of the carnivalesque, Iffland illustrates the tremendous comic variety in *Don Quijote*. In his focus on scenes in which characters actually laugh, he finds "upward" and "downward" laughter (someone laughing at a member of a higher estate, and the inverse), "horizontal" laughter (same social status), and "polidirectional" laughter: "I point all this out to show that in *Don Quijote* we have the entire range of laughter, from the most subversive and liberating forms to those which reinforce hierarchical differentiation. The important thing ... is precisely this richness and variety, the fact that the laughter tumbles in all imaginable directions, coming from extremely diverse individuals."[32]

As the likes of Plato, Lucian, and Montaigne have affirmed, greater knowledge can come at an epistemological cost, as we become less sure of our assumptions. James Wood discusses how such a process is at work in the rise of the novel: "This comedy, or tragicomedy, of the modern novel replaces the knowable with the unknowable, transparency with unreliability, and this is surely in direct proportion to the growth of the characters' fictive inner lives" (10). Painting in broader strokes, Milan Kundera sees in Cervantes the first great novelist whose comic irony "tore the curtain" of our presumptions to knowledge, thereby disorienting but also freeing the reader of *Don Quijote*, who must deploy an active imagination and judgment in order to make sense of the world: "We are laughing not because someone is being ridiculed, mocked, or even humiliated but because a reality is abruptly revealed as ambiguous, things lose their apparent meaning, the man before us is not what he thought himself to be" (*The Curtain* 109). And then there are critics, such as Michael Wood, who claim that Cervantes outdoes the moderns at their own game:

> In Nabokov we have endless grounds for a fine modern distrust, but find ourselves trusting (some of) what our shifty narrator says. In Cervantes the situation is more or less the reverse. Broadly: where there is trust Cervantes finds multiple grounds for mistrust; indeed finds such grounds pretty much everywhere; devotes himself to finding them, gets many of his best jokes out of such moves. (33–4)

Granted, not all of the preceding observations are based on a rigorous historicism. But the dichotomy between the "hard school," insisting on historical context, and the "romantic approach," which seeks to bring out incipient or unappreciated potential meanings, is in certain respects false: both yield valid insights, and either can be taken to a distorting extreme. Of particular interest is the fact that some of the pillars of "romantic" interpretations, supposedly predicated on a disregard for the comic content of the work, can be supported by an analysis of the humour. And the more "modern" types of humour I ascribe to Cervantes are also found in some of his illustrious contemporaries.

In similar ways, Erasmus, Montaigne, and Burton articulate an important refinement to Aristotle's frequently cited maxim that a defining trait of human beings is the ability to laugh. As Montaigne puts it, "Our own peculiar condition is that we are as fit to be laughed at as to laugh" (I, 50). An emphasis on risible humanity dates back at least as far as Diogenes and Democritus. But there is a tendency in early modern humanists to explore the tension between laughing *at* and laughing *with*, between ridiculing folly in others and acknowledging one's own. It is a significant tension because "corrective" laughter sometimes shifts to one that accepts and even validates the folly that occasions it. The rational faculty, which allows us to recognize laughable defects, cedes some of its authority to the affective, and there is an emphasis on the pleasure of laughter itself. Horace provided enduring emblems for such an outlook in his Second Epistle. The bustling banquet hall, and the otherwise rational man from Argos who enjoyed theatrical performances in an empty theatre and laments the "cure" of his well-meaning friends, proved quite suggestive to his humanist descendants. As we shall see below, Erasmus, Montaigne, and Burton give such figures an ambiguity they may not have possessed in their original contexts.

A volatile blend of satirical with humane laughter pervades *The Praise of Folly*, in which the "madness of the Furies" is derided alongside the productive delusions of which we all partake. Although the distinctions between types of madness are not always clear, Folly embeds a tempering mechanism in the form of an additional Democritus: "not even a thousand Democrituses would suffice to laugh at them; and then you'd need one extra Democritus to laugh at the thousand laughers" (49). Democritus is human, therefore also fit to be laughed at. It is worth recalling Folly's injunction to "drink up or get out," and to "blunder along in good company," rather than "demanding that the play no longer be a play" (29). Life in society involves an acceptance of rules and conventions; to refuse to participate simply because one sees the arbitrary nature of convention is more a sign of boorishness than wisdom. Such illustrations of the ludic element at the centre of human intercourse blur the distinction between play and seriousness. Montaigne was also fond of the banquet hall metaphor, and availed himself of the common source (Lucretius, via Horace): "If you know not right living, then give way / To those that do; you've had enough of play, / Of food and drink; 'tis time you left with grace, / Lest lusty youth expel you from the place" (II, 12, p. 366). The coarse and lively atmosphere of the banquet represents for Montaigne the imprecise but pleasurable nature of human interaction. Accordingly, he gives such a venue priority over the sterility of the classroom and book learning. To be sure, the passage in which he cites the banquet, shortly after a reference to Horace's deluded theatre-goer, is highly ambivalent, meant to illustrate the sceptical position that knowledge does not ensure happiness: "What is all that but philosophy confessing her impotence, and sending us back not merely to ignorance, to be under cover, but to stupidity itself, to insensibility and nonexistence?" (p. 366). But Montaigne would concur with Lucretius who, amidst the absence of transcendent meaning in life, encourages us to follow "Nature herself," the fertile cycle of birth and death: "Now put aside all thoughts that are unseemly for your grey head, / Come along, make room for others, leave with your heart light. / So it must be" (*The Nature of Things* bk. III, l. 961–3).

In "Of Democritus and Heraclitus," Montaigne distinguishes between the comic and the tragic outlook, preferring the former: "Pity and commiseration are mingled with some esteem for the thing we pity; the things we laugh at we consider worthless. I do not think there is as much unhappiness in us as vanity, nor as much malice as stupidity. We are not so full of evil as of inanity; we are not as wretched as we are worthless" (I, 50, p. 221). It bears emphasizing that this is an early essay, by a youthful and somewhat severe Montaigne. The passage cited describes ridicule, a satirical laughing *at*. In contrast with tragic commiseration, the comic outlook affirms a separation between subject and object, an analytical distance involving censorious judgment. It is not the novelistic humour discussed above, which entails a narrowing of the gap between subject and object, but rather what "hard critics" would identify as typical of Cervantes's age, an Aristotelian laughter at defects: "For the comic is constituted by a fault and a mark of shame, but lacking in pain or destruction: to take an obvious example, the comic mask is ugly and misshapen, but does not express pain" (*Poetics* 36). But as the use of the first-person plural indicates, Montaigne does not exempt himself ("Our own condition is that we are as fit to be laughed at as able to laugh"). He expresses ambivalence towards a being who possesses a degree of rational function and discernment, and is thus "able to laugh," but who nevertheless remains mired in absurdity. Schiller would describe a similar comic orientation towards experience: "to find everywhere more chance than fate, and to laugh more about absurdity than rage and whine about maliciousness" (*On Naive and Sentimental Poetry* 209).[33] Montaigne's ambivalence has a similar function to Erasmus's extra Democritus, which assures that the laughers themselves are humbled. In his later essays, Montaigne expresses a more lenient, Epicurean sensibility, with greater acceptance of human vanity and delusion. He develops an outlook more humorous than satirical.

Lest we erroneously assign to Montaigne's stoicism a rigid, antisocial bearing – as distinguished from a more humane Epicureanism – it is worth observing Seneca's comments on Democritus and Heraclitus, which is a model for Montaigne's comments above:

> Accordingly, we must allow ourselves to be persuaded of the view that all the vices of the mob are not hateful, but ludicrous, and we should take Democritus as our model rather than Heraclitus ... We must, therefore, take a less serious view of all things, tolerating them in a spirit of acceptance: it is more human to laugh at life than to weep tears over it. There is the further point that the human race is also more indebted to the man who laughs at it than to the one who mourns for it: the first leaves it some measure of optimism, while the second foolishly mourns for what he despairs of being remedied; and when he surveys the world, he who does not hold back his laughter shows a greater mind than the one who does not hold back his tears, since he gives vent to the gentlest of the emotions and thinks there is nothing important, nothing serious, nothing miserable, in the whole great state of life. (*On the Tranquility of the Mind* 135–6)

The sense of humility, and universal complicity in human folly, and the acceptance and tolerance that come of such a view, make Seneca a precursor to Pirandello's "feeling for the other," and James Wood's "comedy of forgiveness," not to mention the humane satire of Erasmus. It is far in spirit from the Aristotelian, corrective laughing *at* deformities or vices, as if they were aberrations from an exalted norm.

In his "Apology for Raymond Sebond," Montaigne again cites Horace, recounting the anecdote of the man from Argos: "Alas, you have not saved me, friends, quoth he, / But murdered me, my pleasure snatched away, / And that delusion that made life so gay (II, 12, p. 366). Montaigne considers the foundations of knowledge tenuous, based on an unstable combination of conjecture, subjectivity, imaginative exuberance and custom. It is thus misguided to base one's happiness on certainty of knowledge. As we observed above, the art of living well involves an acceptance of ignorance, receptiveness to pleasure, and an adaptive flexibility that allows us to interact in human community: "Greatness of soul is not so much pressing upward and forward as knowing how to set oneself in order and circumscribe oneself ... There is nothing so beautiful and legitimate as to play the man well and properly, no knowledge so hard to acquire as the knowledge of how to live this life well and naturally" (III, 13, p. 852). As Montaigne comments in his meditation on the absurdity of vilifying and repressing sexuality: "Our life is part folly, part wisdom" (III, 5, pp. 677–8). Recognizing this central truth about humanity, Montaigne, like Erasmus before him, adjusts his discourse to the subject matter, and the resulting *serio ludere* is presented not just as a mode of philosophical writing, but also as a model for conducting one's life.

Robert Burton joins Erasmus and Montaigne in citing Horace and proclaiming himself a partisan of Democritus. His monumental *The Anatomy of Melancholy* contains virtually every argument for and against leisure surveyed in the present study. The section titled "Exercise rectified of Body and Mind" (II, 2, iv) discusses games of skill and chance, physical recreations and spectacles, types of leisure particular to social class, the *locus amoenus* and good company, the restorative value of indulging the senses, and the connectedness of body and mind. In this same section he cites Vives, Erasmus, Apuleius and Boccaccio. As with Boccaccio, he presents recreation as a sort of antigen: in *The Decameron*, protection is sought from the plague ravishing Florence, and the love-sickness afflicting ladies; in Burton, it is the disease of melancholy, which is shown to be of epidemic proportions. And, as Boccaccio privileges story-telling over the board games present at the country estate, Burton is partial to taking recreation in books: "For what a world of books offers itself, in all subjects, arts, and sciences, to the sweet content and capacity of the reader! What vast tomes are extant in law, physic, and divinity, for profit, pleasure, practice, speculation, in verse or prose, etc.!" (II. ii. 4, p. 88). Burton observes the moral rationale of recreation, and he stresses the importance of moderation, the Horatian "profit" of reading, the allowance of play to avoid the greater evil of idleness (e.g., 84–5). But he also goes far beyond such conventional justifications.

Insofar as it catalogues human dispositions and behaviours that lead to dysfunction and vice, *The Anatomy of Melancholy* is a panoramic satire. Burton recognizes the dangers of excess – in gambling and chess as well as in reading: "or such inamoratoes as read nothing but playbooks, idle poems, jests, Amadis de Gaul, the Knight of the Sun, the Seven Champions, Palmerin de Oliva, Huon of Bordeaux, etc. Such many times prove in the end as mad as Don Quixote" (93). But notable are the rhapsodic accounts of the "sweet delights" contained in certain types of melancholy, reading and study in particular (II. ii. 4). Burton twice mentions the idea that the narration or reading of a thing brings a pleasure comparable to actually seeing or experiencing it (II. ii. 4, pp. 78 and 81). Like Cervantes, whose concern with alleviating melancholy has been noted, Burton's enthusiasm for the tremendous variety and imaginative engagement offered by books frequently overrides the moral and hygienic concerns he cites along the way. A great practitioner of paradox, Burton ambivalently endorses many of the vices he purportedly sets out to remedy.[34] It is therefore not surprising that Horace's man from Argos should repeatedly surface, as in the following discussion of the humours and the power of imagination in melancholy subjects:

> [T]hey are in paradise for the time, and cannot well endure to be interrupt; with him in the poet, *Pol, me occidistis, amici, non servastis, ait* ["In sooth, good friends, you have killed, not cured me, says he]; you have undone him, he complains, if you trouble him: tell him what inconvenience will follow, what will be the event, all is one, *canis ad vomitum* [like a dog to his vomit], 'tis so pleasant he cannot refrain. (I. iii. 4, p. 406)

Like Erasmus, Burton recognizes that there are malignant as well as salubrious varieties and aspects of folly, and that one should curb the former while cultivating the latter. To attempt to eliminate all forms would be inhuman. It is telling that even the highly moralistic Vives cites the man from Argos while discussing the therapeutic value of laughter and the pleasures of the imagination: "pues algunos consiguen por el solo reflejo de la imaginación convencerse de que gozan de los mayores bienes" ("some achieve by a mere reflex of the imagination to convince themselves that they are enjoying the greatest goods" [*Obras completas* III, 9]). According to Vives, Horace's deluded man is not an aberrant exception, but the rule: "Harto sabido es el cuento. Es un fenómeno común en todas aficiones" ("The story is well known. It is a phenomenon common in all passions" [III, 9]).

Here it is important to observe that a source for much of the above, Horace's Second Epistle, does not in fact hold a favourable view of delusion. The man from Argos, sitting happily in his empty theatre, is meant to illustrate that "it is profitable to cast aside toys and to learn wisdom; to leave to lads the sport that fits their age" (437). And the banquet hall image promotes a deferential withdrawal, an acceptance of old age and mortality. In his satire on human follies, Horace sketches a broad landscape of varied and nearly universal madness, with the goal of fostering a corrective awareness of vice (*Satires* II. iii). He even views contests of wit, so popular in Cervantes's Spain, as instigations to man's agonistic nature: "For such sport begets tumultuous strife and wrath, and wrath begets fierce quarrels, and war to the death" (*Epistles*

I. xix). Erasmus, Montaigne and Burton, we might say, went some way towards "romanticizing" Horace.[35] In the following consideration of *Don Quijote* we will see many instances in which the humour deflates not only the mad knight's delusions, but also broader human pretences to *gravitas* and certitude. Furthermore, many of the same comic traits that come in for ridicule are revived in the generous light of Cervantine laughter, which is capable of vindicating the very foolishness it initially derides. In view of the preceding observations on humanist writers, it should be clear that assigning such characteristics to Cervantes's humour need not be symptomatic of viewing *Don Quijote* through the lens of the modern novel. Rather, it involves an appreciation of Cervantes's affinity with some of the greatest writers of the early modern period.[36]

Comic Doubt and Delusion in *Don Quijote*

The "epistemological humour" I refer to above is introduced in the very first words of *Don Quijote* – "En un lugar de la Mancha, de cuyo nombre no quiero acordarme" ("In a village in La Mancha, the name of which I cannot quite recall") – and sustained in the initial presentation of the hero: "*Quieren decir* que tenía el sobrenombre de Quijada, o Quesada, que en esto hay alguna diferencia en los autores que deste caso escriben; aunque por conjeturas verosímiles se deja entender que se llamaba Quejana. Pero esto importa poco a nuestro cuento; *basta que en la narración dél no se salga un punto de la verdad*" ("His surname's *said to have been* Quixada, or Quesada; concerning this detail there's some discrepancy among the authors who have written on the subject, although a credible conjecture does suggest he might have been a plaintive Quexana. But this doesn't matter much, as far as our story's concerned, *provided that the narrator doesn't stray one inch from the truth*" [I, 1, p. 71 my italics]). Faced with such uncertainty, Cervantes encourages us to ponder what sort of precise narrative truth we are dealing with; and the question increases in complexity as we continue reading. One notable instance is when don Quijote and the marginally sane Basque have their furious battle interrupted by the curtailment of the manuscript, and the author meanders through the streets of Toledo inspecting scraps of paper, generating news of a presumed "second author," of the historian Cide Hamete Benengeli who composed the original in Arabic, and of visual illustrations of the characters accompanied by descriptive notes. Our narrator seems aware of the somewhat challenging implications all of this poses to transmitting a faithful account of his hero in

Castilian, but he reassures us in the same terms employed some eighty pages earlier: "Otras menudencias había que advertir, pero todas son de poca importancia y que no hacen al caso a la verdadera relación de la historia, que ninguna es mala como sea verdadera" ("Other details could be observed, but none of them is important, or relevant to the truthful narration of this history – and no history is bad so long as it is truthful" [I, 9, p. 144]). Of course this can only make sense if we are dealing with something other than a factual conception of truth. Close discusses how Cervantes's notion of narrative truth derives from contemporary rhetorical precepts regarding the separation of extrinsic and essential information in storytelling, and the poetics of verisimilitude, of making that which is recounted both plausible and vivid, or "present" (*A Companion*, chs. 4–5). Montaigne has also reflected upon the issue, as when he discusses vivid literary representations of grief and death: "understanding is always enhanced by actual presence, when the eyes and ears have a share in it, organs that cannot be stirred except by incidental details" (III, 4, p. 636). But Cervantes also expands the notion of truth, extending the principles of well or poorly constructed narratives to extra-literary concerns. The humorous subversion that calls into question criteria of textual interpretation insinuates itself into the making sense of lived experience.

The Toledan Merchants episode (I, 4), in which don Quijote affirms the importance of faith and the merchants favour empirical evidence, is an early example of Cervantes playing with – if not "problematizing" – the notion of truth. The interpolated tale of the *Curioso impertinente* (I, 33–5) does so in a more serious and troubling manner. While Part I begins with complicating the notion of narrative truth, Part II starts off by drawing into the humorous field a striking range of knowledge sources, as the priest and barber test the convalescing knight's sanity. In response to don Quijote's *arbitrio* recommending knight-errantry to save Spain, the barber tells the story of the *loco* with *lúcidos intervalos* in Seville. The comic anecdote recalls Horace's man from Argos ("a man who would correctly perform all other duties of life"), and serves the purpose of eliciting a didactic, corrective laughter. Don Quijote will have none of it, and rejects the intended exemplarity of the tale: "¿éste es el cuento, señor barbero … que por venir aquí como de molde, no podía dejar de contarle? ¡Ah, señor rapista, señor rapista …" ("And this is that tale, mister barber … that fitted the bill so perfectly that you could not refrain from telling it? Oh, mister shaver, mister shaver …" [II, 1, p. 47]).[37] He proceeds to give a moral defence of chivalry, deploying a conventional topos of social decline similar to that delivered in his Golden Age speech (I, 11). The curate then voices his doubt regarding the historical existence of the famous knights: "imagino que todo es ficción, fábula y mentira, y sueños contados por hombres despiertos, o, por mejor decir, medio dormidos" ("it seems to me that it's all fiction, fables and lies, and dreams recounted by men after they've woken up, or to be more accurate, half woken up" [II, 1, p. 50]). Rather than mimic the "loco de Sevilla," who, once diverted from his good reason, is completely insane ("que soy Neptuno ... lloveré todas las veces que se me antojare y fuere menester" – "I, Neptune ... will rain as often as I like and is required" [50]), don Quijote gives the following explanation of his belief:

> [L]a cual verdad es tan cierta, que estoy por decir que con mis propios ojos vi a Amadís de Gaula, que era un hombre alto de cuerpo, blanco de rostro, bien puesto de barba, aunque negra, de vista entre blanda y rigurosa, corto de razones, tardo en airarse y presto en deponer la ira; y del modo que he delineado a Amadís pudiera, a mi parecer, pintar y describir todos cuantos caballeros andantes andan en las historias en el orbe, que por la aprehensión que tengo de que fueron como sus historias cuentan, y por las hazañas que hicieron y condiciones que tuvieron, se pueden sacar por buena filosofía sus faciones, sus colores y estaturas. (II, 1, p. 50)

> [[T]ruth so palpable that I can almost say I have seen Amadís of Gaul with my own eyes – he was a tall man with a pale face, a splendid beard even if it was a black one, a look that hovered between gentleness and severity, and sparing of words, slow to lose his temper and quick to recover it; and just as I have described Amadís, I believe I could describe every single knight errant in every single history in the world, because my realization that they were as their histories say they were, together with my knowledge of the deeds they did and the qualities they possessed, enables me to use logic and deduce their features, complexion and stature.]

This is an example of narrative truth in the form of a compelling verisimilitude, of making the character "present" – to use Close's term – before the reader. The vivid detail of don Quijote's description recalls his account of the massing armies in the *rebaños* episode (I, 18) and his famous "knight of the boiling lake" narrative (I, 50), delivered in refutation of the Canon's objections to chivalric romance. In place of the clear exemplarity of the *loco de Sevilla* story, which warns against being fooled by temporary appearances of sanity, we see a defence of belief which, although risible in a literal sense, rests upon venerable aesthetic precepts.

As the barber, in humorous condescension, inquires about the size of Morgante, the distinction between narrative truth and larger epistemological issues becomes thornier: "En esto de gigantes –respondió don Quijote – hay diferentes opiniones, si los ha habido o no en el mundo; pero la Santa Escritura, que no puede faltar un átamo a la verdad, nos muestra que los hubo, contándonos la historia de aquel filisteazo de Golías, que tenía siete codos y medio de altura, que es una desmesurada grandeza" ("With regard to giants," replied Don Quixote, "there are different opinions as to whether they ever existed or not; yet the Scriptures, which cannot be anything less than the absolute truth, show us that they did exist, by recounting the history of that immense Philistine, Goliath, who was seven and a half cubits tall, a vast height" [II, 1, p. 50]). When the narrator at the beginning of Part I says that "basta que en la narración dél no se salga un punto de la verdad" ("provided that the narrator doesn't stray one inch from the truth"), we can either take it as a dismissive joke – *of course this is all make-believe, not really to be compared with serious texts* – or, following Close and others, as an example of how Cervantes is interested in illustrating other sorts of truth (rhetorical, artistic). But when nearly identical terms are applied to the Bible ("no puede faltar un átamo a la verdad"), the implications are more complicated. At the very least, we can say that the Goliath references goes some way, according to contemporary standards of proof, towards legitimizing don Quijote's belief in giants. The knight then adds two additional layers to his argument, referring to the archaeological evidence of large bones found in Sicily, and concluding that, since Morgante was described sleeping indoors, he could not have been so huge. As with don Quijote's literary debate with the canon of Toledo (I, 47–50), part of the humour here resides in the spectacle of a presumed lunatic managing to throw his learned interlocutors off balance. One is inclined to agree with Michael Wood's assertion that where there is certainty, Cervantes finds grounds for doubt.[38]

The *barco encantado* adventure (II, 29) is one of those episodes, like the Cave of Montesinos (II, 23) or the *cabeza encantada* (II, 62), which functions as a sort of concentrated illustration of the mechanisms and concerns of the entire novel, and it contains a striking density of resonances – of image, theme, diction – with other parts of the work. It is also one of the novel's funniest scenes. The comedy ranges from farcical to linguistic, and includes some epistemological games similar to those examined above. As usual, don Quijote's imaginative transcription of the mundane phenomena (the Ebro River, an oar-less boat on the banks) works on the principle of association and signs, although the process has been complicated by recent experiences. A sort of focalization occurs as the narrator modulates into a pastoral register: "llegaron don Quijote y Sancho al río Ebro, y el verle fue de gran gusto a don Quijote, porque contempló y miró en él la amenidad de sus riberas, la claridad de sus aguas, el sosiego de su curso y la abundancia de sus líquidos cristales, cuya alegre vista renovó en su memoria mil amorosos pensamientos" ("Don Quixote and Sancho reached the River Ebro, and it gave Don Quixote great pleasure to see it as he surveyed its delightful banks, its clear waters, its tranquil flow and its abundant liquid crystal, the contemplation of which delights revived a thousand loving thoughts in his mind" [II, 29, p. 261]). The conventionality of the pristine place may be a set-up for another prosaic deflation, but, as elsewhere, Cervantes delights in the very material he mocks: there is fertile interplay between parody and aesthetic pleasure. The crystalline waters, the love associations, the boat – all unmistakably beckon don Quijote, "porque éste es estilo de los libros de las historias caballerescas" ("because this is the way of the histories of knight-errantry" [262]). But he is preoccupied by his recent grotesque visions in the Cave of Montesinos, and by the monkey's equivocal pronouncements on them: "puesto que el mono de maese Pedro le había dicho que parte de aquellas cosas eran verdad y parte mentira, él se atenía más a las verdaderas que a las mentirosas, bien al revés de Sancho, que todas las tenía por la mesma mentira" ("for although Master Pedro's monkey had told him that some of those things had been true and some false, he stood more by the true ones than the others, quite the opposite of Sancho, who was convinced that they were all part and parcel of the same great lie" [261]). The doubt accompanying the interpretative freedom that the narrator instiled in the reader (e.g., II, 5 and 24) has crept into the consciousness of our protagonist.

In addition to foregrounding the question of truth, the accompanying concern of transcendent order emerges at the outset of the episode. The boat signifies that another knight is in trouble, and only a true peer can help: "que no puede ser librado dél sino por la mano de otro caballero" ("and can only be saved by the hand of another knight"). Don Quijote still believes that happenstance is the product of providential *fortuna*, that there is purpose behind seemingly chance occurrences.

Despite the uncertainty occasioned by the sceptical comments regarding our hero's consecrated status by the captives in the Cave of Montesinos ("cuando así no sea, paciencia y barajar" [II, 23, p. 217]), and by his financial inadequacy when asked there to lend money to Dulcinea, don Quijote commands Sancho to prepare for the adventure: "ata juntos al rucio y a Rocinante, y a la mano de Dios, que nos guíe; que no dejaré de embarcarme si me lo pidiesen frailes descalzos" ("tie the dun and Rocinante together to the tree, and may God's hand guide us, because a monastery-full of discalced friars will not prevent me from embarking" [262]). The potential contradiction between a venerable religious order and divine will generates a dissonance, as does the odd juxtaposition of God's *hand* and the bare *feet* of the friars. It is a curious variation on what El Pinciano termed "adjunto de lugar" ("proximity of place" [IX, 399]). Although I would not go as far as to claim that Cervantes is satirizing the friars in this scene, it is worth noting that Juan de Valdés did: "Ora sus, vedme aquí, 'más obediente que un fraile descalço quando es conbidado para algún vanquete'" ("And look at me now, 'more obedient than a discalced friar when invited to some banquet'" [131]). As Barbolani notes in her edition, the Erasmian quip was censored in Spain. In his seminal study of Erasmus's influence on Cervantes, Bataillon observes that "the men of the cloth who appear in Cervantes are almost always comic."[39]

Don Quijote attempts to alleviate Sancho's dismay at leaving behind the animals, and his reference to the mysterious powers that guide them commences the scene's linguistic comedy:

> Don Quijote le dijo que no tuviese pena del desamparo de aquellos animales; que el que los llevaría a ellos por tan longincuos caminos y regiones tendría cuenta de sustentarlos.
>
> – No entiendo eso de *logicuos* –dijo Sancho – , ni he oído tal vocablo en todos los días de mi vida. (II, 29, p. 263)
>
> [Don Quixote told him not to worry about leaving the animals unattended, because he who was going to care for them on a voyage of such longinquity would see to their animals' sustenance.
>
> "I don't know what you mean by longdrinkity," said Sancho, "and I've never heard such a word in all the days of my life."]

Although don Quijote excuses Sancho's misunderstanding of the Latinate "longincuos" ("que no estás tú obligdo a saber latín" – "you are not obliged to know Latin"), the knight resumes his erudite register, albeit with explanatory rephrasing: "*Santiguarnos y levar ferro*; quiero decir, embarcarnos y cortar la amarra con que este barco está atado" ("Cross ourselves and weigh anchor: in other words, board the boat and cut the mooring rope"). Such humour does not serve the exclusive function of undermining chivalric delusion. Sancho's solecisms and facetious etymologies draw attention to the physicality of words, thereby expressing his own corporeal, earthy values. El Pinciano's discussion of linguistic comedy dealing with the "body" of words contains fine illustrations of such comedy: "Vamos, pues, a las figuras; de las cuales digo que unas tocan al cuerpo del vocablo; otras al alma. Las que al cuerpo, o le añaden o quitan; otras ponen o mudan ... Mudando, como si alguno por decir tanto dijesse 'tonto'; añadiendo como por decir lengua latina decir lengua latrina y, por decir latina, decir 'latinaja'" ("Let's consider, then, those of figures; of which I say that some deal with the body of the word; others the soul. Those touching the body, either add to or subtract from it; others put on or change ... Changing, as when someone instead of saying 'so many' should say 'fool' [tanto/tonto]; adding as when instead of saying 'Latin tongue' says 'potty mouth' [latina/latrina] and, instead of saying Latin says dog Latin [latina/latinaja]" [402]).[40] Spitzer demonstrated how the great range of linguistic registers in *Don Quijote* has epistemological implications. Even if, as Close, Martínez Mata and others have argued, this does not involve the radical subjectivity of what Spitzer termed "hybrid reality," Cervantes does examine the dynamic relationship between characters' life (and reading) experience, language, and perception of the world. We will see further instances of this linguistic humour below.

Once underway, don Quijote embarks on a lengthy disquisition regarding the distance they have travelled. There is talk of the astrolabe and Ptolemy, the poles and Equator and the Indies. When, sensibly observing that he can simply look at the shore, Sancho refuses to gauge their position relative to the equinoctial line by checking whether his lice have died, don Quijote delivers himself of the following barrage: "que tú no sabes qué cosa sean coluros, líneas, paralelos, zodíacos, clíticas, polos, equinocios, planetas, signos, puntos, medidas, de que se compone la esfera celeste y terrestre; que si todas estas cosas supieras, o parte de ellas, vieras claramente qué de paralelos hemos cortado, qué de signos visto y qué de imágenes hemos dejado atrás, y vamos dejando ahora" ("because you don't understand about colures, lines, parallels, zodiacs, ecliptics, poles, solstices, equinoxes, planets, signs, points and measurements of which the terrestrial and celestial globe is composed; for if you did understand all these matters, or some of them, you would realize how many parallels we've crossed, how many signs we've seen and how many constellations we've left behind and are leaving behind even now" [264–5]). There is an impressive energy of comic accumulation here, but don Quijote is also indicating one of the virtues of the chivalric genre praised by the Canon of Toledo: "que era el sujeto que ofrecían para que un buen entendimiento pudiese mostrarse en ellos ... Ya puede mostrarse astrólogo, ya cosmógrafo excelente" ("they provided subject matter with which a good intelligence could express itself ... The author can show himself to be an astrologer, a skilled cosmographer" [I, 47, p. 566]). It is also quite similar to Burton's awestruck enumeration of cosmographical topics in his praise of books and study:

> But in all nature what is there so stupend as to examine and calculate the motion of the planets, their magnitudes, apogeums, perigeums, eccentricities, how far distant from the earth, the bigness, thickness, compass of the firmament, each star, with their diameters and circumference, apparent area, superficies, by those curious helps of glasses, astrolabes, sextants, quadrants, of which Tycho Brahe in his Mechanics, optics (divine optics), arithmetic, geometry, and such-like arts and instruments? (II. ii. 4, p. 95)

Of course, Cervantes does not suggest that don Quijote is modelling the type of ideal narrative, based on verisimilitude and variety, outlined by the Canon. Rather than epic *perfección y hermosura*, don Quijote's creation is absurdly hyperbolic, and subverted on numerous counts. For one, his speech is framed by Sancho's virtuosic mishearings and informal etymologies: from Ptolomeo and cosmógrafo, he comes up with "puto y gafo, con la añadidura de meón, o meo, o no sé como" ("with his sexy butts and his tomfoolery, and what's more a great pornographer, or whatever it was you said"), causing one of the few incidences in which the Caballero de la Triste Figura actually laughs. But, as in Burton's wonder at the folly and range of human endeavours, the variety and detail of don Quijote's account carries a peculiar force, as does the "layering effect" – seen also in his discussion of giants – of referencing so many concepts that had contemporary currency.[41]

Don Quijote insists that Sancho conduct the experiment of checking for lice:

> [T]órnote a decir que te tientes y pesques; que yo para mí tengo que estás más limpio que un pliego de papel liso y blanco.

Tentóse Sancho, y llegando con la mano bonitamente y con tiento hacia la corva izquierda, alzó la cabeza, y miró a su amo, y dijo:

– O la experiencia es falsa, o no hemos llegado adonde vuestra merced dice, ni con muchas leguas.

– Pues ¿qué? –preguntó don Quijote – . ¿Has topado algo?

– ¡Y aun algos! –respondió Sancho. (265)

["[S]o I repeat: feel yourself, go fishing for lice, because it's my firm belief that you're freer of them than a sheet of smooth white paper."

Sancho slipped his hand gently in and slowly down towards the back of his left knee, and then he looked up at his master and said:

"Either the whole of the experiment's baloney or we haven't gotten to where you say, not by a long way."

"What?" asked Don Quixote. "Have you found something?"

"Quite a few somethings," Sancho replied.]

Sancho's expressive coinage – the plural "algos" – confirms not only what looking over at Rocinante and the ass on shore tells them (that they have not travelled very far), but also that it was foolish of don Quijote to assume that Sancho would be *limpio*. When the caged don Quijote and Sancho debate the former's presumed enchantment in Part I, there is a similar linguistic, epistemological and scatological humour. To disabuse his master, Sancho asks if he has felt the need to relieve himself, since enchanted knights would not experience such imperatives. But Sancho's terminology confuses don Quijote:

– No entiendo eso de *hacer aguas*, Sancho; aclárate más, si quieres que te responda derechamente.

– ¿Es posible que no entiende vuestra merced de hacer aguas menores o mayores? Pues en la escuela destetan a los muchachos con ello. Pues sepa que quiero decir si le ha venido en gana de hacer lo que no se escusa.

– ¡Ya, ya te entiendo, Sancho! Y muchas veces; y aun agora la tengo. ¡Sácame deste peligro, que no anda todo limpio! (I, 48, p. 575)

["I do not understand what you mean by 'doing numbers,' Sancho; you must be more explicit if you wish me to give you a clear answer."

"How can you not know about doing number one and number two? It's the very first thing you learn at school. Look, what I'm asking is if you've felt the urge to do what you've got to do."

"Oh, now I understand you, Sancho! Yes, yes, often; indeed I am feeling it at this very moment. Do save me from my plight, for things in here are none too clean!"]

Once again, linguistic variety is foregrounded, don Quijote identifying with the more genteel "hacer lo que no se escusa" over Sancho's graphic and earthy "hacer aguas." The brief interrogation proves that no occult force is as work, and don Quijote is released from his cage in order to attend to his bodily function, "de donde vino más aliviado ..." ("from where he returned much eased and comforted" [I, 49, p. 577]). Building on Spitzer and others, Maureen Ihrie has discussed how the linguistic imprecision and vacillations in *Don Quijote*, by characters and author alike, contribute to a cognitive flexibility that is akin to the scepticism of Montaigne and Francisco Sánchez (Ihrie 30–4). In other words, Ihrie reveals a ludic "to-and-fro" on the epistemological level of the work.

The *barco encantado* scene also produces numerous echoes from the *batanes* (fulling mills) episode (I, 20), in which Sancho's uncontrollable corporeality deflates don Quijote's vision of adventure. One is the narrator's adverbial flourish when describing Sancho's surreptitious lowering of his trousers: "bonitamente y sin rumor alguno, se soltó la lazada corrediza con que los calzones se sostenía" ("with great stealth to loosen the running knot that was all that held his breeches up" [I, 20, p. 245]).[42] Sancho also ties the legs of Rocinante, which can be read as a literal intervention in the symbolic agent of chivalric *fortuna*: the knight's giving free reign to the whims of his horse, we recall, represents his confidence in the transcendent significance of all "accidents."[43] And in his attempt to delay don Quijote's departure by saying dawn is near, it is Sancho who claims knowledge of the constellations, and don Quijote – observing that it is too dark even to see the stars – who undermines the speculation with empirical evidence. Sancho concedes this point, while offering two interesting counterarguments: "Así es ... ; pero tiene el miedo muchos ojos, y vee las cosas debajo de la tierra, cuanto más encima en el cielo; puesto que, por buen discurso, bien se puede entender que hay poco de aquí al día" ("That's true enough ... but fear has many eyes, and it can see things under the ground so it's got even more reason to see them up in the sky, but anyway you only need to use your head to realize that it isn't long till daybreak" [I, 20, p. 240]). On the one hand, Sancho entertains the quasi-perspectivistic notion that one's state of mind enhances perception – an idea that will find fertile ground in the underworld and celestial realms of the Cueva de Montesinos and Clavileño episodes. On the other hand, the practical squire falls back on *buen discurso*: they both have a sense of how long it has been dark, and may thus reasonably anticipate the arrival of dawn. This recalls don

Quijote's concluding logic in his discussion of Morgante, his common-sense deduction based on the information that the giant slept indoors.

After the scatological climax on the Ebro ("¡y aun algos!"), which undermines don Quijote's navigational and cosmographical references, Sancho washes his hand: "Y sacudiéndose los dedos, se lavó toda la mano en el río, por el cual sosegadamente se deslizaba el barco por mitad del corriente, sin que le moviese alguna inteligencia secreta, ni algún encantador escondido, sino el mismo curso del agua, blando entonces y suave" ("And he shook his fingers and gave his hand a good wash in the river, along which the boat was gliding with the current, not propelled by any secret intelligence or hidden enchanter but by the flow of the water, as yet calm and smooth" [II, 29, p. 265]). The absence of a transcendent order is perhaps deceptively simple. An indifferent if pleasant natural phenomenon ("el mismo curso del agua") contrasts with the malign forces of an "encantador escondido" – or any secret intelligence, for that matter. Without putting too fine a point on it, we can at least say that such "teleological ambivalence" is inherent to Cervantine irony, forming a distinct subset of his epistemological humour. Don Quijote's final sickness and relegation to the domestic sphere is described with a similar technique: "o ya fuese de la melancolía que le causaba el verse vencido, o ya por la disposición del cielo, que así lo ordenaba, se le arraigó una calentura, que le tuvo seis días en la cama" ("either out of the depression brought on by his defeat or by divine ordination, he was seized by a fever that kept him in bed for six days" [II, 74, p. 586]). As a "hygienic" explanation is entertained alongside a Providential one, the apparent exemplarity of the knight's rejection of folly and his Christian death remains open to question.[44]

As the farce resumes in the collision with the flour-coated millers, the description of a terrified Sancho sustains the tension between divine and prosaic causality: "Púsose Sancho de rodillas, pidiendo devotamente al cielo le librase de tan manifiesto peligro, como lo hizo, por la industria y presteza de los molineros, que oponiéndose con sus palos al barco, le detuvieron" ("Sancho fell to his knees, sending devout prayers up to heaven to deliver him from such a manifest peril – which it did, acting through the quick thinking of the millers, who thrust their poles up against the boat and stopped it" [266]). While his behaviour is similar to the frenzied ceremony and superstition in Erasmus's "The Shipwreck," Sancho's prayers are answered, but in the mundane form of the "industria y presteza" of the millers. Where is the "mano de Dios" or "inteligencia secreta"? As Basilio memorably answered the astonished onlookers at Camacho's wedding a few scenes earlier, "¡No 'milagro, milagro,' sino 'industria, industria!'" ("No miracle, no miracle: ingenuity, ingenuity!" [II, 21, p. 200]). After a narrow escape from drowning, Sancho renews his pieties, this time requesting deliverance from don Quijote: "puesto de rodillas, las manos juntas y los ojos clavados en el cielo, pidió a Dios con una larga y devota plegaria le librase de allí adelante de los atrevidos deseos y acometimientos de su señor" ("Sancho knelt and pressed his hands together and riveted his eyes on heaven and prayed to God in a long and fervent petition to deliver him in the future from his master's foolhardy plans and enterprises" [266–7]). And don Quijote makes a final, frail appeal to divine assistance, before recognizing that his is not the "mano de caballero" capable of prevailing in such an incoherent world: "Dios lo remedie; que todo este mundo es máquinas y trazas, contrarias unas de otras. Yo no puedo más" ("May God send a remedy; for everything in this world is trickery, stage machinery, every part of it working against every other part. I have done all I can" [II, 29, p. 267]). As in the aftermath of Maese Pedro's puppet show, there is nothing left for don Quijote to do but pay for what he has demolished. It is tempting to conclude that Cervantes's protagonist has undergone a transformation similar to that of another salient novel of the period, Marie-Madeleine de Lafayette's *Zayde*: "Lafayette's hero has moved from fortune to chance, from a subjectively coherent though delusional narrative to a world that no longer has such coherence" (Lyons, "From Fortune to Randomness" 168). Don Quijote's exasperation at the "máquinas y trazas, contrarias unas de otras" retains a hint of belief in malign forces (the "trazas"), but his inability to make sense of the chaos ("contrarias unas de otras") brings him close to a modern, *aleatory* notion of experience.

While don Quijote and Sancho are undoubtedly the objects of laughter, the range of their responses and the subject matter encompassed turns our laughter, at first confidently uncomplicated, in sometimes unexpected directions: notions of narrative truth, of the comparative efficacy of chivalric and religious ceremony, of common sense versus theory, as well as elements of pathos and doubt, create complexity of character. Don Antonio's famous plea against Sansón Carrasco's "curing" of don Quijote expresses another aspect of the ambiguity I have been trying to bring out:

> – ¡Oh señor –dijo don Antonio – Dios os perdone el agravio que habéis hecho a todo el mundo en querer volver cuerdo al más gracioso loco que

hay en él! ¿No veis, señor, que no podrá llegar el provecho que cause la cordura de don Quijote a lo que llega el gusto que da con sus desvaríos? ... y si no fuese contra caridad, diría que nunca sane don Quijote, porque con su salud, no solamente perdemos sus gracias, sino las de Sancho Panza su escudero, que cualquiera dellas puede volver a alegrar la misma melancolía. (II, 65, pp. 536–7)

["Oh, my dear sir!" said Don Antonio. "God forgive you for the offence you've committed against the whole world in attempting to restore the funniest madman in it to his senses! Don't you see, sir, that the benefits of Don Quixote's recovery can't be compared with the pleasure that his antics provide? ... And if it weren't uncharitable to do so I'd say that I hope Don Quixote never recovers, because if he does we won't only lose his antics but those of his squire Sancho Panza as well, any one of which is enough to make melancholy itself merry.]

Pleasure ("el gusto") and combating melancholy once again displace rational didactic concerns ("el provecho"). Don Antonio's lament provides a final variation on Horace's man from Argos, although in this case the primary beneficiaries are not the deluded subject, but those with whom he comes into contact ("todo el mundo"). Nevertheless, the effects of Carrasco's remedy are swift and, despite the conventional exemplarity implied in the knight's renouncement of chivalry, don Antonio's concern seems to resonate with that of Horace's disillusioned man: "Egad! you have killed me, my friends, not saved me" (435).

R.B. Gill observed that "[c]omedy not only wishes its form to be appreciated, it demands that our understanding of the strategies of meaning become part of the meaning itself" (244). I have indicated some ways in which *Don Quijote* compels the reader to appreciate the strategies of creating literary meaning, as well as those by which the world beyond the book is ordered. Cervantes explored the satirical "comedy of correction" in the uncompromising Licenciado Vidriera. Although I will argue below that he tired of the severe judgments of such a figure, it is worth recalling that the prologue to the *Novelas ejemplares* invites the reader to approach the stories as a billiards game in the public setting and open air of "la plaza de nuestra república." Such communal, transparent imagery would seem consistent with the didactic function and unambiguous meaning of satire – much like the "romance" stories of the collection serve the ostensible purpose of reinforcing social structure and a clear hierarchy of values. As noted above, *Don Quijote* describes us in very different terms, alone at home, involved in a possibly subversive activity: "estás en tu casa donde eres señor della ... y sabes lo que comúnemente se dice, que debajo de mi manto, al rey mato" ("you are sitting in your own home, where you are the lord and master ... and you know that common saying, 'Under my cloak a fig for the king'" [I, Prólogo]). Given such freedom and lack of the homogenizing laughter of a surrounding community, the reader of *Don Quijote* may delightfully lose his or her bearings.

Such perspective-shifting laughter brings us to a fundamental connection between comedy and play. The distance and doubt created by humour make one aware of alternate ways of making sense of the world, and, consequently, of the possible arbitrariness of established structures of meaning and behaviour. As Huizinga muses, this can lead to a ludic perspective on existence itself:

> Surveying all the treasures of the mind and all the splendours of its achievements we shall still find, at the bottom of every serious judgement, something problematical left. In our heart of hearts we know that none of our pronouncements is absolutely conclusive. At that point, where our judgement begins to waver, the feeling that the world is serious after all wavers with it. Instead of the old saw: "All is vanity," the more positive conclusion forces itself upon us that "all is play." (212)

And so we return to Democritus and Heraclitus, and to Seneca's advocacy of the former: "when he surveys the world, the man who does not hold back his laughter shows a greater mind than the one who does not hold back his tears, since he gives vent to the gentlest of the emotions and thinks there is nothing important, nothing serious, or even miserable, in the whole great state of life" (*On the Tranquility of the Mind* 135–6). A fundamental sense of epistemological instability, experienced by nearly all great thinkers – religious and secular – elicits varying reactions. Cervantes's comic scepticism differs from contemporary cultivators of *desengaño*, of the "old saw" of *vanitas*. We can say that, contrary to Spariosu's assertion (see above p. 26), Cervantes *was* able to consider the possibility that "all is play." But he did so mostly in a festive, un-anxious and non-dogmatic manner. A consideration of a few key sequences of Part II of *Don Quijote* will elucidate further Cervantes's ludic vision.

Ludic Scepticism in *Don Quijote* II

The intricate theatricality of the world in Part II contributes to the sense of disorientation discussed above. From the early encounter with the travelling actors (II, 11) and with the *caballero de los espejos* (II, 12–16), to the *bodas de Camacho* (II, 19–21), the prolonged habitation with the Duke and Duchess, and the entertainments in Barcelona with don Antonio, the atmosphere is highly festive and playful. The question arises as to whether the play is depicted as appropriate or excessive, elitist or popular. Much of the issue hinges on what type of laughter don Quijote and Sancho provoke. Close argues that the Duke and the Duchess exemplify contemporary good taste and decorum, and their laughing play with knight and squire affirms an exclusive, aristocratic norm more-or-less endorsed by Cervantes (*Cervantes and the Comic Mind*). In his insistence on the validity of understanding *Don Quijote* in terms of Bakhtinian carnivalesque, Iffland maintains that the Duke and Duchess are themselves the objects of some satire, and that the Catalán Antonio Moreno, with his connection to Roque Guinart, is a potentially subversive, popular figure (*De fiestas*, especially III). In Iffland's reading, the transition from the controlled precincts of the Ducal palaces to the beach and streets of Barcelona, during the solstice ritual of the Noche de San Juan, marks a movement from an elitist to a communal festivity, and an expansion of the novel's comic range. Redondo, who also investigated the carnival and Lenten imagery of *Don Quijote*, links the festive atmosphere in Part II with a general levity in Spain following the death of the stern Felipe II and the ascent of the more licentious Felipe III (*Otra manera de leer*).

Barber's discussion of the festive in Shakespeare helps us consider Cervantes's depiction of ritual and ceremony in the context of a broader epochal shift:

> The Renaissance … was a moment when educated men were modifying a ceremonial conception of human life to create a historical conception. The ceremonial view, which assumed that names and meanings are fixed and final, expressed experience as pageant and ritual – pageant where the right names could march in proper order, or ritual where names could be changed in the right, the proper way. The historical view expresses life as drama. People in drama are not identical with their names, for they gain and lose their names, their status and meaning – and not by settled ritual:

> the gaining and losing of names, of meaning, is beyond the control of any set ritual sequence. (193)

Compared to a play like *Henry IV.1*, *Don Quijote* may not seem to offer much of an examination, or "problematization" – as Auerbach might put it – of history, kingship, or political legitimacy. Rather, one could say that Cervantes depicts a protagonist who adheres to a "ceremonial view" of life and then, somewhat surprisingly, becomes surrounded by others who derive great pleasure from consciously cultivating such a view. Having ritualistically named himself, his horse and his lady, and then arranging a knighting ceremony at the inn, don Quijote fixes his identity. But even though other characters in the work seem aware that a ceremonial conception is antiquated, it is not clear that they are prepared to embrace Barber's "historical view," which points towards the uprooted subject of modernity.[45] But it is a historical conception of human life that emerges in *Don Quijote*, and adds dimension to its festive atmosphere. For the games played by the characters do not affirm any fixed and final meanings; they are exercises in *imaginación* and *industria*. Much of the novel's comedy is generated by exposing the lack of correspondence between names and meanings, and when the names can no longer be substantiated, the reality that reasserts itself is not always so reassuring.

Sometimes don Quijote and Sancho recognize the fictional identity of their counterparts, as when Sancho comments on the privileged status of the travelling actors in the *carro de la muerte*: "Sepa vuesa merced que como son gentes alegres y de placer, todos los favorecen, todos lo amparan, ayudan y estiman" ("They're a cheerful crowd and they amuse people, you see, so everybody looks after them, everybody protects them and helps them and likes them" [II, 11, p. 118]). His observation would seem to support what Redondo characterized as the festive orientation of contemporary Spanish society, and it partially prefigures the reception our adventurers will receive in many episodes. It is a partial prefiguration because their treatment as *gente de placer* involves a good deal of ridicule along with the privilege. And it is the ridicule, along with the extraordinary measures taken by the Duke and Duchess to create comic spectacles, that makes us wonder whether Cervantes always endorses their merrymaking, or whether they themselves become the comic object. Of particular interest are the moments when Sancho seems to gain the upper hand, inverting the dynamic of deceivers and deceived. His Clavileño narrative and performance as governor involve an unexpected level of agency on his part, at times suggesting a recognition and mastery of the games staged by the Duke and Duchess.[46] The ducal pair also loses control of their games due to unplanned incursions from "reality," for instance in the challenge between don Quijote and Tosilos (II, 56). As we shall see, it is in such moments of friction between the play sphere and reality where the nature of both game and player are most tellingly revealed: when Tosilos falls in love with doña Rodríquez's daughter, when Sancho discovers his true self amidst the tumults of Barataria, when don Quijote and don Diego happen upon the lion cart.

Even a character commonly held up as an exemplar of good sense, moderation, and civic responsibility, don Diego de Miranda, is theatrical. His elaborate outfit and equine adornments inspire don Quijote to name him *el Caballero del Verde Gabán* (II, 17, p. 168), and the two *hidalgos* reflect each other in curious ways.[47] Although there has been some critical debate regarding the significance of don Diego's attire and pursuits, Murillo aptly observes that his outfit "emphasizes the festive and springtime air of this series of adventure."[48] But whereas the Duke and Duchess seem decadent in the single-minded excess of their pursuit of pleasure, don Diego's life corresponds to a presumably sober social and metaphysical order. His regular attendance at mass, acts of charity, and careful maintenance of his domestic sphere round out a life of moderation, piety, and good sense, much like the equilibrium of *otium, negotium, templum* expressed in the prologue to the *Novelas ejemplares*. His pastimes, "de la caza y pesca" ("of hunting and fishing" [II, 16, p. 153]), are "entretenimientos pacíficos y prácticos" ("pacific and practical pastimes" [Redondo, *Otra manera* 270]), and recall Tomé Cecial's recommendation to Sancho: "Harto mejor sería que los que profesamos esta maldita servidumbre nos retirásemos a nuestras casas, y allí nos entretuviésemos en ejercicios más suaves como si dijésemos, cazando o pescando; que ¿qué escudero hay tan pobre en el mundo, a quien le falte un rocín, y un par de galgos, y una caña de pescar, con que entretenerse en su aldea?" ("It would be much better for those of us who are in this accursed service to go back home and amuse ourselves there with gentler activities, like for example hunting or fishing; for what squire is there in the world so poor that he hasn't got a hack, a couple of greyhounds and a fishing-rod to amuse himself with in the village?" [II, 13, p. 129]). The proximity to the domestic sphere, the modesty and moderation – not to mention the edible bounty – would seem to represent Pedro de Guzmán's ideal of *ocio con negocio* (see ch. 1 of this study).

The only minor dissonance in don Diego's life comes from his son, who, instead of applying himself to the more practical and remunerative study of law, is obsessed with poetry. While his literary engagement does not lead him to take up a lance, he does compete in a "justa literaria," an artistic *agon*. Don Quijote defends Lorenzo's vocational choice, appealing to the humanist ideal of allowing the student to follow his own individual inclination. Don Quijote's subsequent apology for poetry, justifying composition in the vulgar languages, describing the relationship between poetry and the other sciences, and art and nature, and again emphasizing the role of reader competence, compels his interlocutors to reconsider his presumed insanity. In his attempt to put literary experience into practice, don Quijote may exemplify excessive and naive reading; but he also critiques unrefined literary taste: "[la poesía] no se ha de dejar tratar de los truhanes, ni del ignorante vulgo, incapaz de conocer ni estimar los tesoros que en ella se encierran. Y no penséis, señor, que yo llamo aquí vulgo solamente a la gente plebeya y humilde; que todo aquel que no sabe, aunque sea señor y príncipe, puede y debe entrar en número del vulgo" ("[Poetry] must not be allowed into the company of rogues or the ignorant, vulgar crowd, incapable of recognizing or appreciating the treasures contained within her. And do not imagine, sir, that by 'vulgar crowd' I mean only the humble lower orders: everyone who is ignorant, even if he is a lord and a pillar of the community, can and should be considered one of the vulgar crowd" [155]). As mentioned above with regard to the discussion of giants, it is important to notice that don Quijote's lucid discourses do not only occur when the subject matter is safely segregated from knight-errantry novels. Like his debate with the Canon of Toledo (I, 47–50), in the company of don Diego and his son don Quijote participates in a fairly serious discussion of aesthetics, in which he sets forth substantive arguments. And so when their discussion later involves ethical and social matters, one is compelled to consider don Quijote's reasons more carefully.

Don Quijote's recklessness before the lions seems to signal a return to insanity. When don Diego attempts to dissuade him, the knight imperiously draws a distinction between the two men: "Váyase vuesa merced, señor hidalgo ... a entender con su perdigón manso y con su hurón atrevido, y deje a cada uno hacer su oficio. Este es el mío, y yo sé si vienen a mí, o no, estos señores leones" ("Sir hidalgo ... pray go away and play with your tame decoy partridge and your intrepid ferret, and let others proceed with their own business. This is my business, and

I know whether or not these lion fellows have come after me" [II, 17, p. 161]). If don Quijote's earlier affirmation of faith sets him at odds with the "empirical" Toledan merchants ("La importancia está en que sin verla lo habéis de creer" – "The whole point is that, without seeing her, you must believe" [I, 4, p. 100]), his challenge to the cart-driver, who is understandably concerned about his livelihood, rises to a Kierkegaardian pitch: "¡Oh hombre de poca fe!" ("Oh you of little faith!" [II, 17, p. 161]). Our "knight of faith," like Abraham, seems prepared to risk a gruesome death in defence of his belief.[49] And as with his physical compulsion of Sancho during the banquet with the goatherds in Part I, the lionkeeper's declaration confirms that there is no willing collaboration with don Quijote's chivalric game: "Seánme testigos cuantos aquí están como contra mi voluntad y forzado abro las jaulas y suelto los leones" ("All of you are witnesses of how I'm being forced against my will to let these lions out" [161]). Gone is the benevolent, nurturing authority don Quijote counselled to fathers with their sons: "y en lo de forzarles que estudien esta o aquella ciencia no lo tengo por acertado, aunque en persuadirles no será dañoso" ("and as regards forcing them to study this or that discipline, I consider it to be a mistake, although there would be no harm in trying to persuade them to do so" [II, 16, p. 155]). As we have seen, when persuasion fails, don Quijote is generally quite prepared to exercise force. It is the freed lion's reaction to him that undermines Kierkegaard's assessment, along with other romantic exaltations of the knight's spiritual virtues: "Hasta aquí llegó el estremo de su jamás vista locura. Pero el *generoso* león, más *comedido* que arrogante, no haciendo caso de las niñerías ni de bravatas, después de haber mirado a una y otra parte, como se ha dicho, volvió las espaldas y enseñó sus traseras partes a don Quijote, y con gran flema y remanso se volvió a echar en la jaula" ("His unparalleled madness reached even this far. But the *noble-hearted* lion, more *inclined to civility* than to despotism, wouldn't take any notice of posturing or bravado; and, having looked this way and that, as described, it turned round, showed Don Quixote its backside and, with the utmost composure and deliberation, lay itself down again it its crate" [164, my italics]). In another of his delightful inversions of species, Cervantes shows the lion possessing some of the qualities claimed by don Quijote's ennobling practice of knight errantry: "De mí sé decir que después que soy caballero andante soy valiente, comedido, liberal, biencriado, generoso, cortés, atrevido, blando, paciente, sufridor de trabajos, de prisiones, de encantos" ("Speaking for myself, I can say that ever since I became a knight errant I have been courageous, polite, generous, well-bred, magnanimous, courteous, bold, gentle, patient, and long-suffering in the face of toil, imprisonment and enchantment" [I, 50, p. 586]). The chivalric ideals enumerated by our knight are not ridiculous; it is his self-aggrandizement and consequent disregard for the situations of others that make him appear, in contrast to the lion, "más arrogante que comedido."

Nabokov's somewhat facetious tallying of don Quijote's defeats and victories as points in a tennis match does in fact reveal a structure and symmetry overlooked by many readers. This dialogic structure, a variation of what Torrente Ballester termed *contar jugando*, is also evident within episodes, in a sort of pendulum movement that confounds efforts to pass definitive judgment on the characters. When don Quijote acknowledges to don Diego the temerity of his behaviour, and provides a justification, he becomes less ridiculous again:

> Todos los caballeros tienen sus particulares ejercicios: sirva a las damas el cortesano; autorice la corte de su rey con libreas; sustente los caballeros pobres con el espléndido plato de sus mesas; concierte justas, mantenga torneos, y muéstrese grande, liberal y magnífico, y buen cristiano, sobre todo, y desta manera cumplirá con sus precisas obligaciones. Pero el andante caballero busque los rincones del mundo, éntrese en los más intricados laberintos; acometa a cada paso lo imposible; resista en los páramos despoblados los ardientes rayos del sol en la mitad del verano, y en el invierno la dura inclemencia de los vientos y de los yelos; no le asombren leones, ni le espanten vestiglos, ni atemoricen endriagos; que buscar éstos, acometer aquéllos y vencerlos a todos son sus principales y verdaderos ejercicios. (II, 17, p. 167)
>
> [Every knight has his part to play: let the knight courtier serve the ladies, add lustre to his king's court with his retinue, maintain poor knights at his sumptuous table, organize jousts, celebrate tourneys and show himself to be important, generous, magnificent and, above all, a good Christian, and if he does all this he will be fulfilling his own particular obligations. But the knight errant must search out the remotest corners of the world, make his way into the most complex labyrinths, at every step attempt the impossible, withstand on desolate plains the burning rays of the midsummer sun and in the winter the harsh inclemency of winds and ice; he must not be alarmed by lions, or dismayed by monsters, or daunted by dragons, because seeking these, attacking those and defeating them all is his principal and proper occupation.]

This is not the first time don Quijote's description of the hard life of the knight-errant casts the courtier in a dubious light. While the nobles of the court would seem to be fulfilling their role as exemplars of beauty and virtue, the emphasis on ceremony and spectacle suggests a superficiality to their activities: their jousts and tournaments, like the entourage of servants, are adornments of the king's majesty. But it is the knight errant who exposes himself to hardship and consequence, in venues that contrast with the sumptuous exhibitionism and safety of the court. The courtier's realm of experience is recreational and aesthetic, while the knight errant's is purposeful. The ambiguity of don Quijote's terminology points to this contrast: each has his particular *ejercicio*, which can suggest "exercise" in the sense of a recreational pursuit, the playing of a role, or an occupation or duty. When, responding to don Diego's warnings before the lion, don Quijote dismissively tells him to attend to his hunting and fishing, "y deje a cada uno hacer su oficio" ("let others proceed with their own business"), a similar fecklessness is implied. One "occupation" is to pass the time pleasantly; the other is to act valiantly. Of course, don Quijote accomplishes very little of practical value during his wanderings. His actions and identity, as we have been discussing in terms of the mimetic impulse, are even more of an aesthetic construct than don Diego's. But his play sometimes takes on unexpected dimension in the perspective it gives on "official society." Don Quijote's melodramatic account of the knight's activities above is, in fact, not so different from something Cervantes took quite seriously, as evidenced when the infantry captain persuades the protagonist to join the military in *El licenciado Vidriera*: "Puso las alabanzas en el cielo de la vida libre del soldado y de la libertad de Italia; pero no le dijo del frío de las centinelas, del peligro de los asaltos, del espanto de las batallas, de la hambre de los cercos, de la ruina de las minas, con otras cosas deste jaez, que algunos las toman y tienen por añadiduras del peso de la soldadesca, y son la carga principal della" ("He praised to the skies the soldier's free life and the easy ways of Italy; but he said nothing to him about the cold of sentry duty, the danger of attacks, the horror of battles, the hunger of sieges, the destruction of mines, and other things of this kind, which some consider to be the extra burdens of a soldier's life, when in fact they are the main part of it" [45]). The old martial values may be risible emanating from the anachronistic knight, but the early modern aristocracy does not fare so well by comparison.

Don Quijote proceeds to demonstrate his self-awareness when he explains the nature of true bravery, which lies between the polar vices of cowardice and recklessness: "y en esto de acometer aventuras, créame vuesa merced, señor don Diego, que antes se ha de perder por carta de más que de menos, porque mejor suena en las orejas de los que lo oyen 'el tal caballero es temerario y atrevido' que no 'el tal caballero es tímido y cobarde'" ("and in this matter of undertaking adventures, Don Diego, believe you me, it is better to lose the game through scoring too many points than through scoring too few, because 'such and such a knight is rash and foolhardy' sounds better in the hearer's ears than 'such and such a knight is timid and cowardly'" [II, 17, pp. 167–8]). Don Diego affirms the reasonableness of don Quijote's discourse, as well as its consistency with the rules of chivalry, and invites him back to his pleasant estate in terms that recall the recuperative stroll in the park at the end of the harrowing experience of *El coloquio de los perros*: "lleguemos a mi aldea y casa, donde descansará vuestra merced del pasado trabajo, que si no ha sido del cuerpo, ha sido del espíritu, que suele tal vez redundar en el cansancio del cuerpo" ("let's make haste to reach my village and my house, where you'll be able to rest from your recent labours – if not labours of the body, then of the spirit, which often also make the body weary" [II, 17, p. 168]). Having concluded one of his most successful adventures, and one that will allow him to express his fortitude of spirit with the additional moniker of *el Caballero de los Leones*, don Quijote bestows upon don Diego a name associated with his own particular *oficio* of recreational hunting: *el Caballero del Verde Gabán*.

Clearly, don Quijote's heroism comes in for much qualification. One of the greatest instances occurs when Sancho deploys his master's own terminology while justifying his cheeky intrusion during the conversation of the Duke and Duchess upon the arrival of the dueña Dolorida:

> – Por lo que tiene de condesa –respondió Sancho, antes que el duque respondiese – , bien estoy en que vuestras grandezas salgan a recebirla; pero por lo de dueña, soy de parecer que no se muevan un paso.
>
> – ¿Quién te mete a ti en esto, Sancho? –dijo don Quijote.
>
> – ¿Quién, señor? –respondió Sancho –. Yo me meto, que puedo meterme, como escudero que ha aprendido los términos de la cortesía en la escuela de vuestra merced, que es el más cortés y bien criado caballero que hay en toda la cortesanía; y en estas cosas, según he oído decir a vuesa merced, tanto se pierde por carta de más como por carta de menos; y al buen entendedor, pocas palabras. (II, 37, p. 328)

["Being as she is a countess," Sancho replied before the Duke could, "I'd agree to Your Graces going to meet her, but being as she is a duenna I think you shouldn't budge an inch."

"Who told you to butt in like that, Sancho?" said Don Quixote.

"Who told me, sir?" Sancho replied. "I butted in all by myself, as well I can, being a squire who's learned courtesy in your school, the school of the most courteous and well-bred knight in all courteousness – and in these matters, as I've often heard you say, as much is lost by a point too many as by a point too few. And a word to the wise is enough."]

Sancho's initiative ("Yo me meto, que puedo meterme") parallels the numerous uninvited impositions of his master. His use of the same card-playing terminology as don Quijote has the effect of reducing the venerable principle of "erring on the side of valor" to cliché, much like when Sancho deflates don Quijote's tendentious metaphor on life and theatre (see above p. 152). The squire's hyperbolic play on "cortesía" recuperates the irony of the lion appearing more "generoso" and "comedido" than the arrogant knight. Sancho exercises a valor on the level of witty conversation rather than heroic action – a terrain highly valued by Cervantes.

The "translator" of the story seems to endorse don Quijote when, back at don Diego's house, he decides to excise a passage from the original text: "Aquí pinta el autor todas las circunstancias de la casa de don Diego, pintándonos en ella lo que contiene una casa de un caballero labrador rico" ("At this point the author describes every detail of Don Diego's house – all the contents of any rich gentleman farmer's dwelling" [II, 18, p. 169]). The materialist historicist's loss is our gain, as the omission is justified on the grounds of narrative truth: "porque no venían bien con el propósito principal de la historia; la cual más tiene su fuerza en la verdad que en las frías digresiones" ("because they aren't relevant to the principal purpose of the history, which derives its strength from its truthfulness rather than from dull digressions" [169]). Don Quijote is the principal source of our laughter – a phenomenon, as we saw, that signals the authenticity of his character (see I, 9). But the previous sequence indicates that, in addition to being funnier than don Diego, he may also be more interesting. Curiously, the "truth" of the narrative at this point of the novel is beginning to reside more and more with Sancho, as he takes don Quijote's teachings and applies them in his own inimitable manner.

The country wedding of Camacho and Quiteria, with its banquet, dances and theatrical spectacle, places don Quijote and Sancho in an overtly festive context, although one that is not free from social discord. What gives the episode a particular richness and resonance with the rest of the novel is the way it allows for the expression of material social concerns within a highly theatrical and literary frame. The destabilizing influence of money – a phenomenon examined by Cervantes in multiple episodes – is framed within the conventional topos of *amor* vs *interés*. Basilio prevails as the community, initially present to celebrate the wealthy Camacho, coalesces in defence of true love, which triumphs over the coercions of money. But the outcome is peculiar for many reasons. On the one hand, it can be seen as another example of literary escapism, a wish-fulfilment that can only occur in fiction. As such, it is an episode that seems to vindicate the archaic and aesthetic values of don Quijote, so recently challenged by his experience with the wealthy and practical don Diego. However, Basilio represents a worldly, modernized, and self-conscious version of romance. In Basilio, virtue prevails with the assistance of guile; or, perhaps more accurately, guile is shown to be a virtue, as his "cheating" of Camacho is validated by the onlookers. And Sancho is again a pivotal figure within the tensions set forth in the episode. He shares with Falstaff a sometimes salutary, sometimes suspect instinct for self-preservation over honour and virtue. It is a disposition that allows him to indulge in the festive atmosphere while also retaining a pragmatism that seems inimical to the spirit of play.

Basilio's qualities manifest themselves in his prowess at games: "él es el más ágil mancebo que conocemos, gran tirador de barras, luchador estremado y gran jugador de pelota; corre como un gamo, salta más que una cabra y birla a los bolos como por encantamento; canta como una calandria, y toca una guitarra, que le hace hablar, y, sobre todo, juega una espada como el más pintado" ("he's the nimblest lad we know, a great pitcher of the bar, a splendid wrestler and a superb pelota-player; he can run like a deer, jump farther than a goat and knock the skittles down like magic; he sings like a lark, and when he plays guitar you'd say he's making it talk, and, above all, he can fence with the best of them" [II, 19, p. 179]). Citing fray Alonso Remon, Redondo has noted how Basilio's games represent a compendium of contemporary rural recreation, with other Cervantine characters rounding out the list: deliverers of rustic witticisms and comic insults ("pullas"), formulaic oral narratives, and puppeteers (*Otra manera de leer* 69–84). A sort of vulgar counterpoint to aristocratic pursuits, such pastimes reflect the conditions of class. Rather than the noble hunt of large game, or the *justas y torneos*, which cultivate and reinforce martial ideals, the rustic bar-throwing, ball games, and running and jumping reflect a subsistence based on capacity for physical labour (we recall Sancho's enthusiastic praise for Aldonza Lorenzo's strong voice and her ability to throw the bar, I, 25, p. 312). In like manner, the *pullas* and oral narratives correspond to what Bakhtin called the *billingsgate* interaction of the lower classes, and the non-textual nature of illiterate narrative. Nevertheless, Basilio is a sort of rustic version of Castiglione's *cortesano*, his array of talents giving him social currency and an allure to the ladies. Quint argues that "the peasants Camacho and Basilio are made to stand in respectively for the moneyed parvenu and the old-style noble of the sword," and that the episode shifts the readers' sympathies, recently claimed by the virtuous and "modern" don Diego, back towards the chivalric values of don Quijote (*Cervantes's Novel of Modern Times* 115–23).

Don Quijote is naturally impressed with Basilio's sword-play, and declares him on that account alone worthy of marrying above his station. But Sancho seems impervious to the notion of play as an indicator of a superior spirit. For him, material advantage takes the day: "bien boba fuera Quiteria en desechar las galas y las joyas que le debe de haber dado, y le puede dar Camacho, por escoger el tirar de la barra y el jugar de la negra de Basilio. Sobre un buen tiro de barra o sobre una gentil treta de espada no dan un cuartillo de vino en la taberna. Habilidades y gracias que no son vendibles, mas que las tenga el conde Dirlos" ("Quiteria would be a right idiot to turn down the jewels and finery Camacho can give her and must already have given her, and go instead for Basilio's bar-pitching and fencing. You won't get so much as a half-pint of wine in a tavern for a good pitch of your bar or a neat thrust with your sword. Those are skills and gifts that aren't saleable, even if Count Dirlos himself has them" [II, 20, p. 187]). On this account, Sancho would seem to side with the "modern" values of commerce, in opposition to his master's chivalry.

The primary game of the episode, then, is an *agon* between the wealthy Camacho and the talented and wily Basilio, and for which the community of revellers will serve as judge. Cervantes also includes a "play within the play," as the dance spectacle featuring the maiden, nymphs, allegorical figures, and savages stages the conflict between love and riches. As Iffland noted, the episode, like the famous debacle with the *rebuznos*, is one in which an *agon festivo* threatens to break out into real strife, the play sphere impinged upon by purposive reality (*De fiestas* III, ch. 4). When don Quijote speculates that the presentation has been skewed in favour of Camacho, Sancho declares himself untroubled by any lack of fair play: "El rey es mi gallo: a Camacho me atengo" ("My money's on the winner – I'm sticking by Camacho" [193]). His cock-fighting exclamation in favour of Camacho shows him siding with the powerful – a vulgar and opportunistic inclination, in don Quijote's view. But Sancho claims to be adjusted to the times ("el día de hoy, mi señor don Quijote, antes se toma el pulso al haber que al saber" – "nowadays, don Quixote, you're more respected for having than for knowing" [194]) and proceeds admirably to hold his own in a discussion about mortality. Indeed, the lavish feast seems to have stimulated his faculties as, upon seeing the bride, he lets fly a barrage of praise in which he applies the linguistic lesson given him during the "colloquy of the squires" (II, 13) by Tomé Cecial: "¡Oh hideputa, y qué cabellos ...!" ("Son of a whore, what hair ...!" [II, 21, p. 196]). The ambivalence of Sancho during the entire scene is characteristic of his progress in Part II, during which his earthy authenticity and materialism generate increasingly powerful oratorical and artistic abilities. His cupidity and cowardice are not merely deflationary counterpoints to don Quijote's exalted values; they have their own vital force. His Falstaffian nature is illustrated when, following Basilio's deception, the two camps draw their swords, and don Quijote brandishes his lance: "Sancho, a quien jamás pluguieron ni solazaron semejantes fechurías, se acogió a las tinajas, donde había sacado su agradable espuma, pareciéndole aquel lugar como sagrado, que había de ser tenido en respeto" ("Sancho, who never found any pleasure or comfort in such exploits, took refuge among the cooking pots from which he'd acquired his delectable skimmings, thinking of this place as sacred, and therefore one that would be respected" [201]). When Lazarillo de Tormes describes "mi paraíso panal" ("my bready paradise" [Tratado II]), it is a sign of his abject desperation, and of the stark absence of the spiritual at the priest's abode. For the corpulent Sancho, the irony is lighter. The food does not represent marginal subsistence, but a joyful indulgence. Sancho's "material spirituality" will be even clearer when we observe how his defence of pleasure and the preservation of life becomes associated not just with food, drink, and a salary, but also with the life of the imagination.[50]

As mentioned, if his embodiment of true love seems to represent an antiquated – or at least incongruously aesthetic – order, in contrast to the new wealth of Camacho, in other ways Basilio expresses quite modern sensibilities. Barber writes that "Shakespeare presents patterns analogous to magic and ritual in the process of redefining magic as imagination, ritual as social action" (193). The non-dogmatically secular sensibilities I have been tracing in Cervantes have much to do with "redefining magic as imagination," and Basilio's famous exclamation upon recovering from his self-impalement is a striking instance, and not an isolated one. The entire episode comprises another series of playful subversions of authoritative metaphysical and literary ideas. Basilio's apparently mortal desperation, brought on by the *bella ingrata*, recalls Grisóstomo's death – an event that his friends attempt to frame in the staid tradition of exalted love poetry, despite Marcela's rational proof to the contrary. But Basilio *pastor* is also something of a *pícaro*, as demonstrated by his surprising revival after winning Quiteria's hand in marriage as a sort of last rite:

> Quedaron todos los circunstantes admirados, y algunos dellos, más simples que curiosos, en altas voces comenzaron a decir:
> – ¡Milagro, milagro!
> Pero Basilio replicó:
> – ¡No "milagro, milagro," sino industria, industria! (200)

> [All the bystanders were astonished, and some of them, more simple-minded than inquisitive, began to cry:
> "A miracle, a miracle!"
> But Basilio replied:
> "No miracle, no miracle: ingenuity, ingenuity!"]

If don Quijote's contemptuous "¡Hombre de poca fe!" at the lionkeeper casts himself in a peculiarly transcendent light, the priest's overture is similarly allusive, although his hand in the wound completes a demystification: "El cura, desatentado y atónito, acudió con ambas manos a tentar la herida, y halló que la cuchilla había pasado, no por la carne y costillas, sino por un cañón hueco de hierro" ("The priest, shaken and astonished, felt the wound with both hands, and found that the blade hadn't passed through Basilio's flesh and ribs but through a hollow iron tube that he'd fitted around them" [201]). The distinction between different reactions to the trick is significant, as it echoes conventional demarcations of reading competence. Some, aligned with the traditional *vulgo*, are *simples*. They are unsophisticated in their processing of the experience, and therefore liable to deception. The *curiosos* are like the *lector discreto*, who can comprehend the true meaning of the text.

A similar division of the public, also involving a hollow tube, occurs in the *cabeza encantada* episode (II, 62). Building on George Haley's analysis of the Maese Pedro episode as a compact exposition of the novel's larger narrative dynamic, Cory Reed examined the *cabeza encantada* as a game that allegorizes the act of reading: "The enchanted head episode illustrates the process of constructing, presenting, and receiving a rhetorical system, which, like the conventions of chivalric romance, may have undesirable effects in the untrained reader" (17). Reed discusses such technological devices in the context of Renaissance interest in *lusus scientiae*, or games of knowledge, in which the apparently magical effects (e.g., a bronze head that can respond to questions) are revealed to be artifice. Such games may thus be appreciated on different levels, according to the condition of the participant: as miraculous phenomena (by the credulous *vulgo*), or as examples of human ingenuity and imagination (by the knowing *discreto*). In the case of the *cabeza encantada*, the disillusionment of the player does not result in destruction of the game, but rather an enjoyment of it in a more refined manner: the reader delights in the artifice, but also retains a certain distance that prevents confusion between art and reality. Which is to say, we are never completely "disillusioned." We enter into the play sphere while retaining a reserve of rationality and judgment, a faculty that mediates between our play identity and our place in the "real world."

In the subaltern world it is often clarifying to *tocar las apariencias con la mano*, as a healthy empiricism dispels ignorance and superstition. It would be an exaggeration to claim that Cervantes is proposing a parallel between religious belief and superstition. However, as Redondo and others have suggested, he does tend to treat issues such as miracles, ostentatious religious ceremony, and marriage with a scepticism and subtlety discordant with the ideological purity of the Counter Reformation.[51] As mentioned, in his study of Avellaneda's attempt to correct and sanitize Cervantes's unruly masterpiece, Iffland shifts the focus from the theological – as contained in Gilman's account – to the social, the concerns of which insistently emerge even in scenes of carnivalesque play: "it should be noted how Cervantes introduces a very serious social issue amidst this episode built upon festive principles. Highlighted here is the very real class conflict that exists between the Camachos and Basilios of the world. Don Quijote ends up championing the latter, as one would expect."[52] While don Quijote's defence of the virtuous and wily Basilio seems a noble protest against the corrosive influence of money, Sancho's backing of Camacho represents a peculiar combination of material, social, and spiritual concerns.

Sancho derives a transcendent feeling from that which he can *tocar con la mano*. For him, the bounty of the country festivities, funded by Camacho's riches, is an Eden made actual, a materialization of don Quijote's lettered *edad dorada*. And so when he is compelled to leave, it is to Sancho an exile, a fall from grace: "y así se dejó atrás las ollas de Egipto, aunque las llevaba en el alma; cuya ya casi consumida y acabada espuma, que en el caldero llevaba, le representaba la gloria y abundancia del bien que perdía; y así, congojado y pensativo, aunque sin hambre, sin apearse del rucio, siguió las huellas de Rocinante" ("and he left the fleshpots of Egypt behind him, even though he was carrying them in his soul; and their skimmings in the stew-pan, by now almost consumed and spent, conjured up visions of the glory and the abundance of the good cheer that he was forsaking; and so, anguished and dejected, even though not hungry, he followed, without dismounting from his dun, in Rocinante's footsteps" [202]). As was clear after the four days with don Diego, don Quijote's imperative to seek adventure, to right wrongs in the age of iron, is inimical to comfort and carefree abundance. Sancho's leave-taking in the footsteps of his master's horse, "asenderado y triste," in some ways resonates with one of literature's momentous exits: "Some natural tears they dropp'd, but wip'd them soon; / The World was all before them, where to choose / Their place of rest, and Providence their guide: / They hand in hand with wand'ring steps and slow, / Through *Eden* took their solitary way" (*Paradise Lost* XII, l. 648–9). While the juxtaposition of Sancho leaving the Bodas de Camacho and the finale of Milton's Christian epic may seem gratuitous, Cervantes's elaborate incorporation and reworking of the pastoral throughout *Don Quijote* involves a good deal of attention to the genre's spiritualization of nature. And, as we have seen, this process involves both demystification (*desengaño*) and revitalization. If Cervantes shows the "erotic pastoral" and the "pastoral of the self" to be problematic, bringing components of the broad Golden Age tradition into conflict, individuality and community are at least partially reconciled in Part II, particularly after Sancho's abdication of his governorship and renewed understanding of his authentic self. Consistent with what Iffland felicitously terms his "fe barriguda" ("fat-bellied faith" *De fiestas* 524), much of Sancho's recuperation of value and meaning depends on a reaffirmation of the physical world. A passage in the "Gambler's Mass" ("Officium lusorum") of *Carmina Burana* anticipates Sancho's spirituality: "Epicurus proclaims: / A sated belly is best off. / The belly will be my god, / a god such as the gullet seeks. / His temple is a kitchen where it smells divine."

Although Sancho laments his exile from the *lugar sagrado* of Camacho's feast, the arrival at the Ducal palaces will seem providential to knight and squire alike. It is the novel's most elaborately theatrical sequence, and presents an arguably decadent human inclination to play. The artifice is so successful that an inspired don Quijote exclaims, somewhat surprisingly, that it is the first time he truly believes himself to be a knight-errant (II, 31). Again, it is not always easy to discern whether the Duke and Duchess are satirized by Cervantes, as critics like Redondo and Iffland maintain, or whether, as Close sought to demonstrate, they represent an approved norm of upper-class leisure and humour. Sancho's debate with the ducal pair regarding the hunt would again seem to lay bare the novel's ambivalence.

When the pacifistic Sancho objects to hunting for its brutality, his exchange with the Duke registers contemporary views on social class and leisure, and reveals Sancho's conception of the role of play in an ideal republic:

> Antes os engañéis, Sancho –respondió el duque – ; porque el ejercicio de la caza de monte es el más conveniente y necesario para los reyes y príncipes que otro alguno. La caza es una imagen de la guerra: hay en ella estratagemas, astucias, insidias para vencer a su salvo al enemigo; padécense en ella fríos grandísimos y calores intolerables; menoscábase el ocio y el sueño, corrobóranse las fuerzas, agilítanse los miembros del que la usa, y, en resolución, es ejercicio que se puede hacer sin perjuicio de nadie y con gusto de muchos; y lo mejor que él tiene es que no es para todos, como lo es el de los otros géneros de caza, excepto el de la volatería, que también es sólo para reyes y grandes señores. Así que, ¡oh Sancho!, mudad de opinión, y cuando seáis gobernador, ocupaos en la caza y veréis cómo os vale un por ciento.
>
> – Eso no –respondió Sancho– : el buen gobernador, la pierna quebrada, y en casa. ¡Bueno sería que viniesen los negociantes a buscarle fatigados, y él estuviese en el monte holgándose! ¡Así enhoramala andaría el gobierno! Mía fe, señor, la caza y los pasatiempos más han de ser para los holgazanes que para los gobernadores. En lo que yo pienso entretenerme es en jugar al triunfo envidado las pascuas, y a los bolos los domingos y fiestas; que esas cazas ni cazos no dicen con mi condición, ni hacen con mi conciencia. (II, 34, p. 307)

["No, you're mistaken there, Sancho," the Duke replied, "because the sport of hunting bears and boars is more suitable and indeed necessary for kings and lords than any other. Hunting is an image of war: it involves stratagems, ruses and traps to defeat the enemy in safety; while practicing it, one suffers extreme cold and intolerable heat, one scorns idleness and sleep, one strengthens one's body and increases the agility of one's limbs, and, in short, it's a sport that can be practiced without harming anybody while giving pleasure to many; and what's best of all about it is that it isn't a sport for every Tom, Dick and Harry, as many other kinds of hunting are, except hawking, which is also reserved for kings and great lords. So, my dear Sancho, you'd better change your mind and, when you're a governor, practice hunting and you'll soon see how you reap the benefit."

"Not likely," Sancho replied. "A governor's place is in the home. A fine thing it'd be if people came to see him on business, tired out from their journey, and he was out in the countryside having himself a good time! A pretty pickle the government would be in if he went and did that! On my faith, sir, hunting and such pastimes are more for loafers than for governors. How I'm going to amuse myself is playing brag at Easter and Christmas, and skittles on Sundays and fiesta-days – that hunting lark doesn't suit my nature or sit easy on my conscience."]

The Duke's defence of hunting is broadly consistent with the parameters of licit recreation considered in Part I of this study. But his conventional appeal to the criterion of harmlessness ("sin perjucio de nadie") as a justification for play is disallowed by Sancho, for whom animals deserve a place in the equation of suffering and compassion. It is the same sort of compassion don Quijote had extended to the plant world during his deliberations on whether to perform his love-sick penitence in the manner of Orlando or Amadís ("¿para qué quiero yo tomar trabajos agora de desnudarme de todo, ni dar pesadumbre a estos árboles, que no me han hecho mal ninguno?" – "why should I take the trouble to strip naked or torment these trees that have never done me any harm?" [I, 26, p. 319]). The Duke also cites the venerable arguments that the hunt teaches strategy and forges a sturdy character and constitution in the rigors of the outdoors. While this recalls don Quijote's praise of chivalric pursuits over the delicate life of the courtier (II, 17), the behaviour of the Duke and Duchess corresponds more to that of the *cortesano*. Moreover, the type of hunting – extolled by the Duke for its exclusivity – and its large entourage comprise a marked contrast with the modest recreational hunting of don Diego, as well as that recommended by Tomé Cecial (II, 13). Indeed, it suggests the sort of excess and precariousness satirized by Zabaleta (see above pp. 107–8). Margaret Greer has considered how Cervantes juxtaposes the Duke and Duchess's inhumane hunt with their mean-spirited pranks on the knight and squire, and contrasts such pastimes with Sancho's humanistic governance: "Through this framing, Cervantes makes the hunt and the evening 'entertainment' that follows the occasion to critique the ethics and cruel practices of the high aristocracy, a critique with a striking kinship to those of Montaigne and Erasmus" (205). What previously possessed both a practical and aesthetic function – martial training and the demonstration of a heroic ethos inherent in the nobility – has become an idle spectacle, the excesses and distortions of which reflect the degraded condition of the first estate.

As governor, Sancho prefers his accustomed pastimes of cards and bowling. Just as the *tratadistas* recommended for the sangleyes in the Philippines (see above pp. 117–18), Sancho would contain such games within prescribed festive days, unlike the Duke and Duchess, who seem to aspire to a perennial state of holiday.[53] Anticipating his governorship, Sancho demonstrates an understanding of the need for a balance between *otium* and *negotium*. The former should not overflow its bounds, compromising the latter ("A fine thing it'd be if people came to see him on business, tired out from their journey, and he was out in the countryside having himself a good time!"). Sancho's productive orientation would seem to challenge the accepted social phenomena of "algunos que ni tienen, ni deben, ni pueden trabajar" ("those who do not, should not, and cannot work"), those for whom ball games, chess, billiards, and reading help while away the time (I, 32). But we will also see that he has an appreciation for play; he does not wholly dismiss, as he did when siding with Camacho over Basilio, "[h]abilidades y gracias que no son vendibles" ("skills and gifts that aren't saleable").

As Étienvre has pointed out ("Paciencia y barajar" 57–8), Castillo de Bobadilla's *Política de corregidores* (1597) is a possible source for Sancho's governing philosophy. Like Sancho, Bobadilla held up the industrious bee as an example for humankind, and disdained those who lived off "el sudor ajeno" ("another's sweat" [380]). While I will argue that Sancho's judgments are generally more compassionate than the Counter-Reformation orthodoxy of Castillo de Bobadilla, the latter's comments on municipal government provide an illuminating perspective for Sancho *gobernador*, and give further support to the possibility that the episode contains satire of the high nobility. In contrast to the big-game hunting of the Duke and Duchess, Bobadilla describes the *ronda* as a "caça nocturna" ("nocturnal hunt") a necessary and productive endeavour. He cites classical examples of the ruler who, "cuando los ciudadanos dormían, y otros estavan en banquetes y juegos entretenidos, el andava vigilante por los muros de la ciudad" ("while the citizens slept, or others were at banquets and diverting games, he walked vigilantly along the city walls" [374–5]). In light of the feasting and playing ducal pair, Sancho seems a prudent governor indeed.[54]

While making the rounds of his *ínsula*, Sancho states his intent to do away with idleness: "vamos a rondar, que es mi intención limpiar esta ínsula de todo género de inmundicia y de gente vagamunda, holgazanes y mal entretenida; porque quiero que sepáis, amigos, que la gente baldía y perezosa es en la república lo mesmo que los zánganos en las colmenas, que se comen la miel que las trabajadoras abejas hacen" ("let's make our rounds: I'm planning to rid this island of all sorts of rubbish and tramps and idlers and layabouts, because I'll have you know, my friends, that useless, lazy people in a society are like drones in a beehive, eating up the honey that the worker bees produce" [II, 49, p. 406]). Does the episode comprise a progressive satire of a decadent nobility, a humanistic affirmation of unpretentious good sense and judgment in the person of Sancho, or an elaborate ploy to set up the naive simpleton for a comic fall? The butler's reaction to Sancho's initiative expresses the multi-directional quality of Cervantes's humour: "Cada día se veen cosas nuevas en el mundo: las burlas se vuelven en veras y los burladores se hallan burlados" ("In this world every day brings a new surprise; jests turn into earnest, and jesters find the tables turned upon them" [406]).[55]

Given Sancho's folkloric roots, his function as judge can be considered within the tradition of the equivocal country trials Huizinga studied, which illustrate again the connections between play and law: "those satirical and comic sessions that used to be held in peasant courts, particularly in Germanic countries, where all sorts of minor offences were judged and punished, mostly sexual ones ... That they are situated midway between play and seriousness is evidenced by the 'Saugericht' of the young men of Rapperswil, from which appeal could be made to the Petty Sessions of the town" (86). Governor Sancho's judgments seem sound enough that few of the townspeople would require appeal to an official jurisdiction. He and his entourage happen upon two men knife-fighting, and find that gaming is the cause of their dispute:

> Vuestra merced sabrá que este gentil hombre acaba de ganar ahora en esta casa de juego que está aquí frontero más de mil reales, y sabe Dios cómo;

> y hallándome yo presente, juzgué más de una suerte dudosa en su favor, contra todo aquello que me dictaba la conciencia; alzóse con la ganancia, y cuando esperaba que me había de dar algún escudo, por lo menos, de barato, como es uso y costumbre darle a los hombre principales como yo, que estamos asistentes para bien y mal pasar, y para apoyar sinrazones y evitar pendencias, él embolsó su dinero y se salió de la casa. (406–7)
>
> [The fact is that this fine fellow here has just won more than a thousand reals in that gaming house over there, and God in heaven knows how he did it, and I was watching the game and decided more than one dispute in his favour, against all the dictates of my conscience; he got up with his winnings, and just when I was expecting him to give me an escudo or two at the very least, as a tip – because it's the normal custom to give one to leading citizens like myself who are there to earn a precarious living, and to support injustice and avoid disputes – he pocketed his money and walked out.]

As in the genre paintings of the period (see Figures 3 and 4), the complicity between the player and spectator represents a violation of Vives's ideal play structure, in which the players cede to the judgment of a presumably just audience ("Remember that those who watch are as the judges of the game, and cede to their rulings without showing signs that you disagree. This way the game is recreation"). Of course, one cheat cannot be sure of honest treatment by another, and the player's refusal to give the corrupt spectator a tip has a humorous logic: "y que para señal que él era hombre de bien, y no ladrón, como decía, ninguna había mayor que el no haberle querido dar nada; que siempre los fulleros son tributarios de los mirones que los conocen" ("and there was no better proof that he was an honest man and not the thief he'd been made out to be than the fact that he hadn't been prepared to give him anything, because swindlers always pay their dues to the onlookers who know them" [407]). The swindler has upheld a veneer of fair play in his very act of cheating the other cheat. For such reasons, Bobadilla, who states that "al Corregidor conviene interponerse en las questiones y renzillas, y escusar que no se vengan a damnificar" ("it is fit for the Mayor to intervene in disputes and arguments, and to prevent them from causing damage" [385]), affirmed that "los muñidores de juegos y los miradores deven ser castigados casi por las mismas penas que los jugadores" ("the game managers and onlookers should be punished by almost the same penalties as the players" [377]). Sancho designates thirty *reales* of the gambler's fine to the incarcerated poor, and the *mirón* is to take one hundred *reales* along with ten years of exile for idleness: "y vos, que no tenéis oficio ni beneficio, y andáis de nones en esta ínsula" ("And you, without job or an income, scrounging your way through life on this island" [408]). While directed at the lowly *vagamundo*, Sancho's decree has unflattering implications for the leisurely Duke and Duchess. Bobadilla explicitly extends the principle: "devrian todos los hombres, para conservarse en sus estados, trabajar y tener sus adaptados oficios y ejercicios" ("all men, in order to preserve themselves in their estates, should work and have their appropriate jobs and activities" [381]); "los Reyes, y Consejos, y Governadores devrian mucho proveer al remedio de la gran ociosidad introduzida en las Republicas, y que se diessen mas las gentes al trabajo, *aunque ricos*, por no degenerar de la propia naturaleza" ("Kings, and Councils, and Governors should very much provide for the remedy of the great idleness introduced in the Republics, and the people should be given to work, *even though wealthy*, in order not to degrade their own nature" [382, my italics]).[56]

Sancho's desire nearly to eradicate *otium* in favour of *negotium*, however, proves excessive – or at least utopian amidst contemporary social realities. The *escribano*'s reply to Sancho expresses a sense of pragmatic compromise that, in light of human imperfection and the destructive results of demanding purity, contains its own wisdom:

> Contra otros garitos de menor cantía podrá vuestra merced mostrar su poder, que son los que más daño hacen y más insolencias encubren; que en casas de caballeros principales y do los señores no se atreven los famosos fulleros a usar de sus tretas; y pues el vicio del juego se ha vuelto en ejercicio común, mejor es que se juegue en casas principales que no en la de algún oficial, donde cogen a un desdichado de media noche abajo y le desuellan vivo. (408)

> ["But you'll be able to flex your muscles on other, lesser gambling dens, they're the ones that do the most damage and cover up the most iniquities: in the houses of high-ranking gentlemen and nobles, famous card-sharpers don't dare to get up to their tricks, and since the vice of gambling has become such common practice it's better for it to happen in top people's houses than at some tradesman's place where they'll trap a poor wretch in the small hours and flay him alive."]

Not only would it be politically risky for Sancho to challenge the gambling house of a powerful aristocrat; the gambling that takes place in such houses is generally better regulated than in the smaller houses, thus providing a more acceptable manner to allow a vice that cannot be completed suppressed. The *escribano*'s accommodation is similar to that of Bobadilla, who stipulates that his prohibitions "no se entiende con algunas casas de cavalleros, o personas ciudadanas principales, donde suelen juntarse a jugar, mas por via de entretenimiento y conversacion, que a juegos rezios, pues alli no se sacan baratos para velas, ni hay otros desordenes que en las tablagerias cosarias, y donde se juegan juegos prohibidos" ("do not apply to some gentlemen's houses, or principal citizens, where they convene to play more for entertainment and conversation than at rough games, since there they do not use the decks to take advantage of each other, nor are there other disorders as in habitual gambling, and where prohibited games are played" [377]). Bobadilla suggests that the card-playing nobles adhere to the ideal of urbane recreation, with its courteous order and conversation. Sancho, perhaps recognizing the limits of a governor's purview before powerful interests, leaves the question open: "Ahora, escribano ... yo sé que hay mucho que decir en eso" ("Now, thanks to the clerk ... I can see that there are lots of ins and outs to this question" [408]).

Étienvre has discussed the debate on gambling houses as another Cervantine endorsement of *eutrapelia*, of his qualified belief that such play may be conducted in an honest, socially acceptable manner: "That, relating to the enunciated. But, on the other hand, as far as the enunciation, all games are of hustlers, there is no entertainment without deception."[57] As colourful scenes from *Rinconete y Cortadillo*, *La ilustre fregona*, and elsewhere confirm, Cervantes was fascinated with uncouth and disorderly card-playing, and his attitude regarding such sanitizing reform is difficult to pin down. A case in point is don Quijote's peculiar stance on another seemingly irrepressible social vice: "Porque no es así como quiera el oficio de alcahuete: que es oficio de discretos y necesarísimo en la república bien ordenada, y que no le debía ejercer sino gente muy bien nacida" ("Because the pimp's trade is no ordinary trade; it must be carried out by intelligent people and it is absolutely essential to any well-ordered society, and only the well-born should exercise it" [I, 22, p. 269]). Don Quijote's remedy for degenerate pimping is similar to that of the *escribano*'s suggestion for gambling: the potential harm can be mitigated through regulation by the upper classes, who are presumably less susceptible to the activity's corruption. Although he does not mention Bobadilla, García Santo-Tomás examined how reformers of the period attempted to contain the social threat of gambling by promoting card-playing only among homogenous gatherings of the upper class, the civilized houses of which contrast with the subterranean gambling dens: "The perils of chance have thus to be reserved for those who can afford them, that is, to the unproductive hands of the privileged. The deck of cards must be an orderly, chivalric, harmless companion to the male urbanite much like the sword, the gloves, the *bigotera*, and the snuff-box, a sign of social capital to be shared with equals on a specific timeframe" (161). As we noted above, this type of reform and accommodation is essentially conservative, meant to solidify existing social structures and identities. We will see a far more ironic representation of social stability, based on rule-bound play and its associated card decks, in *Rinconete y Cortadillo*.

Beyond the specific types of leisure (hunting, gambling, etc.) discussed in Part II of *Don Quijote*, a larger game taking place is the elaborate scenarios created by the Duke and Duchess. The nobles exploit the imaginative aspirations of don Quijote and Sancho, as well as the circumstances of their subjects. Of particular interest are the moments when such circumstances confound the carefully structured spaces devised by the Duke and Duchess, with sometimes unexpected results. One example is the young girl brought to Sancho during his *ronda*: "los consabidores de las burlas que se habían de hacer a Sancho fueron los que más se admiraron, porque aquel suceso y hallazgo no venía ordenado por ellos, y así, estaban dudosos, esperando en qué pararía el caso" ("those who knew about the hoaxes being played on Sancho were the most amazed of all, because this event, this meeting, hadn't been planned, and so they were perplexed as they awaited the outcome" [II, 49, pp. 410–11]). This encroachment of reality on the play sphere consists of another *mujer encerrada* – a literary convention of particular interest to Cervantes, whose numerous enclosed women form the basis of incisive psychological and social analyses. Although it functions as one of the many comic, *entremés*-like interludes that make up Sancho's governorship, there are associations, excesses, and an anticipated denouement that give the scene disturbing, Zayaesque overtones: the girl's total confinement, ten years and counting, imposed by her father on the death of his wife; the male characters' desires and assumptions regarding marriage. In typical Cervantine fashion, the episode also contains a good deal of commentary on narration and reception.

Having disguised herself as a boy, the girl escapes her father's house at night, driven by a universal impulse: "quisiera yo ver el mundo" ("I wanted to see the world" [412]). Her interest had been piqued by news of the entertainments enjoyed beyond her enclosure:

> Cuando oía decir que corrían los toros y jugaban cañas, y se representaban comedias, preguntaba a mi hermano, que es un año menor que yo, que me dijese qué cosas eran aquéllas y otras muchas que yo no he visto; él me lo declaraba por los mejores modos que sabía; pero todo era encenderme más el deseo de verlo. Finalmente, por abreviar el cuento de mi perdición, digo que yo rogué y pedí a mi hermano, que nunca tal pidiera ni tal rogara ... (412)

> [Whenever I heard talk about bullfights and mock battles and plays, I asked my brother, who's a year younger than me, to tell me about these things, and about others that I've never seen; he explained it all as best he could, but this only made me long even more desperately to see it for myself. In the end, to cut short the story of my undoing, I have to tell you that I begged and entreated my brother, and I wish I'd never begged or entreated him to do any such thing ...]

Her endeavour carries strong literary and ludic associations. No only is she motivated by a wish to observe the recreational spectacles of the "real world," her initial attempt to satisfy this curiosity through a narrative account merely serves to increase her desire for first-hand experience, resulting in the siblings donning disguises and sallying forth. It is the quixotic pattern in miniature, pointing again to the perils of narrative, and the possibility that it can lead to action. In the context of the girl's transgression, the entertaining spectacles (bulls, tournaments, theatre) would appear to carry the negative connotations warned of by the moralists examined earlier in this study. Her characterization of the entire affair as the story of her perdition, suggesting she has succumbed to vice, is reinforced by Sancho, whose judgment places an exemplary seal on the episode: "que la doncella honrada, la pierna quebrada, y en casa; y la mujer y la gallina, por andar se pierden aína; y la que es deseosa de ver, también tiene deseo de ser vista. No digo más" ("a lass's place is in the home, and women and hens are lost by gadding, and the woman who wants to see wants to be seen. That's all I've got to say" [414]). But such formulaic pronouncements, like the rhyming couplets with which Juan Manuel concludes his stories in *El conde Lucanor*, or the ready epithets applied by the offended male shepherds to Marcela, fail to encapsulate the complexity of the girl's situation.[58] The extremity of her condition ("ni sé qué son calles, plazas, ni templos, ni aun hombres" – "I don't know anything about streets or squares or churches or even men") brought on a melancholy that seems entirely justified: "Este encerramiento y este negarme el salir de casa, siquiera a la iglesia, ha muchos días que me trae muy desconsolada" ("Being locked up like this and never allowed to leave home, not even to go to church, has been making me feel depressed for a long, long time" [412]). Furthermore, her action has not been rash; she has reflected upon it and attempted to exercise good judgment, "pareciéndome que este deseo no iba contra el buen decoro que las doncellas principales deben guardar a sí mesmas" ("I didn't believe this wish infringed upon the decorum that young ladies of rank are supposed to observe" [412]). We recall that, in contrast to its traditional theological association with hubris, Cervantes often uses "curiosidad" to express a spirit of empiricism and inquiry. The girl's curiosity is not the pathological excess of the "impertinente" of Part I (chs. 33–5), nor is her role-playing as a portal to freedom as transgressive as the picaresque escapade of Avendaño and Carriazo, an adventure that certainly does go against the "buen decoro" of their station. A vague justification of the girl's escape by Sancho's party recalls another similarity with these boys, even as it points to a crucial difference: "todo lo atribuyeron a su poca edad" ("they put it all down to their youth" [414]). If her actions might be accepted as the license of youth, we are reminded that *mocedades* comprise a masculine rite of passage. Given the stifling limitations of her situation, Cervantes seems to critique the patriarchal perspective of Sancho and his men, and to validate the girl's desire to see bullfights, tournaments, and theatre.[59]

The unexpected appearance of the runaway further complicates the Duke and Duchess's entertainment by introducing the disordering force of *eros*. Sancho's insinuation notwithstanding ("the woman who wants to see wants to be seen"), such desire seems to have no part in the girl's motivation to see the world. It is, rather, the male characters who are stricken by her beauty (and that of her brother), and whose plans suggest an uneasy resolution:

> Quedó el maestresala traspasado su corazón, y propuso de luego otro día pedírsela por mujer a su padre, teniendo por cierto que no se la negaría, por ser él criado del duque; y aun a Sancho le vinieron deseos y barruntos de casar el mozo con Sanchica su hija, y determinó de ponerlo en plática a su tiempo, dándose a entender que a una hija de un gobernador ningún marido se le podía negar. (415)

> [The steward was left with his heart transfixed, and he resolved to ask her father for her hand in marriage the very next day, certain that this

> wouldn't be denied to one of the Duke's own servants; and Sancho even felt the inclination to marry his daughter Sanchica to the lad, and decided to raise the matter for discussion when the time was right, in the belief that no prospective husband could be refused to a governor's daughter.]

In the aftermath of the *Bodas de Camacho*, and with the spectre of Marcela looming in the background, such a sense of entitlement and obligation in the realm of love has disturbing implications. As *El celoso extremeño* affirmed, male attempts to coerce and control the love object are doomed to failure.

Sancho's impatient condensation of the girl's narrative provides an interesting correlative to the inadequacy of his popular wisdom, expressed in proverbs. Miffed at her drawn-out account and its accompanying rhetorical gestures ("tantas lágrimas y suspiros"), he suggests a more concise telling: "que con decir: 'Somos fulano y fulana, que nos salimos a espaciar de casa de nuestros padres con esta invención, sólo por curiosidad, sin otro designio alguno', se acabara el cuento, y no gemidicos, y lloramicos, y darle" ("because if you'd just said, 'We're so-and-so and so-and-so, and we left our parents' house to have a bit of fun, in these disguises, just out of curiosity, without any other thought in mind,' that would have been that, without any whining or blubbering or going on and on and on" [414]). Although Sancho's version does hone in on the essence of the activity – "sólo por curiosidad" – it seems clear that Cervantes does not consider the deprivations (ten years' enclosure) that led to her curiosity insignificant. So while Sancho's narrative sensibilities have progressed markedly since his ridiculously circuitous storytelling in Part I, the scene demonstrates once again that the art of separating *verdad* from *frías digresiones* is a subtle one.

The intervention of *eros* in another of the ducal entertainments proffers an unexpected rapprochement and resolution. Don Quijote's battle against the lackey Tosilos in order to restore the honour of doña Rodríguez's daughter is an orchestrated spectacle and, as with the *cabeza encantada* and other deceptions, there are those in the know, and others who think the spectacle is real. But like the elaborate narrative and identity created by Dorotea as Princesa Micomicona (I, 29), this deception is structured upon a consequential reality: doña Rodríquez's daughter has, indeed, been deceived and dishonoured by a nobleman. With a pageantry evocative of the climactic trial scene in *Cantar de mío Cid* (see above pp. 18–21), instructions are given, terms laid out and accepted, the space cleared and platform erected with judges and plaintiffs, positions taken on the field, and drums and trumpets sounded – only to have Mars abruptly make way for Venus: "el niño ceguezuelo a quien suelen llamar de ordinario Amor por esas calles, no quiso perder la ocasión que se le ofreció de triunfar de una alma lacayuna y ponerla en la lista de sus trofeos" ("that little blind boy, commonly known by the name of Love, didn't like to waste this opportunity of triumphing over a lackey's soul and placing it on his list of trophies" [II, 56, pp. 463–4]). The manner of describing the chance intervention of an agonistic eros is comic, another example of Cervantes's delight in mixed allusions.[60] But Cervantes was certainly interested in the disruptive and uncontainable nature of love. We might recall old Carrizales's resolution, following much rational reflection and taking of account, *not* to marry: "Y estando resuelto en esto, y no lo estando en lo que había de hacer de su vida, quiso su suerte que, pasando un día por una calle, alzase los ojos y viese a una ventana puesta una doncella" ("And being resolved in this, but not about what he was to do with his life, his luck arranged that, walking along a street one day, he should raise his eyes and see a young girl in a window," *El celoso extremeño* 102). Nevertheless, the smitten Tosilos's offer of marriage is an antidote to the litigious and combative situation: "no quiero alcanzar por pleitos ni contiendas lo que puedo alcanzar por paz y sin peligro de muerte" ("I don't want to accomplish through strife and struggle what I can achieve in peace and without risk to life" [464]). But if the amorous scheming of Basilio resulted in the conflicting cries of *milagro* and *industria*, doña Rodríguez and her daughter recognize the discrepancy between their real-life malefactor and the adversary staged by the Duke: "¡Este es engaño; engaño es éste! … ¡Justicia de Dios y del Rey de tanta malicia, por no decir bellaquería!" ("This is a fraud, this is a fraud! … Justice, in the name of God and the King against such mischief, not to say villainy!" [465]). The confusion is compounded when don Quijote expounds upon enchanters, and Sancho, by way of illustration, points to the recent transformations of the *Caballero de los Espejos* and Dulcinea. The Duke, irritated by the disruption of the duel, adjusts to the new twist in his comedy, offering to lock up Tosilos for a fortnight, during which the true identity of "este personaje" ("this character") may be elucidated. Of course, this also serves as the Duke's revenge for Tosilos's diverging from his script.

Perhaps realizing that neither the justice of God nor King is likely to offer much recourse, the daughter of doña Rodríguez declares the following compromise: "Séase quien fuere este que me pide por esposa, que yo se lo agradezco; que más quiero ser mujer legítima de un lacayo que no amiga y burlada de un caballero" ("This man who wants me for his wife can be whoever he likes – I'm grateful to him all the same, because I'd rather be the lawful wife of a lackey than the cast-off mistress of a gentleman" [466]). Such practical accommodation in the face of confusion is akin to the ludic orientation of Cipión and Berganza, who are unable to clarify the meaning of their situation: "Pero sea lo que fuere, nosotros hablamos, sea portento o no ... mejor será que este buen día, o buena noche, la metamos en nuestra casa, y pues la tenemos tan buena en estas esteras y no sabemos cuánto durará esta nuestra ventura, sepamos aprovecharnos della" ("Well, anyway, we're speaking, whether it's a portent or not ... Let us make the most of this happy day, or happy night, and since we are so comfortable on these mats and we don't know how long this good fortune of ours will last, let us take advantage of it" [*El coloquio de los perros* 301]). Life itself is recognized as a game in which the wisest approach is, as Folly counselled, "blundering along in good company" rather than being paralysed by uncertainty or demanding a perfectly intelligible order. It is, to recall Barber's characterization, indicative of an "historical" consciousness, in which people recognize their life as drama ("they gain and lose their names, their status and meaning – and not by settled ritual: the gaining and losing of names, of meaning, is beyond the control of any set ritual sequence" [193]). As we noted with Maravall in the introduction to this study, such a vision involves a tactical bearing towards reality: "this world, however apparent it may be, is what confronts one and what must be dealt with; ... precisely because of its condition as illusory appearance, one must wholly enter into the game in terms of whatever becomes present to us" (198). The comic resolution of doña Rodriquez's daughter's situation reminds one of the multiple weddings in Shakespearian comedies. Their contrived nature and failure to resolve satisfactorily all tensions and injustices leave the audience with the rather uneasy sense of role-playing in real life, of the frequently provisional and incommensurate quality of status, meaning and names.

What also leaves a bitter residue to the Tosilos-Rodríguez episode is the dissatisfaction of the spectators, who had anticipated a violent outcome:

> En resolución, todos estos cuentos y sucesos pararon en que Tosilos se recogiese, hasta ver en qué paraba su transformación; aclamaron todos la vitoria por don Quijote, y los más quedaron tristes y melancólicos, de ver

que no se habían hecho pedazos los tan esperados combatientes, bien así como los mochachos quedan tristes cuando no sale el ahorcado que esperan, porque le ha perdonado, o la parte, o la justicia. (II, 56, p. 466)

[To be brief, the upshot of all these doings and sayings was that Tosilos was to be locked up to await the outcome of his transformation; everybody acclaimed Don Quixote's victory, although most people were dejected and depressed because the participants in the long-awaited combat hadn't hacked each other to pieces, just as boys are disappointed when the condemned man they've been awaiting doesn't come out to be hanged, because he's been pardoned either by the aggrieved party or by the judge.]

Cervantes's observations on the human propensity to take pleasure in the suffering of others, and how games themselves can be infused with cruelty, compels the reader to look more closely at the representation of the Duke and Duchess. For while the Duke had given specific instructions to Tosilos about how he was to vanquish don Quijote without injuring him, and how the Clavileño trick was to be performed *sin daño de barras* (352), there are numerous indications of mean-spiritedness and, not least, excess in the behaviour of the ducal pair. Redondo elaborates on a possible political dimension to Sancho's festive governorship: "In a Spain corroded by the [economic] crisis, in which bribery, prevarication and injustice triumph, the peasant, in the frame of a carnivalesque structure, that of a transitory topsy-turvy world, that which corresponds to a mock kingdom, and between outbursts of laughter, makes it possible to express this desire for rectitude and justice that could bring about the restoration of Spain. Festive discourse becomes, in this way, political discourse."[61] The *burlas con veras* technique that Redondo and others divine in Cervantes is consistent with what we have discussed as the humanist *serio ludere* tradition. But even if one does not argue for specific political implications, the strong festive and carnivalesque associations with so many of the episodes in Part II pose the question: when, following the liberating revelries of disguise and "misrule," will the Duke and Duchess return to seriousness, to the responsibilities of purposive existence? In other words, apart from the debatable issues of cruelty or topical references in the jokes, the seemingly exclusive dedication of the nobility to entertainment is a sign of decadence.

Don Quijote and Sancho, the ludic characters *por excelencia*, are the ones who end up articulating boundaries of time and space. Following the Tosilos episode, don Quijote becomes impatient with the leisurely atmosphere of the nobles:

> Ya le pareció a don Quijote que era bien salir de tanta ociosidad como la que en aquel castillo tenía; que se imaginaba ser grande la falta que su persona hacía en dejarse estar encerrado y perezoso entre los infinitos regalos y deleites que como a caballero andante aquellos señores le hacían, y parecíale que había de dar cuenta estrecha al cielo de aquella ociosidad y encerramiento; y así, pidió licencia a los duques para partirse. (II, 57, pp. 466–7)

> [Don Quixote thought it was high time to put an end to his lazy life in the castle, because he imagined that his person was being sorely missed as a result of allowing himself to remain shut up and idle amid the countless luxuries and delights that the Duke and Duchess lavished upon him as a knight errant, and he felt that he was going to have to render a detailed account to heaven of such indolence and seclusions; so one day he requested the permission of the Duke and Duchess to leave.]

While his assumptions regarding the effects of his absence in the real world are delusional, one is inclined to consider don Quijote's aversion to the idleness of the ducal palaces in the context of his critique of courtly life (e.g. during discussion with don Diego), and of contemporary moralists' more generalized condemnation of a superficial and "feminized" urban culture.[62] As noted in our discussion of card playing, García Santo-Tomás points out how such upper-class play could reinforce the nobility of the participants, as with the gambling of gentlemen who showcase *sprezzatura* (159). But the ideals of Castiglione were increasingly problematic amidst the social and economic turmoil of imperial Spain. As we saw, like other reformers and biblical commentaries upon which he draws, Bobadilla stresses the importance of productive use of time: "devrian todos los hombres, para conservacion de sus estados, trabajar y tener sus adaptados oficios y exercicios" ("all men, in order to preserve themselves in their estates, should work and have their appropriate jobs and activities" [381]). Such contexts, familiar to Cervantes, cast an unfavourable light on the ducal pair and the nobility they represent.

When Sancho announces the renunciation of his governorship, the ludic nature of his endeavours is manifest: "y con este presupuesto, besando a vuestras mercedes los pies, imitando al juego de los muchachos, que dicen 'Salta tú, y dámela tú', doy un salto del gobierno, y me paso al servicio de mi señor don Quijote" ("And now I've made up my mind about that, I'll just kiss your feet and copy children playing who shout, 'Jump and let me have it,' and I'll jump out of my government and go back to serve my master Don Quixote" [II, 56, p. 461]). Such role-switching, and its associated transport into alternate realms of experience, is part of a highly theatrical tradition, ranging from Cervantes's own folkloric trickster *Pedro de Urdemalas*, to Calderón's political-theological *Vida es sueño* to Ibsen's Faustian *Peer Gynt*. Redondo has described Sancho's move as an attempt to retain his carnivalesque identity before the Lenten deprivations of the doctor Pedro Recio ("En torno a dos personajes festivos" 172). In a series of articles, Forcione has examined the broader humanistic and literary contexts of Sancho's rise, from a validation of Erasmian folly and the carnivalesque, to the creation of a revitalized pastoral community. My inquiry into the ludic aspect of part II of *Don Quijote* is in many ways consistent with these studies.

A culminating moment in the refinement of Sancho's narrative skills is his re-articulation of the "hexameral poem" atop Clavileño. Forcione considers Sancho an artist figure who, like don Quijote during his *caballero del lago* fantasy (*DQ* I, 50), Periandro in *Persiles y Segismundo*, and Gracián's Critilio and Andrenio (*El Criticón*), challenges a classicist aesthetic that emphasizes verisimilitude and unity, and that would reflect a rational and ordered universe. What challenges this order is the play of the imagination.[63] Sancho describes the origins of his narrative in an act of subordination:

> Yo, señora, sentí que íbamos, según mi señor me dijo, volando por la región del fuego, y quise descubrirme un poco los ojos; pero mi amo, a quien pedí licencia para descubrirme, no la consintió; mas yo, que tengo no sé qué briznas de curioso y de desear saber lo que se me estorba y impide, bonitamente y sin que nadie lo viese, por junto a las narices aparté tanto cuanto el pañizuelo que me tapaba los ojos … (II, 41, p. 353)

> [I felt us going up, lady, just as my master told me, flying through the region of fire, and I wanted to peep out from under my blindfold, though when I asked my master for his permission he wouldn't let me – but I'm a bit on the curious side, keen to know what I'm not supposed to know, so, on the sly and so no one would see me, I pulled the blindfold aside next to my nose …]

It is Sancho's condition as a *curioso* that prompts him to peek – just like the young girl whose transgression he rebukes during his rounds as governor. We have noted the significance of this word in the period and in Cervantes, and we should recall that its meanings include "inquisitive" and "creative."[64] Both senses apply to Sancho: his inquisitiveness supposedly compels him to look; but rather than passively beholding forbidden knowledge, he delivers a peculiar narrative to an incredulous audience. Again, there are numerous echoes from Part I. While Sancho's narrative skills have developed considerably since his ridiculous account of the very specific number of goats transported across the river (I, 20), both stories have a certain tactical motivation: with the goat narrative, it is to detain his master; with Clavileño, it is to *compete* with his master (and the Duke), that is, to affirm his active participation in the creation of fictions. As we noted above, the surreptitious uncovering of his formidable buttocks during the night of the *batanes* strangely prefigures his action on Clavileño (Unwilling to relinquish his clasp of the mounted don Quijote's thigh, Sancho lowered his drawers "bonitamente y sin empacho" I, 20). But if Sancho's fully exposed haunches sallied forth into the dark night to perform a base if salubrious function (the production of excrement), the very slight exposure of the "eyes of his mind" is sufficient to bring forth an entire cosmos. Not only does his tale rival don Quijote's account of Montesinos (more on this below), but it can also be seen as a response to the Duke's fictions. As Redondo observes, "the squire clearly indicates that he is playing, entertaining his interlocutors and having fun himself, that he knows very well what he is doing."[65] Having self-consciously accepted the role of *bufón*, Sancho turns the tables on the Duke and Duchess, who cannot call his bluff without destroying their own illusion.[66]

Forcione examined how Sancho's Clavileño tale functions as a counterpart to don Quijote's Knight of the Lake narrative as a sort of Ariostan challenge to classicist order and authority. It is also indicative of the squire's rising dynamism, in absolute terms and in relation to his master. The parallel between Sancho's tale in Part II and don Quijote's account of the Cave of Montesinos is made explicit by the knight himself: "Sancho, pues vos queries que se os crea lo que habéis visto en el cielo, quiero que vos me creáis a mí lo que vi en la cueva de Montesinos. Y no os digo más" ("Sancho, since you want people to believe what you saw in the sky, I want you to believe what I saw in the Cave of Montesinos. I say no more" [II, 41, p. 355]). Like the Duke, don Quijote is forced into complicity by the fabulating Sancho. But don Quijote's underworld journey is replete with moribund imagery, and a sense of decay and inadequacy. While the *aporia* of unredeemed heroes in the Cave is emblematized by re-shuffling a card deck ("paciencia y barajar"), the regenerative vigour of Sancho's narrative is expressed by a different sort of play, his cavorting with the multi-coloured goats:

> Y sucedió que íbamos por parte donde están las siete cabrillas, y en Dios y en mi ánima que como yo en mi niñez fui en mi tierra cabrerizo, que así como las vi, ¡me dio una gana de entretenerme con ellas un rato…! Y si no lo cumpliera me parece que reventara. Vengo, pues, y tomo, y ¿qué hago? Sin decir nada a nadie, ni a mi señor tampoco, bonita y pasitamente me apeé de Clavileño, y me entretuve con las cabrillas, que son como unos alhelíes y como unas flores, casi tres cuartos de hora, y Clavileño no se movió de un lugar, ni pasó adelante. (II, 41, pp. 353–4)
>
> [And, as it so happened, we were going along by the side of the Seven Sisters, that we also call the Seven Little Goats in my part of the world, and I swear to God and my immortal soul that having been as I was a goatherd as a little lad, as soon as I saw them I felt the urge to go and play with them a bit. And if I hadn't satisfied that urge I reckon I'd have burst. So what am I going to do about it then? Without a word to a soul, or to my master either, I slipped as quiet as quiet from off Clavileño and I went to play with the goats, and they're as pretty as petunias or as flowers, for nearly three-quarters of an hour, and Clavileño didn't budge an inch from where he was standing.]

As with the imperatives of his digestive tract and his explosive laughter following the *batanes* episode (I, 20), Sancho's urge to play with the goats is irrepressible ("si no lo cumpliera parece que reventara"). But if those other compulsions emanate from the belly, asserting Sancho as a primarily physical being, his play impulse in Part II is equally associated with the spirit and imagination. The spasmodic, spontaneous flow of his narrative ("Vengo, pues, y tomo, y ¿qué hago?") wonderfully reflects the childlike associations of Sancho's account, inspired by his own early life experience. The contemplative distance and order of the cosmos, and the introspection of the pastoral *locus amoenus*, merge into palpable familiarity as Sancho descends from his mount to frolic among the goats. In don Quijote's cave narrative, the ravages of time are evident in Durandarte's mummified heart and Belerma's reduced beauty, and Dulcinea appears in her "fallen" state as a peasant in need of money (II, 23). Sancho's artistry reverses time, and there is even, for the sake of play, a fermata during Clavileño's swift progress through the spheres. Such parallels and inversions vis-à-vis don Quijote's storytelling reveal the success of Sancho's apprenticeship as his master's squire, and his ascendant role as a representative of "las fuerzas expansivas de la vida" ("the expansive forces of life" [Redondo, "En torno a dos personajes festivos" 172]). This exuberance and creative force is strongly linked to the ludic inclination, a faculty that – as Torrente Ballester commented, taking from Goethe – is both child-like and highly innovative. As we discussed above, it is also the principle that ultimately justifies Rodrigo Caro's erudite inquiry into games: "¿Qué mejor entretenerse que en aquello que en primer lugar merece este nombre? ¿Qué más inculpable diversión que en los sencillos juegos de la niñez?" ("what better entertainment than in that which originally deserves this name? What more harmless diversion than in simple childhood games?" [II, 259]).

As noted, Sancho's association with life and vitality has a strong pastoral element – most memorably expressed when he attempts to coax his moribund master back into the fields dressed as shepherds, "porque la mayor locura que puede hacer un hombre en esta vida es dejarse morir, sin más ni más, sin que nadie le mate, ni otras manos le acaben que las de la melancolía" ("because the maddest thing a man can do in this life is to let himself die, just like that, without anybody killing him or any other hands except the hands of depression doing away with him" [II, 74, p. 589]). Indeed, a significant measure of don Quijote's decline is his confused reticence upon stumbling into the *Arcadia fingida* a few scenes earlier: "se halló don Quijote enredado entre unas redes de hilo verde, que desde unos árboles a otros estaban tendidas; y *sin poder imaginar qué pudiese ser aquello*, dijo a Sancho [etc.]" ("Don Quixote found himself entangled in nets of green thread hanging between the trees; and *unable to imagine what this could be*, he said to Sancho" [II, 58, p. 476, my italics]). The recreation of the nobles, whose mimetic play is inspired by pastoral poetry, recalls the "hygienic" rural retreat in Boccaccio: "porque por agora en este sitio no ha de entrar la pesadumbre ni la melancolía" ("because for the present no sadness or grief is going to find its way into this place" [477]).[67] But don Quijote is increasingly unable to allay his melancholy; his play is more and more tenuous, and, as a consequence, his mind is less able to affirm his chivalric identity. Just a few pages prior to the discovery of the feigned Arcadia, don Quijote's comments before the carved images of saints reveal his state:

"Ellos conquistaron el cielo a fuerza de brazos, porque el cielo padece fuerza, y yo hasta agora no sé lo que conquisto a fuerza de mis trabajos" ("They conquered heaven by force of arms, for heaven suffers violence, and so far I do not know what I conquer by force of toils" [473]). Here it is instructive to recall our consideration of don Quijote's certainty following Rocinante's debacle at the end of the Marcela and Grisóstomo episode: "Y si no fuese porque imagino ... ¿qué digo imagino?, sé muy cierto, que todas estas incomodidades son muy anejas al ejercicio de las armas, aquí me dejaría morir de puro enojo" ("And if it were not that I imagine ... no, I do not imagine: I know for a certain fact – that all these discomforts are inseparable from the exercise of arms, I should be ready to die of sheer rage, here and now" [II, 15, p. 194]). While there is little reason to question the sincerity of the religious ceremony surrounding Alonso Quijano's death, the most consistent thread during the decline of his chivalric play is not a spiritual awakening or gradual acknowledgment of his folly, but rather a waning of his imaginative powers and a corresponding increase in sadness – the very emotion to which the prologue states opposition. As Sancho's exhortation above suggests, the force acting upon don Quijote is neither occult ("la mano de Dios"), nor heroic ("la mano de caballero andante"); it is the power of the afflicted mind ("las de la melancolía"). The logic of his assertion to Sancho in Part I holds true: when he is no longer able to imagine and affirm the consistency of his experience with his identity as knight errant, he does let himself die. If Clavileño is an ancestor of one of the magical horses in the *Arabian Nights*, don Quijote's decline is partly due to his inability to match Scheherazade's imaginative stamina.

Sancho's development, on the other hand, not only involves an expanding imaginative faculty, but also an increasingly social sensibility. If his refusal to sit and eat next to his master with the goatherds (II, 20) points to the deficiencies in both don Quijote's imagined community and in Sancho's wilful independence, the banquet with Ricote and his band of "pilgrims" is a resounding affirmation of brotherhood transcending linguistic, national and religious divisions:

> – *Español y tudesqui, tuto uno: bon compaño.*
>
> Y Sancho respondía: *Bon compaño, jura Di!*
>
> Y disparaba con una risa que le duraba una hora, sin acordarse entonces de nada de lo que le había sucedido en su gobierno; porque sobre el rato y tiempo se come y bebe, poca jurisdición suelen tener los cuidados. (II, 54, p. 450)

> ["*Espagnol et tudeski, tuto uno, bon compagno.*"
> And Sancho would repy:
> "*Bon compagno, jura Di!*" and he'd explode in a burst of laughter that lasted an hour, without a thought for what had happened during his governorship: because cares and worries don't wield much power while we're eating and drinking.]

The communication via signs and hybrid language, the bonding over food and drink, and the laughter that banishes preoccupations make for a scene of carnivalesque revelry. It also suggests a respite from history. Despite being a highly playful episode, the encounter with Ricote and his companions is also one of the most "problematic" scenes in *Don Quijote*, as Cervantes explicitly refers to the expulsion of the *moriscos*. The eating and drinking in good company have their accustomed therapeutic effects, suspending the indignities suffered by Sancho during his governorship, and diverting Ricote, who has graver worries to contend with. Apart from the sympathetic amiability of Ricote, the most acute implication of injustice comes in the form of his comment on the pilgrims' arrival in Germany, where "cada uno vive como quiere, porque en la mayor parte della se vive con libertad de conciencia" ("everyone lives as he pleases, because in most of the country there's freedom of conscience" [451]). For this reason Dunn has suggested that Ricote and his pilgrims represent a potentially subversive liminal community, a social arrangement that opposes official ideology (*Spanish Picaresque* 310). If Marcela's escape into the wilds comprises a challenge to the masculinist pastoral – not to mention the social expectations of the town in which she was raised – the Ricote scene is an appealing instance of what Turner called "spontaneous *communitas*": "Is there any of us who has not known this moment when compatible people – friends, congeners – obtain a flash of lucid mutual understanding on the existential level, when they feel that all problems, not just their problems, could be resolved, whether emotional or cognitive, if only the group which is felt (in the first person) as 'essentially us' could sustain its intersubjective illumination" (48). If this community does represent any sort of threat, that is, if the scene contains satire of national policy, Cervantes does so with his accustomed subtlety and ironic ambivalence.[68] It is not a sustained and consistent critique. Considering Turner's observation that spontaneous *communitas* (unlike ideological and normative *communitas*) is short-lived ("This illumination may succumb to the dry light of next day's disjunction"), it is fitting that Sancho and Ricote affirm their bonds in a festive, intoxicated state – unlike the sober Marcela, for example. Forcione reads the scene within Cervantes's intricate examination of the pastoral genre, and sees in it the articulation of a more ethical and fundamentally human alternative to the excesses of the predatory erotic pastoral and the antisocial pastoral of the self: "Cervantes has gone from eros to agape, from passion consumed in itself to *amicitia*, from solipsism to communion, from self to community or, we might say, to the essential condition of purity in which the self and community are one, in which man can only exist as friend, companion and neighbour."[69] It is hard to imagine Sancho reaffirming a preference for eating in solitude, whatever liberties it affords. He has come to understand the essentially human and ludic virtue of "blundering along in good company."

3 The *Novelas ejemplares*: *Ocio*, Exemplarity, and Community

The explicit game imagery with which Cervantes presents his collection of stories places the *Novelas ejemplares* squarely within the tradition of *eutrapelia* – a quality not lost on Fray Juan Bautista, who, in his "Aprobación" of the collection, writes that "la verdadera eutropelia está en estas *Novelas*" ("true *eutropelia* is in these *Novelas*" [45]). As noted above, the public space, the implied utility of the stories, the partaking of them in harmonious balance with the serious activities of work and worship, all point to the conventional Aristotelian-Horatian concept of edifying entertainment. In play terms, the tradition of exemplarity corresponds to the highly structured, rule-bound realm of *ludus*. As we observed, a prime example of such literary recreation is Juan Manuel's *El conde Lucanor*, with its clear and repetitive structure, specific applicability of the situations represented, and authoritative and controlling narrative voice that seeks to preclude any ambiguity of meaning – which is to say, any creative act of interpretation. Anybody who has performed the most cursory reading knows that such is not the case in the *Novelas ejemplares*. Despite the conventional references to exemplarity, the traditional moral and theological vocabulary deployed throughout the stories, and even the seemingly unambiguous instances of vice punished and virtue rewarded, the reading experience of Cervantes's stories is much closer to the fluid, improvisational play of *paidia*. Rather than adhering to precept and submitting to a controlling authority, the reader of the *Novelas ejemplares* is engaged in the creative, spontaneous, imperfect collaboration of dialogue. The dialogic principle informs the collection at multiple levels: from the pairing of characters who must constantly negotiate meaning and identity, the multiplicity of literary genres which are represented in unorthodox proximity, and the representation of collaborative and agonistic games, to the dynamic between author and reader.

The *Novelas ejemplares* afford the opportunity to re-examine the entire range of humanist views on education, play, the imagination, and social cohesion. The metaphorical game with which Cervantes presents his collection – the *mesa de trucos* – will serve as a touchstone as we consider the many illustrations of specific games and leisure activities within individual tales. Cervantes's representations of cards, story-telling, hunting, and music broadly corroborate the views expressed by the early modern moralists, theorists, and physicians discussed in the first section of this study. Gambling frequently involves strife and deception; noblemen hunt; women are warned to beware music and private reading. But the *Novelas ejemplares* also contain nuanced explorations of the very inclination to play, to imitate, and to indulge in artifice, in free time as well as in real life. As the exception often illustrates the norm, we will begin with what is in many ways Cervantes's least playful creation.

Agonistic and Restrictive Play in *El licenciado Vidriera*

> Our mind likes to think it has not enough leisure hours to do its own business unless it dissociates itself from the body for the little time that the body really needs it.
>
> They want to get out of themselves and escape from the man. That is madness: instead of changing into angels, they change into beasts; instead of raising themselves, they lower themselves. (Montaigne III, 13, p. 856)

Perhaps more than any other of the *Novelas ejemplares, El licenciado Vidriera* eludes classification. The indeterminate genre is, to a large extent, consistent with the protagonist's lack of clear identity. Tomás, young but of imprecise age, is awakened from his solitary slumber beneath a tree, refuses to recall the name of his birthplace, and proclaims his wish to serve a master so that he may improve himself through studies. While the boy does eventually commit himself to a scholarly vocation, and university life is presented as an appealing alternative to court society, relatively few pages are dedicated to these formative years. Tomás undergoes various transformations –of dress, name, milieu, mental state – and these changes correspond to shifts in the representational mode: from the pleasantries of student life, the vicissitudes of military duty, the marvellous variety beheld by the cultural tourist, and the spectacle of a cynic railing against a disordered society, to an exemplary death in battle. Such a structure allows for the exposition of themes including the dangers and proper use of knowledge, the vanity of the court, and the relative merits of charity, letters, and arms.[1]

A look at the primary comic techniques employed by Cervantes will clarify a central ambiguity of *El licenciado Vidriera*. While the transparency of glass may represent clear and piercing vision, the licentiate's brittle body (or psyche) impedes interaction between him and society. The humour thus involves a combination of social satire and comedy of character. In his psychosomatic predicament, the paranoid glass man resembles the Bergsonian automaton, a character whose particular mania ossifies his personality: "this view of the mechanical and the living dovetailed into each other makes us incline towards the vaguer image of *some rigidity or other* applied to the mobility of life, in an awkward attempt to follow its lines and counterfeit its suppleness" (Bergson 38). The licentiate's corporeal angst is a comic materialization of what we might call his professional deformation: his intellectual detachment, glorification of a certain kind of knowledge, and his uncompromising stance towards fellow human beings. As Bergson observed – like Frye in his discussion of the "blocking figure," or "senex" of the comic mode (*Anatomy of Criticism*) – such a personage is normally the object of a derisive laughter, and ultimately defeated. While the licentiate's final inability to remain in society superficially resembles this type of expulsion, the circumstances of his exit contain an irony that complicates the conventional comic structure. The product of serious reflection ("de pensado" [74]), Rueda's sane commentaries cannot match Vidriera's stand-up routine of satirical commonplaces (his remarks "de improviso") for popularity, and the disgruntled licentiate leaves after a final lamentation on the corruptions of the court. These elements underscore the socially satirical content of the story. Following the comic, negative exemplarity of Vidriera's disgust with court society, Cervantes provides the dramatic, positive exemplarity of Rueda's death as a patriot. But there is no real resolution, tragic or comic, in large part because the shortcomings depicted in society do not seem to justify the extremity of Vidriera's condition.

El licenciado Vidriera is linked to the picaresque primarily through its satirical elements, as Vidriera's sharp wit and sense of alienation make for a derisively critical perspective on society. Américo Castro maintains that, compared to picaresque narrators, Cervantes's protagonist possesses a clear-eyed temperance: "With regard to Vidriera, his moralizing, ironic and clear-sighted criticism is nothing like the sombre and bitter diatribes that the typical heroes of the picaresque novel hurl at the universe."[2] While such a contrasting vision is valid with regard to most of Cervantes's fiction, Castro's observation does not square with the present story. The variety of humour contained in works like *Guzmán de Alfarache* and *La pícara Justina* (from satirical derision to carnivalesque festivity) surely surpasses that of *El licenciado Vidriera*. It might be more accurate to say that *El licenciado Vidriera* engages with a particularly pessimistic and socially derisive tendency within the picaresque. As we shall discuss below, Cervantes explores a similar aspect of the genre in the more self-conscious and generically allusive *El coloquio de los perros*. Both tales ultimately critique the misanthropic vision, although in different ways: Vidriera, through the emphasis on his pathology; the dialogic dogs in their ongoing attempts to keep each other's back-biting in check. As we will discuss below, the satirical voice is considerably refined and developed in the latter tale.

A consideration of Tomás's early experiences and education reveals how much he departs from other Cervantine protagonists. From the companions who travel to picaresque underworlds (*Rinconete y Cortadillo*, *La ilustre fregona*), to conversing dogs (*El coloquio de los perros*), and Sancho's chivalric apprenticeship with don Quijote, we are reminded of Cervantes's abiding interest in character development as part of a dialogic process, through conversation and shared experiences. It is a process we also observed in the humanist writings on education, in which book-learning is expanded by experience, sociability is cultivated through play, the body tended along with the mind. While *El licenciado Vidriera* occasionally gestures towards these ideals, they are either distorted, abandoned, or entirely absent from the protagonist's education.

The solitary, modestly attired Tomás, happened upon as he sleeps by the river Tormes, expresses a desire to serve the two high-born students and improve his social standing through a successful university career – elements that, again, seem to signal a generic orientation towards the picaresque. But, just as the two roguish youths surprise us with their embrace and amicable fidelity in the exposition of *Rinconete y Cortadillo*, Tomás's relationship to the students quickly departs from the picaresque norm: "Y como el buen servir del siervo mueve la voluntad del señor a tratarle bien, ya Tomás Rodaja no era criado de sus amos, sino su compañero" ("[A]nd since a servant who gives good service gets treated well, Thomas Rodaja became his masters' companion, and no longer their servant" [44]). His later relationship to the infantry captain he meets on the road returning to Salamanca bears a similar quality of companionship: "Hicieron camarada, departieron de diversas cosas, y a pocos lances dio Tomás muestras de su raro ingenio y el caballero las dio de su bizarría y cortesano trato" ("They shared lodgings, chatted about various things, and Thomas soon gave signs of his unusual talent and the gentlemen of his magnificent and courtly bearing" [44]). Rather than the *mozo de muchos amos* (servant of many masters) typical of the picaresque, Tomás becomes a sort of companion to various social types. His resulting exposure to arms and letters presents the complementary realms of contemplation and action – and exposes his deficiencies in both.

In his equal relationship to these would-be masters, Tomás applies his intellect to conversation and observation rather than to the scheming and deception of a Lazarillo or Guzmán. Moreover, the university experience of Tomás is free of student pranksters, humiliating initiation rituals, and revolting and/or insufficient food. In *El licenciado Vidriera*, the university does not represent the conventional picaresque haven but rather a scholarly utopia. As a point of comparison, we might consider the tantalizing tuna beaches in *La ilustre fregona*: "allí van, o envían, muchos padres principales a buscar a sus hijos, y los hallan; *y tanto sienten sacarlos de aquella vida como si los llevaran a dar la muerte*" ("many high-born fathers go there – or send others there – to search for their sons, and they find them; and *it pains them to be taken from that life as if they were being taken to execution*" [141, my italics]). For Tomás, scholarly life has an equal allure, as he decides to leave the home of his noble companions: "pero como le fatigasen los deseos de volver a sus estudios y a Salamanca – *que enhechiza la voluntad de volver a ella a todos los que de la apacibilidad de su vivienda han gustado* – pidió a sus amos licencia para volverse" ("but as he was anxious to return to his studies and to Salamanca, *whose charms make everyone who has enjoyed the pleasure of living there determine to go back*, he asked his masters' leave to return" [44, my italics]). Of course, such idealizations seldom escape the tinge of irony in Cervantes, and Tomás's immersion in the life of the mind ultimately results in the detached, critical perspective that feeds his lunacy. We will consider this perspective further below.

On the way back to Salamanca, Tomás's acquaintance with the captain results in a postponement of his studies, and the consideration of military life:

> Alabó la vida soldadesca; pintóle muy al vivo la belleza de la ciudad de Nápoles, las holguras de Palermo, la abundancia de Milán, los festines

> de Lombardía, las espléndidas comidas de las hosterías; dibujóle dulce y puntualmente el *aconcha, patrón; pasa acá, manigoldo; venga la macarela, li polastri, e li macarroni*. Puso las alabanzas en el cielo de la vida libre del soldado y de la libertad de Italia[.] (45)
>
> [He praised the soldier's life, and gave him a vivid picture of the beauty of the city of Naples, the delights of Palermo, the prosperity of Milan, the banquets of Lombardy, and the splendid food of the inns. He gave a delightful and exact account of the way they shouted, "Here, landlord," "This way, you rogue," "Let's have the *maccatella*, the *polastri* and the macaroni." He praised to the skies the soldier's free life and the easy ways of Italy.]

The picaresque tuna-fishing beaches in *La ilustre fregona*, the scholarly retreat of Tomás in Salamanca, and the soldier's life as presented by the captain each set forth idealized, alternative realms of experience. Like the world described in the anonymous poem, *La vida del pícaro*, these realms can be seen as variations on the *menosprecio de corte* tradition – an aspect of *El licenciado Vidriera* that is elaborated through the insane licentiate's experience at court. As oppositional alternatives to the strictures of court society, the counterworlds are associated with freedom from oppressive structure. But the captain's presentation of army life quickly acquires some deflating perspective through a narrator whose author had some experience in the field: "pero no le dijo nada del frío de las centinelas, del peligro de los asaltos, del espanto de las batallas, de la hambre de los cercos, de la ruina de las minas, con otras cosas deste jaez, que algunos las toman y tienen por añadiduras del peso de la soldadesca, y son la carga principal della" ("but he said nothing to him about the cold of sentry duty, the danger of attacks, the horror of battles, the hunger of sieges, the destruction of mines, and other things of this kind, which some consider to be the extra burdens of a soldier's life, when in fact they are the main part of it" [45]). The narrator proposes an alternative image of military life in which the "dominant" (*la carga principal* vs. *añadiduras*) is a stark realism. (Sancho Panza, we recall, felt his early chivalric adventures did not correspond to don Quijote's account during his enthusiastic recruiting of his neighbour.) The descriptive ability and selective representation of the captain find in Tomás a favourable reception: "En resolución, tantas cosas le dijo, y tan bien dichas, que la discreción de nuestro Tomás Rodaja comenzó a titubear y la voluntad a aficionarse a aquella vida, que tan cerca tiene la muerte" ("In short, he told him so many things and in such an attractive way, that our Thomas's judgement began to waver, and his will to be set on that way of life, where death is always so near at hand" [45]). The foreboding tone of this resolution and its repercussions at the story's end notwithstanding, Tomás's journey with the soldiers functions as an extension of his education, an empirical complement to his intellectual life as a student. In this sense, it would seem to conform to the humanist educational ideal outlined above. However, Tomas's refusal to commit himself formally to the captain's company, joining the soldiers with no official obligations or duties, is symptomatic of the detachment that mars not only his education, but his relationship to society.

The limitations of the intellectual orientation are clearest when Tomás is afflicted by his strange illness. As the previous comments suggest, rather than a drastic change brought about by the poisoned fruit, his malady is an exaggeration of his withdrawn personality. The insane Vidriera's lack of appetite, austerity of dress, irregular sleeping patterns and distance from others can be seen as an extension of a fear grounded in his own corporeality, and his neglect of the physical and affective aspects of existence are apparent prior to his ingestion of the fruit. Ruth El Saffar finds the poisoning artistically deficient: "Cervantes reveals his misunderstanding of his character by having recourse to poison to explain the madness which afflicts Tomás. There is an underlying unity between the young Tomás and the crazed Licentiate which Cervantes appears to obscure by introducing poison to explain the transformation" (*Novel to Romance* 56). Tomás's rejection of the lady, creating the unconventional situation of a beautiful female courting an unwilling male, reveals his recreational proclivities. They are, unsurprisingly, cerebral rather than corporeal: "Pero como él atendía más a sus libros que a otros pasatiempos, en ninguna manera respondía al gusto de la señora" ("As he was more devoted to his books than to other pastimes, he did not respond at all to the lady's fancy" [52]). Since exclusive dedication to books was sufficient to drive Alonso Quijano insane, El Saffar is right in pointing out the superfluousness of the poison fruit. As we have been observing, Cervantes's images of ideal recreation include the exercise of both mind and body. Vidriera's deviation may be viewed in light of Vives's dictum: "Se ha de procurar, mientras lo permitan la salud y el tiempo, que el juego, al par que diversión, sea ejercicio del cuerpo" ("One must see to it, while health and time permit, that the game, while diverting, also provide exercise for the body" [*Diálogos*, "Las leyes del juego"]); or Montaigne's warning against an exclusive dedication to books: "The mind is exercised in books, but the body, whose care I have not forgotten either, remains meanwhile inactive, droops and grieves. I know of no excess more harmful to me, or more to be avoided in my declining years" (III, 4, 630).[3]

The Agonistic Intellect: Cruel Comedy and Vidriera's Humourless Vision

"porque sobre la ajena necedad todos discurren y todos se adelantan antes al convicio que al encomio"

["because over the foolishness of others everyone pontificates and all outdo each other at insults rather than at praise"]

(Gracián, *Agudeza y arte de ingenio* Disc. XXXVII)

The licentiate's intellectual detachment informs the tone and the function of his humour. Vidriera implicitly asserts his own superiority by constantly pointing out the folly of those around him. What such a cynical perspective overlooks, of course, is the critic's own complicity in human imperfection. To refer again to James Wood's terminology, Vidriera produces the satirical comedy of "correction" rather than the novelistic comedy of "forgiveness." It is tempting to claim that Vidriera is a thoroughly non-ludic being, a "spoil-sport" who refuses to participate, to enter into prescribed social, sentimental, and professional roles;[4] however, his railing against society comprises a form of recreation that enjoyed great prestige in early modern Spain – virtuosic wordplay and contests of wits. As Gracián notes in the citation above, people are much more entertained by put-downs than by praise. Furthermore, it is telling that his well-known work on wit, *Agudeza y arte de ingenio*, strongly favours the acerbic wordplay of the likes of Gracián, Quevedo and López de Ubeda. *El licenciado Vidriera* is arguably Cervantes's closest approximation to this literature of virtuosic *desengaño*.

A recollection of Erasmus's exuberant satirist will help us more clearly delineate the character of Cervantes's cynic. Vidriera and Folly both discern the pervasiveness of vice and mendacity, but the conclusions they draw are very different. For Vidriera, the illusory quality of social appearance indicates a world of treacherous hypocrisy, and necessitates vigilance and withdrawal. His view is akin to Critilio, the prudent elder of Gracián's *El Criticón*: "Por tan dificultoso tengo yo alcançarle solidez a la frágil vida como al delicado vidrio, que para mí, hombre y vidrio todo es uno: a un tris dan un tras, y acábase vidrio y hombre" ("I find it just as difficult to find solidity in fragile life as in delicate glass, so for me, man and glass is all the same: with a snip and a snap, glass and man are done for" [Crisi XII]). Folly, we recall, acknowledges the deceptiveness of appearances while advocating tolerance and participation: "In short, if you take away the illusions, you ruin the whole fable ... Now what else is the life of mortal men but a kind of fable in which the actors appear on stage under the disguise of different masks? ... They are but shadows of real persons, yet there's no other way to put on the show" (*The Praise of Folly* 28). Vidriera's refusal to participate in society clearly likens his clear-sightedness to the impoverished wisdom condemned by Folly: "he won't even acknowledge the common rule of the barroom, drink up or get out – all of which amounts to demanding that the play should no longer be a play" (29). Vidriera's reply to the husband of the woman he slighted in the clothes-market of Salamanca illustrates his antipathy to Erasmian folly: "'Hermano licenciado Vidriera ... más tenéis de bellaco que de loco.' 'No se me da un ardite' – respondió él –, 'como no tenga nada de necio'" ("'Brother Glass ... you are more of a rogue than a fool.' 'I don't care a bit,' he answered, 'as long as I'm not stupid'" [55]). For Vidriera, naiveté and foolishness can only be negative attributes. Green has noted that this part of the story consists of "the tradition, centuries old in the folklore of many nations, of *preguntas y respuestas*," and that the agonistic nature of such contests is emblematic of Vidriera's relationship to society ("El *Licenciado Vidriera*" 217).

Vidriera and his group of approving spectators fulfil a function similar to Erasmus's thousand Democrituses, constantly revealing and laughing at the folly around them. And Cervantes does provide the "one extra Democritus": it is the reader, who, from the distance created by the ironic third-person narrator, recognizes the contradictory nature of the critical laughers' sense of superiority. We recall that during a significant part of her speech, sitting "among the poetic gods," Folly attacks the madness of the "Furies," the more serious vices such as greed, sacrilege, lust. It is Erasmus's distinction between two types of madness, and, correspondingly, two types of deception, that makes *The Praise of Folly* so distinct from the *desengaño* tradition. For if Vidriera, like Gracián's Critilio, is constantly wary of the madness of the

Furies, he fails to appreciate the other type of derangement. The madness Folly condones as her own occurs "whenever some genial aberration of the mind frees it from anxiety and worry while at the same time imbuing it with the many fragrances of pleasure" (39).[5] In one of his most attractive witticisms, Vidriera condemns flattery as he satirizes the court: "yo no soy bueno para palacio, porque tengo vergüenza y no sé lisonjear" ("I'm no good for palaces, because I'm bashful and don't know how to flatter" [56]). The content of such ironic censure recalls Folly's comment on the sycophancy of courtiers: "The rest of their talent is just barefaced flattery" (68). But Folly also praises flattery of a different kind, one which she claims as "my flattery," described as "the honey and spice of all human intercourse" (46). This other type, which differs from the adulation of courtiers in degree as well as in its motivation, has to do with common courtesy, those compliments that boost self-esteem and facilitate social interaction. The rigid licentiate is blind to such nuances, and his stern rejection of flattery corresponds to his anti-social behaviour. Despite seeing in this trait a measure of dignity, Rosales recognizes its destructive consequences: "His being requires space; his dignity distances him from others. Perhaps for this reason the licentiate does not dare to flatter, because flattery eliminates distance, the moral dignity that establishes a distancing respect between men. If the licentiate fell into any sort of flattery he would break."[6] As we have been observing, Cervantes knows that such a critical outlook quickly becomes dogmatic and un-philosophical, and, in praxis, precludes essential aspects of experience, especially those relating to living in human community. Despite his superior vision, the cynical licentiate is in some ways the most foolish character of the story.

The spoilsport, as Huizinga observed, is a threat to society for precisely the reason observed by Folly: "By withdrawing from the game he reveals the relativity and fragility of the play-world in which he had temporarily shut himself with others. He robs the play of its *illusion* – a pregnant word which means literally 'in play' (from *inlusio, iludere* or *inludere*). Therefore he must be cast out, for he threatens the existence of the play-community" (*Homo Ludens* 11). As we saw, the young licentiate had never completely "shut himself with others" in society in the first place; he maintained a noncommittal distance. But even at his most antisocial stage as a cynical railer, Vidriera is a curiously non-threatening figure. In part, this is because of what El Saffar identified as an inhibiting effect of the role he assumes vis-à-vis his onlookers: "The crowd has disarmed him both by identifying him as mad and by engaging him so mercilessly that it undermines him even at his own game by forcing him to release his over-all knowledge in bits and pieces which never find their way into a coherent and potentially dangerous alternate system" (*Novel to Romance* 59). One would be hard-pressed to speculate on what Vidriera's "over-all knowledge" might be, other than a general misanthropy. As El Saffar suggests, Vidriera does not represent an instance of Turner's liminality; there is no sense that he might form a counter-society, a subversive *communitas* around him. But another important reason why he is not seditious is that his torrent of sardonic witticism signals his participation in a highly-esteemed form of play, one with roots in popular culture but which was refined by some of the most cultivated minds of Cervantes's Spain.

Vidriera's "one-liners" can be found in collections such as Rufo's *Las seiscientas apotegmas*, Luis de Pinedo's *Libro de chistes*, and in El Pinciano's examples in his chapter on comedy (*Philosophia Antigua Poética* Ep. IX). A rather innocuous jibe, for example, is directed at men who dye their beards in order to appear younger (67–8). It is a conventional joke – like derision of women and their *afeites* – which can also be found in *Guzmán de Alfarache* with a similar concluding pun (II, i, 3, p. 522). Some critics see in Vidriera's commentaries commonplace aphorisms, others incisive revelations. Rosales, for example, calls Vidriera a "hero of sincerity," who is unwilling to conceal the sordid reality of his fellow citizens, and whose intense awareness of this reality makes it impossible for him to share any intimacy with those around him (108–11).[7] Riley has observed that Vidriera's aphoristic outbursts do not so much reveal a consistent or ironic attitude as a penchant for sardonic wit: "However honest they may be, most of them aim more at cleverness than accuracy, and the high proportion of unpleasant remarks surely says something about the character that made them, and something not very nice" (190). Whether or not the licentiate's remarks consist of mere exercises of wit or revelatory social truths, there seems to be a consensus regarding the bitterness of his humour. Erasmus understood that such an austere outlook is not only profoundly unsociable, but also ethically flawed:

> Even if a certain mutual benevolence does grow up between these severe devotees of virtue, it can never be securely grounded or long lasting when men are so morose of temper and sharp of sight that they study the vices of their friends like eagles or the serpent of Epidaurus. Of course they shut their eyes to their own vices, and never realize what a sack of faults and

> follies is hanging from their own shoulders. It's the nature of human life that no individual can be found who's not subject to great vices and faults. (*The Praise of Folly* 21)

It is worth recalling Schiller's comments regarding good character, which present the inverse of Folly's foolish stoic, and of Vidriera: "Severity with one's self combined with leniency toward others is a sign of the truly excellent character" (*Letters on the Aesthetic Education of Man* 124).

As Riley suggests above, it is somewhat inaccurate to identify Vidriera as a standard-bearer for clear-eyed *desengaño*, uncompromising in his desire to reveal the world in its unsavoury essence. Such a characterization would suggest a moral commitment, where in fact a bilious disposition and desire to elicit laughter at all costs (recall Aristotle's *bomolochos*) may be closer to the truth. Maxime Chevalier, who identifies Vidriera's remark regarding the "paciencia de un tahúr" ("patience of a card player") as a particular category of witticism – "la paradoja del pecador" ("the paradox of the sinner") – promoted by Quevedo (*Quevedo y su tiempo* 130–3), has studied the tremendous popularity of verbal witticisms in early modern Spain, tracing source material as varied as classical antiquity, the oral and folkloric traditions, collections of *faceciae* and novellas. As Chevalier notes, ethical reform is not the primary goal of such witticisms: "Giving nicknames is not aimed at reforming conduct; the nickname stings, bites, and wounds. It pertains to the category of aggressive wit defined by Freud, wit that so frequently manifested and manifests itself in small circles, whichever they may be, and especially in the courtly circles of the Golden Age."[8] We can say, then, that Vidriera, despite his detachment, does indeed engage in a form of play: his activity falls within the ludic categories of Quevedo and his circle, described by Chevalier as "contiendas de mentiras" ("contests of lies" [20]), "justas verbales" ("verbal jousts" [20]), "auténtica actividad lúdica" ("authentic ludic activity" [28]), "juguetes de ingenio" ("toys of wit" [131]), etc. It is a highly agonistic game, the opposite of the sociable conversation held up as the humanist recreational ideal we considered above. Rather than dialogue, which, even when contentious, is a dynamic, collaborative form of communication, Vidriera's utterances are primarily a form of monologic attack, creating distance between speaker and object. One is tempted to characterize the vogue of *agudeza* in early modern Spain as a regression to "prerational play." Rhetorical virtuosity is not deployed to create order or to unify a community around a consensus of approximating truth. It is like El Cid's verbal assaults on the Infantes de Carrión which, as we noted above, was consistent with Huizinga's account of primitive systems of justice: "Here it is not the most meticulously deliberated juristic argument that tips the balance, but the most withering and excoriating invective" (84).

The vituperative glee in *El licenciado Vidriera* is thus part of a long tradition of contest, and of generating laughter based on attack and ridicule. The insane licentiate's tremendous popularity – at court and in public square alike – illustrates the appeal of such humour to primal, prerational impulses. The behaviour of the young boys in the town reveals, in un-sublimated form, the nature of the game: "Los muchachos, que son la más traviesa generación del mundo, a despecho de sus ruegos y voces, le comenzaron a tirar trapos, y aun piedras, por ver si era de vidrio, como él decía" ("Boys, being the most mischievous creatures in the world, in spite of his pleas and shouts began to throw rags at him, and even stones, to se if he really was made of glass as he said" [54]). Vidriera's tongue-lashing at their harassment causes a modification in their behaviour: "Por oírle reñir y responder a todos le seguían siempre muchos y los muchachos tomaron y tuvieron por mejor partido antes oílle que tiralle" ("When they heard him tell them off they always followed him in crowds, and the boys thought it would be a much better game to listen to him than to throw things at him" [55]). They find their destructive desires can better be gratified by listening to Tomás's verbal assaults; the linguistic *agon* represents a tenuous sublimation of physical violence. In distinguishing between tragic and comic suffering, El Pinciano makes a rather extreme concession by claiming that not only insult and ridicule but even death may be comic, provided that the losses are socially acceptable, or even desirable:

> Y la diferencia que ay de los temores trágicos a los cómicos es que aquéstos se quedan en los mismos actores y representantes solos, y aquéllos passan de los representantes en los oyentes; y ansí las muertes trágicas son lastimosas, mas las de la comedia, si alguna ay, son de gusto y passatiempo, porque en ellas mueren personas que sobran en el mundo, como es una vieja zizañadora, un viejo avaro, un rufián o una alcahueta. (Epístola IX, 385)

> [And the difference between tragic and comic fears is that the latter remain in the actors themselves, and the former pass from the actors to the listeners; and so tragic deaths are painful, but those of comedy, if there are any,

are pleasurable and entertaining, because with them die people the world can do without, like a nagging old woman, a greedy old man, a pimp or a procuress.]

A notable aspect of Vidriera's comic assaults is that they breach the conventional boundaries of acceptable social targets – or, at least, they too insistently implicate those around him, removing the distance that makes such laughter safe.[9]

One of the period's most irrepressible wits, la Pícara Justina, observes just how delicate the dynamic between jokester and public can be. As she holds forth during a meal, the traditional associations of communion and companionship are desecrated by her singular focus on *agudeza*, and the shift in the attitude of her audience reveals the agonistic underpinnings of their association:

> [Q]ue al paso que iban riendo mis agudezas, iban envidiando mi buen entendimiento, y así iban resfriando la risa, hasta tanto que se murió de frío, y después de muerta la enterraron la pena. Pero mi orgullosa pujanza tenía vendados mis ojos para no echar de ver que ya el placer había reconocido las riberas de su fin y que aquella gente no estaba para gracias[.] (273–4)

> [At the same time they laughed at my witticisms, they envied my fine intelligence, and so their laughter cooled, to such a degree that it died of cold, and following its demise they buried the pain. But my proud vigour veiled my eyes from seeing that pleasure had already recognized the limits of its shore, and that those people were not in the mood for jokes.]

The acrid ferment of pride and envy that destroys the recreational repast for Justina and her audience is like the unsavoury and fleeting bond that also exists between Vidriera and the throngs that egg him on.

Early in the licentiate's Italian journey there occurs an episode that, in its humane and irenic interaction, provides a significant contrast to the dominant tone of the story. On the voyage to Genoa, some of the disagreeable aspects of the soldier's life that the captain had failed to mention become manifest: a stormy passage frightens Tomás and delivers a soggy and tattered company to its destination. The fear and perils of the voyage, however, are forgotten amidst the festivities arranged by the captain: "pusieron en olvido todas las borrascas pasadas con el presente *gaudeamus*" ("they forgot all about the storms of the past in the merry-making of the present" [47]). As with Sancho, Ricote, and his fellow pilgrims, a life-affirming indulgence in food and drink displaces preoccupations over bodily harm; and the company's accommodating host transports them further into the festive realm with an impressive enological display:

> Y habiendo hecho el huésped la reseña de tantos y tan diferentes vinos, se ofreció de hacer parecer allí, sin usar de tropelía, ni como pintados en mapa, sino real y verdaderamente, a Madrigal, Coca, Alaejos, y a la Imperial más que Real Ciudad, recámara del dios de la risa ... Finalmente, más vinos nombró el huésped, y más les dio, que pudo tener en sus bodegas el mismo Baco. (48)

> [And when mine host had gone through all these different wines, he volunteered to bring in, without recourse to trickery or sleight of hand, the genuine Madrigal, Coca, Alaejos and Ciudad Real (which deserves to be called Imperial rather than Royal) which is sacred to the god of laughter ... In short, our host named and offered them more wines than Bacchus himself can have had in his vaults.]

The emphasis on wine, Bacchus, and laughter creates a colourful scene of mirth. But Tomás is not merely an observer of this epic geographical review, for the entire spectacle is interactive: the famous regions and cities appear in a felicitous metonymy as various bottles are not only named, but passed around and consumed as well. The participatory element is assured by the unifying function of the wine, which symbolically and literally links the feasters to the scene represented to them. It is this vital element that becomes foreign to Tomás, who, parting company with the captain and his men, soon resumes his distanced, analytical perspective.

Vidriera's evaluation of artists reveals some nuance that is absent in his own capacity as a performer. Of theatrical troupes, for example, Vidriera says, "son necesarios en la república, como lo son las florestas, las alamedas y las vistas de recreación, y como lo son las cosas que honestamente recrean" ("they are necessary to the State, in the same way as woods, groves, restful landscapes, and all those things which provide honest recreation" [67]). This is consistent with Cervantes's appeal in the prologue to the *Novelas ejemplares,* and also recalls the stroll into the "Espolón" by Peralta and Campuzano at the end of *El coloquio de los perros*. Similarly, Vidriera's distinction between the theory and practice of poetry, along with his support of the few excellent poets who are unappreciated by the *vulgo*, represents some familiar aesthetic values:

> ¿Qué diré del ladrar que hacen los cachorros y modernos a los mastinazos antiguos y graves? ¿Y qué de los que murmuran de algunos ilustres y excelentes sujetos donde resplandece la verdadera luz de la poesía que, *tomándola por alivio y entretenimiento de sus muchas y graves ocupaciones*, muestran la divinidad de sus ingenios y la alteza de sus conceptos, a despecho y pesar del circunspecto ignorante que juzga de lo que no sabe y aborrece lo que no entiende, y del que quiere que se estime y tenga en precio la necedad que sienta debajo de doseles y la ignorancia que se arrima a los sitiales? (59–60, my italics)

> [You should see how these modern young puppies bark at the hoary old mastiffs. Not to mention those who snipe at some of those illustrious and worthy persons in whom the true light of poetry shines, and *who find it a comfort and recreation among their many serious occupations*, who show the divine nature of their genius and the nobility of their thoughts, in spite of those meddlesome ignoramuses who pass judgement on what they do not know, and hate what they cannot understand; and those who only want praise for the stupid folk who sit beneath canopies, and the ignorant who cling to the seats of the mighty.]

The licentiate's recognition that poetry provides entertaining relief from weighty concerns – along with the reference to honest recreation in the previous passage – comprises yet another reference to *eutrapelia*, and suggests that his views on art may not be as unaccommodating as his social commentary.

It is important to recall that the moral element of *eutrapelia* is requisite, but is not necessarily its explicit end. As noted above, Aristotle was concerned with defining a licit form of entertainment based on a mean between the activities of the *bomolochos* (the buffoon) and the *agroikos* (the boor): the entertainment should respect rules of propriety and moderation so as not to incite people to vice, but the enjoyment taken in it has no inherently edifying function. Vidriera's description of the experience provided by theatre and poetry seems consistent with this. Like nature ("florestas," "alamedas"), art provides a recreational space separate from the workplace and everyday traffic. In a similar vein, Vidriera observes how actors are ideal members of a commonwealth: "*en el sudor de su cara ganan su pan* con inllevable trabajo, tomando continuo de memoria, hechos perpetuos gitanos, de lugar en lugar y de mesón en venta, desvelándose en contentar a otros, *porque en el gusto ajeno consiste su bien propio*" ("*they earn their bread by the sweat of their brow* with intolerable hard work, always learning things by heart. They're perpetual gypsies wandering from village to village and from inn to inn, losing sleep in order to give pleasure to others, because their own profit lies in that satisfaction they give to the public" [66, my italics]). Not only do they obey the biblical injunction following humanity's fall (*En el sudor de tu rostro te sustentarás*); the reciprocal relationship between artist and public includes but also transcends material concerns, bringing about a well-being of a different order, one that can only be achieved through recreation. Thomas Mann, who, in addition to being an insightful reader of *Don Quijote* was also keenly interested in the transformations achieved through play (see above p. 40), has his picaresque protagonist make the following observation on the allure of the theatre: "What unanimity in agreeing to let oneself be deceived! Here quite clearly there is in operation a general human need, implanted by God Himself in human nature, which Müller-Rosé's abilities are created to satisfy. *This beyond doubt is an indispensable device in life's economy, which this man is kept and paid to serve*" (*Felix Krull* I, 5, my italics). Felix's observation is strikingly similar to the qualified endorsement of illusion we noted, a few pages above, in Erasmus: "Now what else is the life of mortal men but a kind of fable in which the actors appear on stage under the disguise of different masks? ... They are but shadows of real persons, yet there's no other way to put on the show" (*The Praise of Folly* 28). We might say that Vidriera's appreciation of the theatre borders on that of Felix Krull, while failing to make the extension – implicit in Felix, explicit in Folly – to accepting the theatrical quality of social existence. Vidriera insists on a clear delineation between art and life. For him, the illusion of theatre remains separate from larger deceptions: "Tienen más, que con su oficio no engañan a nadie, pues por momentos sacan su mercaduría a pública plaza" ("They have this in their favour too: they deceive no one by their trade, for they are always showing their merchandise in public, for all to see and judge" [66]). The spectacles of the theatre, staged in public without any pretence to reality, belong to a category of deception outlined by Alemán's *pícaro*: "La tercera manera de engaños es cuando son sin perjuicio, que ni engañan a otro con ellos ni lo quedan los que quieren o tratan de engañar" ("The third type of deceptions is when they are without damage, they neither deceive another nor do those who want or try to deceive become deceived" [*Guzmán de Alfarache* II, i, 3]).

Like the *mesa de trucos*, the theatrical performance is sanitized by the light of the public space, where everyone can presumably enjoy an artifice harmlessly, since they knowingly indulge in a fiction.

Vidriera's abuse of puppeteers is odd in light of his praise of theatre, and seemingly signals a return to his more censorious and sombre vision:

> De los titireros decía mil males: decía que era gente vagamunda y que trataba con indecencia de las cosas divinas, porque con las figuras que mostraban en sus retablos volvían la devoción en risa, y que les acontecía envasar en un costal todas o las más figuras del Testamento Viejo y Nuevo y sentarse sobre él a comer y beber en los bodegones y tabernas; en resolución, decía que se maravillaba de como quien podía no les ponía perpetuo silencio en sus retablos, o los desterraba del reino. (66)

> [Of puppeteers he said thousands of bad things: he said they were vagrants, who treated divine things without due respect, because they made a mockery of worship with the figures they put on in their shows, and sometimes they would stuff in a sack all or nearly all the figures in the Old and New Testament and then sit on the sack to eat and drink in the eating-houses and taverns. In short, he said he was amazed that the powers that be didn't put an end to their shows or banish them from the realm.]

This description calls to mind the roguish protagonists of *El retablo de las maravillas*, vagabonds who incorporate biblical figures in their ironic representation. But in Cervantes's satirical *entremés*, the hypocritical townspeople are more the target of derision than the con artists. To be sure, Cervantes also reveals an interest in the trickster as artist with Ginés de Pasamonte (another puppeteer) in the second part of *Don Quijote*, not to mention the crafty protagonist of *Pedro de Urdemalas* – characters who are much closer to the outlook of Mann's Felix Krull. With regard to Vidriera's objection to combining laughter and feasting with religious elements, nobody in Counter-Reformation Spain should be called prudish for voicing a concern with sacrilege. But the carnivalesque quality of the description is striking. Making "a mockery of worship" is similar to what the two tricksters accomplish in *El retablo de las maravillas* – and, as we saw, the result of Sancho's frantic pieties during the *barco encantado* episode. It should hardly be surprising that Vidriera could not appreciate, as Cervantes (and Erasmus) did, the aesthetic and ethical appeal of combining the divine and the comic. What is one to make of these ambivalent, apparently contradictory views? I would suggest that the fact that Vidriera expresses artistic values that seem consistent with those of his author is not, as with don Quijote, a manifestation of a fruitful complexity of character. I agree with El Saffar, who argues that Cervantes did not quite know what to do with this solitary character of impoverished sensibilities. Vidriera's limited perception is, she maintains, "paralleled by Cervantes's failure to grasp his character as a whole and his inability to fully distinguish narrator and character within the work. In both cases the result is a fragmented production whose parts, though individually interesting, fail to cohere into a convincing whole" (*Novel to Romance* 56).

It should by now be clear how Vidriera diverges from the ambiguous, capacious, humorous vision embodied by characters such as Folly, Sancho Panza and don Quijote, and even some *pícaros*. Vidriera's reductive, unsympathetic treatment of his fellow beings is, as Cervantes clearly illustrates, pathological. As Rosales observed regarding Vidriera's outlook: "Understanding is not always generous. But Cervantine understanding always was; this attitude towards life is in no way characteristic of Cervantes."[10] The disillusioned character who joylessly uncovers the pitfalls of life and shortcomings in others failed to sustain its author's interest. In the space of little over a page, Cervantes has him cured, further satirizes the court in its complete lack of interest in a sane man, and then sends Rueda to an exemplary death in military service. The precipitous ending to this strange story leaves an impression of resignation, both on the part of the licentiate, who sees no other option than to leave society and take up arms, as well as that of Cervantes, who rarely closes off a work so definitively.

The Picaresque and Play in *El coloquio de los perros*

El coloquio de los perros, like *Don Quijote* and *El retablo de las maravillas*, contains play at the very premise of its fictional situation. Along with its frame tale, *El casamiento engañoso, El coloquio de los perros* presents multiple images of games and players, and various types of recreation take place, from Berganza's frolicking with the students in the Jesuit school to Cañizares's demonic escapes to the Pyrenees. The Ensign's entrance into the fictional world of the manuscript of the dogs' colloquy creates the central image of play, and it models the reader's own participation in Cervantes's peculiar *eutrapelia*. Affirming the freedom and security of the play realm, the Ensign points out that if the reader does not find the activity pleasurable, it can be set aside without consequence: "que no tienen [esos sueños o disparates] otra cosa de bueno si no es el poderlos dejar cuando enfaden" ("whose only virtue is that you can leave them alone when they annoy you" [295]). As noted, the rules for the reader's activity are in large part prescribed by genre. *El coloquio de los perros* both incorporates picaresque satire and articulates a formal critique of the genre. The narrative structure, with Berganza giving an account of his life to Cipión, contains the picaresque narrator within a larger, layered context of a dialogue framed by a meta-text. Not only is dialogue between characters a primary engine of the narration; the picaresque genre – its narrative dynamic, its satirical view – is *dialogized*, that is, interrogated by an additional voice and perspective (as we will discuss below, a different variation on this phenomenon occurs in *La ilustre fregona*). Finally, the entire colloquy bears an important relationship to the redemption of another roguish character, the Ensign of *El casamiento engañoso*. Amidst the evil and capriciousness of the dogs' picaresque world, we shall see the cultivation of a peculiar optimism in which play is affirmed in its most positive and unique function, and which is consonant with humanist ideals of leisure.

El casamiento engañoso illustrates the social as well as narrative implications of a particular type of play. It is a combination of *mimesis* and *agon*, corresponding to the basic satirical situation of the mutual confidence game, or "robber robbed." Consistent with its picaresque orientation, the principal ludic vocabulary has to do with cards, of which a good deal of moral and metaphoric import is exploited – their association with deception and greed, erotic overtones, and the combination of skill and chance. The *posada* where Campuzano and doña Estefanía initially meet is a typical gaming venue, and a concentrated sequence of play imagery and concepts begins as Campuzano contemplates the tantalizingly veiled woman:

> Y aunque le supliqué que por cortesía me hiciese merced de descubrirse, no fue posible acabarlo con ella, cosa que me encendió más el deseo de verla. Y para acrecentarle más –*o ya fuese de industria o acaso* – sacó la señora una muy blanca mano con muy buenas sortijas. Estaba yo entonces bizarrísimo, con aquella gran cadena que vuesa merced debió de conocerme, el sombrero con plumas y cintillo, el vestido de colores a fuer de

> soldado, y tan gallardo a los ojos de mi locura que me daba a entender que *las podía matar en el aire*. (283–4, my italics)
>
> [Although I begged her out of courtesy to unveil herself, there was nothing doing, and this increased my desire to see her. It was still further increased by the fact that, *whether by accident or by design*, she let me catch a glimpse of a snowy-white hand adorned with very fine jewels. At that time I was looking very smart, with that big chain which you must have seen me wearing, my hat with plumes and bands, my coloured uniform so dashing, to my crazy way of thinking, that it seemed *I could conquer a woman just by looking at her*.]

Of course, the appearance of the white hand is not at all a chance occurrence, but rather the skilful manipulation of Estefanía, whose action achieves its intention of piquing her victim's interest. Estefanía's visual rhetoric mirrors the story-telling strategy of Campuzano, whose anticipatory remarks to the dogs' colloquy have the same effect on his audience, Peralta: "Todos estos preámbulos y encarecimientos que el alférez hacía antes de contar lo que había visto *encendían el deseo* de Peralta" ("All these preambles and commendations with which the Ensign prefaced his account of what he had seen *aroused the curiosity* of Peralta" [293, my italics]). Since we readers stand at one remove from Peralta, the mischievous parallel of Estefanía / Campuzano and narrator / narratee indicates that our reading activity may be very unlike the wholesome recreation promised by the prologue's *mesa de trucos*, and is in fact a sort of picaresque confidence game, in which the reader is both accomplice and dupe of an unreliable narrator. A painting by Georges de La Tour, who had read Cervantes's *Novelas ejemplares*, provides a visual corollary. "The Cheat with the Ace of Diamonds" (1630–4) is set in a tavern, with the roguish cheat on the left, a treacherous seductress in the centre, and a willing dupe in his finery on the right. The pleasurable distraction of the pretty servant girl serving wine compounds the deception (see Figure 6).[11] Campuzano's cocky hunting metaphor reinforces his libidinous motivation. Significantly, the figure of being able to "shoot birds on the fly" ("las podía matar en el aire"), also suggests rhetorical capability, a high level of wit or *agudeza*.[12] And the *ojos de mi locura* refer to Campuzano's moral blindness, an inversion of the "ojos" of the "entendimiento" and the "cuerpo" that will emerge renewed at the other side of *El coloquio de los perros*.

Figure 6 Georges de La Tour, *Cheater with the Ace of Diamond*, 1635 (oil on canvas). Louvre, Paris, France / Giraudon / The Bridgeman Art Library.

Campuzano's degradation is principally illustrated in his failure to exercise the higher faculties of reason and understanding, a shortcoming he acknowledges in hindsight. The following passage offers a summary of the principle motifs that will be played out in the two stories:

> Yo, que tenía entonces *el juicio*, no en la cabeza, sino en los carcañares, haciéndoseme *el deleite* en aquel punto mayor de lo que en *la imaginación* le pintaba y ofreciéndoseme tan a la vista la cantidad de hacienda, que ya la contemplaba en *dineros* convertida, sin hacer otros discursos de aquellos a que daba lugar *el gusto*, que me tenía *echados grillos al entendimiento*, le dije que yo era el venturoso y bien afortunado en haberme dado el cielo, casi por *milagro*, tal *compañera*, para hacerla señora de mi voluntad y de mi hacienda[.] (285–6, my italics)

> [At that time I had my brains in my heels rather than in my head, and as the *pleasure* seemed just then greater even than I had *imagined* it, and all that property in front of me as good as *cash* already, without stopping to look for any arguments beyond *my own wishes*, which *had quite overcome my reason*, I told her that I was the most fortunate of persons to have been presented with this heaven-sent *miracle*, a *companion* like this to be the mistress of my will and my possessions.]

The enslavement of Campuzano's judgment consists of visual attraction followed by an irrepressible urge to pursue his desire. His initial acquaintance with the lady follows this pattern ("quedé abrasado con las manos de nieve que había visto y muerto por el rostro que deseaba ver" – "I was inflamed with passion at the sight of those snowy hands, and dying to see her face" [284]), and the ocular emphasis of the scene contributes to its thematic exposition: the "eyes of the body," which can be easily delighted and deceived, are set against the "eyes of the soul." Castiglione gave an account of this traditional tension, as he exhorted the courtier to

> turn within himself to contemplate what he sees with the eyes of the mind, which begin to be penetrating and clear-sighted once those of the body have lost the flower of their delight; and in this manner, having shed all evil, purged by the study of true philosophy, directed towards the life of the spirit, and practised in the things of the intellect, the soul turns to contemplate its own substance, and as if awakened from deepest sleep it opens the eyes which all men posses but few use [.] (IV, 339)

The process described by Castiglione, including the different types of vision, the inward contemplation and reference to sleep, bears a striking resemblance to Campuzano's somnolent and ultimately eye-opening journey through the manuscript of the dogs.

Play and the Liminal Underworld Experience

Campuzano learns through painful experience, transmuted into the art of the manuscript, what the prescient Preciosa knew at the outset of *La gitanilla*, wisely laying out the following conditions to her suitor:

> Primero, tengo que saber si sois el que decís; luego, hallando esta verdad, habéis de dejar la casa de vuestros padres y la habéis de trocar por nuestros ranchos, y tomando el traje de gitano, habéis de cursar dos años

en nuestras escuelas … Y habéis de considerar que en el tiempo de este noviciado podría ser que cobrásedes la vista, que ahora debéis de tener perdida, o, por lo menos, turbada, y viésedes que os convenía huir de lo que ahora seguís con tanto ahínco. (86)

[To begin with, I shall have to find out if you are who you say; then, when this has proved true, you will have to leave your parents' house and exchange it for our camps, and taking gypsy garb, spend two years in our schools … And you must bear in mind that during the period of this novitiate you might recover your sight, which you must have lost now or which at any rate must be blurred; and you might then see that you must flee from what you now so zealously pursue.]

Andrés is called upon to prove himself in play, as he takes up the trappings of gypsy life for a determined period of time, after which he may freely choose to marry or to leave. The initiation rites, complete with a speech from the wise elder ("un gitano viejo"), signal Andrés's entrance into a peculiar association: "y sentándose Andrés sobre un medio alcornoque, pusiéronle en las manos un martillo y unas tenazas, y al son de dos guitarras que dos gitanos tañían, le hicieron dar dos cabriolas" ("and when Andrés had sat down on the stump of the cork oak, they put a hammer and tongs in his hand, and to the sound of two guitars played by two of the gypsies, they made him caper about a few times" [100]). The gypsy community is an ambivalent liminal realm, combining elements of don Quijote's speech on the Golden Age (freedom, equality, nature's bounty) and those of a sinister underworld (incest, thieving, killing of unfaithful wives). Turner's notion, as discussed above in relation to *Don Quijote*, is suggestive for a number of the *novelas*:

Liminality may involve a complex sequence of episodes in sacred space-time, and may also include subversive and ludic (or playful) events. The factors of culture are isolated, in so far as it is possible to do this with multivocal symbols … such as trees, images, paintings, dance forms, etc., that are each susceptible not of a single meaning but of many meanings. Then the factors or elements of culture may be recombined in numerous, often grotesque ways, grotesque because they are arrayed in terms of possible or fantasied rather than experienced combinations. (27)

La gitanilla and *Rinconete y Cortadillo* present initiations into societies that subvert, but also represent, in distorted form, significant aspects of official society.

The ambivalence of the liminal experience is important because *La gitanilla*, like *Rinconete y Cortadillo* and *La ilustre fregona*, does not simply depict the protagonist's rescue from a lower world of vice, followed by re-integration in an ideal society. The lower worlds represent liberation and novel experience, accompanied by implicit as well as explicit critique of official society – often, as we have seen, as a variation of the *menosprecio de corte* tradition. In *La gitanilla*, the suspect character of the upper world is succinctly illustrated by Preciosa's encounter with the noblemen of the esteemed order of Calatrava, who appear more dedicated to idleness than any spiritual or military calling: "Asomóse Preciosa a la reja, que era baja, y vio en una sala muy bien aderezada y muy fresca muchos caballeros que, unos paseándose y otros jugando a diversos juegos, se entretenían" ("Preciosa looked in at the window, which was a low one, and saw a room which looked cool and richly furnished, with a great number of gentlemen, who were enjoying themselves, some walking about and others playing various games" [72]). Forcione, who discusses the numerous references to gambling addiction and penury in the court of Felipe III, points out the dramatic contrast between the idle noblemen's offer of gambling tips – "Entren, entren las gitanillas, que les daremos barato" ("Come in, let the gypsy girls come in, for we'll give them some of our winnings" [72]) – and the pious reception by Andrés's father: "Subid, niñas, que aquí os darán limosna" ("Come up, girls, for they'll give you alms here" [92]).[13] At any rate, the gambling noblemen do not seem to represent the civilized ideal of aristocratic card playing and *sprezzatura* hoped for by some reformers (see Santo-Tomás, 159). Rather than a simplistic, Manichean vision, *La gitanilla* presents a critique of the decadent court society as well as the gypsy underworld, often using the latter to shed satirical light upon the former. In addition to testing and legitimizing the foundations of his union with Preciosa, Andrés's play experience affords a renewed understanding of his own society.[14]

El casamiento engañoso offers a more problematic sense of redemption than the *novelas* referenced above, and only at the end of its accompanying tale. Campuzano thinks he has secured a luxurious existence in his impulsive union with Estefanía. But their hedonism is threatened when a startled entourage arrives at the house, and Hortigosa's animated reprimand deflates the false utopia: "¡Milagros veo hoy en esta casa! ¡A fe que se ha ido bien del pie a la mano la señora Estefanía, fiada en la amistad de mi señora!" ("I can hardly believe my eyes. I must say Doña Estefanía has gone too far, taking advantage of my lady's good nature!" [288]). Both the miracle of riches observed by Campuzano in the house and the ideal of companionship he saw in Estefanía are dispersed. Doña Estefanía tries to salvage the situation by suggesting that a hidden meaning lies behind the appearances: "No reciba vuesa merced pesadumbre ... y entienda que no sin misterio ve lo que ve en esta su casa" ("Don't be upset ... and be sure that what you are seeing here in your home is not what you think" [288]). Although her attempt to insinuate the enigmatic character of appearances involves little more than a simple irony, hers is another statement that will find a complex resonance in *El coloquio de los perros*.

After realizing the deception, Campuzano seeks to resolve the situation by exercising on Estefanía "un ejemplar castigo" ("an exemplary punishment" 290). But again, what he takes to be chance intervenes ("Pero la suerte ... ordenó que en ninguna parte donde pensé hallar a doña Estefanía la hallase" – "However luck ... determined that I couldn't find Doña Estefanía, hard though I looked" [290]), and Campuzano falls into a deep sleep in the church of San Llorente. Just as what precipitated his downfall was not chance but the intention of Estefanía, the beginning of his redemption – his slumber rather than finding and beating his "wife" – is strongly associated with Providential design.[15] The traditional moral vocabulary and didactic tone are reinforced by the progressively constrictive spaces, ending in the tomb-like empty chest: "Aquí me tuvo de nuevo Dios de su mano. Fui a ver mi baúl, y halléle abierto y como sepultura que esperaba cuerpo difunto, y a buena razón había de ser el mío si yo tuviera entendimiento para saber sentir y ponderar tamaña desgracia" ("But I could feel the hand of God upon me again. I went to look at my trunk and found it open, like a tomb awaiting a corpse, and the corpse might well have been me, if my mind had been up to appreciating the full weight of my misfortune" [290]). The game of mutual deception ends in a draw: the material gain sought by Estefanía was illusory, and Campuzano's concupiscence has left him deceived and diseased. Even though he would like simply to leave the experience behind and begin anew, or *volver a barajar*, he is left with a tangible reminder that this particular game has infringed on real life; it has not been carried out "sin daño de barras." Rather than a "castigo ejemplar" of Estefanía, we are given the more complex exemplarity of Campuzano's convalescence at the hospital, which includes the mysterious yet highly cohesive and relevant *Coloquio de los perros*.

It is on its principle level of plot structure, theme and point of view that *El coloquio de los perros* most resembles picaresque narrative.[16] This level of the tale includes Berganza's episodes with different masters (the picaresque *mozo de muchos amos*), and the panorama of degradation and hypocrisy that his low perspective affords. The world experienced by Berganza is primarily characterized by violence, treachery, and vindictiveness, in which vice is present at birth and thrives in society. The constable and the court clerk, for example, are complicit with prostitutes in the predatory extortion of foreigners: "Estas les servían de red y de anzuelo para pescar en seco ... andaban siempre a caza de extranjeros" ("These women acted as net or hook to make their catches for them ... They were always on the hunt for foreigners" [324]). It hardly needs to be emphasized that this is not the beneficial *caza y pesca* of Diego de Miranda or Tomé Cecial in *Don Quijote*. As Cipión remarks upon hearing of the facility with which Berganza learns to attack the bulls, "No me maravillo, Berganza; que como el hacer mal viene de natural cosecha, fácilmente se aprende el hacerle" ("I'm not surprised, Berganza, for since wrong-doing comes naturally, one easily learns it" [302]). His use of the impersonal reflexive marks no distinction between men and dogs, and the rest of Berganza's story affirms many similarities between the species.

The peculiar physiognomy of our *pícaro* has varied implications. On the one hand, the protagonist of *Guzmán de Alfarache* and *Lazarillo de Tormes* can be seen to be parodied as a back-biting dog. This function accords with the tale's underlining of humanity's feral nature. On the other hand, there are canine qualities, as well as aspects of Berganza's own particular character, that suggest possibilities of exemplarity in a low place. In spite of the fact that malice comes easily to Berganza (demonstrated both in his vocation at the slaughterhouse and his penchant for slander as he tells his story), Cipión brings up some laudable canine characteristics during the dogs' initial conjectures about their sudden gift of speech: "Lo que yo he oído alabar y encarecer es nuestra mucha memoria, el agradecimiento y gran fidelidad nuestra; tanto, que nos suelen pintar por símbolo de la amistad" ("What I have heard extolled is our good memory, our gratitude and our great loyalty; to such an extent that they often depict us as the symbol of friendship" [300]). Aphoristic commonplaces perhaps, but both qualities – fidelity and memory – are central to the thematic exposition of the frame tale, from Estefanía's betrayal of Clementa's trust to the indelible mark of deceit on Campuzano's mind (and body); and both are developed further in the dialogue. Berganza demonstrates his fidelity in his confrontation with the servant girl who momentarily succeeds at bribing him into complicity in her carnal encounters with her fellow slave: "Pero, en efeto, llevado de mi buen natural, quise responder a lo que a mi amo debía, pues tiraba sus gajes y comía su pan, como lo deben hacer no sólo los perros honrados, quien se les da renombre de agradecidos, sino todos aquellos que sirven" ("but in fact, carried away by my natural goodness, I decided to do my duty to my master, for I was drawing my wages from him and eating his food. After all, this is the duty not only of honest dogs, who are famous for their gratitude, but of all who serve" [320]). As illustrated in the episode of the shepherds, it is this sort of civic-mindedness (provided, of course, that one accepts the premise of forced servitude!) that is lacking among the wolfish humans of *El coloquio de los perros*. Berganza's use of his keen canine memory is also edifying, from his review of Latin during his free time at the merchant's house, to his leisurely reflections on topics such as human vice and the discrepancy between the reality and literary representation of pastoral life.

As with many Cervantine characters, Berganza is depicted during crucial moments of cognitive and moral development, and his education takes many forms. Berganza's stay at the Jesuit school is the most optimistic of his episodes, presenting an image of good-humoured companionship. Like Tomás in *El licenciado Vidriera*, Berganza is enthralled by student life ("corren parejas en ella la virtud y el gusto, y se pasa la mocedad aprendiendo y holgándose" – "for virtue and pleasure go there hand in hand, and one spends one's youth in learning and in enjoying oneself" [317]), and he sees travelling as an extension of his education ("el andar tierras y comunicar con diversas gentes hace a los hombres discretos" – "travel and meeting different people teaches men wisdom" [332]). As with many *pícaros*, Berganza's principle education consists of frequently unsavoury life experiences: "¡Oh, qué de cosas te pudiera decir ahora de las que aprendí en la escuela de aquella jifera dama de mi amo!" ("Oh, the things I could tell you that I learned in the school of my butcher-master's lady!" [306]). But unlike Vidriera, whose quest for knowledge leads to isolation, Berganza's education exhibits elements of Montaigne's and Erasmus's notions of arriving at wisdom through experience – disorderly though it may be – rather than through rigid book-learning.

While Berganza does display moments of genuine insight, Cipión points out that his pontifications are occasionally sententious. Such is the case when Berganza claims to see higher forces at work in the shaping of his life: "Considera, Cipión, ahora esta rueda variable de la fortuna mía: ayer me vi estudiante, y hoy me ves corchete" ("Think, Scipio, how the wheel of fortune turned for me: yesterday I was a student and now I'm a constable" [323]). Guzmán de Alfarache frequently explained his world in terms of allegory and providential structure, and many of Cipión's responses to Berganza can be seen as critical allusions to Alemán, as well as to *Lazarillo de Tormes*: "Asi va el mundo, y no hay para qué te pongas ahora a exagerar los vaivenes de fortuna, como si hubiera mucha diferencia de ser mozo de un jifero a serlo de un corchete" ("That's the way of the world, and there's no reason why you should start exaggerating the swings of fortune, as if there were much to choose between serving a butcher and a constable" [323]). Indeed, Cipión himself considers the vicissitudes of Fortune's wheel as a possible clarification of the witch's oracle; but this exegesis, like Berganza's above, proves unsatisfactory. In both cases, such a facile imposition of meaning is rejected because, upon closer inspection, it seems inapplicable to the dogs' empirical experience. The absence of signifying structures, as we shall see, bestows upon Cipión and Berganza a peculiar, frightening freedom, not unlike the *mimesis* of the improvising actor: at work is the unscripted play of possibility within a limiting framework – a somewhat anxious version of the prologue's *mesa de trucos*.

Berganza's stint as the *perro sabio* in the drummer's travelling curiosity show recalls, as a colourful example of popular entertainment, the wandering tricksters of *El retablo de las maravillas*, as well as the avaricious fishermen who forcibly take the metamorphosed Lazarillo on the road as an exhibition in Juan de Luna's *Segunda Parte del Lazarillo*.[17] The "conjuring" show in Montilla, which features a judicious and physically gifted dog, illustrates both the complexity of humour and the fragility of the play realm. The first *conjuros*, to which the dog refuses to react, involve satirical commonplaces: the drummer entreats Berganza to jump for the *viejo verde* who dyes his beard (similar to jokes in *Guzmán de Alfarache* and *El licenciado Vidriera*), for the pretentious doña Pimpinela, and for the student who signs with a false title. Recalling the one festive scene of *El licenciado Vidriera*, he then asks the dog to jump for a number of famous wines, to which Berganza, following his signal, responds affirmatively. The drummer proceeds in this vein, announcing the wise dog's ability to imbibe great quantities of wine, and to sing and perform a variety of dances expertly. The promise of such a spectacle commands the rapt anticipation of the townspeople, but the following *conjuro* results in chaos, as it inadvertently turns into a real incantation: "Volved, hijo Gavilán, y con gentil agilidad y destreza deshaced los saltos que habéis hecho; pero ha de ser a devoción de la famosa hechicera que dicen que hubo en este lugar" ("Come back, Gavilán, my boy, and go through again all those jumps you've done so nimbly and skilfully; but you must take your orders from the famous witch who they say came from this village" [335]). Thinking he has merely alluded to popular lore, the drummer's entertainment has unintentionally crossed the line into reality, inciting the indignation of one of his spectators. The offended Cañizares puts a chaotic end to the show with her cursing and insults. In Maese Pedro's puppet show, a deluded don Quijote takes the theatrical illusion for reality; in *El retablo de las maravillas*, the townspeople are duped into creating a non-existent illusion based on their real social obsessions; in the *perro sabio* scene, the entertainment presented deteriorates because it touches on matters of consequence for a spectator. As in Erasmus's "Exorcism," the play realm is contaminated by real life. Like Chanfalla and la Chirinos at the end of *El retablo de la Maravillas*, the roguish drummer is unfazed by the destruction of his spectacle, since he has made a good profit. The drummer might have avoided the debacle had he exercised the moderation of the *eutrapelos* – as the narrating Berganza comments, his manner of entertaining is more reminiscent of the *bomolochos*: "mostróse aquel día chocarrero en demasía" ("he surpassed himself with his games that day" [334]).

It is with the drummer that Berganza develops a critical attitude towards popular entertainment, and a number of his judgments recall those of Vidriera. While serious actors labour in memorizing lines and travelling the countryside ("made perpetual gypsies," as Vidriera remarked), the puppeteers are idle purveyors of cheap entertainment, who most likely resort to thievery in order to fund their drinking. Berganza's primary concern with regard to theatre is its degraded state. His master the playwright is unable to hold an audience's attention, ridiculous poets are obsessed with minutiae of historical detail and bizarre syntax and metrical form, and the *entremeses* in which he participates provide nothing but farcical humour aiming to please a vulgar audience. If the spectators of Berganza's tumultuous *entremeses* display a derelict laughter involving the basest sensibilities ("con que daba que reír a los ignorantes" – "with which he made the ignorant laugh" [354]), Cañizares also reveals an impoverished laughter, as described in her "anointings," in hallucinatory transports to demonic orgies in the Pyrenees: "pues mientras se ríe no se llora" ("for you can't weep while you're laughing" [343]). Such laughter is escapist, promoting denial rather than insight. In anticipation of the process through which the dogs (particularly Berganza) develop a comprehending, humorous outlook, and the liberating implications this process has with regard to the convalescent Ensign, it is worth underscoring that Cañizares's laughter involves a turning away from the painful realities of her life. A genuine sense of humour, as discussed above, involves the ability to create pleasure from the very elements that cause distress.[18]

A consideration of the few instances of genuine humour in *El coloquio de los perros* will serve as a transition to a discussion of the play element. The laughter of the four lunatics in the hospital of Valladolid following the *arbitrista*'s economic plan of public fasting demonstrates a significant element of distance and self-effacement: "Riyéronse todos del arbitrio y del arbitrante, y él también se riyó de sus disparates" ("They all laughed at the scheme of the schemer, and he laughed himself at his crazy ideas" [357]). Such laughter reveals the men's ability to detach themselves from their obsessions momentarily, and suggests a comprehension of the potential arbitrariness and insignificance of their respective projects. Although the children's amusement in the Jesuit classroom lacks a cognitive function on the part of the participants, it is a vital ingredient in the story's only image of harmonious community. By carrying the forgotten notebook to class, Berganza endears himself to the laughing schoolchildren, who embrace the happy dog as a playmate: "con lo cual tenía una vida de rey, y aun mejor, porque era descansada, a causa que los estudiantes dieron en burlarse conmigo, y domestiquéme con ellos de tal manera que me metían la mano en la boca y los más chiquillos subían sobre mí" ("and as a result I lived like a king, and even better, for my life was an easy one. The students took to playing games with me, and I got so tame with them that they would put their hands in my mouth, and the smaller ones would get on my back" [316]). The scene of recreation and trust between the powerful canine and small children represents an inversion of the episode of the wolf-like shepherds, and the playfulness of the students is emphasized by their joking *with* him ("burlarse conmigo") – a significant contrast to the typical picaresque students, who joke at the expense of others (burlarse *de*).[19] The delight the children take in feeding Berganza salads and muffins in order to see him eat "como si fuera persona" ("as if I were human") recalls the effects of Lucius's appetite on his masters in *The Golden Ass*: "They no longer worried about the losses they were sustaining; they were astonished at the portentous spectacle of an ass as gourmet, and they split their sides with uncontrollable laughter" (bk. 10). Berganza's pleasant student experience ("yo pasaba una vida de estudiante sin hambre y sin sarna" – "I lived the life of a student, free of hunger and of the itch" [317]) combines recreation and study ("corren parejas en ella la virtud y el gusto, y se pasa la mocedad aprendiendo y holgándose" – "for virtue and pleasure go there hand in hand, and one spends one's youth in learning and in enjoying oneself"), recalling Erasmus's contention that youth learn best when enjoying themselves: "I'm not sure anything is learned better than what is learned as a game" (*Colloquies* 625). Berganza's praise of the Jesuits' edifying pedagogy reveals an intriguing aesthetic element: "como les pintaban la fealdad y horror de los vicios y les dibujaban la hermosura de las virtudes, para que, aborrecidos ellos y amadas ellas, consiguiesen el fin para que fueron criados" ("how they depicted for them the ugliness and horror of vice and portrayed for them the beauty of virtue, so that hating the former and loving the latter, they might attain the end for which they were created" [316]). This process of vivid representation, involving intense experience complemented by reflection, is in fact central to the elaborate coherence of *El casamiento engañoso* and *El coloquio de los perros*.

The story's first explicit reference to play follows the Ensign Campuzano's relation of his recent misfortunes to his friend, Peralta, who seeks to console Campuzano by observing that the relationship that was the source of his troubles is over:

> – Desa manera –dijo el Licenciado –, entre vuesa merced y la señora doña Estefanía, pata es la traviesa.
>
> – Y tan pata – respondió el Alférez –, que podemos volver a barajar; pero el daño está, señor Licenciado, en que ella podrá deshacer de mis cadenas y yo no de la falsía de su término; y, en efeto, mal que me pese, es prenda mía. (291)
>
> ["In that case," said the licentiate, "as far as you and Doña Estefanía are concerned, you're quits."
>
> "And so much so," answered the Ensign, "that we can shuffle the cards and start again; but the trouble is, Licentiate, that she can get rid of my chains, but I can't get over the dirty trick she played on me. The fact is that whether I like it or not I've got the consequences for keeps."]

As noted above, the use of card-playing imagery is particularly appropriate to the Ensign's situation, since both he and doña Estefanía have attempted to play out similar schemes in a comedy of mutual deception. The re-shuffling of the cards presents the attractive possibility of a new beginning, suggesting the exhilarating combination of uncertainty and optimism one feels upon being dealt a new hand. Frye has pointed out that "cards and dice are common in descent narratives, because of their overtones of fatality and chance" (*The Secular Scripture* 124). The central romance elements of fatality, chance, and the hoped-for metamorphosis in the lower world are present in Cervantes's final pair of exemplary tales, and also as Durandarte considers the possibility that don Quijote may represent the key to the prophecy of his disenchantment ("paciencia y barajar" [II, 23]). For Campuzano, whose previous "hand" has proven unsuccessful and whose moral failures are painfully indicated by his past actions, the possibility of re-shuffling his cards might seem particularly liberating. In a realization of a significant discrepancy between games and real life, however, Campuzano acknowledges that the consequences of his past action are still with him, in the form of syphilis. If his physical convalescence is contingent on the prescription of copious sweating, Campuzano's spiritual recuperation is achieved through contemplating his past life, a redemptive process of which the strange dialogue of Cipión and Berganza clearly forms a part. Central to this dialogue's bearing on the Ensign's recovery is its contribution to his self-awareness through an imaginative exploration of the very impulses that landed him in the hospital; and the process is initiated by his conscious reflection upon and the telling of his experience with doña Estefanía to Peralta. The structure of Cervantes's narrative thus points to Campuzano as the principle participant and beneficiary of the recreation, allowing him, by story's end, to accompany his friend outside with a sense of renewal. But the elaborate architecture also indicates other players, pointing inward, to Cipión and Berganza (and Cañizares), and, as is typical in Cervantes, outward, to the reader.

The discussion between Campuzano and Peralta regarding the mysterious manuscript contains Huizinga's essential structure of play. The "playing field" is the physical manuscript, which Peralta will read while the Ensign takes a nap. Campuzano and Peralta then attempt to agree on the rules of their game, which gives rise to a few sticking points. As one might expect, there is discord regarding the plausibility of the situation: in spite of the Ensign's appeal to the authority of ocular and aural observation committed to paper, Peralta refuses to accept as fact that the dogs had use of speech and reason. But acceptable conditions are soon reached, as Peralta agrees to read the story as fiction: "Como vuesa merced … no se canse más en persuadirme que oyó hablar a los perros, de muy buena gana oiré ese coloquio" ("Provided you don't weary yourself further in persuading me that you heard the dogs speaking ... I shall be very happy to listen to this colloquy" [295]). It is significant that Peralta insists on designating the account as fiction before he will read it, as this assures for him that the activity is completely removed from what Huizinga called "the sphere of necessity or material utility": he can now read for pleasure, free from the obligation to confront the potentially disturbing (or portentous) implications of real-life talking dogs. These rules having been agreed upon, Peralta accepts the manuscript in an attitude of levity: "le tomó riyéndose y como haciendo burla de todo lo que había oído y de lo que pensaba leer" ("he took it, laughing and apparently making a joke of all that he had heard and of what he was expecting to read" [295]).

The *admiración* and *maravilla* referred to by Campuzano and Peralta as well as by Cipión and Berganza, along with the various disputes and instances of uncertainty and anticipation, bespeak a form of play, a rule-bound agon with tension, transport, and surprise. Huizinga characterizes this peculiar disposition: "The play-mood is one of rapture and enthusiasm, and is sacred or festive in accordance with the occasion. A feeling of exaltation and tension accompanies the action, mirth and relaxation follow" (132). Peralta's tentative mirth ("laughing and apparently making a joke") is fitting as he anticipates the enchanting ambiguity of the aesthetic space, in which rational criteria often dissipate amidst the potency of the experience. Huizinga elaborates on this inherent ambivalence:

> [A]s we have already pointed out, the consciousness of play being "only pretend" does not by any means prevent it from proceeding with the utmost seriousness, with an absorption, a devotion that passes into rapture and, temporarily at least, completely abolishes that troublesome "only" feeling. Any game can at any time wholly run away with the players. The contrast between play and seriousness is always fluid. (8)

Gadamer has also commented on the ambiguity of play which seems to be acknowledged by Peralta's attitude: "The player knows very well what play is, and that what he is doing is 'only a game'; but he does not know what exactly he 'knows' in knowing that" (102). In like manner, Ife discusses how the story examines an issue at the heart of contemporary misgivings over fiction: "What Cervantes seems to be doing in the *Coloquio de los perros* is asserting with particular eloquence the independence of aesthetic and rational belief, and illustrating in the process the fact that literature is little more than an organised form of language depending almost entirely for its impact on inherent properties of language" (60). Cervantes's two mastiffs explore these enigmatic aspects of play, and suggest what is at stake when humans partake of such games.

The dialogue of Cipión and Berganza involves many significant ludic elements, although their activity does not, for them, take place outside the sphere of necessity or material utility: the mystery of their identity is at stake in the realization of their stories, and the solution is complicated by both time constraints and the unreliability of the information they have to consider. All of these elements make for an excellent play structure from the reader's perspective. But what is intriguing about this story is that the characters themselves develop, amidst the uncertainties of their situation, an attitude of play. As we shall see, although such an attitude is largely a reaction to the apparent lack of necessity and meaning in their world, the play response is not to be mistaken for a cynical or frivolous outlook. It involves, rather, a spirit of scepticism and humour, and a highly collaborative ethos.

Dialogue and the Digressive Quest for Meaning in *El coloquio de los perros*

> Berganza amigo ... retirémonos a esta soledad y entre estas esteras, donde podremos gozar sin ser sentidos desta no vista merced que el cielo en un mismo punto a los dos nos ha hecho. (299)
>
> [Berganza, my friend ... let's go off quietly over there to those mats, where we may enjoy unobserved this unprecedented blessing which heaven has granted to both of us at one and the same time.]

Rather than the sun-bathed public enjoyment of the prologue's billiards table, the dogs' colloquy is a hidden, nocturnal endeavour. But the dark implications of the mastiffs' meeting are immediately tamed by their amiability and collaboration while setting the rules for their interaction. As the dogs express surprise at their ability to speak, and speculate on how this could be, explanations range from the eschatological-allegorical – talking dogs as a portent of impending doom – to the deductive: since dogs have long been held up as emblems of positive qualities (fidelity, friendship, memory), perhaps their linguistic proficiency is not so surprising. Unable to clarify the mystery, they agree upon a *modus operandi*:

> Pero sea lo que fuere, nosotros hablamos, sea portento o no, que lo que el cielo tiene ordenado que suceda, no hay diligencia ni sabiduría humana que lo pueda prevenir, y, así, no hay para qué ponernos a disputar nosotros cómo o por qué hablamos ... y no sabemos cuánto tiempo durará esta nuestra ventura, sepamos aprovecharnos della y hablemos toda esta noche, sin dar lugar al sueño que nos impida este gusto, de mí por largos tiempos deseado. (301)
>
> [Well, anyway, we are speaking, whether it's a portent or not; for what heaven has ordained should happen, no human endeavour or wisdom can prevent; and so there is no point in our starting to dispute about how or why we are speaking ... and we don't know how long this good fortune of ours will last, let us take advantage of it, and talk all night, without allowing sleep to rob us of this pleasure, which I have so long desired.]

Berganza concurs that they should waste no time enjoying their unexpected capacity, and anticipates the disordered form of his discourse: "Empero ahora, que tan sin pensarlo me veo enriquecido deste divino don de la habla, pienso gozarle y aprovecharme dél lo más que pudiere, dándome priesa a decir todo aquello que se me acordare, *aunque sea atropellada y confusamente*" ("However, now that I see myself so unexpectedly endowed with this divine gift of speech, I intend to enjoy it and take advantage of it as much as I can, making haste to say everything I can remember, *even if it is all jumbled up and confused*" [301, my italics]). The dogs will, by necessity, practice what Montaigne preferred: the nonlinear, digressive, chance-informed discourse of "prompt speech."[20]

As interlocutor, Cipión's role is to keep the narrating Berganza on task: "escucha, y si te cansare lo que te fuere diciendo, o me reprehende o manda que calle" ("listen to me; and if what I tell you wearies you, check me or tell me to be quiet" [302]). The relationship between speaker and listener grows complicated as Cipión increasingly feels compelled to interrupt. Since Berganza is unable to refrain from criticizing the vices he has observed in the world around him, Cipión intervenes on grounds both moral and aesthetic:

> – ¿Al murmurar llamas filosofar? ¡Así va ello! ¡Canoniza, canoniza, Berganza, a la maldita plaga de la murmuración y dale el nombre que

> quisieres, que ella dará a nosotros el de cínicos, que quiere decir perros murmuradores. Y, por tu vida, que calles ya y sigas tu historia.
> – ¿Cómo la tengo de seguir si callo?
> – Quiero decir que la sigas de golpe, sin que la hagas que parezca pulpo, según la vas añadiendo colas. (319)
>
> [– You call slandering philosophizing? So that's how it is! Fine, Berganza, make a virtue of this cursed plague of backbiting, and give it any name you like; it will cause us to be called cynics, which means backbiting dogs. Now, for pity's sake, be quiet and go on with your story.
> – How am I to go on if I'm to be quiet?
> – I mean you should follow it consecutively without making it look like an octopus by the way you keep adding tails.]

Not only does Cipión object to the mean-spiritedness and potential hypocrisy of satire; he abhors the resulting shapelessness of Berganza's narrative, its tentacled digressions giving rise to the monstrous form of an octopus.

As we have seen, what Montaigne warns of as "a varying and formless body, which can be neither tied nor grasped" (II, 12, p. 419) is not entirely negative. Cipión resembles the primary "literary critic" in *Don Quijote*, the Canon of Toledo, who argues for verisimilitude and proportion, also to avoid the "formless body" of digressive, open-ended and fantastic narrative (I, 47–8). But despite the substantial authority of the Aristotelian tradition invoked by Cipión and the Canon, neither of Cervantes's two masterpieces consistently conforms to such precepts. Part of the seismic tremors that emanate from Cervantes throughout literary history is due to the way in which his narratives contain a dynamic similar to that of Montaigne's *Essays*, what Rigolot called "[r]eflexive operations ... grafted onto the main logical thread of the discourse" ("Problematizing Renaissance Exemplarity" 15). The largely monologic genres of epic, pastoral, exemplary tale, give way to heteroglossia, generic cross-contamination (and fertilization), unexpected combinations and spontaneous shifts. One result is a hitherto unprecedented consciousness of the artificiality of artistic or conceptual constructions, and a novel interest in holding them up against the chaotic vitality of the quotidian. The ungraspable, formless body of the octopus (and the mind) simultaneously threatens meaning and holds out the possibility for renewed understanding and experience.

The initial stages of the dogs' dialogue, with Cipión and Berganza negotiating the rules of their storytelling and arguing about issues such as decorum and the definition of philosophizing, exhibit the "to-and-fro movement" of play. As noted above in relation to Montaigne, the dialogue form itself comprises a sort of conceptual tennis match. Gadamer's observation is worth reviewing in the present context: "In order for there to be a game, there always has to be, not necessarily literally another player, but something else with which the player plays and which automatically responds to his move with a countermove" (105–6). Cervantes's method of description also assumes this to-and-fro quality, particularly in scenes of confusion and farce. The effect, as in the following spate of conjectures caused by Cañizares's exposure in the hospital courtyard, involves the creation of tension about the meaning and the outcome of the particular circumstances. It is an epistemological to-and-fro:

> Acudió la gente del hospital, y viendo aquel retablo, *unos decían*: "Ya la bendita Cañizares es muerta …" *otros, más considerados, la tomaron el pulso …* por do se dieron a entender que estaba en éxtasis y arrobada … *Otros hubo que dijeron*: "Esta puta vieja, sin duda debe de ser bruja" … *Curiosos hubo que se llegaron a hincarle alfileres* por las carnes … [Cañizares] creyó, y creyó la verdad, que yo había sido el autor de su deshonra; y así, arremetió a mí[.] (344–5, my italics)

> [The people from the hospital came out, and when they saw the scene, *some said*, "Old Cañizares is dead …" *Others, more practical, took her pulse …* came to the conclusion that she was in an ecstasy … *There were others who said*: "There's no doubt this old whore must be a witch" … *Some curious people went as far as to stick pins right up to the head* into her flesh … [Cañizares] thought, and thought rightly, that I had been the cause of her dishonour. So she attacked me]

As with much else in *El coloquio de los perros*, the to-and-fro sets forth various possibilities, approximating the truth of the situation, but without any clear resolution. As Nabokov indicated in his scoring of the episodes in *Don Quijote* as a tennis match, Cervantes's playful mode of representation – the constant sense of "move and countermove" on the level of dialogue, description, episode, and genre – creates a background sense of order even where chaos is the primary impression.

Berganza's autobiography proceeds in fits and starts, and the digressive exchanges between narrator and narratee are as compelling as the main story line. Of particular interest is the dogs' discussion of hypocrisy and the limits of satire. Having found it difficult to refrain from criticizing, Berganza retracts a promise he has made to bite his own tongue every time he slanders: "Lo que yo dije no fue poner ley, sino prometer que me mordería la lengua cuando murmurase. Pero ahora no van las cosas por el tenor y rigor de las antiguas; hoy se hace una ley y mañana se rompe, *y quizá conviene que así sea*" ("What I said wasn't intended as a law, but a promise that I would bite my tongue when I was guilty of backbiting; but nowadays things aren't as strict as they used to be in times gone by. Today you make a law, and tomorrow you break it, *and perhaps it's right that it should be so*" [321, my italics]). Berganza's rationale recalls Montaigne's critique of the rigidity of laws and his awareness of the inadequacy of fixed precepts before the complexity of experience.[21] There follows an ironic defence of duplicity, as Berganza notes that virtuous acts have greater impact in plain view of the public than in the dark corner of the hospital. But when Cipión points out that, were he human, he would be called a hypocrite, Berganza's justification seems persuasive: "No sé lo que entonces hiciera; esto sé que quiero hacer ahora, que es no morderme, quedándome tantas cosas por decir que no sé cómo ni cuándo podré acabarlas" ("I don't know what I'd do then; but I know what I want to do now, and that's not to bite myself, when I have so many things left to say that I don't know how or when I can get through them" [321]). Rather than fall on his own sword, Berganza wants to proceed with his narrative, to take advantage of the opportunity they have been granted and not agonize over whether his conduct has been ideal. This is one of the many cases in which Cervantes illustrates the impoverishing effects of imperatives. Other instances, memorable for the extremity of their premises, include the playwright who cannot stage his performance without an exact hue of purple in the robes for his cardinals (*El coloquio de los perros* 351), the poet composing an epic exclusively in proparoxytone metre ("esdrújulamente") and without verbs (355), and Sancho's pastoral narrative, predicated on don Quijote remembering precisely how many goats have been shuttled across the river (*Don Quijote* I, 20). A salient aspect of Berganza's refusal to observe similarly strict rules is the way in which narrative and ethical concerns are intertwined: were he to punish himself for every minor transgression, the very instrument of the telling (his tongue) would be rendered useless. Better to acknowledge shortcomings and continue narrating. Perhaps the imperfections themselves will be a source of insight and pleasure.

The moment of greatest confusion and potential narrative aporia comes when Berganza recounts his meeting with the witch, Cañizares, who maintains the dogs are humans transformed at birth, and whose "oracle" would point to their future redemption. Claiming to convene with her devil and other witches in drug-induced transports, Cañizares represents an extreme of the disordered imagination. Unsure whether the orgiastic gatherings take place physically as well as mentally, she quixotically explains that "todo lo que nos pasa en la fantasía es tan intensamente que no hay diferenciarlo de cuando vamos real y verdaderamente" ("everything that happens to us in our imagination happens in such an intense way that it can't be distinguished from the times when we go really and truly" [340]). Berganza's contemplation of the hideously naked witch as she lies motionless in a claustrophobic cell is the nightmarish anti-climax of the story. Cañizares's promise to return with information pertaining to the dogs' redemption in human form evokes but ultimately travesties the romance motif of the hero's underworld journey. Her activity involves the opposite of dialogue; it is a solitary indulgence that leads to solipsism and alienation from human community. In her assumed identity as a witch, and the vertiginous experience of her nocturnal escapes, Cañizares would seem to indulge in Caillois's most chaotic and antisocial combination of play:

> The alliance of *mimicry* and *ilinx* leads to an inexorable, total frenzy which in its most obvious forms appears to be the opposite of play, an indescribable metamorphosis in the conditions of existence. The fit so provoked, being uninhibited, seems to remove the player as far from the authority, values, and influence of the real world, as the real world seems to influence the formal, regulated, and protected activities that characterize the wholly inhibited games subsumed under the rules of *agon* and *alea*. The association of simulation and vertigo is so powerful and so inseparable that it is naturally part of the sphere of the sacred, perhaps providing one of the principal bases for the terror and fascination of the sacred. (75–6)

The cultish character of Cañizares's "anointings" indeed conveys a sense of the sacred, even as the conventional sense of piety is inverted. Overcome by fear and disgust, Berganza drags the grotesque body *out* into the open air of the courtyard, where he can more calmly reflect upon the mystery of her evil and her wisdom. As the witch finds herself, at daybreak, in public view in the courtyard, the entire scene collapses into farce and confusion, and Berganza flees.

At this point in the narrative Cipión intervenes to discuss the meaning of the witch's oracle:

> Volverán a su forma verdadera
> cuando vieren con presta diligencia
> derribar los soberbios levantados
> y alzar a los humildes abatidos
> por mano poderosa para hacello. (346)
>
> [They will return to their true form
> when they see the mighty speedily brought down
> and the humble exalted by that hand which has the power to perform it.]

As when the dogs initially try to make sense of their speech, a variety of exegetical techniques are applied. Part of the humour in Cervantes's story lies in the way he sustains an implied tragic structure in the background of the canine dialogue (are these dogs the victims of a cruel fate, compelled to solve a sorceress's riddle in order to save themselves?), only to have this structure dissipate in an anti-climax of senselessness. The dual quality of ancient riddles, which were, according to Huizinga, "a ritual element of the highest importance and yet essentially a game" (110–11), is present in the prophecy of the dogs. It is an enigma, the solution of which has ontological implications for Cipión and Berganza. The demented alchemist and mathematician who reside in the hospital are also engaged in the solution of "magical questions": finding the philosopher's stone, the fixed point, and squaring the circle. Apart from the obvious material advantages sought by the alchemist, these two characters pursue a sort of "sacred knowledge" that will bestow upon them the special distinction of glimpsing the mysterious workings of the world.[22] Huizinga describes some of the typical conditions for the riddle competition as follows: "In principle there is only one answer to every question. It can be found if you know the rules of the game ... You have to know the secret language of the adepts and be acquainted with the significance of each symbol ... for the various categories of the phenomena" (110). These conditions are reflected in the dogs' prophecy, but the entire process is complicated by certain peculiarities of their situation and of Cervantes's narrative structure.

The dogs think the words (which allude, as Forcione noted, to Virgil and the Magnificat) are maybe an allegorical reference to Fortune's

Wheel. But since they have already observed the fluctuations of fortune many times, Cipión offers the following possibilities:

> [M]e doy a entender que no en el sentido alegórico sino en el literal, se han de tomar los versos de la Camacha; ni tampoco en éste se consiste nuestro remedio, pues muchas veces hemos visto lo que dicen y nos estamos tan perros como ves ... Digo, pues, que el verdadero sentido es un juego de bolos, donde con presta diligencia derriban los que están en pie y vuelven a alzar los caídos y esto por la mano de quien lo puede hacer. Mira, pues, si en el discurso de nuestra vida habremos visto jugar a los bolos, y si hemos visto por esto haber vuelto a ser hombres, si es que lo somos. (347)

> [I gather that it is not in the allegorical but in the literal sense that Camacha's verses are to be taken. However, the answer to our problem does not lie here either, for we have often seen what they say and we are still dogs as much as ever we were ... I tell you then that the meaning is just a game of ninepins, in which those who are standing are quickly knocked down and those who fall down get up again, and this by the hand of him who is able to perform it. Consider then whether we have ever seen this game of ninepins and whether in doing so we have become men again, if indeed that is what we are.]

The constructive and pleasurable play of the prologue, and the accompanying hope to find exemplary meaning in the oracle, have been reduced to a bowling game. The repetitive cycle of the ninepins suggests the futility of the dogs' situation, much like the seemingly endless re-shuffling of the card deck expresses the hopeless resignation of the spell-bound captives in the Cueva de Montesinos (*Don Quijote* II, 22–3). Both games emblematize a low point in hallucinatory, nightmarish narratives. A precursor image of the repetitive game as emblem of meaninglessness is found in *La Celestina*, in Pleberio's despairing image of the world as a "juego de hombres que andan en corro" ("game of men who go in circles").[23] Despite the structural similarities, however, the two underworld narratives exemplify the different visions of Cervantes's great novel and his story collection, a distinction intimated by our observation of the radically divergent images of the reader in the respective prologues: the subjective, private individual in *Don Quijote*; citizens convening in the *plaza* in the *Novelas ejemplares*. Forcione has argued that the traditional moral and theological vocabulary of *El coloquio de los perros*, however bleak, serves as a conventional admonition to a fallen humanity. In this it contrasts significantly with *Don Quijote*:

> The assault on the ideal model, the fabric of romance, in the Cave of Montesinos creates a metaphysical absence ... which is far more threatening than the demonic mistreatment of the divine in Berganza's underworld vision. The model is rent beyond all repair, and all that remains is a world totally disenchanted in the neutral continuum of time, implacably flowing in its destructive course, while a pathetic hero tries unsuccessfully to render his life and his relation to the world about him meaningful through a scheme of ideals which has no warrant other than his own isolated subjectivity. (*Cervantes and the Mystery of Lawlessness* 53)

As an image of play emblematizing the hero's plight, the card-shuffling of Durandarte anticipates the enigmatic peasants of Cézanne, ritualistically dealing the cards as modernity renders their way of life obsolete, captivated in a "collective solitaire" (see above, Figure 4). In the case of *El coloquio de los perros*, the quest for meaning may have led to a dead end, but dialogue will suggest a path to redemption, in the form of return to an exterior and public space of recreation.

Play and the Exemplarity of Process

In Cervantes as well as in Montaigne, the principle of dialogue poses a challenge to the tradition of exemplarity. Given its peculiar structure, *El coloquio de los perros* is a story that proceeds by way of discussion; its narration takes place within a dialogue. This structure does, not, as in *El conde Lucanor*, result in authorial control and fixing of meaning. Rather, it embeds a dynamic process of "point and counterpoint" that qualifies any pronouncement. We noted above how this ludic to-and-fro movement also pervades the *Essays* of Montaigne: his learning of Greek, arithmetic and geometry "in the form of amusement and exercise" (I, 26); his likening of conversation to playing tennis, in which speaker and listener have active, creative roles, bringing forth meaning in a collaborative if imprecise endeavour (III, 13). The static model of Example, associated with pedantry, book learning, schools, and the passive acceptance of authority, is called into question: "every example is lame, and the comparison that is drawn from experience is always faulty and imperfect" (III, 13, p. 819). Instead Montaigne advocates lively conversation, the tavern, and laughing self-deprecation along with satire. What emerges from such notions of learning, conversation, and reading is an exemplarity of process rather than of product. Herein lies both the modernity and modesty of his project. While meaning is rarely fixed and knowledge is inconclusive, the *Essays* continuously model the workings of an agile and independent mind.

"Of the art of discussion" contains many of the points of contact between Montaigne and Cervantes presently under consideration: satire of pedantry and general human folly, the chance-determined and "groping" nature of thought, the partiality of examples, the spirit of *serio ludere*, and an examination of the relationship between external conformity and internal freedom. If Montaigne compares vigorous conversation to the tournament, and truth to the quarry of hunters, he is careful to emphasize (like the contemporary tracts on licit entertainment considered above) the absence of dire consequence in the ideal *agon* of conversation. In fact, although he claims to enjoy rough and boisterous opposition, it is the ordered, rule-bound structure of conversation that Montaigne seems most eager to preserve. Quint observes that such an "order, like the larger social order for which it seems to serve as a model, becomes an end in itself. It depends on the rational capacities of the speakers to keep discussion on track and to the point, but even more on their mutual commitment to preserve the form of conversation over and above its matter and the positions they defend" (*Montaigne and the Quality of Mercy* 113). Montaigne returns to the image of the king to illustrate the crucial point that deference to authority and rules, while necessary and conducive to social stability, is not necessarily at odds with individual integrity: "What I myself adore in kings is the crowd of their adorers. All deference and submission is due to them, except that of our understanding. My reason is not trained to bend and bow, it is my knees" (III, 8, p. 714). Montaigne's defence of freedom of judgment and thought represents a peculiar combination of political obedience with inner autonomy. In light of France's destabilizing religious and class schisms, it represents a moderate alternative to rigid authoritarianism.[24] It is worth recalling a Cervantine phrase that is also politically suggestive: "Debajo de mi manto, al rey mato" ("Under my cloak, a fig for the king," *Don Quijote* I, Prólogo). While Cervantes is certainly encouraging the reader to judge his fiction freely, the question remains as to what extent he depicts life in society as oppressive, thus necessitating the private refuge of the text. In other words, are the independent readers and thinkers of Cervantes and Montaigne meant as corollaries to a disaffected, and thus potentially unruly, subject?

We saw above how Cipión and Berganza illustrate that dialogue is imprecise, digressive, and does not always lead to clear resolution, and that Montaigne depicted this phenomenon within a single consciousness ("having undertaken as exercise and sport to maintain an opinion contrary to my own" [II, 12, p. 426]). As with the play of authentic conversation, the structure of thought is not so much a dialectic as a meandering process. And although his *Essays* are a monument of erudition, a testament to time spent alone with books, reading itself is for Montaigne a form of dialogue, a type of ideal recreation: "And every day I amuse myself reading authors without any care for their learning, looking for their style, not their subject. Just as I seek the company of some famous mind, not to have him teach me, but to come to know him" (III, 8, p. 708). Here the sense of dialogue's playful competition – not to mention the didacticism of exemplarity – has been replaced entirely by a sense of companionship. Montaigne's account of recreational reading goes beyond the scholarly topos referred to above by Pedro de Covarrubias: "que mejor compañia que la de los libros en los quales estan presentes los claros varones passados: las nobles hazañas: los virtuosos exemplos" ("what better company than that of books in which are present illustrious men of the past, noble feats, virtuous examples" [57]). It is closer to Quevedo's famous image of solitary reading:

> Retirado en la paz de estos desiertos,
> con pocos, pero doctos libros juntos,
> vivo en conversación con los difuntos,
> y escucho con mis ojos a los muertos.[25]
> (Soneto 131, "Desde la Torre")
>
> [Retired in the peace of these wastelands,
> together with few, but learned books,
> I live in conversation with the deceased,
> and listen with my eyes to the dead.]

Montaigne's good company provides the amiable and spirited counterpoint that allows for not only understanding, but a kind of communion. The constant foregrounding of alternative points of view and, consequently, the limitations of one's own perspective, instil a humility that bodes well for the imperfect give-and-take of social interaction.

At the conclusion of *El coloquio de los perros*, the failure of Berganza's narrative to reveal the dogs' origins (and thus their fate) does not prevent them from proceeding with their dialogue. Like Montaigne,

Cervantes appreciates *desengaño,* he understands that under close scrutiny things are not as substantial as we assume. "Of experience" contains the following evocation of the vanities of Ecclesiastes: "I, who boast of embracing the pleasures of life so assiduously and so particularly, find in them, when I look at them thus minutely, virtually nothing but wind. But what of it? We are all wind. And even the wind, more wisely than we, loves to make noise and move about, and is content with its own functions, without wishing for stability and solidity, qualities that do not belong to it" (III, 13, p. 849). But rather than moralize about the "vanity of vanities," he accepts this fact of existence and, as it were, moves on. In like manner, the canine and human protagonists of *El coloquio de los perros* find in their disillusionment no reason to deny the enjoyment of their dialogue. As Berganza says, "pero no por esto dejemos de gozar deste bien de la habla que tenemos y de excelencia tan grande de tener discurso humano todo el tiempo que pudiéramos, y, así, no te canse el oírme contar lo que me pasó" ("But don't let us for that reason fail to enjoy this blessing of speech that we have and the great honour of possessing the gift of speaking like humans for as long as we can. So don't get bored with hearing me tell you what happened" [347]). Here the optimistic ethos of the prologue's play reasserts itself. The dogs continue their tale, and, as daybreak puts a temporary end to their stories and the Ensign awakens from his nap, the author and reader from the frame tale agree that, despite not being able to verify the story's truth, their activity is worthwhile:

> – Aunque este coloquio sea fingido y nunca haya pasado, paréceme que está tan bien compuesto que puede el señor alférez pasar adelante con el segundo.
>
> – Con ese parecer –respondió el alférez – , me animaré y disporné a escribirle, sin ponerme más en disputas con vuesa merced si hablaron los perros o no.
>
> – –
>
> – Señor alférez, no volvamos más a esa disputa. Yo alcanzo el artificio del coloquio y la invención, y basta. Vámonos al Espolón a recrear los ojos del cuerpo, pues ya he recreado los del entendimiento.
>
> – Vámonos –dijo el aférez.
>
> Y con esto se fueron. (359)
>
> [– Although this colloquy may be faked and may never have happened, it seems to me so well composed that you may continue with the second, Mr. Ensign.

– Since you think so –answered the Ensign – I'll go ahead and write it, without getting into more disputes with you about whether the dogs talked or not.

– –

– Mr. Ensign, let's not return to that argument. I appreciate the art and invention of the colloquy, and let that suffice. Let's go to the Espolón and refresh the eyes of our body, for we've already refreshed those of the understanding.

– Let's go –said the Ensign.

And with that, off they went.]

Instead of digging in their heels over whether or not such an event really could have taken place, the two friends affirm the value of their game, the imaginative participation in a fictional world. Like Montaigne reading authors "looking for their style, not their subject," Peralta drops his demand for factual truth, citing his appreciation of "the art and invention." Also in the spirit of the Frenchman, they complement their mental recreation by going outside to refresh the body. This brings us back to the hygienic currents of thought that extended throughout early modern Europe, and which Cristóbal Méndez had so efficiently summarized in his promotion of walking: "Que mas quereys que todas las potencias animales (como tengo dicho) en esto se exercitan ... en lo que se oye y vee el sentido comun: y en lo que podeys ymaginar y fantasear la ymaginativa y fantasia. Y en lo que quisieredes pensar: la memoria y cogitativa todo esto passeando os lo podeys hazer" ("What more could you want than that all of the physical capacities (as I have said) in this are exercised ... the common sense in that which is heard and seen, the faculties of the imagination and fantasy in what you can imagine and fantasize about. And of what you might want to think, memory and cognition, all of this you may do while strolling" [139]). Like the physician Méndez, Cervantes understood the cognitive faculties to be inseparable from the physical organism. The care of the body and the spirit, like the recreational stroll through the Espolón and the imaginative journey through the *coloquio*, are not wholly distinct endeavours.

Pleasurable and instructive companionship, instrumental in the Ensign's physical and moral convalescence, redeems the narrative space, and points to the possibility of community. As we noted above, against a despairing backdrop of disease, predation and hypocrisy, Cervantes kindles a peculiar sort of optimism. When the two friends in the frame of *El coloquio de los perros*, agreeing on the virtue of the story despite the lack of resolution regarding its meaning or application, prepare to return to the world of human interaction, the reader must imitate them, for the story has ended. This is not the servile imitation of example, but rather a realization that our activity as readers has been parallel to that of the friends. We, too, have partaken not of a lesson, but an experience, not a product but a process. The dialogue of the two dogs, and then of the human companions, reverberates in the companionship of Cervantes's mind and our own. It is possible that our moral sensibilities have developed; it is quite probable that our literary judgment has improved; it is nearly certain that the experience has given pleasure, which is, as Montaigne affirms, "one of the principal kinds of profit" (III, 13, p. 834). As early modern Europe became increasingly conflictive and authoritarian, such sensibilities were overcome by dogmatic rhetoric and satirical extremes. But Montaigne and Cervantes left supreme models of nuanced thought and interchange that posterity has, to our benefit and peril, alternately adopted and ignored.

Rinconete y Cortadillo and *La ilustre fregona*: Picaresque Freedom and Festive Play

Rinconete y Cortadillo seems to invert the stark and conventional satire contained in *El licenciado Vidriera* and *El coloquio de los perros*: while Monipodio and his cohorts are morally degenerate, their society is rather harmonious. The oddly affirmative qualities revealed in the underworld of *Rinconete y Cortadillo* are corroborated by its festive tone, which is distinct from the cynicism exuded by Vidriera as well as the trepidation, humour and resignation displayed by the dogs. One can make sense of this contrast by placing *Rinconete y Cortadillo* – along with *La ilustre fregona* – within a particular vein of picaresque representation: instead of bitter satire on vice and social alienation, the lawless world represents a realm of wish-fulfilment and freedom. The elements of violence, deception and poverty are still prominent in this tendency, but they are frequently attenuated in farce.

As we have been emphasizing, the play realm should not be associated with frivolity, or escapist evasion of substantive concerns. Cervantes's festive stylizations of the picaresque in *Rinconete y Cortadillo* and *La ilustre fregona* are also meditations upon contemporary society. Monipodio's family of thieves, for example, is a sort of liminal community, with its initiation ceremonies and particular rules and hierarchies. But rather than presenting a viable alternative, Monipodio's underworld is a grotesque reflection of official society, and in fact deeply complicit with it. For the boys it functions as a "parenthetical space," a formative interlude from which they will presumably emerge. But if the picaresque interludes of Andrés Caballero in *La gitanilla* and Carriazo and Avendaño in *La ilustre fregona* have a functional relationship to their final reaffirmation of identity and integration into society, there is no clear sense as to where Rinconete and Cortadillo are going to "return." Furthermore, the knowledge they gain from their experience, like the reading of the mysterious manuscript by Peralta and Campuzano, is ambiguous. Discussing play in terms of Dilthey's *Erlebnisse*, Turner provides a useful optic for considering the boys' experience:

> Such an experience is incomplete, though, unless one of its "moments" is "performance," an act of creative retrospection in which "meaning" is ascribed to the events and parts of experience – even if the meaning is that "there is no meaning." Thus experience is both "living through" and "thinking back." It is also "willing or wishing forward," i.e., establishing goals and models for future experience in which, hopefully, the errors and perils of past experience will be avoided and eliminated. (18)

The conscious reflections by Campuzano and Peralta, and by Rinconete and Cortadillo, at the end of their experiences, at moments when they are preparing to resume their lives, strongly suggest the type of experience and cognitive mediation characterized by Turner. There is the implication that the experience in the play realm will beneficially inform their anticipated return to reality, although Cervantes leaves the "goals and models for future experience" vague. The precise sense of the "exemplarity" is again left up to the reader's conjecture.

The Festive Mode of the Picaresque

> Un muchacho asturiano ... respondió que el oficio era descansado y de que no se pagaba alcabala, y que algunos días salía con cinco y con seis reales de ganancia, con que comía y bebía y triunfaba como cuerpo del rey, libre de buscar amo a quien dar fianzas y seguro de comer a la hora que quisiese, pues a todas lo hallaba en el más mínimo bodegón de toda la ciudad. (*Rinconete y Cortadillo* 200)

> [An Asturian boy ... said that it was any easy trade and that you didn't pay any duty, and that some days he made five or six *reales* profit. With

that he could eat, drink and live splendidly, without needing to look for a master to whom he would have to give guarantees; and knowing that he could eat at any time he wished, for he could find food at all times of the day in any cheap eating-house in the city.]

Although *Rinconete y Cortadillo* lacks the degree of character development, social preoccupations and episodic plot characteristic of picaresque novels, the tale of the two boys' meeting, journey to Seville, and experience at Monipodio's house comprises a relatively undiluted engagement with aspects of the picaresque. There is no meta-textual frame tale, no deflationary or perspectivistic exposure to opposing genre conventions. And although the incorporation of the picaresque is self-conscious in its stylization, *Rinconete y Cortadillo* is not a picaresque parody, but rather a concentration on what we are calling the "festive" tendency of the genre.[26] The typical picaresque autobiographical narration, in which the protagonist's self-justification to an implied reader is a central component, is dispatched with rapid, almost perfunctory brushstrokes in *Rinconete y Cortadillo*. Diego Cortado supplies the basic elements of marginality – an inauspicious past, and journeying: "mi tierra no es mía, pues no tengo en ella más que un padre que no me tiene por hijo y una madrastra que me trata como alnado; el camino que llevo es a la ventura, y allí le daría fin donde hallase quien me diese lo necesario para pasar esta miserable vida" ("the place I came from is not my own part of the country. All I have in it is a father who doesn't treat me as his son and a stepmother who treats me in the way stepchildren are usually treated. I am going where chance directs, and I shall stop wherever I find someone who will give me the wherewithal to get through this wretched life" [193]). As in *La ilustre fregona*, a primary focus is on the bathetic appeal of the picaresque world, represented in *Rinconete y Cortadillo* by the inn, the road, and the city. Inverting a traditional theme, Cortado expresses a *menosprecio de aldea*: "Enfadóme la vida estrecha del aldea y el desamorado trato de mi madrastra" ("The restricted life of the village and my stepmother's unloving attitude made me fed up" [197]). As with Tomás's Italian travels in *El licenciado Vidriera*, the varieties of experience presented by the urban landscape contain a powerful allure for the young adventurer.

Compared to the epistemological, ethical, and aesthetic inquiries generated by the conversations in *El coloquio de los perros*, dialogue in *Rinconete y Cortadillo* is rudimentary, consisting of brief biographical summaries and, later, witty repartee. Following their introductions, the boys' first act is to dupe the muleteer in a card game. Their collaborative cheating at cards affirms their bond, and presents the sort of play – feared by the *tratadistas* discussed above – that will be emblematic of the entire story.[27] They proceed to rob a fellow traveller during their journey to Seville, and then enter the delinquent world of basket-carriers ("esportilleros") and, finally, Monipodio's house. The action takes place on a somewhat flat and theatrical plane of the third-person narrative present, and at the end of the tale there is no explanatory imposition of form, but rather bemused reflections on the part of Rinconete.[28]

Despite its brevity, the opening exchange of life stories contains an element of narrative collaboration similar to what we observed with Cipión and Berganza. As in the beginning of *El coloquio de los perros*, there takes place a negotiation between the two boys, in which the older (Rincón), noticing the reticence of the younger, offers the following conditions: "*para obligar a vuesa merced que descubra su pecho* y descanse conmigo, le quiero obligar con descubrirle el mío primero; porque *imagino que no sin misterio nos ha juntado aquí la suerte*, y pienso que habemos de ser, déste hasta el último día de nuestra vida, verdaderos amigos" ("*to make you open your heart freely to me*, I am going to put you under an obligation by opening mine first. I do this because *I imagine there's some good reason why fate has brought us together here*, and I think we are destined to be true friends from now until our dying day" [194, my italics]). The participatory play spirit in *El coloquio de los perros* ("De buena gana te escucho, por obligarte a que me escuches cuando te cuente, si el cielo fuere servido, los sucesos de mi vida" – "I will listen to you very willingly, to oblige you to listen to me when I tell you, if heaven grants it, the events of my life" [347]) is present in Rincón's desire to establish a mutual obligation in their narratives. Also, the mysterious meaning Rincón anticipates in their encounter recalls aspects of the dogs' enigmatic union in speech. In both stories, rather un-picaresque elements of trust, friendship and favourable dispositions (*buen natural, buena gracia*) are emphasized in the protagonists. And if the *miserable vida* Cortado claims as his lot seems to be reflected in the villainous underworld of Seville, the positive, communal qualities mentioned above will also resound in Monipodio's patio.

The prestidigitation and linguistic display of the two boys in the plaza of Seville illustrate the nature of Cervantes's picaresque narrative. From the *bernardinas*, or nonsensical prattle, Cortado uses to confound the "sacristán" (205), to the slang (*germanía*) that signals the identity of the urban criminal (206–7), Cervantes again foregrounds the ludic nature of language. Rincón's response to the offer of employment by the soldier anticipates his reactions at the end of the story, and can be seen as an indication of Cervantes's fascination with the representational possibilities of the delinquent world: "no le quería dejar tan presto, hasta ver, a lo menos, lo que tenía de malo y bueno" ("he didn't want to leave it [the life of independent pícaro] so soon, until he had at least weighed up the pros and cons" [202]). As with Campuzano's account of doña Estefanía's deception in *El casamiento engañoso*, such material should also remind the reader to take a critical stance before the narrator's rhetorical strategies. The brilliant and attractive surface may conceal an unpleasant reality.

In spite of their lowly backgrounds, the boys are driven by curiosity more than prospects for material gain: "aunque se les ofrecían algunas ocasiones de tentar las valijas de sus medios amos, no las admitieron, por no perder la ocasión tan buena del viaje de Sevilla, donde ellos tenían grande deseo de verse" ("although they had some chances to rob the bags of their temporary masters, they didn't take them, so as not to lose the splendid chance of the journey to Seville, where they very much wanted to go" [199]). The great city's draw was also felt by the travellers present at Grisóstomo's funeral in *Don Quijote*, who invited the knight to join them as they took their leave: "Don Quijote se despidió de sus huéspedes y de los caminantes, los cuales le rogaron se viniesen con ellos a Sevilla, por ser lugar tan acomodado a hallar aventuras, que en cada calle y tras cada esquina se ofrecen más que en otro alguno" ("Don Quixote said goodbye to his hosts and to the travellers, who begged him to come with them to Seville, because it's just the place to find adventures – on every street and round every corner they're simply waiting for you, more of them than anywhere else in the world" [I, 14]). Consistent with his genre, however, don Quijote opts to remain in the wilds of La Mancha, where he imagines he might serve Marcela. Even when Cortado is overcome by temptation and robs the Frenchman upon entering the city, the theft is described in a colourful personification which reminds us of Lazarillo's assault on the priest's food chest, or don Quijote's heroic slaughter of the wine-skins: "no se pudo contener Cortado de no cortar la valija o maleta que a las ancas traía un francés de la camarada; y así, con el de sus cachas le dio tan larga y profunda herida, que se parecían patentemente las entrañas" ("Cortado ... could not refrain from cutting the bag or valise that a certain Frenchman in the company was carrying on the crupper of his mule. So, with his yellow-handled knife he gave it such a long and deep wound that its insides were open for all to see" [199]).[29] Similar elements appear in Rincón's description of his initiation into vice: "Pero habiéndome un día aficionado más al dinero de las bulas que a las mismas bulas, me abracé con un talego, y di conmigo y con él en Madrid, donde con las comodidades que allí de ordinario se ofrecen, en pocos días saqué las entrañas al talego, y le dejé con más dobleces que pañizuelo de desposado" ("But one day, being more fond of the cash from the bulls than the bulls themselves, I made off with a bag of money and ended up with it in Madrid. Taking advantage of the sort of opportunities that crop up there, I very soon took the stuffing out of that bag and left it with more creases than a bridegroom's handkerchief" [195]). Comic personification of the booty, the urban atmosphere of mischief and opportunity, and ironic interplays between the material and the spiritual figure throughout *Rinconete y Cortadillo*. The picaresque life is described as a jovial apprenticeship, and even threats of dire consequence – as when the boys recoil at the sight of the galley ships upon entering Seville – as well as actual scenes of punishment, are highly attenuated. An inconsequentiality surrounds the entire picaresque experience, which is presented as a youthful adventure. As Casalduero noted, "Despite the bearing and appearance of Monipodio, despite the ruffians, we have the sensation of finding ourselves in an infantile world, in a game, in which the puerility of the players prevents them from seeing the deception. So innocent is this world, that Rincón and Cortado completely dominate it."[30]

It is worth emphasizing again that the "puerility" of the play realm should not be confused with frivolity. Just as Torrente Ballester cited Goethe's notion of childhood play to highlight the creative vitality of don Quijote's *mimesis* (see above p. 208), it can be said that the play of *Rinconete y Cortadillo* involves substantial cognitive, ethical and social considerations. Turner's characterization of leisure is pertinent:

> Leisure is also: (1) *freedom to* enter, even to generate new symbolic worlds of entertainment, sports, games, diversions of all kinds. It is, furthermore, (2) *freedom to* transcend social structural limitations, freedom to *play* … with ideas, with fantasies, with words (from Rabelais to Joyce and Samuel Beckett), with paint (from the Impressionists to Action painting and Art Nouveau), and with social relationships … Here far more than in tribal or agrarian rites and ceremonies, the ludic and experimental are stressed. (37)

The entrance into "new symbolic worlds" of the picaresque communities, in which the combinations of social relationships stimulate reflection by the boys, affirms the fundamental spirit of inquiry that is part of play. The "ludic and experimental" will be even more apparent in *La ilustre fregona*, in which the protagonists undergo numerous transformations and transitions between symbolic worlds.

Monipodio's Criminal and Ludic Community in *Rinconete y Cortadillo*

As in *El coloquio de los perros*, the self-conscious incorporation of genre conventions in *Rinconete y Cortadillo* underlines the play quality of art: a particular representational system is actualized according to conventions that are recognized by the reader. *El coloquio de los perros* contains an extensive illustration of the play element at work in the aesthetic experience as the reader reflects upon a dramatization of both creation and reception of the narrative. In Monipodio's comic underworld, the emphasis is more on play's social function, that is, its role in the forming and maintenance of human community. If Marcela's pastoral *communitas* forms an ideal if somewhat vague alternative to the patriarchal organization of her town of origin (*Don Quijote* I, 12–13), the two astonished boys find Monipodio's realm to be nearly as structured as the society they had left behind.

When approached by a young thief regarding their obligation to pay dues to Monipodio, Cortado, who had anticipated an existence free of structure and obligation, expresses a degree of disillusionment: "Yo pensé … que el hurtar era oficio libre" ("I thought … that stealing was a free trade" [206]). Nevertheless he genially accepts the rules: "pero pues así es, y en cada tierra hay su uso, guardemos nosotros el désta" ("But since things are this way, and every country has its customs, let us observe those of this country" [206]). The "customs-house" ("aduana") is the first of many elements that point to Monipodio's society as a distorted mirror image of official society. Following much comic dialogue combining religious vocabulary with thieves' slang and malapropisms, the boys' misgivings increase; so, too, does their curiosity. As Cortado expresses it: "Pero pues nuestra suerte ha querido que entremos en esta cofradía, vuesa merced alargue el paso; que muero por verme con el señor Monipodio, de quien tantas virtudes se cuentan" ("But since our fate has decreed that we should join this brotherhood, let's get moving, for I'm dying to meet Mr. Monipodio, of whose many virtues I hear so much" [209]). Their acceptance of the aleatory nature of the situation ("pues nuestra suerte ha querido") corresponds to the story's central image of card-playing, and conveys the sense of buoyant opportunism with which the boys undertake their adventure. On the other hand, the highly structured process of examination, re-naming, and integration, strongly suggests the phenomenon of initiation rites. Turner's account of such processes, particularly with regard to their cognitive effects on the initiands, is relevant to Cervantes's tale: "The novices are taught that they did not know what they thought they knew. Beneath the surface structure of custom was a deep structure, whose rules they had to learn, through paradox and shock" (42). As we shall see, aspects of the "deep structure" of Andalusian society are revealed to the boys during their peculiar experience of descent.

The anticipation and ceremony surrounding Monipodio's entrance into the courtyard of his house, the gravity and authority of his presence, and his central role during the procedures and conflicts that follow all contribute to a scene of festive travesty of official order. The monarch of thieves appears before a colourful company of subjects ("en poco espacio se juntaron en el patio hasta catorce personas de diferentes trajes y oficios" – "Within a short time there were about fourteen persons assembled in the patio in different dress and belonging to different professions" [210]), including "dos bravos y bizarros mozos" ("two fine swaggering young fellows"). Monipodio is elaborately presented as a being at once grotesque, demonic and comical, a "Lord of Misrule" or Erlking presiding over his court of goblins. The carnivalesque elements of Monipodio include his ragged dress, sunken eyes, hyperbolic shagginess and shoe size, as well as his role as a travesty of the king figure. His court resembles a Bakhtinian "variation of carnivalesque hell" (*Rabelais and His World* 391–4). Bakhtin's discussion of the Erlking as a saturnalian uncrowned king, a figure both demonic and affirmative in his material, bodily presence, and who is surrounded by a grotesque coterie, points to both Monipodio and the Falstaff of *The Merry Wives of Windsor*; it also calls to mind Sancho Panza presiding over his governor's banquet.[31]

After further ceremony ("todos los que aguardándole estaban le hicieron una profunda y larga reverencia" – "all those who were waiting for him bowed long and low to him" [212]), the two boys come before Monipodio, who examines their abilities in order to determine their worthiness for his community. They must demonstrate their wit and resourcefulness in order to pass Monipodio's test and win general approval. The mock conventionality of the scene heightens its playfulness, as Rincón, who delivers the first clever response, takes on the appearance of a chivalric hero visiting the court of a foreign king:

> [Monipodio] preguntó a los nuevos el ejercicio, la patria y padres.
>
> A lo cual Rincón respondió:

– El ejercicio ya está dicho, pues venimos a vuestra merced; la patria no me parece de mucha importancia decilla, ni los padres tampoco, pues no se ha de hacer información para recebir algún hábito honroso. (212)

[[Monipodio] asked the newcomers about their trade, where they came from and who their parents were.

To which Rincón replied, "The trade speaks for itself, since we have come to you; where we come from doesn't seem to matter much, nor who our parents are, because you don't have to provide this sort of information even to enter an order of nobility."]

The boy's reasoning scores highly with Monipodio, whose sense of decorum recognizes the wisdom of a thief keeping such personal information secret, since it can only heighten his dishonour should he come to justice.[32] Rincón's *discreción* persuades Monipodio to take a preliminary step towards admitting the two boys into his company, as he dubs them with the names that give the story its title: "Pues de aquí adelante … quiero y es mi voluntad que vos, Rincón, os llaméis *Rinconete,* y vos, Cortado, *Cortadillo,* que son nombres que asientan como de molde a vuestra edad y a nuestras ordenanzas" ("Well, from now on … I wish and indeed insist that you, Rincón, shall be called 'Rinconete', and you, Cortado, 'Cortadillo', which are names just right for your age and our rules" [212]). Clamurro, who points out the parallel between Monipodio's judging and that of Sancho during his governorship of Barataria (*Beneath the Fiction* 92–4), emphasizes how the linguistic play – the "various verbal games" – in the story is linked to its social focus: "while there are obvious instances of puns, malapropisms, and shared (i.e., mutually controlled and enjoyed) verbal play, a major role in *Rinconete y Cortadillo* is also played by the acquisition of the totally new jargon, the code of another 'world.' The special, foreign language – the discourse as code – of the new social group is both a necessary tool and a verification of authentic belonging" (76–7).

When Monipodio examines the elementary card-sharping ability of the two novices, he expresses a belief in progress and elevation through studies: "quería saber, hijos, lo que sabéis, para daros el oficio y ejercicio conforme a vuestra inclinación y habilidad" ("I should like you to tell me, boys, what you know, so as to give you the duty appropriate to your inclination and talent" [214]); "que asentado sobre ese fundamento media docena de liciones, yo espero en Dios que habéis de salir oficial famoso, y aun quizá maestro" ("for half a dozen lessons on top of this foundation I should think would make you a first-rate operator, and even master of the craft" [215]). Such an attitude recalls the optimism of the young Tomás at the outset of *El licenciado Vidriera*, when one of the noblemen asks him how he plans on honouring his parents ("By the fame I win through my studies … because I have heard that even bishops start off as men"). As will be discussed further below, *La ilustre fregona* contains another case of education according to individual proclivity: "había de ir Avendaño a Salamanca, donde por su gusto tres años había estado estudiando las lenguas griega y latina, y su padre querría que pasase adelante y estudiase la facultad que quisiese" ("Avendaño was to go to Salamanca, where at his pleasure for three years he had been studying Greek and Latin, and his father wanted him to continue and study whichever field he liked" [143]). Carriazo and Avendaño's free pursuit of their inclination leads away from the hallowed halls of Salamanca, to picaresque Andalucía. The humanist educational ideal, defended by don Quijote while discussing don Diego de Miranda's son (*Don Quijote* II, 18), yields divergent results throughout Cervantes's works. As with the varied representation of games under discussion, Cervantes is always aware that the freedom associated with such pursuits can lead to good or ill.

Cortadillo's triumphant flourish of wit and valor as he assures the group that they need fear no leaks under torture ("¡como si tuviese más letras un *no* que un *sí*!" – "As if a 'yes' had more syllables than a 'no'!" [216]) sounds victory for both of the boys, and they get an enthusiastic reception into the thievish kingdom by sovereign and subjects alike:

> – ¡Alto, no es menester más! –dijo a esta sazón Monipodio – . Digo que sola esta razón me convence, me obliga, me persuade y me fuerza a que desde luego asentéis por cofrades mayores y que se os sobrelleve el año del noviciado.
>
> – Yo soy dese parecer –dijo uno de los bravos.
>
> Y a una voz lo confirmaron todos los presentes, que toda la plática habían estado escuchando, y pidieron a Monipodio que desde luego les concediese y permitiese gozar de las inmunidades de su cofradía, porque su presencia agradable y su buena plática lo merecía todo. (216)
>
> ["Stop, that's enough," said Monipodio at this point. "This statement alone convinces me, and obliges me to let you become full members at once and dispense with the year of probation."
>
> "I agree to that," said one of the toughs.

And with one voice all the company agreed, for they had been listening to the whole conversation, and they begged Monipodio to allow them straight away to enjoy the immunities of the brotherhood, because their pleasant bearing and good conversation well deserved this reward.]

Thus the picaresque adventure of the two boys leads not to marginality, expulsion or cynicism, but rather to a boisterous scene of celebratory inclusion. Strikingly, it is the social graces of the boys ("su presencia agradable y su buena plática") that endear them to the group. Within the distorted values of Monipodio's society, Rinconete and Cortadillo appear as variants of Aristotle's *eutrapelos* and Castiglione's courtier. The abundance of Monipodio's speech, with its redundancies, malapropisms and gradations ("quiero y es mi voluntad," "popa y soledad," "esta razón me convence, me obliga, me persuade y me fuerza") amplifies the festivity of the scene. The membership privileges of complete liberty to indulge in wine and food ("piar el turco puro; hacer banquete cuando, como y adonde quisieren, sin pedir licencia a su mayoral" – "drink wine without water in it, have a party whenever, however and wherever they wished, without asking leave of their chief" [216]) recall the Bodas de Camacho (*Don Quijote* II, 19–21). One suspects Sancho just as easily might have been recruited to this picaresque underworld as he was the chivalric enterprise of his neighbour. The broader significance of such parallels, as we have been noting, is how they reveal Cervantes's fascination with initiation into alternate realms and the accompanying transformation of identity. But the new identity, while opening possibilities of experience and understanding, retains, as we saw with children's play, elements of the original. In other words, the character is aware that he or she is involved in play (in this case, *mimesis*). In the instances of the liminal realms we have seen – Marcela and her shepherds (*Don Quijote*), the gypsies (*La gitanilla*), Monipodio and company – it is tempting to speculate to what extent the characters are cognizant of implicitly critiquing the "real world" in their participation in counter-societies. As noted in relation to Iffland's study of Cervantes and Avellaneda, don Quijote himself can be seen as a "Lord of Misrule" re-naming and presiding over a world that overturns official values, with Sancho as minion and minister (*De fiestas* II).

Amidst the arrival of the constable looking for the purse Cortado had stolen, the conflict between Cariharta and Repolido, and the administration of duties, the company of thieves and prostitutes continues to respect the authority of Monipodio, deferring to him for the maintenance of order. Huizinga argues that play is intrinsic to human community: "civilization cannot exist in the absence of a certain play-element, for civilization presupposes limitation and mastery of the self, the ability not to confuse its own tendencies with the ultimate and highest goal, but to understand that it is enclosed within certain bounds freely accepted. Civilization will, in a sense, always be played according to certain rules, and true civilization will always demand fair play. Fair play is nothing less than good faith expressed in play terms" (211). Giamatti's comments on particularities of the play element in the urban sphere are pertinent to present considerations: "If a family is an expression of continuity through biology, a city is an expression of continuity through will and imagination – through mental choices making artifice, not through physical reproduction" (50). Monipodio's patriarchal status, the preponderance of familial terms ("hijos," "hermana Cariharta," "madre Pipota," etc.) and the specialized slang (*germanía*) of his community further the sense of a continuity forged "through will and imagination." Part of the fun, of course, is that the "good faith" expressed in Monipodio's community is at the service of ruffians, whores, and thieves.

The disruption resulting from the constable's inquiry into the stolen purse only confirms the sense of shared community. Monipodio furiously responds to the threat posed to his society: "¡Nadie se burle con quebrantar la más minima cosa de nuestra orden, que le costará la vida!" ("Let no one make light of breaking our rule in the slightest degree, or it'll cost him his life!" [217]); but he also offers assistance to anyone who might be withholding the purse out of financial need ("y si se encubre por no pagar lo derechos, yo le daré enteramente lo que le toca, y pondré lo demás en mi casa, porque en todas maneras ha de ir contento el alguacil" – "and if it's being concealed so as not to pay the dues, I will pay the lot on my own account, because the constable must be satisfied whatever happens" [217]). And there is general consternation at the lack of progress towards resolving the case: "todo lo cual fue poner más fuego a la cólera de Monipodio y dar ocasión a que toda la junta se alborotase, *viendo que se rompían sus estatuos y buenas ordenanzas*" ("all of which added flames to Monipodio's anger, and made the whole gathering get excited, *seeing that their statutes and good ordinances were being broken*" [217, my italics]). The scene does receive comic resolution, as the two boys agree between themselves to divulge the booty, with

Rinconete proudly announcing how his young companion did not stop at the purse, acquiring also the sacristan's handkerchief, *por añadidura*. The newly-anointed *Cortadillo* thus receives from Monipodio (whose function as a cruel *justiciero* has been narrowly defused) the honourable epithet of *el Bueno*, and order is restored, with a general, legitimizing approval of the community: "De común consentimiento aprobaron todos la hidalguía de los dos modernos y la sentencia y parecer de su mayoral" ("By common consent, they all applauded the splendid behaviour of the two newcomers and the judgement and decision of their leader" [218]).

Vis-à-vis the "official" world of Seville, Monipodio and company appear to be a society of cheats. As Huizinga commented, the cheat "pretends to be playing the game and, on the face of it, still acknowledges the magic circle" (11). But this formulation bears further refinement, which will allow us to get to the heart of Cervantes's satire. It is not simply the case that Monipodio's people pay lip service to official values while hypocritically gaining advantage for themselves. His ruffians, thieves, and prostitutes are employed to support the vengefulness, greed, and lust of mainstream society. Monipodio's festive and cohesive community thus provides an incisive perspective on conventional values, such as honour and love. With La Pipota, who shares attributes with Cañizares (*El coloquio de los perros*) and is a descendent of Celestina, Cervantes imbues the story with an Erasmian satire of religious ceremony.

Making her second of two entrances just as the jovial company is preparing their feast, Pipota has urgent matters on her mind: "y más que antes que sea mediodía tengo de ir a cumplir mis devociones y poner mis candelicas a Nuestra Señora de las Aguas y al Santo Crucifijo de Santo Agustín, que no lo dejaría de hacer si nevase y ventiscase" ("Anyway before midday I must go and carry out my devotions and place my candles before the altars of Our Lady of the Waters and the Holy Crucifix of St Augustine, which I'd have to do even if it snowed or blew a gale" [219–20]). Such confidence in the redemptive power of Catholic ritual (Ganancia requests that candles be placed before three saints of her own) recalls Sancho's frenzied gesticulations on the *barco encantado* (*Don Quijote* II, 29) and, as noted during our consideration of that episode, Erasmus's "The Shipwreck." The irony is compounded in *Rinconete y Cortadillo* by the fact that the supreme justice to which the characters appeal is at odds with the civil justice they hope to escape.

As she requests a drink of wine before departing, and is offered a two-litre helping by Escalanta, Cervantes illuminates the colourful essence of his character:

> [S]e le puso en las manos a la devotísima, la cual, tomándole con ambas manos, y habiendo soplado un poco de espuma, dijo:
>
> – Mucho echaste, hija Escalanta; pero Dios dará fuerzas para todo.
>
> Y aplicándosele a los labios, de un tirón, sin tomar aliento, lo trasegó del corcho al estómago[.] (221)

> [[S]he put it in the hands of the devout old woman, who taking it with both hands, and blowing off some foam, said: "You've poured a lot out, daughter Escalanta; but God will give me strength for all my tasks."
>
> And putting it to her lips, without taking a breath, she transferred it from the measure to her stomach in one go[.]]

Pipota's firm, two-handed grip, her dispersal of the foam, and the culminating lusty swig make her appeal to divine assistance seem almost appropriate. This energetic description is in the carnivalesque spirit, recalling Celestina's most affirmative moments at church and table, and Sancho's unaffected revelry with Ricote and the pilgrims (*Don Quijote* II, 54).

The episode of the feuding couple, Juliana la Cariharta and Repolido, with a rapid, farcical exposition and finale, is a sort of *entremés* within the story. In its combination of elevated registers with degraded circumstances, a lack of serious consequence amidst threats of destruction, and final emphasis on festivity and inclusion, the interlude reinforces the centrality of play in *Rinconete y Cortadillo*. Fittingly, the origin of the conflict between ruffian and prostitute is gambling. As la Cariharta explains it, "estando jugando y perdiendo, me envió a pedir con Cabrillas, su trainel, treinta reales, y no le envié más de veinticuatro, que el trabajo y afán con que yo los había ganado ruego yo a los cielos que vayan en descuento de mis pecados" ("as he was gambling and started to lose, he sent me his boy Cabrillas to ask me for thirty *reales*, and I sent him only twenty-four, and may God grant that the labour and anxiety I had to get them be set against my sins" [224]). That la Cariharta hopes her hard work – engaging in sexual relations with her clients – might tip the scales of divine judgment in her favour is another of the tale's travesties of theological discourse. *En el sudor de tu rostro te sustentarás*, indeed.

The entrance of the maltreated prostitute returns the community to disarray, again disturbing the ordered integrity of their republic. Her appeal to "¡La justicia de Dios y del Rey …!" ("the justice of God and the King"!) momentarily erases the antipathy of the two codes, expressed by Pipota above. Monipodio presents a circumvention of this potential dissonance, offering a third realm of justice: "Sosiégate, Cariharta … que aquí estoy yo, que te haré justicia. Cuéntanos tu agravio, que más estarás tú en contarle que yo en hacerte vengada" ("Calm down, Cariharta … for I'm here and I'll see that justice is done. Tell us what they've done to you, for it'll take longer for you to tell us about it than for me to see you revenged" [224]). Stepping forth as the ultimate authority within his community, Monipodio, like don Quijote, offers himself as a righter of wrongs, particularly disposed towards assisting a damsel whose honour has been compromised. If Monipodio is more successful than the knight in restoring justice, his damsel is at least as prosaic as the rustic maids encountered in *Don Quijote,* from Maritornes to the peasant women at the outskirts of Toboso. Carnivalesque inversion is sustained by the description of the abuse suffered by Cariharta, which seemingly alludes to the dishonouring of the Cid's daughters at the hands of the Infantes de Carrión: "esta mañana me sacó al campo, detrás de la güerta del Rey y allí, entre unos olivares, me desnudó, y con la petrina, sin excusar de hierros, que en malos grillos y hierros le vea yo, me dio tantos azotes, que me dejó por muerta" ("this morning he dragged me out behind the Huerta del Rey, and there, among some olive trees, he stripped me and with his belt, without bothering to hold the buckle (curse him and may I see him in fetters) he whipped me so many times that he left me for dead" [225]). As the Infantes' brutality leads to the final scene of ordered justice rather than savage revenge, with the Cid arguing his case before the king (see ch. 1 of this study), the pimp Repolido will eventually be reduced to obedience by Monipodio. The interlude of Cariharta and Repolido follows the *entremés* conventions of *palos,* music and dancing, and the final scene of reconciliation precludes any sense of serious consequence from the physical violence or compromised honour.

The feasting imagery in *Rinconete y Cortadillo* represents further carnivalesque elements: "Fue contenta la Juliana de obedecer a su mayor, y así, todos volvieron a su *gaudeamus,* y en poco espacio vieron el fondo de la canasta y las heces del cuero. Los viejos bebieron *sine fine;* los mozos adunia; las señoras, los quiries. Los viejos pidieron licencia para irse. Diósela luego Monipodio" ("Juliana was happy to obey her chief, so they all went back to their merry-making, and soon saw the bottom of the basket and the dregs of the wine-skin. The old men drank without stopping; the young ones freely; the ladies without stinting themselves. The old men asked to be excused, and Monipodio gave permission immediately" 226). Huizinga describes how the play spirit infuses the *gaudeamus*: "In the very nature of things the relationship between feast and play is very close. Both proclaim a standstill to ordinary life. In both mirth and joy dominate, though not necessarily – for the feast too can be serious; both are limited as to time and place; both combine strict rules with genuine freedom. In short, feast and play have their main characteristics in common" (22). Of course, Monipodio's feasting is a travesty of the synthesis of corporeal and spiritual recreation represented in a work like Erasmus's "Godly Feast" (see above pp. 60–1). It is, rather, the sort of hedonistic indulgence that captivates Sancho, heedless of limitations of time and space, during the Bodas de Camacho (*Don Quijote* II, 19–21). Consistent with Sancho's aspirations to remain indefinitely at Camacho's feast, the "festive" picaresque mode holds forth the dissolute utopia of permanent holiday.[33]

Rinconete Reflects: Distance, Morality, and the Aesthetic Experience

"Todos los vicios, Sancho, traen un no sé qué de deleite consigo."

(*Don Quijote* II, 8)

["All vices, Sancho, bring with them some kind of delight."]

The curious amalgam of harmony and vice that holds the community together compels Rinconete to remain for a few months. It is uncertain whether the lesson Rinconete has already drawn from his experience (i.e., Monipodio's community is vile and hypocritical) is equivalent to the promised *ejemplo* that might be gained from his anticipated stay-over. There is a dissonance between moral and aesthetic concerns that calls into question the exemplarity so earnestly promised at the outset of the stories, and associated with the enigmatic *mesa de trucos*. A basic premise of this study is that an artwork, as play, can never be completely explained; understanding requires an experience, or actualization, of it. The picaresque realms presented in these stories might be considered in relation to Jung's observations on archetypes: "The concepts of complex psychology are, in essence, not intellectual formulations but names for certain areas of experience, and though they can be described they remain dead and irrepresentable to anyone who has not experienced them" (270–1). Rinconete's final observations reveal a fascination with the potential experience before him, coupled with rational reflection on it. While the reflection inclines him to reject Monipodio, the fascination draws him in. This tension is as pertinent to the story's "meaning" as any concise formulation – which, we recall, is also absent at the end of *El coloquio de los perros.*

Following the action of *El coloquio de los perros*, the two friends discuss their experience, and propose a regenerative stroll in the garden, "Y con esto, se fueron" ("And with this, they left" [359]). The end of one story's action gives rise to further action in another (the characters from *El casamiento engañoso*). By the end of *Rinconete y Cortadillo*, the two boys have effectively been relegated to the role of observers, and the closing of the action, as Ganchoso is the last of the company to see them off, elicits their reaction: "Con esto se fue, dejando a los dos compañeros admirados de lo que habían visto" ("With this he left, leaving the two comrades amazed at what they had seen"). Rinconete's reactions include emotional, intellectual, aesthetic, and moral registers:

> Y *reíase de* la otra buena vieja de la Pipota ... *le suspendía* la obediencia y respeto que todos tenían a Monipodio ... *Consideraba* lo que había leído en su libro de memoria y los ejercicios en que todos se ocupaban ... *propuso en sí de aconsejar* a su compañero no durasen mucho en aquella vida tan perdida y tan mala, tan inquieta, tan libre y tan disoluta. *Pero, con todo esto,* llevado de sus pocos años y de su poca experiencia, *pasó con ella adelante algunos meses*, en los cuales le sucedieron cosas que piden más luenga escritura, y así se deja para otra ocasión contar su vida y milagros, con los de su maestro Monipodio, y otros sucesos de aquéllos de la infame academia, que todos serán de grande consideración y que podrán servir de ejemplo y aviso a los que las leyeren. (240, my italics)

> [And he laughed at the good old woman, Pipota ... *He was no less astounded by* the obedience and respect they all felt for Monipodio ... *He thought of* what he had read in the memorandum book and the practices in which they were all engaged ... *he made up his mind to advise* his companion that they should not spend much time in that evil and abandoned way of life, so uncertain, lawless and dissolute. *But all the same,* carried away by his youth and lack of experience, *he spent some months longer*

> *with the community*, during which things happened to him which require more time than this to tell; and so the account of their life and marvelous doings is left for another occasion, with those of their master Monipodio and other events which took place in that infamous academy, all worth consideration and capable of serving as an example and warning to those who may read them.]

Rinconete's staying on with Monipodio is justified by the *escarmiento*, or moral warning, that the representation of vice can serve. As in many picaresque tales, however, such negative examples also contain a good deal of comic entertainment, and the entertainment sometimes borders on a tacit approval of the activities and situations presented, potentially evoking feelings of identification on the part of the reader. Rinconete's reactions acknowledge these complexities, and Cervantes was clearly interested in the possibilities such representation offers ("things happened to him which require more time than this to tell"). The authorial decision, discussed above, in the house of don Diego de Miranda (*Don Quijote* II, 18) provides an illustration by contrast. The narrator refers to the representation of "las circunstancias de la casa de don Diego, pintándonos en ella lo que contiene una casa de un caballero labrador rico" ("every detail of Don Diego's house – all the contents of any rich gentleman farmer's dwelling" [169]) only to decide that such details are not essential to the story, "la cual más tiene su fuerza en la verdad que en las frías digresiones" ("which derives its strength from its truthfulness rather than from dull digressions" [169]). The "circunstancias" of Monipodio's house, on the other hand, comprise the "truth" of this particular narrative, and merit sustained attention, focalized by the two curious boys: "Miraban los mozos atentamente las alhajas de las casa … se atrevió Rincón a entrar en una sala baja … y vio en ella dos espadas de esgrima y dos broqueles de corcho … En la pared frontera estaba pegada a la pared una imagen de Nuestra Señora" ("The boys examined the furnishings of the house with care … Rincón ventured into one of the two small rooms … [and saw in it] two fencing swords and two cork shields … There was one of those badly-printed images of Our Lady stuck on the wall opposite" [209–10]). The life of a country nobleman may be ethically edifying, but it is in many ways less interesting than that of a king of thieves.

In addition to the satisfaction of curiosity, the underworld escapade is justified by a certain quality shared by the canine Berganza: "Era Rinconete, aunque muchacho, de muy buen entendimiento, y tenía un buen natural" ("Rinconete, although only a boy, was very intelligent and good-natured" [239]). The boy's intellect and moral faculty allow him to retain a mediating consciousness throughout his experience. It is appropriate that the narrator attributes Rinconete's desire temporarily to remain in the underworld of Monipodio to his age. *La ilustre fregona* also suggests that lawlessness is the prerogative of youth. And experiences of disorder, which Cervantes repeatedly depicts as youthful rites of passage, contribute to cognitive and moral development. Cervantes understood what later thinkers and writers would spend much time examining.[34] Turner's comments on play theory are again relevant:

> Sutton-Smith, who has been recently examining the continuum of *order-disorder* in games ... goes on to say that "we may be disorderly in games [and, I would add, in the liminality of rituals, as well as in such "liminoid" phenomena as charivaris, fiestas, Halloween masking, and mumming, etc.] either because we have an overdose of order, and want to let off steam [this might be called the "conservative view" of ritual disorder, such as ritual reversals, Saturnalia, and the like], or because we have something to *learn* through being disorderly. (28)

We discussed above, with Erasmus and Montaigne, how "being disorderly" could reveal that the agents of order in any given culture are, to a large degree, arbitrary, or even foolish; but this does not mean that they are not desirable. Even if Rinconete and Cortadillo do not "learn" this, the distorted mirror Cervantes holds up to contemporary Spanish society in Monipodio's community might well affect such an understanding in the reader. Valle-Inclán pointed to an illustrious predecessor to his own grotesque aesthetic: "El esperpentismo lo ha inventado Goya ... Los héroes clásicos reflejados en los espejos cóncavos dan el Esperpento. El sentido trágico de la vida española sólo puede darse con una estética sistemáticamente deformada" ("Goya invented *esperpentismo* ... The classical heroes reflected in concave mirrors give us the *Esperpento*. The tragic sense of Spanish life can only be found with a systematically deformed aesthetic" [*Luces de Bohemia* XI]). As Monipodio's *mundo al revés* indicates, Valle-Inclán might well have extended his heritage farther back, through Quevedo and Cervantes. Our observations of the festive quality of Monipodio's community notwithstanding, the complicity of official society with the grotesque underworld gives the tale disturbing undertones.

Jung's description of the trickster archetype offers further insight into the picaresque adventure of *Rinconete y Cortadillo*:

> [T]he living effect of the myth is experienced when a higher consciousness, rejoicing in its freedom and independence, is confronted by the autonomy of a mythological figure and yet cannot flee from its fascination, but must pay tribute to the overwhelming impression. The figure works, because secretly it participates in the observer's psyche and appears as its reflection, though it is not recognized as such. (269–70)

The boys' fascination with the folkloric-archetypal Monipodio might well have infected the readers of Cervantes's Spain, who may have recognized in the house of thieves a warped reflection of their own society.[35] As Colin Thompson points out in his account of *eutrapelia*'s "indirect form of moral discourse" (272), Cervantes plays with the reader by putting the moral judgment in the voice of two *pícaros* "who seem to be blind to the fact that they too are implicated in the life they are condemning, as if they could emerge unscathed by maintaining their distance and using their intelligence to correct their leader's malapropisms and to point out the gang's religious hypocrisy" (277). Noting the story's linguistic play (with register, *germanía* and malapropism, 273), Thompson suggests that Rinconete "is presented as morally superior to the gang only because he can use language more accurately" (281). Of course, such implications would lead the attentive reader to question his or her own moral status before the characters. The luminous optimism expressed in the game imagery of the collection's prologue, which emerges most profoundly from the nightmare world of *El coloquio de los perros*, flickers ironically amidst Monipodio's comic society of sinners at the end of *Rinconete y Cortadillo*.

Generic Interplay in *La ilustre fregona*

La ilustre fregona is in some ways one of the most picaresque of the *Novelas ejemplares*; it also contains the most thorough romance resolution, ending in *anagnorisis*, reunion, restoration, and multiple weddings. Many readers have commented on the varying aspects of rupture and unity resulting from this peculiar composite. Jorge Checa describes the story in terms of Bakhtinian *heteroglossia*, and illustrates a dialogic principle at work on the generic level of the story. Rather than as parody, the picaresque elements in *La ilustre fregona* should be understood in terms of what Bakhtin calls "auto-critical discourse" (*The Dialogic Imagination*, ch. 1), a concept well-suited to the frequently self-conscious art of Cervantes. Given the interplay of picaresque and romance within a single work, auto-critical discourse is operative in *La ilustre fregona* to a greater degree than in *Rinconete y Cortadillo*, where it is achieved through the ironic reflections of the two boys. In *La ilustre fregona*, picaresque and romance elements exist in a state of mutual interrogation, creating a tension with regard to which representational mode is more verisimilar, and which structure will ultimately be played out: while the consolidating resolution of romance seems to prevail by the end of the tale, it was the picaresque inclination of the boys that caused the providential convergence at the inn in Toledo, and the story ends in a picaresque flashback by Carriazo.[36] By integrating the two representational systems to such a degree, Cervantes revitalizes both, and illustrates the natures of their appeal.

The generic complexity of *La ilustre fregona* also results in the characters undergoing multiple transformations, thus joining a long line of Cervantine metamorphoses that includes Ginés-Maese Pedro (*Don Quijote*), the protagonist of *Pedro de Urdemalas*, and Tomás-Vidriera. In play terms, this highly theatrical aspect of Cervantes's narratives provides an examination of *mimesis* – both in Auerbach's sense of the way an author "represents reality," and in the more specialized sense of the character's inclination to play-act, to take on roles. Consistent with Caillois's argument (ch. 6), the mimetic inclination of these characters is associated with a potential threat to the social order. The fact that the boys' engagement with the picaresque world is primarily recreational makes *La ilustre fregona* especially pertinent in the context of the contemporary debates surrounding leisure. While the delinquent underworld, with its card-sharping and thievery, would seem a perfect illustration of illicit play, there is a sense that the boys' *mimetic* involvement in the picaresque entails a rite of passage, a liminal state from which they return at least partially enlightened.

If for Rinconete and Cortadillo the liminal picaresque experience contributes (albeit ambiguously) to their moral and cognitive development, in *La ilustre fregona* there is a more explicit lesson to be learned. Looming behind the overarching structure of romance and restitution is the rape committed by Carriazo's father. Carriazo's lust for adventure, which he sates through his picaresque identity, may be understood as a corollary to his father's transgression. The mostly comic violence and lust of the boys' underworld journey comprises a relatively safe indulgence and mastery of the father's more destructive impulse. In a sense, they atone for the father's sin through their picaresque play. The structure is thus similar to that of *El casamiento engañoso* and *El coloquio de los perros*. An initial sexual transgression of grave consequence is followed by an imaginative, highly ludic exploration of the conditions and inclinations that gave rise to it.

The motive behind the high-born Carriazo's delinquency broadly corresponds to Huizinga's criteria for play: "It is an activity which proceeds within certain limits of time and space, in a visible order, according to rules freely accepted, and outside the sphere of necessity or material utility" (132). Rather than material necessity, Carriazo is "llevado de una inclinación picaresca, sin forzarle a ello algún mal tratamiento que sus padres le hiciesen, sólo por su gusto y antojo" ("Carried by a picaresque inclination, without being forced into it by any poor treatment from his parents, but only by his pleasure and fancy" [139]). While from the character's standpoint what prevails in picaresque life is an exhilarating disorder, from a representational perspective that order, to continue with Huizinga's definition, could not be more "visible." As in *Rinconete y Cortadillo*, Cervantes explicitly deploys the genre conventions of the picaresque. But instead of the bleak determinism of poverty and delinquency associated with many picaresque works, we have a realm of freedom and festivity. The purest expression of this tendency of picaresque representation is contained in the anonymous poem, *La vida del pícaro* (1600):

> Tu, picaro, de gradas haçes sillas,
> y, sin respeto de la justa media,
> a tu plaçer te asientas y arrodillas.
>
> No aguardas que el relox te de la media …
>
> No saves de jaraves ni socroçio,
> porque la enfermedad del cuerpo huye
> de aquellos que procuran risa y oçio. (v. 248–56)

[You, picaro, make seats of steps, / and, without respect to the just mean, / sit or kneel at your pleasure. / You do not wait for the clock to give you its signal … / You know nothing of syrups nor poultice, / because sickness flees the body / of those who have laughter and leisure.]

The picaresque existence is presented as a salubrious alternative to conventional life, a hygienic indulgence in pleasurable leisure and laughter. Dunn commented that the poem "could be described as an "urban pastoral" insofar as it is "anticommercial and anti-industrial, and it takes no account of the floods, the plagues, the miseries of winter, the hostility of sedentary citizens" (*Spanish Picaresque Fiction* 241). Indeed, the *pícaro* enjoys an eternal spring ("Aqui se llama Março el mes de Octubre" – "Here they call March the month of October" [v. 121]), and exercises a carefree and opportunistic mobility: "Si alavan el año en Sevilla, / en veinte dias a Sevilla marcha, / y en la mitad aprende su cartilla. / Si el de Valladolid, de alla desmarcha" ("If the year in Seville is praised, / in twenty days he goes to Seville, / and in the middle he learns his trade. / If that [the year] of Valladolid, he sets forth from there" [v. 227–30]). But if Dunn is correct to characterize the poem as escapist in its lack of engagement with unsavoury social realities, we might recall Iffland's observation that such nomadism could itself be subversive, an image of *el mundo desterritorializado* ("the deterritorialzed world," *De fiestas* 101). In *La ilustre fregona*, Carriazo's voluntary *mimesis* (to which he soon recruits his friend, Avendaño) has its associated pastimes and itinerant lifestyle: "En tres años que tardó en parecer y volver a su casa, aprendió a jugar a la taba en Madrid, y al rentoy en las ventillas de Toledo, y a presa y pinta en pie en las barbacanas de Sevilla" ("In the three years it took him to arrive and return to his house, he learned to play sheep-bone in Madrid, cards at the inns of Toledo and the low walls of Seville" [139–40]). We will consider the characteristics of their "picaresque leisure" at more length below, along with the countervailing forces of "reterritorialization" it will incite. For the time being, it is worth pointing out that the "taba" – a primitive dice game played with an animal bone – recalls the juvenile diversion sketched in Erasmus's dialogue "Knucklebones" (see above p. 60).

The picaresque realm of play is associated with Spring and youth, typical regions (Madrid, Toledo, Seville, and the tunneries of the southern coast) and venues (the *venta*), and offers an abundant variety of experience:

> ¡Oh pícaros de cocina, sucios, gordos y lucios, pobres fingidos, tullidos falsos, cicateruelos de Zocodover y de la plaza de Madrid, vistosos oracioneros, esportilleros de Sevilla, mandilejos de la hampa, con toda la caterva

innumerable que se encierra debajo deste nombre *pícaro*! Bajad el toldo, amainad el brío, no os llameís pícaros si no habéis cursado dos cursos en la academia de la pesca de atunes. ¡Allí, allí, que está en su centro el trabajo junto con la poltronería! Allí está la suciedad limpia, la gordura rolliza, la hambre prompta, la hartura abundante, sin disfraz del vicio, el juego siempre, las pendencias por momentos, las muertes por puntos, las pullas a cada paso, los bailes como en bodas, las seguidillas como en estampa, los romances con estribos, la poesía sin acciones. Aquí se canta, allí se reniega, acullá se riñe, acá se juega, y por todo se hurta. Allí campea la libertad y luce el trabajo; allí van, o envían, muchos padres principales a buscar a sus hijos, y los hallan; y tanto sienten sacarlos de aquella vida como si los llevaran a dar la muerte. (141)

[Oh *pícaros* of the kitchen, dirty, fat and sleek, feigning poverty, false cripples, purse-snatchers of Zocodover and the main square of Madrid, flamboyant purveyors of prayers, basket carriers from Seville, underworld servants, with all the innumerable rabble that goes under the banner of *pícaro*! Lower your pretentiousness, trim your gallantry, don't call yourselves *pícaros* if you haven't passed two years of courses in the academy of the tuna fisheries. There, there at its centre is work together with idleness! There is pure filth, plump portliness, prompt hunger, abundant satiety, undisguised vice, constant gambling, frequent altercations, death at any moment, insults at every step, dances as at weddings, song-verses as in print, ballads with stirrups, poetry without action. Here is confession, there is denial, over there is arguing, there is gambling, and everywhere is thievery. There liberty reigns and work shines; many high-born fathers go there – or send others there – to search for their sons, and they find them; and it pains them to be taken from that life as if they were being taken to execution.]

With the energy of hyperbolic description that recalls the Pícara Justina at her most enthusiastic, and a festive ethos consistent with *La vida del pícaro*, Cervantes's interest in the picaresque is expressed in a prolixity equal to that of the Canon of *Don Quijote* as he praises the potential of chivalric romances ("despite all his strictures on such books he did find one positive quality in them: they provided subject matter with which a good intelligence could express itself, because they made available a broad and spacious canvass on which the pen could wander unhindered" [I, 47]). In both *La ilustre fregona* and *Don Quijote*, the imaginative identification of the protagonists corresponds to a creative engagement on the part of the artist. The predictable strife of gambling and lewd behaviour intimated by the *zarabanda* and *chacona* would, according to the prologue's edifying promise of the billiards table, cause the reader to anticipate an eventual condemnation of the boys' picaresque adventure.

But rather than belabour the story's didacticism, we might note the impassioned resistance of the young boys whose fathers bring them back to a respectable life ("y tanto sienten sacarlos de aquella vida como si los llevaran a dar la muerte"). Montaigne touches upon a similar phenomenon:

> I know I have taken boys out of begging into my service, who soon after have left me, my kitchen, and their livery, just to return to their former life. And I found one of them afterward picking up mussels in the dump heap for his dinner, and neither by entreaties nor by threats could I tear him away from the savor and sweetness he found in indigence. Beggars have their splendors and their sensual pleasures as well as rich men, and, it is said, their political dignities and orders. (III, 13, pp. 829–30)

While offering no explicit moral or social edification, Montaigne's observations help elucidate the spirit of *La ilustre fregona*, the curtailment of the visit with don Diego de Miranda (*Don Quijote* II, 18), and the "political dignities and orders" of Monipodio's community. The material comforts and social rectitude of a well-to-do household can prove unsatisfying to both the adventurous youth and the artist; the ludic disposition seeks out alternative realms of experience. As Thompson and others have observed, the pleasure produced in the characters who indulge these inclinations, and in the reader who vicariously experiences them, is an integral part of Cervantes's *eutrapelia*, of his diverting of the "afligido espíritu" ("afflicted spirit"). And, as we shall see, the tale's moral force is curiously bound up with this pleasure.

The entertainment value – or *deleite* – of the picaresque having been established, how does Cervantes convey his story's *enseñanza*, its ostensibly exemplary purpose? As noted above, the ethical component of *La ilustre fregona* is not exclusively contained in the romance resolution, but rather in the tension between romance and picaresque. The aesthetic and ethical concerns are intricately connected. As a rite of passage, the picaresque experience allows the boys to indulge, confront, and expiate transgressive inclinations. While the romance resolution represents the boys' return to their proper state – and a re-alignment of genre and social class – the existence of the picaresque alongside romance gives *La ilustre fregona* a comprehensive representational range, accommodating realms of experience (and their associated recreations) that idealistic genres typically ignore. Cervantes's generic amalgamation is an aesthetic correlative to the philosophical-theological notion of human beings as "mixed" (see ch. 1 of this study).

La ilustre fregona shares some satirical elements with *Rinconete y Cortadillo*, *El licenciado Vidriera*, and *El coloquio de los perros*, although it does not offer any sustained examination of social ills. When Avendaño and Carriazo, having just abandoned their studies, hear two young muleteers discussing the harsh penal system in Sevilla, the theme of judicial abuse comes to the fore: "¡Cuántos pobretes están mascando barro no más de por la cólera de un juez absoluto, de un corregidor, o mal informado, o bien apasionado! Más ven muchos ojos que dos: no se apodera tan presto el veneno de la injusticia de muchos corazones como se apodera de uno solo" ("How many wretches are chewing mud for nothing more than the ire of an absolute judge, of a poorly informed or riled up magistrate! Many eyes see more than two: the poison of injustice does not take power so quickly over many hearts as it does over one" [148]). But the second muleteer cuts his interlocutor short, introducing a more ethereal subject: "Predicador te has vuelto … y según llevas la retahila, no acabarás tan presto, y yo no te puedo aguardar; y esta noche no vayas a posar donde sueles, sino en la posada del Sevillano, porque verás en ella la más hermosa fregona que se sabe" ("You have become a preacher … and the way you are going through the litany, you won't soon be done, and I can't wait for you; and tonight don't go to lodge where you usually do, but at the inn of the *Sevillano*, because you will see there the most beautiful kitchen-maid that is known" [148]). As with Cipion's reprimands of Berganza in *El coloquio de los perros*, we see a suppression of the impulse to indulge in sententious digressions. Cervantes's habitual curtailment of such commentary is consistent with his refusal to give his stories the overt didacticism of conventional exemplarity. Once again, the vicissitudes of experience take precedence over the inculcation of precepts.

The generic dissonance, or hybridity, of *La ilustre fregona* corresponds to its associations of leisure activity with social identity. After an initial mention of two noblemen in Burgos ("dos caballeros principales y ricos"), the narrator announces that the protagonists of the story are their sons, and these boys soon display interests outside of the activities conventionally pertaining to them. Upon returning from his first picaresque sally, Carriazo is morose, his mind continuously occupied by recollections of the tunnery. Yet the traditional antidotes to melancholy seem ineffectual: "Ni le entretenía la caza, en que su padre le ocupaba, ni los muchos, honestos y gustosos convites que en aquella ciudad se usan le daban gusto. Todo pasatiempo le cansaba, y a todos los mayores que se le ofrecían anteponía el que había recibido en las almadrabas" ("The hunt, in which his father occupied him, did not entertain him, nor did the many, honest and pleasurable banquets that were customary in that city please him. Every pastime tired him, and to all the major ones offered him he preferred the one he had experienced at the tuna beaches" [143]). His recreational proclivities are no longer consonant with his social class. With his consuming urge to participate in the adventurous realm that has captured his imagination, Carriazo bears a resemblance to Alonso Quijano. If Carriazo's escapism is less deluded because of his youth and the contemporary reality of his locus of adventure (i.e., the tuna beaches), his picaresque world is nevertheless almost as idealized as the chivalric world of Alonso Quijano, and his fantasies are likewise compromised by some very mundane cuts and bruises. Like Quijano, a former *amigo de la caza* who rejects his comfortable routine, Carriazo becomes indifferent to his former pastimes. It is significant that the language used to describe the feasts ("honestos y gustosos convites que en aquella ciudad se usan") recalls the ideal recreation set forth in the prologue ("ejercicios honestos y agradables"). Carriazo sees in the tuna beaches a *lugar ameno*, even if they are not the "alamedas" (poplar groves) and "fuentes" (fountains) of the prologue: "y todos sus deseos entregó a aquellas secas arenas, que a él la parecían más frescas y verdes que los Campos Elíseos" ("and he surrendered all his desires to those dry sands, which to him seemed fresher and greener than the Elysian Fields" [142]). As with don Quijote taking an inn for a castle, Carriazo imaginatively transforms prosaic phenomena. He represents another Cervantine examination of the mimetic impulse, which, as we have seen, can easily blur the lines between play and reality.

The various metamorphoses of the boys give their adventure a highly theatrical quality. Instead of returning directly to Burgos from his first trip to the tunnery, Carriazo stops in Valladolid in order to revive his original countenance: "Estúvose allí quince días para reformar la color del rostro, sacándola de mulata a flamenca, y para trastejarse y sacarse del borrador de pícaro y ponerse en limpio de caballero" ("He was there for fifteen days to restore his complexion, transforming it from mulatto to Flemish, and to renovate himself and make himself over from base *pícaro* to unsullied gentleman" [142]). Unlike the situation of Campuzano, who must suffer the consequences of his ill-advised adventure in *El casamiento engañoso* (as he himself realized, he cannot simply *volver a barajar*), there is the sense that Carriazo can leave behind his picaresque experience and re-enter society in Burgos as one makes a change of wardrobe – as Sancho playfully switched from governor back to squire. Changing name, appearance, and occupation, Carriazo resembles the protean trickster. But whereas Cervantes's theatrical trickster, Pedro de Urdemalas, feigns both shepherd and noble, Carriazo is a nobleman who convincingly becomes a *pícaro* and water-carrier ("aguador"). Calling to mind the two friends newly outfitted as *esportilleros* (basket carriers) in Seville (*Rinconete y Cortadillo*), both Carriazo and Avendaño transform themselves entirely in Madrid, en route back to the picaresque world: "Vistiéronse a lo payo con capotillos de dos haldas, zahones o zaragüelles y medias de paño pardo. Ropero hubo que por la mañana les compró sus vestidos y a la noche los había mudado de manera que no los conociera la propia madre que los había parido" ("They dressed like country boys in coarse, loose jackets, wide trousers or overalls, and dun-collared stockings. There was a clothier who in the morning bought their suits and by night had transformed them so that not even the mother that bore them would have recognized them" [146]). Also as in *Rinconete y Cortadillo*, the narrator plays along with the artifice of the boys, alternating between their real and play names. Such ludic narrating points to a fundamental parallel between the *mimesis* of the boys and the representational designs of Cervantes. Wardropper has described how the trickster ethos permeates Cervantes's artistic vision, comprising the entertaining component of his broader practice of *delectare et prodesse* in the *Novelas ejemplares*: "In each one the art of illusionist is not limited to the protagonists and the primary events. It extends to the majority of the characters and their acts. The stories form a fabric of playful and innocent illusions. The *tropelía* turns out to be the artistic mode chosen by Cervantes to express in a novelistic way *eutrapelia*."[37]

It should be kept in mind that the metamorphoses in the *Novelas ejemplares* do not always represent a playful or theatrical ethos on the part of the character. Costanza's transformation, like that of Preciosa (*La gitanilla*) and Isabel (*La española inglesa*), involves the non-ironic realization of a romance structure, representing an affirmation of truth and order. Furthermore, Costanza's is not a freely chosen transformation, but rather the work of external forces.[38] But in spite of the different natures of the transformations these characters undergo, and the ambiguity of the noble *pícaros* as well as the beautiful and virtuous kitchen maid, their identities possess a certain "authenticity," a constancy of character beneath the appearances. The experience during their transformation brings an enhanced comprehension of themselves and their relationship to society. As we shall see, the fact that Carriazo is ultimately unable to wipe the slate as clean as the narrator suggests above ("ponerse en limpio de caballero") serves as a comic affirmation of the pertinence of his play to "real life."

Assuming that one's social status and activities should correspond to – indeed, confirm – one's identity, there is an irony when the boys compose the deceiving letter to explain to their parents the deviation on the way to Salamanca: "habiendo nosotros sus hijos, con madura consideración, considerado cuán más propias son de los caballeros las armas que las letras, habemos determinado de trocar a Salamanca por Bruselas y a España por Flandes" ("we your children, with mature consideration having considered how much more appropriate to gentlemen are arms than letters, have determined to exchange Salamanca for Brussels and Spain for Flanders" [146]). As in *El licenciado Vidriera*, both arms and letters are cited as potential, legitimate roles to fulfil, each with its particular venue and mode of behaviour. The presentation of these three roles – two legitimate, the third, chosen, escapist – again points to an element of play within "serious society," that is, the necessarily conventional quality of social organization and interaction, and the different realms of experience pertaining to these conventions. As seen above, a similar theatricality in official society is suggested, by way of comic inversion, in the structured hierarchy of Monipodio's community in *Rinconete y Cortadillo*. Rebhorn's discussion of "masking" in the Renaissance underlines the social function of *mimesis*: "Like many others in the Renaissance, he [Castiglione] conceives social activity as essentially a matter of playing a series of roles, each entailing certain predetermined attitudes and modes of activity, status of relationships, and types of dress and deportment – in other words, each having its appropriate, *figurative mask*" (14). As Rebhorn indicates, the individual's freedom depends on an ability to comprehend and use such roles, rather than merely to cling to one in superficial imitation. We noted earlier in this study (ch. 1) that Cervantes's sense of role-playing was closer to the expressive sociability of Castiglione than to the Machiavellian manipulations of Gracián. Recalling Barber's account of an important transition in the period, we can say that Cervantes also tends to represent a consciousness of life as more historical than ceremonial: "the gaining and losing of names, of meaning, is beyond the control of any set ritual sequence" (Barber 193). As a consequence, the characters bear a good measure of the burden of figuring out and asserting who they are. And they often do so through play.

Interrogation and Validation of the Fictional World in *La ilustre fregona*

Cervantes's criticism of *La Celestina* for its earthy content ("libro, en mi opinión divi-, / si encubriera más los huma-," – "a book, in my opinion divi- /, had it covered up more of the huma-" [*Don Quijote* I]) should be taken with a grain of salt. The author of *Don Quijote, El coloquio de los perros,* and *La ilustre fregona* was certainly attracted to the lower realm, and the ugly, malodorous, and lewd Argüello would be able to hold her own among Celestina's bawds (and so, too, could Maritornes and Cañizares). Just as Berganza let one of his new masters spit in his mouth as part of a routine inspection, but is repulsed by the prospect of a kiss from Cañizares, Carriazo would be hanged, relinquish his friendship with Avendaño, and perform a series of exploits that would be the envy of don Quijote before capitulating to the desires of Argüello: "Mirad, Tomás: ponedme a pelear con dos gigantes y en ocasión que me sea forzoso desquijarar por vuestro servicio media docena o una de leones, que lo haré con más facilidad que beber una taza de vino; pero que me pongáis en necesidad que me tome a brazo partido con la Argüello, no lo consinteré si me asaetean" ("See here, Tomás: have me do battle with two giants and in a position that forces me to break the jaws, in your service, of half a dozen or a dozen lions, which I'll do with more alacrity than drinking a cup of wine; but that you should oblige me to take up *la Argüello* in my arms, is something to which I will not assent though they fill me with arrows" [174]). At the inn in *Don Quijote,* the grotesque Maritornes functions as a reality principle that ridicules the knight's delusions. The negative power of Argüello, however, is set off against the virtuous and beautiful Costanza, who is not the figment of a deluded imagination. The mutual animation resulting from the Argüello / Costanza contrast corresponds to the tale's intermingling of two distinct genres.

The nocturnal scene of rustic festivity at the inn brings the picaresque and romance into contact again. Taking the guitar and a prefatory expectoration in the manner of la Gananciosa (*Rinconete y Cortadillo* 231), Carriazo's *chacona* comically transforms the wench whose advances had caused him such distress: "Cambio el son, divina Argüello, / más bella que un hospital; / pues eres mi nueva musa, / tu favor me quieras dar" ("I change my tune, divine Argüello, / most hospitable beauty / since you are my new muse, / should you want to give me your favours" [168]). An inversion of the sublime Costanza, Argüello has become the queen of carnivalesque revelry. As we saw above (ch. 1) the *chacona*, along with the *zarabanda*, was considered illicit recreation because of its uninhibited, salacious movements. Carriazo acknowledges as much, although his personification of the very dance includes a curious defence of such charges: "¡Cuántas fue vituperada / de los mismos que la adoran! / Porque imagina el lascivo / y al que es necio se le antoja" ("How many times was she insulted / by the very ones who adore her! / Because the lewd imagine / and the foolish desire her" [169]). It is up to the participants and spectators to prevent such activity from deteriorating; only those who are already lewd or foolish see anything harmful in it. But Cervantes is aware of the responsibility of the artist not to incite such poor dispositions, and Carriazo proposes to move on to some more venerable material. The commentary recalls, in miniature, the discussions surrounding *eutrapelia*, which emphasize the mutual obligations of speaker and listener to uphold decorum.

If the *chacona* tilts the balance away from the *eutrapelos* and towards the *bomolochos* (or *chocarrero*), Carriazo provides an alternate justification as he sings of the positive effects of such ribald celebration:

> Hállase allí el ejercicio
> que la salud acomoda,
> sacudiendo de los miembros
> a la pereza poltrona.
>
> Bulle la risa en el pecho
> de quien baila y de quien toca,
> del que mira y del que escucha
> baile y música sonora. (169)

[There is found the exercise / that accommodates health, / shaking the limbs / from lazy indolence.

Laughter bubbles in the chest / of those who dance and those who play, / those who watch and those who listen.]

The laughter of the dancers and players is contagious, infecting even those who observe the spectacle – implying, of course, Cervantes's readers as well. But there is also a therapeutic quality to the vigorous movements of the dance. Such a justification is consistent with the hygienic views on recreation considered above (ch. 1), in which moral considerations are secondary to physiological benefits. Méndez (*Libro del ejercicio corporal y de sus provechos* 1553) had allowed some dancing for women and, in his promotion of activities that give rise to "plazer y alegría," he offers the following list: "assi se puede esgrimir: jugar picas con el espada y broquel. luchar: baylar: -ançar: y assi cosas desta manera con que os holgueys. Y dezimos todo eso: para que tome cada uno lo que mejor le estuviere" ("so can one fence, play lances with the sword and shield, wrestle, dance, stroll; and in such things with which you enjoy yourselves. And we say all this so that each may take that which is most suitable" [138]). Carriazo's defence of the dance reinforces the sense that Cervantes's literary *eutrapelia* is not necessarily predicated on exemplarity. As Jones argued, "recreation is good at least in part since it purifies the pernicious humors caused by idleness. And, more importantly, Cervantes applied this doctrine as a justification for imaginative literature without an obvious moral content, including prose fiction."[39]

It is when Carriazo attempts to complement his boisterous recreation with more exalted material that the suspect character of his audience asserts itself: "y en tanto que Lope se acomodaba a pasar adelante cantando otras cosas de más tomo, sustancia y consideración de las cantadas, uno de los muchos embozados que el baile miraban, dijo sin quitarse el embozo: '¡Calla, borracho! ¡Calla, cuero! ¡Calla, odrina, poeta de viejo, músico falso!'" ("and as Lope was getting ready to proceed singing other things of greater import, substance and consideration than those already sung, one of the masked onlookers of the dance said, without removing the mask: 'Be quiet, drunkard! Quiet, you lush! Quiet, you wineskin, old-school poet, false musician!'" [170]). Apparently following Cervantes's promise in his prologue that each story contains material of "substance and consideration," the conscientious Carriazo attempts to introduce more dignified subject matter in his songs. But just as this material is not elucidated for us in the prologue for reasons of narrative economy ("si no fuera por no alargar este sujeto, quizá te mostrara el sabroso y honesto fruto" – "and were it not to avoid drawing out this subject, maybe I'd show you the tasty and honest fruit" [Prólogo]), Carriazo has no opportunity to expound on his new subject matter. If this outburst of angry invective, along with the general violence which follows, represents the *vulgo* the "modern" Lope de Vega aspired to entertain, the spectator's accusation that Carriazo is a poet of the old school ("poeta de viejo") recalls Vidriera's lament on the degradation of the contemporary artistic milieu ("You should see how these modern young puppies bark at the hoary old mastiffs" [*El licenciado Vidriera* 59]). Once again, Cervantes presents a scene of farcical violence destroying the aesthetic space. But rather than shoddy artistry, as with Berganza's *perro sabio* show (see above p. 241), the curtailment of the present spectacle is due to deficiencies in the audience.

The arrival of the authorities only achieves a temporary calm, as the exalted ballad of an admirer of Costanza elicits further outrage in the rustic audience. But this reaction does not merely illustrate the unhappy fate of artists in a vulgar world ("¡Infelice estado de los músicos, murciélagos y lechuzos, siempre sujetos a semejantes lluvias y desmanes!" – "Unlucky lot of musicians, bats and debt collectors, always subject to such showers and misfortunes!" [172]). Barrabás the muleteer offers a coherent commentary on linguistic register and decorum:

> ¿quién diablos te enseñó a cantar a una fregona cosas de esferas y de cielos, llamándola lunes y martes, y de ruedas de fortuna? Dijérasla, noramala para ti y para quien le hubiere parecido bien tu trova, que es tiesa como un espárrago, entonada como un plumaje, blanca como una leche, honesta como un fraile novicio, melindrosa y zahareña como una mula de alquiler, y más dura que un pedazo de argamasa; que como esto le dijeras, ella lo entendiera y se holgara; pero llamarla embajador, y red, y moble, y alteza, y bajeza, más es para decirlo a un niño de la dotrina que a una fregona. Verdaderamente que hay poetas en el mundo que escriben trovas que no hay diablo que las entienda. (173)

> [Who in the world taught you to sing to a kitchen maid about the spheres and heavens, calling her Monday and Tuesday, and wheels of fortune? You should have said to her, a pox on you and whomever approved of your song, that she is rigid as an asparagus, vain as plumage, white as milk, virtuous as a new friar, prudish and obstinate as a rented mule, and harder than a slab of mortar; had you told her this, she would have understood it and been pleased; but to call her ambassador, and net, and mobile, and highness, and lowness, is more suitable to tell an orphan of charity than to a kitchen maid. Truly there are poets in the world who write verses that no devil may understand.]

What begins as a derision of comic dim-wittedness in the base sensibilities of an irascible audience Cervantes develops into a perspectivistic humorous confrontation. By foregrounding the complex linguistic relationship between interlocutors and the world they attempt to describe, the episode recalls don Quijote's dialogue with Sancho as they attempt to gauge their progress on the *barco encantado* (*Don Quijote* II, 29). As the rules of the poet's game are questioned, cast in an almost ridiculous light, one cannot say for sure who is more laughable, the crooner or the muleteer. Barrabás understands little about the expressive value of poetic imagery, but, in illustrating the conventionality of such images in his comic enumeration, he shows just how poetry's power of expression can be compromised. Checa noted how this sort of language game is emblematic of the dialogic character of the entire story: "precisely because the prevarications of Barrabás and his substitutive language *degrade* a prestigious and somewhat elitist language, they also contribute to laying bare the arbitrary roots of that learned language, that is, its equally conventional basis. So is dramatized the struggle (or mutual questioning) of artistic codes that reproduce, on a small scale, that of the entire text."[40]

Cervantes certainly appreciated Rojas's comic contextualization of the sentimental register of *Cárcel de amor* in Sempronio's bemused incomprehension of Calisto in the first act of *La Celestina*. A similar poetic language contributed to the capitulation of Alonso Quijano's intellect at the outset of *Don Quijote* ("La razón de la sin razón que a mi razón se hace ..." ("The reason for the unreason to which my reason is subjected" [I, 1]). When the same type of amorous idealism affects Avendaño and, like Calisto and don Quijote, his adoration of the woman borders on blasphemy, Cervantes is clearly interested in more than parody. An *agon* is established between two opposing representational modes, and neither is clearly privileged. In the scene above it is the prosaic element that temporarily prevails over the conventions of romance: "Todos los que escucharon a Barrabás recibieron gran gusto, y tuvieron su censura y parecer por muy acertado" ("All who listened to Barrabás greatly enjoyed it, and judged his censure and opinion to be right on the mark" [173]). In an earlier manifestation of this generic "to-and-fro," Carriazo provoked the romantically inclined Avendaño: "Pues ¿qué piensas hacer con el imposible que se te ofrece en la conquista desta Porcia, desta Minerva y desta nueva Penélope, que en figura de doncella y de fregona te enamora, te acobarda y te desvanece?" ("Well, what do you plan on doing with this impossibility you are faced with in the conquest of this Portia, this Minerva, this new Penelope, who in the form of maiden and kitchen maid enamours you, cows you, and dissipates you?" [164]). Avendaño realizes that he is being mocked, and defends himself: "Haz la burla que de mí quisieres, amigo Lope, que yo sé que estoy enamorado del más hermoso rostro que pudo formar naturaleza y de la más incomparable honestidad que ahora se puede usar en el mundo" ("Make fun of me as you like, friend Lope, but I know that I am in love with the most beautiful face nature could form and the most incomparable virtue that can now exist in the world" [164]). And the story will, in fact, back up Avendaño's claim to have encountered real subject matter that is commensurate with his exalted idiom.

When Carriazo retains the tail from the four parts of the ass he has gambled away at the card-table, the playful character of his picaresque existence is evident. The logic of Carriazo's claim causes laughter among his fellow gamblers, although some pedants dispute the case: "hubo letrados que fueron de parecer que no tenía razón en lo que pedía, diciendo que cuando se vende un carnero o otra res alguna no se saca ni quita la cola, que con uno de los cuartos traseros ha de ir forzosamente" ("there were learned men who were of the opinion that he was unjust in his demand, saying that when a sheep or other beast is sold the tail is not taken or removed, that it by force must go with one of the back quarters" [181]). Carriazo points out that his activities pertain not to the rules of *negotium* appealed to by the pedants, but to a more flexible standard of *otium*: "que a lo de ir la cola junto con la res que se vende viva y no se cuartea, que lo concedía; pero que la suya no fue vendida, sino jugada, y que nunca su intención fue jugar la cola" ("that with regard to the tail going with the live animal that is sold and not quartered, he conceded; but his was not sold, but gambled, and it was never his intention to bet the tail" [181]). When the gamblers persist in challenging his claim, Carriazo makes them think twice with a convincing display of ferocity: "como estaba hecho al trato de las almadrabas, donde se ejercita todo género de rumbo y jácara y de extraordinarios juramentos y boatos, voleó allí el capelo y empuñó un puñal que debajo del capotillo traía, y púsose en tal postura, que infundió temor y respeto en toda aquella aguadora compañía" ("since he was formed in the trade of the tuna beaches, where one practices all manner of ostentation and curses and extraordinary oaths, he tossed off his hat and gripped the dagger he carried beneath his cloak, and put himself in such a posture, that he infused fear and respect into that entire water-carrying company" [182]). His virtuosic *mimesis* of a picaresque persona calls to mind Guzmán de Alfarache's violent linguistic and physical display (see ch. 1 of this study), as well as the genre paintings of the period, in which the gamblers grip the sword and dagger handles that are always near the centre of the composition (see Figure 2, above).

We can underscore the multiple transgressions of Carriazo's gambling by recalling the recreational play outlined by Vives in "Las leyes del juego" (*Diálogos*). With regard to one's playing companions, Vives remarks: "Sean graciosos, joviales y corteses, con los que no haya peligro de riñas ni disputas en que digas o hagas cosa torpe o indecente" ("May they be amusing, jovial and polite, with those who pose no danger of arguments or disputes if you say or do something rude or indecent" ["Ley segunda"]). Concerning the amount one should bet, he warns: "ni se ha de apostar tanto que te inquiete el juego y te sepa mal perder, porque así no sería juego, sino tormento" ("nor is one to bet so much that it perturbs your play and makes losing bitter, because in this way it would not be play, but torment" ["Ley cuarta"]). That players who ran out of money were betting their clothes, livestock, and even other human beings (e.g. servants) was another symptom of excess in the period. Deleito y Piñuela refers to the letters of the French priest, Juan Muret, who observes in Felipe IV's Spain a deception that exceeds Carriazo's "tail trick": "The same writer confirms that there was one who, having lost his carriage and team of mules, wagered the driver, deceiving the one who won it from him, making him falsely believe that he was a slave."[41] After more than winning back his losses, Carriazo takes pity on his opponent, who has begun beating his own head against the floor in despair: "Lope, como bien nacido y como liberal y compasivo, le levantó y le volvió todo el dinero que le había ganado y los diez y seis ducados del asno, y aun de los que él tenía repartió con los circunstantes" ("Lope, being well born and generous and compassionate, helped him up and returned to him all the money he had won from him and the sixteen ducats from the ass, and even the remaining coins he distributed to those present" [182]). Despite the obvious excesses and degradation of his activity, he has managed to display what Enrique Santo-Tomás termed the *sprezzatura* of noble play. Carriazo's peculiar display of wit, violent recklessness, and generosity corresponds to the basic tension Cervantes has given to his character, a nobleman playing the role of *pícaro*. If his manner of playing partly expresses his high birth, his immersion in the game – like the broader underworld adventure of the two boys – casts doubt on an essentialist distinction between noble and humble identity.

Female recreation is also examined in *La ilustre fregona*. It is interesting that Avendaño should deliver his love letter to Costanza under the guise of a prayer for her tooth-ache, as readers of *La Celestina* would recall the association of Melibea's *dolor de muelas* with the love malady. Costanza's attitude upon accepting the text, and the reading venue she chooses, allude to some of the key terms of contemporary debates: "y ella, con mucho gusto y más devoción, se entró en un aposento a solas, y abriendo el papel vio que decía desta manera" ("and she, with much pleasure and more devotion, entered her room alone, and opening the paper saw that it said the following" [178]). Her pious bearing to the supposed devotional text would coincide with the only sort of reading generally considered licit for women in early modern Spain. On the other hand, the pleasure she expresses ("con mucho gusto"), and the private space of her reading ("se entró en un aposento a solas") might suggest a more ambivalent reading situation.[42] Is this an echo of *Don Quijote*'s independent and subversive reader ("you are sitting in your own home, where you are the lord and master"), or of Peralta's uneasy mirth as he receives his diseased friend's manuscript of *El coloquio de los perros* ("he took it, laughing and apparently making light of all that he had heard and of what he was expecting to read")? There is, in fact, little ambiguity surrounding Costanza's behaviour. She displays a sincere piety ("es devotísima de Nuestra Señora; confiesa y comulga cada mes" – "she is a devotee of Our Lady; she confesses and takes communion every month" [189]), appropriately attends to her needlework ("no hay mayor randera en Toledo" – "nobody in Toledo exceeds her in needlework"), sings well, but in private ("a la almohadilla" – "to herself"), and discretely refuses to hear Avendaño's songs: "bien es verdad que de cuando en cuando le da alguna música, que ella jamás escucha" ("it is true that he sometimes gives her some music, to which she never listens" [190]). While Costanza's impeccable modesty and obedience correspond to her ideal beauty and virtue, her behaviour and spheres of activity are like those of Leonora of *El celoso extremeño*, with her recreations of needlework, fairy tales, and landscape tapestries: "Las figuras de los paños que sus salas y cuadras adornaban, todas eran hembras, flores y boscajes. Toda su casa olía a honestidad, recogimiento y recato: aun hasta las consejas que en las largas noches de invierno, en la chimenea, sus criadas contaban, por estar él presente, en ningún género de lasciva se descubría" ("The figures on the canvases that adorned his rooms were all of females, flowers and woodland scenes. His entire house smelled of honesty, seclusion and modesty: even the stories told by his female servants, at the hearth during the long winter nights, since he was present, revealed not the slightest hint of lewdness"

[*El celoso extremeño* 10]). While the "honesty" and "modesty" of the house would seem to echo the wholesome *ejercicios honestos y agradables* touted in the collection's prologue, Carrizales exceeds the propriety of *eutrapelia*, as he encloses his young wife in a state of infantile innocence. Gage's study of early modern notions of therapeutic art underlines the restrictiveness of Carrizales: "Unlike images of nudes or of pagan deities, which [Giulio] Mancini insisted should be withdrawn from the public eye and placed in locations under the strict control of the head of household, no objections could be marshalled against placing before the eyes of men and women of any rank and condition landscape paintings, including images of shepherds, animals, and the seasons, as well as perspectival scenes and cosmographical works. The genre of landscape was not only unobjectionable, it was positively healthful" (1188). The "flores y boscajes" allowed by Carrizales accord with the period's views on permissible, even hygienic art; but his exclusion of any member of the masculine gender, either represented or in the flesh, human or animal, run counter to broadly accepted mores. And it will be a particular member of the Sevillian leisure class ("Hay en Sevilla un género de gente ociosa y holgazana" – "There is in Seville a class of useless and idle people usually known as men about town" [106]), idle and unproductive, whose curiosity will spur him to infiltrate Carrizales's monastic fortress. Through a travesty of the narrative convention of the helpless damsel liberated by a dashing hero, Cervantes critically examines the polar conditions of repression and license. The moneyed Loaysa, privileged by class and good looks, is not so different from the dissolute pícaro: "Estos son hijos de vecino de cada colación, y de los más ricos della; gente baldía, atildada y meliflua, de la cual y de su traje y manera de vivir, de su condición y de las leyes que guardan entre sí, había mucho que decir; pero por buenos respectos se deja" ("These are the richer young men from every parish, lazy, showy, plausible people, about whose dress and manner of living, and whose customs and rules of conduct a good deal could be said; but we'll leave that aside for good reason" [106–7]).

La ilustre fregona's Costanza does not possess the appealing vigour of *La gitanilla*'s Preciosa, whose *agudezas* and spectacular dancing make her a female character who is able to balance a degree of independence and assertiveness while still maintaining her virtue. It is significant that in *La ilustre fregona, El celoso extremeño* and *La gitanilla*, music plays an ambivalent and central role. Music presents the moral threat of temptation, but also vitality and festive union. As we observed above, it may have the potential to stimulate the disordering affective faculties, but enjoyment of music was, in the opinion of many during the period, also a sign of humanity: "Y si tampoco deste huelgan señal es efficaz que son mal compuestos y peor condicionados y de aquellos me guarde dios" ("And if they also do not enjoy this, it is an effective sign that they are poorly composed and even more poorly conditioned, and may god protect me from such people" [Pedro de Covarrubias fols. 17r–18]). Cervantes may not cast Costanza in the ironic light of the sternly pious Isabella in Shakespeare's *Measure for Measure*. But she does not possess the dimension of some of his more memorable female characters, and her restricted recreational spheres reflect this condition.

Whereas Carriazo's picaresque engagement has, as we have seen, an overtly playful quality, Avendaño affirms a complete sincerity and commitment in his role as Costanza's suitor. But "Lope el Asturiano" continues his parody, insinuating the artifice of his friend's sentimental world in a deflationary comparison with his own recreational realm:

> ¡Oh amor platónico! ¡Oh fregona ilustre! ¡Oh felicísimos tiempos los nuestros, donde vemos que la belleza enamora sin malicia, la honestidad enciende sin que abrase, el donaire da gusto sin que incite, y la bajeza del estado humilde obliga y fuerza a que le suban la rueda de la que llaman Fortuna! ¡Oh pobres atunes míos, que os pasáis este año sin ser visitados deste tan enamorado y aficionado vuestro! Pero el que viene yo haré la enmienda de manera que no se quejen de mí los mayorales de las mis deseadas almadrabas. (165)

> [Oh platonic love! Oh illustrious kitchen maid! Oh happy times ours, when we see that beauty enamours without malice, virtue inflames without burning, gracefulness gives pleasure without inciting, and the lowliness of a humble condition obliges and forces that wheel they call Fortune to lift her up! Oh my poor tunas, that must pass this year without being visited by this your dedicated and beloved! But next year I will make it up in such a way that the chiefs of my beloved tuna beaches do not complain of me!]

Carriazo's exalted oratory recalls don Quijote's acorn-inspired discourse on the Golden Age, which is comically deflated by its reception by both Sancho and the goatherds (*Don Quijote* I, 11). In the scene above, the derision comes from Carriazo's juxtaposition of his own desires with those of Avendaño, maintaining the same lofty register for each realm: he casts himself in the light of a passionate suitor pining for his tunas, drawing a comparison to Avendaño in a way that pays no great tribute to Costanza. It is the sort of comic contrast that El Pinciano terms "adjunto de lugar," the less indecorous of his two examples being this: "fue gracioso un mayordomo de un cavallero pobre que, dando cuenta a su señor del gasto de aquel día, entre otras partidas, tenía una que dezía: 'de quitar el estiércol de la cavalleriza y la barba de su merced, tres reales'" ("The butler of a poor gentleman was funny when, giving an account to his master of the day's expenses, among other entries, he had one that said: 'for removing the manure from the stable and the beard from your grace, three *reales*'" [López Pinciano IX]). The generic *adjunto*, or juxtaposition, of *La ilustre fregona* generates a broader comic range than such deflations initially suggest.

From the above exchange one might anticipate a rather unforgiving subversion of the sentimental realm – something along the lines of Berganza's revelation of the artificiality of the pastoral romance in *El coloquio de los perros*. Indeed, Avendaño takes offence at his friend's ribbing: "Ya veo, Asturiano, cuán al descubierto te burlas de mí. Lo que podías hacer es irte norabuena a tu pesquería, que yo me quedaré en mi caza, y aquí me hallarás a la vuelta" ("I see, Asturiano, how plainly you make fun of me. What you could do is leave with good tidings to your fishing, and I'll stay here at my hunt, and here you'll find me upon your return" [165]). He announces his dedication to his new pursuit ("mi caza"), and sends Carriazo on his way to the tunneries. It is at this point, however, that Carriazo affirms the bond of friendship between the two boys. As he reveals in his response to his offended friend, the elements of *amistad* and good will significantly qualify the nature of his joking: "Por más discreto te tenía ... y ¿tú no ves que lo que digo es burlando? Pero ya que sé que hablas de veras, de veras te serviré en todo aquello que fuere de tu gusto" ("I thought you were more astute than that ... and didn't you see that I say this in good fun? But now that I know that you are in earnest, in earnest I'll serve you in everything that should be to your pleasure" [165]). Rather than a derisive humour of ridicule and separation (*burlarse de*), Carriazo assures his friend that he is joking *with* him, and he pledges to remain in Toledo in Avendaño's service. This sort of humour is consistent with Cervantes's general preference of humane *sátiras de luz* over derisive *sátiras de sangre*, and with the nature of the humour examined in *Don Quijote* above. To refer back to the phrase of James Wood, we could say that Cervantes creates a "comedy of forgiveness" on the level of genre, as neither the picaresque world of Carriazo nor Avendaño's sentimental romance is invalidated, despite the comic effects of their combination in a single story. Even as the embellishments of each genre are exposed, so are its claims to human experience and aspirations.

Avendaño wonders, in his enamoured perplexity, what sort of mysterious forces are acting upon him:

> Costanza se llama, y no Porcia, Minerva o Penélope; en un mesón sirve, que no lo puedo negar; pero ¿qué puedo yo hacer, si me parece que el destino con oculta fuerza me inclina y la elección con claro discurso me mueve a que la adore? Mira, amigo: no sé cómo te diga ... de la manera con que amor el bajo sujeto de esta fregona, que tú llamas, me le encumbra y levanta tan alto, que viéndole no le vea y conociéndole le desconozca. (164)
>
> [Costanza she is called, and not Portia, Minerva or Penelope; she serves at an inn, I can't deny; but what can I do, if it seems to me that destiny with hidden force inclines me and choice with clear discourse moves me to adore her? Look, my friend: I don't know how to explain ... the way with which the low person of this kitchen maid, as you call her, is praised and raised so high by love, that seeing her I don't see her and knowing her I don't know her.]

In the *barco encantado* episode (*Don Quijote* II, 29), we recall, the *oculta fuerza* assumed by don Quijote turns out to be the simple, non-teleological momentum of the river's current. Pedro Rincón supposed an occult destiny behind his meeting with Diego Cortado ("imagino que no sin misterio nos ha juntado aquí la suerte" – "I imagine there's some good reason why fate has brought us together here" [194]), and Cipión and Berganza contemplate the mystery of their union at length. As we saw, neither story elucidates the mystery. Nor, as this study has been suggesting, does Cervantes ever spell out the mystery he insinuates in the prologue, the words of which seem to echo in Avendaño's speech: "que pues yo he tenido la osadía de dirigir estas novelas al gran Conde de Lemos, algún *misterio* tienen escondido que las *levanta*" ("since I have dared to direct these stories to the great Count of Lemos, they possess some secret *mystery* that *elevates* them" [Prólogo my italics]). The sense of active resignation that emerges in *El coloquio de los perros* ("Pero sea lo que fuere, nosotros hablamos, sea portento o no" [301]) also animates Avendaño as he struggles to understand his predicament: "Finalmente, sea lo que se fuere, yo la quiero bien" ("In sum, whatever the case may be, I love her well" [165]).

In *La ilustre fregona*, the reconciling structure of romance is ultimately realized, lifting Costanza from the underworld of the inn and affirming the noble identities of the characters. But if romance prevails, the picaresque is also legitimized. Within this dialogue of genres, the picaresque fulfils a role of comic subversion, exposing both the conventionality of romance and certain impulses and aspects of experience that it excludes. Checa points out how neither realm of experience is clearly privileged by Cervantes: "The conclusion is not ... that through the evocation of the tuna beaches, the text postulates a greater 'sincerity' or 'authenticity' of the transgressive anxieties latent in each individual; it attempts, rather, to recognize their existence and show how the modality of *romance*, to the extent it channels or represses them, tends to base its mollifying message on the sublimation of our more disruptive passions."[43] Cervantes recognizes that the *mimetic* play impulse that takes the boys to their Southern picaresque adventure is, indeed, potentially destabilizing. It is a liminoid experience that could compromise their own nobility and, in its lawlessness and licentiousness, it represents a threat to official values. But rather than simply have the idealized realm of exalted love and exemplary nobility triumph over abject delinquency and lust, he allows the latter to be aired in its ambivalent appeal. Cervantes thus demonstrates once again that his is not a naive art, unaware of the reductive structures by which we read and live. He also displays an interest in presenting visions of beauty and order, ideal worlds that are examined without necessarily being undermined. It is this integrated tension of scepticism and engagement, of irony and sincerity, which characterizes some of Cervantes's best writings, and which makes *La ilustre fregona* a prime exponent of the ludic vision.

Conclusion

We have seen that the entire range of contemporary thought on licit and illicit leisure finds expression in Cervantes. Often his players are in accord with conventional views: cards and gambling lead to violence and dissolution; respectable women sometimes while away their time with needlework. Rather than give an unqualified endorsement of play, Cervantes is acutely attuned to its dangers, from the solipsism of unreflective mimesis to the cruelty of turning others into objects of play. But in his awareness of the myriad social, ethical, political, theological, and physiological considerations brought to bear on play, Cervantes also articulated new possibilities of reading and writing. His textual spaces of play present *magias parciales* (to appropriate Borges's term again) in many senses. We alternate between getting caught up in the mimesis, in the creation of a peculiar illusion, and having this illusion repeatedly broken by a distancing awareness of the scaffolding and machinations of the artwork. The magic is also partial because the delineation between the fictional world and purposive reality is not absolute; we never enter into an entirely hermetic realm. Cervantes's ludic readers are thus idle and active simultaneously: we are at leisure, our activity is free of material consequence; yet we actively mediate the mysterious relationship between our game and the reality to which we will return. The choice not to do so is one of the few freedoms Cervantes withholds. To recall the ambivalent terms of persuasion deployed throughout *Don Quijote* and the *Novelas ejemplares*, we can say that the structuring of his narratives "invites and indeed compels" us to be active readers.

From the early modern Spanish thinkers designating some leisure activities as *indiferentes*, to Schiller, who maintained play's ethical and ideological neutrality, to Huizinga's contention that "play as such is outside the range of good and bad" (11), there is a tradition of asserting the play sphere's autonomy. But there has also persisted the inclination to recruit play to the service of purposive reality. Satire, and the didactic tradition of exemplarity, are the clearest cases of laying such claims to imaginative literature. The resulting tensions – which date back at least as far as Plato and Aristotle – between justifying play and pleasure on their own terms, and viewing them as means (or obstacles) to more "serious" ends, have never been resolved. Cervantes was keenly aware of what we noted Gadamer observing centuries later: "[t]he player knows very well what play is, and that what he is doing is 'only a game'; but he does not know what exactly he 'knows' in knowing that" (102). We still do not know. But Cervantes increases the possibility that ours is the enlightened ignorance of genuine inquiry and self-reflection.

The liberal citations of Erasmus and Montaigne in this study were meant to illustrate that a recognition of "modernity" in Cervantes's art – the irony and scepticism, the exploration of subjectivity, the awareness of the provisional nature of human knowledge, a sensitivity to the continuum of madness and sanity – need not be the product of anachronistic theorizing. Cervantes's striking innovations involve, rather, a creative engagement with fundamental concerns of early modern Europe.

> I who am king of the matter I treat, and who owe an accounting for it to no one, do not for all that believe myself in all I write. I often hazard sallies of my mind which I mistrust, and certain verbal subtleties at which I shake my ears; but I let them run at a venture. I see that some gain honour by such things. It is not for me alone to judge them. I present myself standing and lying down, front and rear, on the right and the left, and in all my natural postures. (*Essays* III, 9, pp. 720–1)

Montaigne understood that his pronouncements and musings are not fully under his control, that they acquire their own peculiar independence ("I let them run and venture").[1] This is due partly to the chance combination of words, of the play of meaning that is never fully under the control of the writer, and partly to the subjectivity of those who receive the words ("It is not for me alone to judge them"). Cervantes, who expressed a similar idea to his reader at the outset of *Don Quijote* ("you can say of the story whatever you like"), took the romance hero down from his pedestal and examined him, as Montaigne did with himself, "standing and lying down, front and rear, on the right and the left, and in all [his] natural postures." Consistent with the tradition of *serio ludere,* the results were both comic and profound.

Cervantes, like Montaigne, appreciated Ecclesiastes's humbling admonition regarding humanity's essential insubstantiality. As noted above, Montaigne remains unfazed: "But what of it? We are all wind. And even the wind, more wisely than we, loves to make noise and move about, and is content with its own functions" (III, 13, p. 849). Pascal would find this sanguine outlook infuriating, and repeatedly assert the abject condition of human beings who flee from the knowledge of Ecclesiastes: "But take away their distractions and you will see them wither from boredom. Then they feel their hollowness without understanding it, because it is indeed depressing to be in a state of unbearable sadness as soon as you are reduced to contemplating yourself, and without distraction from doing so" (III, 70, p. 16). As William Hildebrand noted, "For Pascal, ennui does not so much usurp or incorporate the capital sins as become the condition on which they depend. It defines the existential structure of humanity apart from God" (299). For this reason, play for Pascal can only consist of a blinding and dangerous distraction, a temporary palliative for the *acedia* that knowledge of mortality brings. His famous "wager" is not play, but a grim calculation of risk management on a metaphysical scale. For his part, instead of promoting a pious *desengaño* and a mind fixed on the final things, a misanthropic withdrawal from society, or a cynical and sophistic manipulation of others, Cervantes exhibits the ludic disposition of Montaigne. The most eloquent embodiments of this disposition are Sancho as he tries to convince his melancholy master to reject death and to join him in pastoral escapades (*Don Quijote* II, 74), and the mastiffs Berganza and Cipión as they agree to tell each other their stories, *sea portento o no* (*El coloquio de los perros* 301).

We will conclude with a slightly earlier, Italian illustration of the risks and rewards of play. Writing his famous letter from the confinement of a small farm, aged and disillusioned with his lot, Machiavelli gives Francesco Vettori an account of his quotidian activities. After a morning of foraging, some poetry reading, and a repast, he goes to an inn, where a few locals are to be found: "With these I sink into vulgarity for the whole day, playing at *cricca* and at trich-trach, and then these games bring on a thousand disputes and countless insults with offensive words, and usually we are fighting over a penny, and nevertheless we are heard shouting as far as San Casciano" (*Letters* No. 137).

Contentiously immersed in their cards and dice, the great thinker and his tavern companions are like another moralizing canvass by La Tour, Caravaggio, or ter Brugghen, succumbing to just the sort of degradation about which the *tratadistas* warned. Even so, Machiavelli notes a positive function: "So, involved in these trifles, I keep my brain from growing mouldy." This is what Pascal would have called a futile distraction from *acedia*, and Machiavelli himself tires of it. But then comes one of the great portraits of the individual at leisure:

> On the coming of evening, I return to my house and enter my study; and at the door I take off the day's clothing, covered with mud and dust, and put on garments regal and courtly; and reclothed appropriately, I enter the ancient courts of ancient men, where, received by them with affection, I feed on that food which only is mine and which I was born for, where I am not ashamed to speak with them and ask them the reason for their actions; and they in their kindness answer me; and for four hours of time I do not feel boredom, I forget every trouble, I do not dread poverty, I am not frightened by death; entirely I give myself over to them.

The change of costume and entrance into a special space, the transformation of self and suspension of time, the communion with other minds – all of this corresponds to the enchanted realm of play. It also corresponds to Aristotle's supreme pleasure, achieved through contemplative leisure (*Ethics*). Machiavelli's account confirms Pedro de Covarrubias's reprimand of nobles who claim that gambling saves them from being alone ("no ay solo salvo el mal acompañado"), and it resonates profoundly with Montaigne's description of reading (III, 8), as well as that of Quevedo, also in a state of exile, which we considered above ("con pocos, pero doctos libros juntos, / vivo en conversación con los difuntos, / y escucho con mis ojos a los muertos" – "together with few, but learned books / I live in conversation with the deceased, / and listen with my eyes to the dead"). Machiavelli eloquently describes the experience of reading as both transport and relevance, of distraction and of pertinence to real-life concerns. A demonic inversion of such recreation is achieved by Cañizares in her hallucinatory escapades in *El coloquio de los perros*. In Alonso Quijano's library in *Don Quijote* there are distorted glimpses of Machiavelli's literary retreat. But it is the reader Cervantes welcomes in the prologue to his masterpiece who most fully approximates the Italian's image of solitary and well-accompanied leisure. And we are invited back, during our "hours of recreation," in the *Novelas ejemplares*.

As we observed above with Huizinga, a ludic disposition can arise even from the sombre knowledge of Ecclesiastes: "In our heart of hearts we know that none of our pronouncements is absolutely conclusive. At that point, where our judgement begins to waver, the feeling that the world is serious after all wavers with it. Instead of the old saw: 'All is vanity', the more positive conclusion forces itself upon us that 'all is play'" (212). A playful bearing recognizes the provisional nature of truth, and seeks out new patterns and possibilities of meaning amidst the fragments of former certainties. It inoculates us against the rigidity of body and mind brought on by the routines of purposive reality, and by the very passage of time. To return to this study's opening citation, we can conclude that Cervantes indeed does appreciate, with Montaigne, "the value of pleasure, play, and pastime. I would almost say that any other aim is ridiculous" (*Essays* III, 3).

Notes

Introduction

1 See, for example, Nerlich, Fuchs, Gaylord, and Forcione ("Afterword").

2 Diego del Castillo was prominent among many advocates of the hunt. Vives gives the most famous account of the dangers of women reading. Alfonso X was the seminal Spanish thinker on chess. Cristóbal Méndez was at the forefront of advocates for physical recreation. We will discuss all of these figures below.

3 Cotarelo y Mori discusses the relative tolerance of the authorities through the first half of the seventeenth century, in part under the thrall of Lope's triumph on the stage. The uprisings within the Peninsula, and political and religious challenges from without, partly account for the increasingly restrictive attitudes and ordinances in the second half of the century (see Cotarelo y Mori, Introduction and 36–8).

4 The heightened profile of play's role in childhood development is evidenced in a recent cover article in the *New York Times* magazine, in which Robin Marantz Henig discusses work by evolutionary biologists and experimental neuroscientists exploring the cognitive, physical and social benefits of play. As we shall see, many of these hypotheses are strikingly similar to those of Erasmus, Vives, and late-medieval "hygienic" thought on recreation. For a discussion of the range of play functions in early modern Europe, see McClure's article on Tasso and Italian parlour games (751). For a summary of the history of theories of play, see López de Sosoaga López de Robles.

5 As Martínez-Bonati observed, genre is "a kind of game, one kind of activity … in which readers are engaged as they enjoy their reading. We can postulate that when the reading is done well, the receptive activity is congruent with the objective structure" (114).

6 Jolles offers the following description of the affinities and oppositions between the three types: "Als hochgemute Ritter verachten wir den einfältigen Hirten und den durchtriebenen Schelm; als zufriedene Hirten verschmähen wir die Unbeständigkeit des Schelmen und die Ehrsucht des Ritters; als schelmische Bohemiens spotten wir über die Beschränktheit des Bukolischen und über die Hirngespinste des Rittertums. Schelm und Ritter vertreten zusammen das Abenteurliche und Bewegliche gegenüber dem ruhebliebenden und ortsgebundenen Hirten; Ritter und Hirt verteidigen gemeinschaftlich ihren ehrlichen Namen gegenüber dem Schelmen, der in bösem Rufe steht; Schelm und Hirt kosten die Freude des Lebens, wo sich der Ritter abmüht und quält" ("As proud knight we disdain the simple shepherd and the cunning rogue; as content shepherds we spurn the rogue's inconstancy and the knight's obsession with honour; as roguish bohemians we mock the restricted nature of bucolic life and the delusions of knighthood. Together, the rogue and the knight represent the adventurous and the itinerant, as opposed to the tranquil and static shepherd; the knight and the shepherd commonly defend their honourable name, as opposed to the rogue, who is of ill repute; the rogue and the shepherd savour the joy of life, whereas the knight struggles and torments himself" [112–13]). According to Huizinga, "There are two play-idealizations *par excellence*, two 'Golden Ages of Play' as we might call them: the pastoral life and the chivalrous life. The Renaissance roused both from their slumber to a new life in literature and public festivity" (180–1). For his discussion of civilization as play, see especially chapters 1 and 11.

7 As the title of his essay suggests (*El* Quijote *como juego*), Torrente Ballester has given an account of what such a game involves from a novelist's perspective. Felix-Bonati approaches the issue more theoretically (see especially 114–37).

1. Leisure and Recreation in Early Modern Spain

1 "[U]na actividad originaria, creadora, vital por excelencia –que es espontánea y desinteresada – ; otra actividad que se aprovecha y mecaniza aquélla y que es de carácter utiliatrio. La utilidad no crea, no inventa, simplemente aprovecha y estabiliza lo que sin ella fué creado" (Ortega y Gasset 632).

2 Thomas Karshan notes how Nabokov, in *Speak, Memory*, argues for the inventive function of play, asserting that *Homo poeticus* precedes *Homo sapiens* (108).

3 See Ehrmann and Spariosu. In a representative critique, Yovanovich maintains that Huizinga sets up an opposition between play and rationality, and that his account of civilization privileges the ascendance of seriousness

and purpose, at the expense of the ludic spirit (see *Play and the Picaresque*, Introduction). Also citing Nietzsche, Kaiser maintains that Ortega y Gasset and Huizinga epitomize the nineteenth-century ludic ethos, "the quasi-anthropological theory that civilization is rooted in contest" (Kaiser 23).

4 Yovanovich made a similar point: "'paidia' has yet to be properly studied" (9).

5 Ife points out the fallacy of countering Plato with an Aristotelian appeal to verisimilitude, since heightened plausibility merely increases the basic problem, which is the medium itself, the way fiction, making deceptive use of language, sweeps us up into an illusion (see, for example, Ife 50–3). As I will point out below in the discussion of mimesis, Aristotle's notion of catharsis represents a more effective reply to Plato, since it deals with the same mysterious phenomenon, literature's appeal to the emotions.

6 Karshan traces how Nabokov's literary game par excellence, *Pale Fire*, a work which conditions us to "read playfully," has its roots in Pope, Erasmus, Lucian and Menippean satire (ch. 6).

7 It is worth noting Caillois's elaboration in light of twenty-first century Spain: "To take one example, it is clear that in Ancient Greece, the stadium games illustrate the ideal of the city and contribute to its fulfilment, while in a number of modern states national lotteries or parimutuels go against the professed ideal. Nevertheless they play a significant, perhaps indispensable, role to the precise degree that they offer an aleatory counterpart for the recompense that – in principle – work and merit alone can provide" (66). It is notable that Spain's famous Christmas lottery, *el gordo*, is experiencing maximum participation and interest during its period of greatest economic crisis – that is, precisely when the principles of work and merit risk losing legitimacy. The 2011 Christmas lottery commercial, "La fábrica de los sueños" ("The dream factory") creates a narrative depicting *alea* not as arbitrary chance but as wish-fulfilment dream, as a recompense for belief (see http://www.antena3.com/videos-online/especiales/loteria-navidad/2011/llega-fabrica-suenos_2011111500054.html).

8 James Iffland has studied the ambivalence of carnivalesque festivity, its unstable shifting in function from "escape valve" to potentially subversive challenge (see especially *De fiestas* 167–76).

9 The translator, Meyer Barash, proposes the terms "Dionysian" and "Rational" to express Caillois's use of "*sociétés à tohu bohu*" and "*sociétés à compatibilité*," respectively (see note 25, p. 187).

10 Kaiser's elaboration of the stage metaphor recalls Bakhtin's account of carnivalesque culture, which is indeed a "world in play," albeit with temporal limitations: "It belongs to the borderline between art and life. In reality, it is life itself, but shaped according to a certain pattern of play … In fact,

carnival does not know footlights, in the sense that it does not acknowledge any distinction between actors and spectators" (*Rabelais and His World* 7).

11 Even after Odysseus's killing of the suitors, the doling out of summary justice continues, as the perfidious women are lynched, and then Melanthius is dealt with: "They hauled him out through the doorway, into the court, / lopped his nose and ears with a ruthless knife, / tore his genitals out for the dogs to eat raw / and in manic fury hacked off hands and feet" (*The Odyssey* bk. 22, ll. 501–4). We will see, by comparison, how much closer the Cid and his men are to the rational ethos of institutionalized justice, despite the spectacular violence of the battle scenes.

12 The *El Cid* translations to English are from Paul Blackburn (Norman: University of Oklahoma Press, 1998).

13 Ife illuminates the linguistic and social dynamic in his hypothetical discussion of insulting a fellow Englishman: "Wherein does the forcefulness of my insult lie? Not, surely, in its truth (it has none), but in his awareness of my intention to offend, an awareness that stems as much from paralinguistic factors – my tone of voice, the look on my face and the circumstances of our meeting – as from his understanding of the propositional content of the words "You bastard" and the role they conventionally play in the personal antagonisms of speakers of English … If he chooses to rise to my insults he does so because he has understood my intention to produce an effect in him and because he is willing to provide the intended response. Without his comprehension and cooperation there can be no insult" (68). For an exquisite illustration of a breakdown of the "reviling match," we can observe a twentieth-century antithesis of El Cid, namely, Joel and Ethan Coen's "The Dude." In the following scene, The Dude's reaction to his opponent's taunts during a bowling tournament, his cowed appeal to the factual accuracy of the latter's claims, reveals his misunderstanding of the "paralinguistic factors" described by Ife:

> *Jesus Quintana*. You ready to be fucked, man? I see you rolled your way into the semis. Dios mío, man. Liam and me, we're gonna fuck you up.
>
> *The Dude*. Yeah, well, you know, that's just, like, your opinion, man. (Deakins et al. *The Big Lebowski*)

I would like to thank Thomas R. Clasen who, a propos of nothing in particular, brought this scene to my attention.

14 It is also worth noting that, although the poem depicts the primacy of the Cid's actions and virtue over the blood of the Infantes, the degraded state of the latter is characterized as an aberration, as Minaya Álvar Fáñez

asserts: "Sangre sois de los Beni-Gómez, que ha dado condes de prez y de valor; pero ya vemos hoy en día las aberraciones que engendra. Y doy a Dios gracias de que los infantes de Aragón y Navarra pidan la mano de mis primas doña Elvira y doña Sol. Antes fueron vuestras mujeres legítimas y vuestras iguales; ahora tendréis que besar sus manos y llamarlas señoras, y las serviréis aunque os pese" ("You are of the Beni-Gómez family, from which have come worthy and valiant counts. Now we know better what their tendencies are these days. For this reason I thank God that the infantes of Navarre and Aragón have asked for my cousins, doña Elvira and doña Sol; they used to be your equals and you held them in your arms; now, you will kiss their hands and call them 'my Lady' and humbly acknowledge yourselves their servants, and that ought to get to you" [III, 49, p. 323]). The promotion of the Cid's bloodlines effectively legitimizes individual virtue with exalted ancestry, again suggesting the work's liminal state between the prerational and rational orders.

15 "There may be a certain connection between all the various methods employed by man since the beginning of time to avoid being caught up in an interminable round of revenge. They can be grouped into three general categories: (1) preventive measures in which sacrificial rites divert the spirit of revenge into other channels; (2) the harnessing or hobbling of vengeance by means of compensatory measures, trials by combat, etc., whose curative effects remain precarious; (3) the establishment of a judicial system – the most efficient of all curative procedures" (Girard 20–1). The episode under consideration in *El Cid* would seem to fall within points 2 and 3, although the poem's emphasis of the piousness of the hero and his men suggests elements of number 1 as well.

16 For a recent discussion of the political implications of Golden Age theatre that calls for a more nuanced understanding particularly of Lope's allegedly propagandistic orientation, see Forcione, *Majesty and Humanity*.

17 Burke provides a summary of the development of the very notion of free time: "In Latin the term *otium*, part of the complementary opposition of *otium* and *negotium*, *vita contemplativa* and *vita activa*, which replaced Aristotle's rather different contrast between the theoretical and the practical life, was defined by the Romans, redefined by the Church Fathers, and transformed by medieval monks to form part of their vocabulary of contemplation, before the word was revived and adapted once again by Renaissance humanists. For the Romans, *otium* was the complementary opposite of political activity or *negotium*, associated in particular with the seasonal withdrawal of the upper classes from the city to their country villas. For Tertullian and Jerome, on the other hand, *otium* was a pejorative

term, more or less 'idleness', though Augustine and Ambrose showed less hostility. For medieval monks, it referred to their essential activity, religious meditation, while for humanists it denoted the life of study as opposed to the 'business' of trade and politics" (139–40). These diverse definitions and associations, from the pejorative to the therapeutic, find expression in the early modern thinkers under consideration in the present section.

18 "Finally we should be careful, as in all other human actions, to suit the person, place, and time, and to be duly adapted to the circumstances, so that our play, as Cicero says, *fits the hour and the man*" (Aquinas, *Summa* 168.2, p. 219).

19 Alemán's best-selling picaresque novel expresses Gracián's sentiment well: "No los hicieron cabezas para comer el mejor bocado, sino para que tengan mayor cuidado; no para reír con truhanes, sino para gemir las desventuras del pueblo; no para dormir y roncar, sino para velar y suspirar, teniendo como el dragón continuamente clara la vista del espíritu" ("Heads were not made in order to eat the tastiest bite, but in order to be most careful; not to laugh with knaves, but to lament humanity's misfortunes; not to sleep and snore, but to stay awake and sigh, like the dragon keeping the sight of the spirit continuously clear" [*Guzmán de Alfarache* I, iii, p. 397]).

20 To be sure, Castiglione did also possess a tactical, political orientation, as the rather Gracianesque comment by Federico demonstrates: "I say that to be praiseworthy and highly thought of by everyone, and to secure the good will of the rulers whom he serves, the courtier should know how to order his whole life and to exploit his good qualities generally, no matter with whom he associates, without exciting envy" (*The Courtier* 114). McClure discusses how, following his confinement in Ferrara's Sant'Anna, Tasso, in his dialogue *Gonzaga II*, moves away from Castiglione's idealism, toward what we would recognize as a more Gracianesque vision: "The shrewd courtier must know when to conceal his superior talent and learning, must be willing to subordinate himself, and must be a master of dissimulation (*l'infinger*), identified as 'one of the great virtues' of the day" (782). Teja examines Tasso's interest in competition, chance and skill, and how the game is a metaphor and proving ground for dealing with *agon* and *fortuna* in real life ("El juego cortés en un diálogo de Tasso (1582)"). Both McClure and Teja discuss the development of Tasso's concept of play in relation to his sense of personal and political crisis.

21 For discussions of a progressive limiting of the Western concept of leisure, see Pieper, Wind, and de Grazia. Schiller expresses the *topos* of deterioration within the classical world: "If at the Olympic Games the peoples of

Greece delighted in the bloodless combats of strength, speed, and agility, and in the nobler rivalry of talents, and if the Roman people regaled themselves with the death throes of a vanquished gladiator or of his Libyan opponent, we can, from this single trait, understand why we seek the ideal forms of a Venus, a Juno, an Apollo, not in Rome, but in Greece" (*Letters* 130–1). In a note, Schiller cites the taste for bullfighting in Madrid as indicative of contemporary Spain's proximity to the Roman rather than the Greek model.

22 I am indebted to my colleagues, Lorina Quartarone and Matthew Lu, for help with the original Greek.

23 "[E]l que busca placeres tiene que recordar siempre que el fin del juego es la vuelta a lo serio" (Wardropper 156).

24 "[L]a *Summa* no se refiere a la utilidad" (Jones 28).

25 Aquinas refers to this anecdote (168.2). Jones cites the same sources, and points out that El Pinciano uses the same justification for imaginative literature (Jones 23).

26 King Lear's famous lines before Edgar on the heath provide a pointed contrast to the measured optimism expressed in Guzmán: "Is man no more than this? Consider him well. Thou ow'st the worm no silk, the beast no hide, the sheep no wool, the cat no perfume. Ha! here's three on's more sophisticated. Thou art the thing itself; unaccommodated man is no more but such a poor, bare, forked animal as thou art" (*King Lear* III. 4. 105–10). Lucretius had offered a similar image of feeble humanity: "A human baby's like a sailor washed up on a beach / By the battering of the surf, naked, lacking in the power of speech, / Possessing no means of survival, when first Nature pours / Him forth with birth-pangs from his mother's womb upon Light's shores" (V, l. 222–5).

27 Karshan relates this moment to Lolita's fleeting transformation while playing tennis: "A window seems cut through onto that 'unshakeably illogical world' which Nabokov advertised as 'a home for the spirit' in 'The Creative Writer' and which he substantiated in *Speak, Memory*" (171–2).

28 Méndez does qualify some of his praise of games, and his reasons are similar to those of some of the moralistic writers under consideration (Alcoçer, Zabaleta). For example, despite the nobleman's praise of his card-playing son in the passage above, Méndez voices reservations regarding the dangers of gambling: "La verdad es que tales habilidades ni las quiero para los mios: ni ninguno de mis amigos querria que sus hijos las tuviessen" ("The truth is that I do not want such abilities for my sons, nor do any of my friends for theirs" [124]). In similar manner, his description of the benefits of hunting includes the following comic deflation: "yo moriame

de hambre: y dava al diablo la caça: y aun la cavada de los hoyos" ("I was dying of hunger, and cursed the hunt, and even the digging of the fox-holes" [126]).

29 As we consider the play types deemed appropriate to the lower classes, it is worth keeping in mind Mauricio Molho's observation regarding the primary experience reflected in popular culture: "Su función radica en la misma función del pueblo, que es el trabajo. La literatura popular –canción, romance, cuento, historieta, etc. – ritma (o mejor dicho, ritmaba) la actividad trabajadora, y correlativamente el descanso, de las masas laboriosas" ("Its function resides in the very function of the commoners, which is labour. Popular literature – songs, ballads, stories, anecdotes, etc. – put rhythm (or, better said, used to put rhythm) to the activity of labour, and, correspondingly, to the repose, of the labouring masses" [19]).

30 Tolstoy's scene, much more than an illustration of the therapeutic value of work, is framed by the visit of Levin's intellectual brother, who takes a sort of Guevaraesque view on country life: "for Sergei Ivanovich the country was, on the one hand, a rest from work and, on the other, an effective antidote to corruption, which he took with pleasure and an awareness of its effectiveness" (237). Sergei relishes the country as a venue for idleness, and pleasing pastimes: he borrows some fishing rods for diversion, engages his brother in agonistic conversation, and solves chess problems. Even his figures of speech are ludic: "how I love this rustic idleness. There's not a thought in my head, you could play ninepins in it" (239). Levin, who is less of a systematic thinker, experiences the country in spiritual and vitalistic terms – a sort of spirituality that, in the wake of fallen man's obligation to live off the sweat off his brow, is associated with productive work: "For Konstantin Levin the country was the place of life, that is, of joy, suffering, labour" (237). When the happily perspiring Levin is offered drink and food by an old peasant, class distinctions fade further: "'Have a sip of my kvass! Good, eh?' he said with a wink" (252); "'Here, master, try a bit of my mash' … The mash tasted so good that Levin changed his mind about going home for dinner. He ate with the old man and got to talking with him … He felt closer to him than to his brother, and involuntarily smiled from the tenderness he felt for this man" (254). If not the boisterous carnivalesque of Sancho's bonding with Ricote and the other pilgrims with the wine-filled bota, the kvass and mash communion contains, like the episode in *Don Quijote* (II, 54), a humble affirmation of common humanity. For a discussion of an emerging "gospel of work" in 19th-century novelists (Tolstoy, Gogol, and Turgenev in particular), along with an increasing scepticism regarding leisure, see Karshan (113–20).

31 Montaigne was also a devoted reader of Lucretius (for some observations of his influence, see Greenblatt, *The Swerve* ch. 11). We will observe below Erasmus's appropriation of the banquet hall image from *De Rerum* (bk. III, l. 931–51).

32 In his introduction to the edition, Étienvre discusses the work within the dialogue tradition, calling it "una diversión estética, un juego (erudito, por supuesto, pero ameno) sobre los juegos" ("an aesthetic diversion, a game (erudite, to be sure, but pleasing) about games" [*Días geniales o lúdricos* LVI]). See also Étienvre's discussion of Caro's literary pretensions, along with his decision not to publish the work, given his awareness of the greatness of the likes of Juan de Valdés and El Pinciano (XC–XCVIII).

33 "[E]l amor de Rodrigo Caro a esta existencia retirada, medio campesina y medio ciudadana, medio solitaria y medio sociable, tan pronto vuelta hacia la antigüedad como encarada con el presente, entremezclada de peregrinas noticias y de cercanía española" (del Campo 275).

34 Friedrich, 121. For his account of the *dignitas hominis* and *miseria hominis* traditions, from their classical, Old Testament and early Christian sources through Montaigne's ambivalent stance, and on to Pascal and La Fontaine, see pp. 118–23.

35 Maravall describes a sort of "dignity of man" ethos taken to an extreme distortion: "El hombre del Barroco … siempre preferirá la naturaleza transformada por el arte a la naturaleza simple" ("The baroque individual, who always preferred nature transformed by art to simple nature," *La cultura* 467–8).

36 "[D]ebieran preocuparse de los libros pestíferos, como son; *Amadís, Esplandián, Florisandro, Tirante, Tristán,* cuyas insulseces no tienen fin y diariamente salen de nuevas; *Celestina,* alcahueta, madre de maldades, y *Cárcel de amor* … La mujer ha de arrojar de sí todos estos libros con la misma enérgica repulsión como si fuesen víboras o escorpiones" ("they should be worried about pestilential books, such as *Amadís, Esplandián, Florisandro, Tirante, Tristán,* whose dullness has no end and are daily renewed; *Celestina,* procuress, mother of evils, and *Cárcel de amor* … The woman must cast from herself all such books with the same energetic repulsion as if they were snakes and scorpions" [*Educación de la mujer cristiana*]). Ife emphasizes that Vives's critique of fictions is an exceptionally informed one, that it comes from a profound understanding of the experience of reading rather than from priggishness: "If men of Vives's intellectual distinction can liken writers of fiction to poisoners of common wells we may be sure that what is interesting about these attacks is not that they raise bigotry and gratuitous abuse to the level of a fine art, though undoubtedly many examples

do this, but that they proceed from a serious and deeply-felt anxiety about the effects of fictional literature in general on the reading public" (14).

37 Renson discusses how the conception of play in Vives is grounded in his ethical and social concerns, and how it in some ways anticipates the more limited function of play I associate with the Enlightenment: "Vivès, l'humaniste engagé, reconnaissait que l'érudition la plus approfondie n'est pas un but en soi-même, mais que la valeur des résultats obtenus par l'étude réside dans l'application au bien-être commun de l'humanité. Son plaidoyer en faveur du jeu prouve ce même souci de réalisme éducatif, car il accentua le fait que l'on ne devrait pas seulement jouer pour le plaisir du jeu, mais pour apprendre quelque chose" ("Vives, the engaged humanist, recognized that the most profound erudition is not a goal in itself, but that the resulting value obtained through study resides in its application to the common good of humanity. His plea on behalf of play demonstrates the same concern as educational realism, since it accentuates the fact that one should not merely play for the pleasure of the game, but to learn something" [481]).

38 "I suggest we spend this hot part of the day not in playing games (a pastime which of necessity disturbs the player who loses without providing much pleasure either for his opponents or for those who watch) but rather in telling stories, for this way one person, by telling a story, can provide amusement for the entire company." Discussing parlour games of the Italian nobility, McClure distinguishes between the agonistic goal of "victory" as opposed to "imitation of some aspect of everyday life" (752).

39 In the introduction to his edition, Sieber uses this term, "entre paréntesis," for situations experienced by many characters in Cervantes's *Novelas ejemplares*, as well as for the reader (I, 15). Clamurro elaborates on the social and linguistic characteristics of these spaces (195–6).

40 Experience may be the teacher of fools, but no reader of Erasmus considers that epithet without mischievous ambivalence: "The man of learning hides behind the volumes of the ancients, and derives nothing from them but empty verbal formulas. The fool, approaching the problem directly and venturing upon it boldly, acquires true prudence from his experience" (*The Praise of Folly* 27).

41 For similarities between the two figures, see Marcel Tetel, who writes of "a conviction, both for Castiglione and Montaigne, that a greater challenge for order and harmony is created when one starts from an apparent disorder and that order and harmony eventually emanate from a cumulative and converging process and not from the imitation of an absolute model" (74).

42 Montaigne's rejection of imitation and pedantic book knowledge as educational goals, and his claims that the fruits of study should be the ability to judge rather than the readiness to act are seen by Hampton as signs of a subversion of traditional humanist pedagogy, and as aristocratic in spirit (see especially 141–55). Hampton also discusses Montaigne's "inward turn" as a proto-Cartesian moment: "This new model might be seen as the transition between humanism and the Cartesian self, which inaugurates the modern era. For though Descartes initially defines his *Discours de la méthode* as an exemplary story, he soon rejects both the body and history, choosing to ground the *cogito* on the disembodied ahistorical 'self' which Montaigne freed from physical and temporal contingency forty years earlier" (186).

43 Incorporating the play categories of Caillois, Rigolot discusses the theatrical element in Montaigne as the favoured mode of play: "Pour reprendre les catégories proposées par Roger Caillois, on peut comprendre pourquoi les *Essais* refusent l'*agôn*, l'*alea* et l'*ilinx*. Par les activités compétetives (la chasse ou les échecs) on prend au sérieux les régles toutes arbitraires qu'on se donne (*agôn*); par les jeux de hasard (les cartes ou les dés), on se soumet inconditionnellement aux arrêts du sport pour de futiles raisons (*aléa*); par la recherche du vertige, on tente inconsidérément d'ébranler la stabilité de ses perceptions (*ilinx*). Seule l'illusion théâtrale permet de devenir 'autre' en échappant à l'aliénation et donc, en un sens, de devenir soi-même (*mimicry*)" ("Taking up again the categories proposed by Roger Caillois, one can understand why the *Essais* reject *agon*, *alea* and *ilinx*. In competitive activities (the hunt or chess) one takes seriously the completely arbitrary rules that are given (*agon*); in games of chance (cards or dice), one submits unconditionally to the cessation of sport for futile reasons (*alea*); for the pursuit of vertigo, one attempts carelessly to undermine the stability of the perceptions (*ilinx*). Only the theatrical illusion permits becoming 'other' by escaping alienation and so, in a sense, becoming oneself (*mimicry*)" [337]). Also suggesting overlap between Castiglione and Montaigne (see Tetel), Quint discerns an ideal of "studied *sprezzatura*" in Montaigne (60).

44 "That is why we like noise and activity so much. That is why imprisonment is such a horrific punishment. That is why the pleasure of being alone is incomprehensible. That is, in fact, the main joy of the condition of kingship, because people are constantly trying to amuse kings and provide them with all sorts of distraction. The king is surrounded by people whose only thought is to entertain him and prevent him from thinking about himself. King though he may be, he is unhappy if he thinks about it" (45). See especially section IX ("Diversion") of *Pensées*.

45 "De las Representaciones y comedias se sigue otro gravísimo daño, y es que la gente se da al ocio y deleyte y regalo y se divierte de la milicia con los bayles deshonestos que cada día inbentan estos faranduleros y con las fiestas Vanquetes y comidas se hace la gente de España muelle y afeminada e inabil para las cosas del travajo y guerra" (Castro Archivo General de Simancas, Gracia y justicia 993–2 [1598]: fol. 5).

46 For a discussion of a theological shift in emphasis during the period from charity to productive work, see Redondo (*Otra manera* 42). Hawthorne's "The Maypole of Merry Mount" posits the clash between a festive community and a sternly religious one: "The future complexion of New England was involved in this important quarrel. Should the grizzly saints establish their jurisdiction over the gay sinners, then would their spirits darken all the clime and make it a land of clouded visages, of hard toil, of sermon and psalm forever" (30). Discussing the early church's opposition to *eutrapelia*, Wardropper notes that "Este ideal aristotélico tenía poco atractivo para la Iglesia primitiva, parte de cuya misión era la de reorientar la vida de la civilización pagana, con su alegre despreocupación vital, hacia una aceptación de la seriedad de la vida cristiana. En tal empresa se citaba y se discutía mucho un versículo del Evangelio según San Lucas: '¡Ay de vosotros, los que ahora reís; porque gemiréis y lloraréis!'" ("This Aristotelian ideal had little appeal for the early Church, part of whose mission was to reorient the life of pagan civilization, with its joyful, untroubled vitality, toward an acceptance of the seriousness of Christian life. In this endeavour a particular verse from the Gospel according to Luke was frequently cited and discussed: 'Woe to you who laugh now; for you will moan and weep!'" [154]). Wardropper describes precisely the tension depicted in Hawthorne's Puritan parable. More to the point, he also characterizes the stern mentality we noted in Mateo Alemán's narrating protagonist: "no para reír con truhanes, sino para gemir las desventuras del pueblo" ("not to laugh with knaves, but to moan the misfortunes of the people" [*Guzmán de Alfarache* I, iii, p. 397]).

47 As documented in Cotarelo y Mori, a number of those who debated the permissibility of theatre in the period appealed to the concept of *indiferente*. Melchor de Cabrera y Guzmán, a Madrid lawyer, provides useful background and a definition in his discussion of *las comedias* in 1646: "Los que las miraron a differente viso, y habiendo más particularmente reconocido sus effetos, affirman ser *acto indiferente*; desta opinión son lo común de los santos doctores y personas que han tratado el punto, particularmente Santo Tomás, fray Marco Antonio Camos, fray Manuel Rodríguez, Castillo de Bobadilla, D. Francisco de Amaya, y otros que ellos refieren …

Y aquello se dice y es indiferente que contiene medianía, y puede caer á una y otra parte según Cicerón y los gramáticos. Y es indubitable que aun tampoco son indiferentes por contener mucho bueno y nada digno de reprobar" ("Those who looked at them in a different light, and having more particularly recognized their effects, affirm them to be *indifferent action;* of this opinion is the most part of the saintly doctors and people who have considered the point, particularly Saint Thomas, friar Marco Antonio Camos, friar Manuel Rodríguez, Castillo de Bobadilla, Sir Francisco de Amaya, and others whom they cite ... And that which is called and is indifferent contains moderation, and can fall to one side or the other, according to Cicero and the grammarians. And it is doubtless that nor are they indifferent by containing much good and nothing worthy of reproof" [Cotarelo y Mori 96a–b]). Like many others, the Augustinian Friar Gaspar de Villarroel, also in 1646, ascribes the same quality to playing cards: "Es el ejemplo ordinario el de los naipes, porque siendo el juego indiferente y habiéndose inventado para honesta diversión, toman algunos ahí cierta ocasión de pecar. Y si ellos depravan el instrumento, no por eso habemos de condenar al que lo hizo" ("The typical example is cards, because being indifferent and having been invented for honest diversion, some make of it an opportunity to sin. And if they deprave the instrument, not for this should we condemn the one who invented it" [Cotarelo y Mori 599a]). For a compact overview of play types in early modern Spain, see Deleito y Piñuela, 204–28.

48 "Parece casi imposible construir todo un relato metafórico calculado sobre una partida de ajedrez, a no ser que se quiera realizar una proeza estilística" (Étienvre *Márgenes* 287). Such stylistic (and structural) exploits would be undertaken centuries later, by the chess aficionado Nabokov.

49 "[E]l 'ajedrez moralizado' se remonta desde luego a la Edad Media, pero entonces se presentaba el juego, por ejemplo en Jacobus de Cessolis, como una imagen de la sociedad. Hay que esperar el Renacimiento para que se imponga la metáfora ajedrecística como parangón de estrategia" (Étienvre *Márgenes* 286).

50 For a discussion of Calderón's use of chess to examine such a shift in *El Rey Don Pedro en Madrid*, see Forcione, *Majesty and Humanity* (135, and 267–8).

51 Compare this with Aristotle on friendship: "And friendship seems to be present by nature in a parent for a child and in a child for a parent, not only in human beings but also in birds and most animals, and for animals alike in kind toward one another, and especially among human beings, which is why we praise those who are friends of humanity" (*Ethics* 1155a17–21).

52 Zabaleta's portrait of "El tahúr" (I, ch. 10) is also of interest. In his edition, Cristóbal Cuevas García points out Zabaleta's debt to Pedro de Covarrubias, Francisco de Alcoçer and Luque Faxardo (168, note 62).

53 Caravaggio's "The Cardsharps" (ca. 1594) is probably the most famous example of the genre. For a discussion of theses paintings within the pictorial genre, see Feigenbaum. For a summary of the slang – so prevalent in picaresque narratives – used to refer to the different parties in such scenes of deception, from perpetrators to victims, see Deleito y Piñuela, 213–18: "A estos ganchos se les llamaba también 'dobles' (en contraste con el jugador 'sencillo' y de buena fe, que era igualmente llamado 'bueno' o 'blanco,' en oposición al 'negro' o 'fullero'), 'muñidores,' 'abrazadores' y 'enterradores'" ("These hooks [accomplices] were also called 'doubles' (in contrast with the 'simple' and good-faith player, who was also called 'good' or 'white,' in opposition to the 'black' or 'cardsharp'), 'fixers,' 'huggers' and 'gravediggers'" [214]). Feigenbaum notes that pictorial depictions in the period emerge from moralizing traditions (the soldiers dicing for Christ's clothes, the Prodigal Son) and the *commedia dell'Arte*, but that they also document social reality: "Gambling was so pervasive in Europe during the Renaissance that not to engage in it would have been considered exceptional" (154).

54 See the Exhibition Catalogue essays by Ireson and Wright, and House (Ireson and Wright).

55 "Todo jugador, en verdad, no hace ya más que reincidir en bazas remotas. Su juego es una repitición de juegos pasados, vale decir, de ratos de vivires pasados. Generaciones ya invisibles de criollos están como enterradas vivas en él: son él, podemos afirmar sin metáfora" (Evaristo Carriego 79–80). In tango music as in the card game, Borges sees the sort of communion that can take place in authentic recreation, the *conversación* extolled by a number of the *tratadistas* under consideration: "La milonga es una de las grandes conversaciones de Buenos Aires; el truco es la otra. El truco lo investigaré en capítulo aparte; básteme dejar escrito que, entre los pobres, el hombre alegra al hombre" ("The milonga is one of the great conversations of Buenos Aires; the truco is the other. The truco I will investigate in a separate chapter; let it suffice to note that, amongst the poor, man gladdens man" [Evaristo Carriego 58]).

56 Quint contextualizes Montaigne's attitude in terms of class: "Such Stoic self-sufficiency is easily aligned with the ideals of aristocratic autonomy, personal bravery and political independence – in short, of 'honour' – that inform the duel" (*Montaigne and the Quality of Mercy* 71). A corollary is Simmel's discussion of the hero's confidence that he is immune to chance, that

the outcome of his adventure will confirm his exceptional identity ("The Adventure").

57 For an overview of attitudes toward chance in Spain, see Green (vol. II, ch. IV). Lyons discusses a shift in seventeenth-century France from a Boethian, providential notion of fortune, to a more modern, Aristotelian-based concept of *hasard*, or randomness ("From Fortune to Randomness in Seventeenth-Century Literature").

58 "El mundo de Pascal es el de Lucrecio (y también el de Spencer), pero la infinitud que embriagó al romano acobarda al francés. Bien es verdad que éste busca a Dios y que aquél se propone libertarnos del temor de los dioses" (*Otras inquisiciones* 99).

59 Citing legal debates on lotteries from the eighteenth century onwards, Levitt reveals the theological implications of such a game: "The 'English' or 'pure chance' view was that for a game to be a lottery, the 'selection and award of the prize must be determined by pure chance in which man's choice or will has no part and which is undeterminable by human reason, foresight, sagacity or design until the same has been accomplished'" (5). As noted below, Borges would make much of such implications. For a discussion of how Borges himself selectively subscribes to the Lucretian concept of the universe, deploying words instead of atoms in an unending creation and destruction of order, see Coleman.

60 For a discussion of these debates, see Poppi.

61 "No podían ser muy eficaces los castigos contra el juego cuando éste constituía un monipolio del Estado, el cual llegó a percibir por tal concepto hasta 50.000 ducados anuales" (Deleito y Piñuela 228).

62 In the goliardic poem, "Decius, God of Dice," there are similar elements of devotion, gambling away one's very clothes, and solace in drink, often in a register that parodies religious discourse: "It irritates / My gambling mates / To pawn their clothes for payment, / When I am dressed by far the best / They cast lots for *my* raiment"; "Then everybody calls for dice / And throws a round or two for drinks; / What wintry winds may blow, what breaths of ice, / Scarce anybody thinks" (Whicher 269, 271).

63 For a discussion of Gaspar de los Reyes's *Tesoro* in the context of Golden Age religious and secular poetry, see José Manuel Rico García, to whom I am grateful for bringing this work to my attention.

64 "[L]a mecánica del juego consistiría en interpretar la copla que le ha correspondido a cada 'dama' o 'señora' – tras arrojar los dados o escoger una carta de la baraja que previamente habría que haber configurado con las cuatro suertes – mediante la suma de los valores simbólicos que subyacen en los cuatro elementos, para al final terminar averiguando las cualidades

del personaje masculino que se esconde tras de ellas. Se trataría, por lo tanto, de un juego de parejas en el que cada dama buscaría el varón que se acercase más a los cánones del amor cortés" (Sanz Hermida 611).

65 "[L]a aparición del sexo masculino tiene razón de ser como un [sic] parte del engranaje de la máquina de este divertimiento, pero no como parte activa del mismo. Así, este juego se presenta como una diversión cortesana en el que la reina y su séquito podían hacer alarde de su erudición simbólica y de sus conocimientos de tonadas y romances" (Sanz Hermida 613–14).

66 Recall Papargyriou's observation that postmodern works tend to emphasize the *aleatory* aspect of reading (25). Julian Barnes's Braithwaite, puzzling over Flaubert and his legacy, delivers insightful ridicule of postmodern non-teleological narratives, giving us, in the process, a sort of extreme version of a *Libro de las suertes*: "After all, if novelists truly wanted to simulate the delta of life's possibilities, this is what they'd do. At the back of the book would be a set of sealed envelopes in various colours. Each would be clearly marked on the outside: Traditional Happy Ending; Traditional Unhappy Ending; Traditional Half-and-Half Ending; Deus ex Machina; Modernist Arbitrary Ending; End of the World Ending; Cliffhanger Ending; Dream Ending; Opaque Ending; Surrealist Ending; and so on. You would be allowed only one, and would have to destroy the envelopes you didn't select. *That's* what I call offering the reader a choice of endings; but you may find me quite unreasonably literal-minded" (*Flaubert's Parrot* 89).

67 "[S]i se consultaban según un rito determinado, podían satisfacer el sentimiento religioso que iba unido a la curiosiad" (Navarro Durán 21).

68 See, for example: "Ejecutoria del pleito litigado por Pedro Díaz de Gurbizta" (Archivo de la Real Chancillería de Valladolid: Registro de ejecutorias 2217.0022 (1617), fol. 2); "Pleito de Alfonso María Brasa" (Pleitos criminales 1887.00133 (1752)); "Ejecutoria del pleito litigado por Pedro Cobeta" (Registro de ejecutorias 638.0017 [1794]).

69 The entry for Tyche in the Oxford Classical Dictionary registers its varying notions, from pure arbitrary chance (the domain of Aristotle's *automaton*) to ill or favourable fortune. The cults of Tyche in Athens and Thebes manifest both the human recognition of the presence of chance, along with our irrepressible desire to influence it – that is, a simultaneous acknowledgement and negation of chance.

70 Internet gambling amplifies this danger, as players interact from the solitude of their respective electronic devices. The US government's ban on such play assumes a higher potential for addiction (see Levitt et al.).

71 "Jugaban los clérigos frecuentemente por mero entretenimiento a los dados, tablas, naipes, entre sí y con otras personas seglares honestas, en sus casas ... o en otros lugares. Pero también debieron jugar, puesto que se les prohíbe, públicamente, delante de los seglares y con ellos en casas de juego a juegos 'deshonestos y prohibidos', 'como son dados, o juegos de naipes ... ni otros juegos prohibidos en sus casas, ni vayan a jugar a las casas donde oviere la tal tablajeria', jugando 'dineros secos', no por mero entretenimiento, sino para obtener ganancias" (Sánchez Herrero 173).

72 "Sobre: acusarles de plabaras unjuriosas a unos frailes del convento de San Francisco, extramuros de la citada villa, cuando estaban jugando al mojón en el pinar de la misma (decirles bigardos regulares, que llevaban a las mozas al pinar, que forzaban a las mujeres y otras cosas)" ("Lorenzo Aguayo," Archivo de la Real Chancillería de Valladolid, Pleitos Criminales. Caja 0246.0002, 1564). The insult of "bigardo," now meaning licentious and idle, had its origins in slanderous suspicion of the Franciscans: "Término injurioso, del qual la gente mal considerada suele usar quando trata con irreverencia a algún religioso, y no saben lo que dicen, ni lo consideran. Traxo origen de los begardos, frayles de la orden de San Francisco tercerones, dichos en Italia los fatricelos y en latín *fraires de paupere vita*. Fueron hereges, cuya cabeça fué un Pedro Juan, y moraron en Francia, en la provincia de Narbona y Tolosa y en otras partes, cerca de los años de nuestra Redención de mil y trezientos y catorze, siendo Romano Pontífice Juan XXII, por quien fueron condenados" ("Injurious term, which poorly intentioned people tend to use when they treat with irreverence a man of the cloth, and they do not know what they say, nor do they consider it. It originated in the begardos, friars of the order of San Francisco tertiaries, called in Italy the fratricelos and in Latin the *friars of poverty*. They were heretics, whose head was one Pedro Juan, and they lived in France, in the province Narbonne and Toulouse and in other parts, around the years of our Redemption of thirteen hundred and fourteen, being the Roman Pontiff John XXII, by whom they were condemned" [Sebastián de Covarrubias, *Tesoro*]).

73 "Reuníanse en ellas personas de calidad, para converser y pasar el rato con varios esparcimientos. Se charlaba lindamente, prodigándose las sutilezas ingeniosas, celebrábanse concursos de cuestiones intrincadas, adjudicando premios a quienes las resolviesen, y se rifaban o vendían objetos varios, tales como bolsillos, medias, guantes, baratijas, adornos más o menos valiosos, y hasta comestibles y bebidas" (Deleito y Piñuela 210).

74 "Pero el juego era el alma de tales reuniones, aunque se practicase con cierto decoro. La plabra 'conversación' solía ser un eufamismo, que disimiluba aquel vicio" (Deleito y Piñuela 211).

75 Aristotle commented on the phenomenon: "Goodwill seems like something that has to do with friendship, though it surely is not friendship, since goodwill arises toward people one does not know, and without their being aware of it, but friendship does not … [G]oodwill is also of sudden origin, as happens in connection with those engaged in athletic competition, since people become goodwilled toward them and share their wishes, but would not share their action in any way, for as we said, they become goodwilled suddenly and like them superficially" (*Ethics* ll66b30–1167a).

76 For a description of the *juego de cañas* and its associations with chivalry and the Reconquista, see Defourneaux, 132–3.

77 "Don Martín de Basurto Alguacil Mayor," Archivo de la Real Chancillería de Valladolid, Pleitos criminales, Caja 281.0005, 1691.

78 As his comments on play portend, Camos was not a particularly subtle judge of literature. Ife's comments are to the point, and illustrate a broader tendency we are tracing in attitudes toward play: "When Fr. Marco Antonio de Camos recommends a book like Luis de León's *De los nombres de Cristo* he is subscribing to a behaviourist attitude toward books and readers: put the right book in the right hands and the result is instant virtue … Good men produce good books and a good book in turn produces a good reader, but a reader whose role remains essentially passive" (54–5).

79 Ife examines the frequently blurred distinctions between "aesthetic" and "rational" belief in literary debates of early modern Spain (see especially chapters 2 and 3). The definitive reference for debates for and against *mimesis* in the Spanish *comedia* is Cotarelo y Mori.

80 "The mimetic character of a sports contest such as a horse race, a boxing match or a football game is due to the fact that aspects of the feeling-experience associated with a real physical struggle enter the feeling-experience of the 'imitated' struggle of a sport. But in the sports experience, the feeling-experience of a real physical struggle is shifted into a different gear. Sport allows people to experience the full excitement of a struggle without its dangers and risks. The element of fear in the excitement, although it does not entirely disappear, is greatly diminished and the pleasure of the battle-excitement is thus greatly enhanced. Hence, if one speaks of the 'mimetic' aspects of sport, one is referring to the fact that it imitates a real-life struggle selectively" (288–9).

81 Ercilla invokes this idea when characterizing Spanish decadence *vis-à-vis* the *araucanos*. In his discussion of *schole*, de Grazia discusses the challenge of leisure in fortunate civilizations: "In war the virtues of men come forth for a united effort; in peace and prosperity men lose their temperance and justice toward one another and become overbearing. The greater the abundance

of blessings that fall to men, the greater will be their need for wisdom, and wisdom is the virtue that cannot appear except in leisure" (10).

82 "[L]a propia inclinación de los clérigos a vagabundear; a la literatura, recitación o charlatanería; a los juegos de manos, acrobacia y mímica; a la danza y el baile" (Sánchez Herrero 176).

83 For an analysis of this scene within the context of early modern political and metaphysical thought, see Forcione, "At the Threshold of Modernity," especially 41–7.

84 "[Q]ue yendo alli compañias de representantes y querriendo Recitar comedias Lo hiciesen en el otro / ospital y en su corral y no en otra parte Alguna Y que pudiesen tener en el Juego de barras sin que ninguna persona pudiese tener el dicho juego por granjeria de los baratos del en ningun tiempo ni dia ni en ninguna parte de la dicha ciudad de çacatecas sino fuere Los her -manos de dicho / ospital para que con lo que dello se sacase se acudiese a la cura y Regalo de los en -fermos" ("passing through a company of actors and wanting the recite plays they were to do it in the courtyard of the other hospital and in no other place and they were to have there bar-games [croquet] without anyone using such games for betting at any time or place of said city of Zacatecas unless it were to be the brothers of said hospital so that with the proceeds they saw to the curing and care of the sick" ["Real Cédula a la Audiencia de Guadalajara" AGI, Indiferente 450, L.A7, 1 (1622): 48–9]).

85 "[Q]ue ninguno de los dichos generales les pueda obligalles a que hagan las dichas fiestas ni hazer ningun repartimiento para ellas mas de lo que ellos Voluntariamente quisieren hazer" ("Real Cédula a los generales de las flotas" AGI, Indiferente 1953, L.5 (1607): 336–336V).

86 "[E]n el alcaiceria que llaman Parian, extramuro desta ciudad" ("Expediente sobre los baratos de los juegos de sangleyes" AGI Filipinas, 22, R.6, N.10, 8 [1636]).

87 "Estos chinos tienen de costumbre quando hacen las fiestas a su luna por el mes de febrero Jugar cinco dias con Unas tablillas como a pares O nones en el suelo sobre una esterilla. alla en su Tierra Juegan quince dias que son las de la creciente de la luna y aca todos los gobernadores Mis antecessors (teniendo muchos pareceres de Theologos como yo Las Tengo de que se puede hacer con buena consciencia) Les an dado los dies dias mas para Jugar de los quales sean a Puerta becdado" ("Expediente sobre los baratos de los juegos de sangleyes" AGI Filipinas, 22, R.6, N.10, 8 [1636]).

88 In 1678, Diego de Villatoro, a magistrate in the court of Manila, refers to the same benefits and dangers that were noted by his predecessors: "Refiere que a los Indios y negros Libres y esclavos y otras Naciones se les

permiten Juegos en diferentes Pue –blos por el interes que de ellos sacan los Alcaldes Mayores de las Provincias y sus oficiales de que resultan los inconvenientes de rovos a las casas y a las Iglesias y ha –ber muchos Vagamundos faltando a sus lavores" ("It refers that the Indians and free blacks and slaves and other nations are permitted games in different towns for the profits that from them the mayors of the provinces and their officials derive, from which result problems of thefts of houses and churches, and there being many vagabonds neglecting their work" ["Petición de Villatoro sobre prohibir juegos de sangleyes," AGI Filipinas 28, N.122 (1678): fol. 859v]). Despite the usefulness of the proceeds towards maintaining infrastructure ("el prozedido de los baratos para gastos de fortificaciones"), the social costs of gambling addiction are high: "de que resulta perder las haziendas de los Vezinos de Manila y mercaderes de chi – na y desesperados los Infieles se ahorcan, y lo Christi – anos se Uyen y dejan sus mugeres y familias" ("from which follow the loss of property of the citizens of Manila and merchants of China and the desperate infidels hang themselves, and the Christians flee and leave their wives and families" [fol. 860v]).

89 "Respuesta al governador de Filipinas" AGI Filipinas 21, R.12, 1 (1638). This document also refers to a limited allowance of such play, based on "muchos pareceres de teologos."

90 For all *Los baños de Argel* references, I use the translation of Fuchs and Ilika (University of Pennsylvania Press, 2010). I am grateful to Beatrice Pinzan for bringing to my attention the scene of garden recreation in this play.

91 "porque conbenga para hallarse siempre juntos en los rebates y aver causa para velar en los pueblos donde residian se permitia que jugasen de noche a los naypes y de dia a los birlos, de manera que estoviesen siempre juntos porque de no lo estar demas de las dichas causas se causaban muchas muertes de christianos y robos de caballos y otras cosas" ("Confirmación de provisión sobre juego" AGI Patronato 276, N.4, R. 147, 1 [1530]: 1).

92 "Desde antiguo tenían los soldados privilegio para establecer mesas de juego en los cuerpos de guardia. El 20 de abril de 1629 expidió Felipe IV cédula dirigida al duque de Alba, virrey capitán general de Nápoles, ordenando que sólo se permitiesen esas mesas (o 'tablas de juego', como entonces se decía), si bien con la prohibición de que en ellas se jugase a los dados, por considerarse de los más peligrosos este juego de azar, dominante en los campamentos" ("Since long ago the soldiers had the privilege of establishing gaming tables in the defense corps. On April 20 of 1629 Phillip IV issued a dispatch to the Duke of Alba, viceroy captain general of Naples, ordering that only these tables (or 'game boards', as they were

then called) be permitted, if with the prohibition that dice be played on them, as this game of chance was considered most pernicious, prevalent in the encampments" [212]).

93 "[O]tros excessos mayores en ofensa de dios nuestro señor"; "Ni den lugar que las dichas Mugeres casadas ni solteras ni Biudas Jueguen" ("Prohibición juego de naipes y dardos a las mujeres: México" AGI, Patronato 183, N. 1, R.7, 1 [1583]: p. 1).

94 "[A]lgunos grados de Parentesco como hijos e hijas con sus padres, maridos con mugeres, hermanos con hermanas" ("Carta del virrey conde de Monterrey" AGI, México 23, N.73, 1 [1597]).

95 "[S]e han causado y de cada dia causan muchos danos a los vezinos y pobladores de aquellas partes especialmente a los mercaderes y tratantes por que dizque con el juego que ay en ellas muy desordenado lo qual visto por los de nuestro concejo de las yndias queriendo proveer como sea escusen estos ynconvenientes fue acordado que debia mandar directamente por vos e yo tovelo por bien por ende yo vos mando que proveays como no se lleven a ninguna parte de las dichas nuestras yndias naypes ny dados ningunos" ("Real Cédula a los oficiales de la Casa de Contratación" AGI Indiferente 1962, L.5, 1 [1538]: 665–6).

96 "[U]na de las principales cosas que en esta tierra destruya a las gentes especialmente a mercaderes es el juego por ser desordenado ... e por jugar ocultamente e interbenyiendo en dichos juegos juramentos falsos e otros fraudes" (Mendoza, AGI, Patronato 180, R. 76 [1539]: 1).

97 "Acabados estos días de dicha pasqua como quedan picados los dichos sangleyes acuden a pedir otra nueba licencia a unos governadores por otros diez diaz, los quales la conseden porque dan por ella quatro y sinco mil pesos; y en el dicho termino prorrogado no se libran mas baratos a las dichas justicias" (Espina, AGI, Filipinas 41. N. 53 [1638]). For the use of "picar" in the passage above, Covarrubias provides an illustration of a phenomenon frequently observed in the artists and moralists of the period: "Picarse y estar picado en el juego, pesarle de perder y porfiar en jugar" ("To hook oneself and to be hooked on gambling, to regret losing and persevere in the game," Sebastián de Covarrubias *Tesoro*).

2. Solitary, Collaborative, and Complicit Play in *Don Quijote*

1 Iffland describes Cervantes's treatment of the apocryphal book as a festive ritual sacrifice: "El *Quijote* de Avellaneda ha sido mandado *hacia abajo*, hasta las puertas del infierno; ha sido sujeto de un tratamiento denigrante (una pelota para los diablos); y finalmente, ha sido 'destripado.'

La trayectoria descendente a la que ha sido sujeto en el *Segundo tomo* no se detiene en la puerta del infierno, a juzgar por las palabras del diablo vuelto crítico: pide que se eche *a sus abismos*, esto es, a la parte más baja de este sitio bajo por antonomasia" ("The *Quijote* of Avellaneda has been sent *downwards*, to the gates of hell; it has been subjected to a denigrating treatment (a ball for devils); and finally, it has been 'disembowelled.' The descending trajectory to which it has been subjected in the *Second tome* does not stop at the door of hell, judging by the words of the devil-as-critic: he asks that it be cast *into the abysses*, that is, to the lowest part of this quintessentially low place" [506]). Iffland also points out the association between inflated objects – blown-up bladders in particular – and carnivalesque insanity (505).

2 The presentation of a book as a "juguete" was not uncommon. Other notable examples include López de Ubeda's *Pícara Justina*, Gaspar Lucas Hidalgo's *Diálogos de apacible entretenimiento*, and Gracián's *Héroe*. As in Cervantes, the innocuous term is deceptive, adorning works containing a range of serious and potentially subversive references. The Inquisition, for example, did not take lightly Lucas Hidalgo's "juguete."

3 "Porque la movilidad encauzada, intencional, no tiene que tener conotaciones negativas, mientras que el errar aleatorio o vagabundear, sí las tiene, incluso cuando no se trata de un loco" (Iffland *De fiestas* 192).

4 "Tampoco debemos pasar por alto que es el cura Pero Pérez el que más se empeña en llevarle de vuelta a casa, y que lo termina haciendo en compañía de los agentes de la autoridad real. Es decir, las dos caras de la soberanía política, Mitra y Varuna, cooperan en la reterritorialización del guerrero, quien en efecto está definido como loco, deforme, usurpador (ejerce una autoridad que no le corresponde)" (Iffland *De fiestas* 204).

5 "[N]uestro héroe, ideado a partir de mecanismos arraigados en la cultura festiva popular, se levanta automáticamente de cada una de sus caídas (si bien es verdad que lo hace con menos energía en la última etapa de su carrera). Hacerlo morir no sólo es la respuesta digna al manicomio de Toledo sino que erige un obstáculo más o menos infranqueable para futuras falsificaciones" (Iffland *De fiestas* 562).

6 "Don Quijote es lo que ha volado de los nidos de antaño. El nido es el propio Quijano, que se ha quedado vacío por su voluntad, para morir sencillamente. El pájaro –don Quijote – seguirá volando" (Torrente Ballester 202).

7 For those who simply "have no work" ("ni tienen"), play represents a way to "pass time," and thus prevent dissolute idleness. A representative contemporary petition to the king claims such a role for the theatre: "Nace también de las comedias demás de la recreación universal, un engaño del

tiempo que en el ocioso es de gran fruto y en el más ocupado es importante, pues al uno quita de vicios, si no de ejecutarlos, de trazarlos, y al otro (como se dijo) le sirve de dar cuerda al pensamiento; pues es cierto que todos los que acuden a las comedias se reducen a gente ociosa o a gente virtuosa y ocupada, y ni a los primeros hace la comedia peores, ni a los últimos menos buenos, pues a los unos les sirve la comedia de freno y suspensión de los vicios, y a los otros de espuela para la virtud y trabajo, de cuyo fruto los unos y los otros se defraudan si del todo se quitan las comedias" ("In addition to universal recreation, theatrical works also provide a trick of time which in the idle is of great benefit and in the most occupied is important, since it removes vices from the one, if not to carry them out, to plan them, and to the other (as was said) it serves to encourage thought; it is certain that all who come to the theatre are either idle people or virtuous and occupied people, and neither are the former made worse by theatre, nor are the latter made less good, since for the first theatre serves as an attenuation and suspension of vices, and to the others a spur to virtue and work, the fruit of which everyone is defrauded if theatre is taken away" ["Memorial impreso dirigido al rey D. Felipe II, para que levante la suspensión en las representaciones de comedias," Madrid, 1598. In Cotarelo y Mori 422b]). The notion that one can "trick time" ("defraudar el tiempo") supports the idea that leisure was "invented" in the early modern period (see Burke).

8 "Original y explícito a la vez, el juego cervantino se vale de los juegos – y particularmente del más vulgar entre ellos, los naipes – como de un lenguaje común que se vuelve, bajo su pluma, lenguaje de creación. Y ese lenguaje, como cualquier otro lenguaje o, mejor dicho, el lenguaje en general, no sirve a Cervantes para representar la realidad, sino para trastocarla: con naipes del montón, baraja tópicos" (Étienvre *Márgenes* 42).

9 "[E]l *Quijote* se cuenta 'jugando', el 'juego' es su modo propio de estar contado. La correlación, pues, entre material narrable y técnica narrativa es adecuada. ¿Hay algo más lógico que el contar jugando la historia de un juego?" (Torrente Ballester 82).

10 Karshan notes that to "read playfully" is to remain sensitive to the ironies and multiple possible interpretations of a literary work (204), and that such a "reader becomes what Nabokov thought any good reader should be, a co-author. One comes to feel that *Pale Fire* is not the words on the page but the shadows they cast, that its art really exists not as a material object but as a possible entity in the mind of the reader, and that its life is its infinite possible afterlives" (231). It is worth pointing out again that Karshan grounds Nabokov's notion of literary play in the early modern humanist tradition.

11 Grandbois (69) notes that, while *tablas* is an early form of chess, the rendering of "backgammon" by some modern translators (Grossman and Rutherford included) is legitimate, given the game's many iterations – sometimes involving dice – during its development.
12 See George Haley's account of the Maese Pedro episode as an emblem of the entire novel's representational dynamic. For the complicated cultural dynamic of literary appropriations of popular, oral culture, see Mauricio Molho, *Cervantes: raíces folklóricas*, especially 37–45.
13 Ife, who traced the rise in private readership with a heightened concern in the period with the dangers of fiction, makes the following comments in his discussion of Campuzano's reading in *El coloquio de los perros*: "Cervantes shows here, as he does in *Don Quijote*, that if an assembled audience will fall under the spell of a skilful narrator so that it will lose track of time and space, how much more easily will a private reader, stripped of the protective company of his fellows and locked away in a solitary world of his own imaginings, how much more easily will he succumb to the rapture of a book" (62). James Wood recently observed how the very privacy of reading facilitates communication and coherence: "Reading fiction feels radically private, because so often we seem to be stealing the failed privacies of fictional characters. This is the privacy not of solitude but of clandestine fellowship; together, the reader and his fictional acquaintance complete, or voice, a new ensemble. Their failed privacies are incorporated into the reader's more successful privacies" ("Why" 36).
14 "No hay en ellas [*Novelas*] ninguna conversión auténtica – ni de rango social, ni de personalidad, ni de especie biológica. Lo que pasa en ellas es que se quitan ilusiones" (Wardropper 165).
15 Alfred Appel's fine introduction to his annotated *Lolita* is another case in point. I attempted to fill in some of these gaps in "*Don Quijote* and *Lolita* Revisited" (Scham 2008).
16 For a discussion and critique of such approaches, see Forcione, *Afterword* (334–51).
17 For the different types of pastoral, including the "pastoral of the self" and the "erotic pastoral," see Poggioli. For a discussion of their appropriation in Cervantes, see Forcione ("Marcela and Grisóstomo"), and Finello (135–7).
18 It is worth recalling Boccaccio's observation that men had at their disposal a range of distractions from this type of melancholy, including hunting and horseback-riding. His collection offers both to men and women an additional remedy, storytelling. In their enactment of fiction – their *mimetic* play – Cervantes's pastoral characters again offer, through the

extremity of their actions, a concentrated image of what such recreation (imaginative literature) entails.

19 For a discussion of feminist aspects of Cervantes's pastoral, see Hart, Gabrielle, and Rivers.

20 For an interesting variation, note don Quijote as he prepares to counsel Sancho on the art of governing: "Entrados, pues, en su aposento, cerró tras si la puerta, y hizo casi por fuerza que Sancho se sentase junto a él" ("Once they were in the room Don Quixote shut the door behind him and almost pushed Sancho down into the chair by his side" [II, 42, p. 357]). The less authoritative posture is perhaps tied to his knowledge of Sancho's rise, poised to enter the world on his own.

21 Dickens had a comparable appreciation of the compulsions of laughter, and its varying effects – therapeutic, disruptive, threatening. The Panzine Sam Weller of *The Pickwick Papers* observes with trepidation as his father attempts, like Sancho, to suppress his laughter: "Here the old gentleman shook his head from side to side, and was seized with a hoarse internal rumbling, accompanied with a violent swelling of the countenance, and a sudden increase in the breadth of all his features" (632). The sanguine Senior Weller's cultivation of "a kind o' quiet laugh" is meant to conceal his mirth from the dour Mrs Weller, who is perturbed by her husband's laughter. Both father and son, recognizing the danger of repression, agree that the "quiet laugh" is "too much in the appleplexy line" (632).

22 "El niño sin juguete, el que se ve obligado a inventarlo en una verdadera operación de *bricolage*, actúa como don Quijote: el más leve y lejano parecido le sirve para transmudar lo real y crea así el mundo en que puede jugar. Señala la silla y decreta: Esto es el barco, y yo soy el capitán. Y, en tanto dura el juego, la silla es barco y el niño es capitán, y aunque el niño sabe que se trata de una convención – de ahí el ingrediente irónico de todo niño que inventa su juguete – , se irrita cuando alguien no acepta lo convenido y niega la condición de barco a la silla y de capitán al niño" (Torrente Ballester 115–16).

23 For discussion of such distinctions, and the range of parody, see Karrer.

24 According to Close, Spitzer, building upon Castro, "opened up for Cervantes the rich quarry of prismatic reality, self-conscious narrative, and fictional viewpoint" (*Cervantes and the Comic Mind* 2). Close focuses on Bakhtin's theory of the carnivalesque as the hinge upon which much "romanticising" theory turns. For a thoughtful argument against closing off such a potentially fruitful and in fact historical approach, see the review article of Iffland ("Laughter Tamed"). In a study that opens up *Don Quixote* to a rich philosophical heritage, Martínez-Bonati, like Close, argues

that Cervantes's humour has a limited epistemological reach: "As if with a smile, it is suggested that madness is only another form of rationality. But, I insist, the suggestion is not serious. This game is openly humoristic, for not only is the validity of traditional common sense not questioned by the *Quixote*, but it is posited as a foundation for all of the ironic construction" (120).

25 "El capítulo de la eutrapelia, del divertimiento espiritual, es sumamente importante en la historia del desenvolvimiento humano; haciendo la historia de la ironía y del humor tendríamos hecha la de la sensibilidad humana, y, consiguientemente, la del progreso, la de la civilización" (Azorín 44).

26 "Hoy no habría persona de mediana sensibilidad – no ya de extremada – que pudiera sonreír ante estas cosas. Al contrario: nos entristecerían. La sensibilidad ha ido evolucionando" (Azorín 44).

27 See *Rabelais and His World*, ch. 1. I have reassessed Nabokov's reading of *Don Quijote*, and the extensive influence of Cervantes on his own novelistic practice in "*Don Quijote* and *Lolita* Revisited."

28 As Martín de Riquer suggests, Cervantes may have in mind one of the *tractatus ludorum* considered earlier in this study (see Riquer's introduction to Luque Faxardo's *Fiel desengaño contra la ociosidad y los juegos*).

29 Here we might recall the above-mentioned allegory of chess in Canalejas's *Libro del juego de las Damas*: "y aun el varon entendido saca el precioso desengaño de su semejanza con las cosas de este mundo" ("and even the learned man derives precious disillusionment from its similitude with the things of this world" ["Al lector"]).

30 The influential Galenic school of medicine described mechanisms of laughter according to such an integrated view of the human organism: "La causa de la risa no es otra, a mi parecer, más que una aprobación que hace la imaginativa viendo y oyendo algún hecho o dicho que cuadra muy bien; y como esta potencia reside en el celebro, en contentándole alguna de estas luego lo menea, y tras él los músculos de todo el cuerpo" ("The cause of laughter is no other, in my opinion, than an approval by the imaginative faculty seeing and hearing some deed or saying which fits well; and as this faculty resides in the brain, in telling it something of this sort it begins to shake, and after it the muscles of the body" [*Examen de ingenios* ch. 6]). Like Huarte, the French physician Laurent Joubert identified the origins of laughter in the mind, which then set off hot and cold humours causing convulsions in the heart, in turn affecting the rest of the body via the pericardium; an excesses could potentially fatal – the very "appleplexy" feared by Sam Weller and son in Dickens's *Pickwick Papers* (see above, note 23).

31 Citing Cervantes's use of irony, parody and paradox, James Parr contends that *Don Quijote* is better understood within the Lucianic-Horatian satirical tradition than as an early example of "realism" (97–102). In addition to exposing pedants and the proximity of man and beast, Parr maintains that the principal function of the satire is "the repudiation of a sociopolitical ideology," which he conceives as "a somewhat subversive message about the futility of trying to resurrect a largely illusionary golden age" (101–2). Trueblood has discussed laughter and sympathy, as well as therapeutic laughter in *Don Quijote*. For a focus on the humour generated by the incorporation of chivalric elements, see Eisenberg.

32 "Señalo todo esto para mostrar que en *Don Quijote* tenemos la gama completa de la risa, desde las formas más subversivas y liberadoras hasta las que refuerzan la diferenciación jerárquica. La importancia ... es justamente esta riqueza y variedad, el hecho de que la risa se vuelca en todas las direcciones imaginables, partiendo de individuos extremadamente diversos" (Iffland, *De fiestas* 50–1).

33 Of course, perceiving everywhere chance rather than fate does not *necessarily* correspond to a comic outlook, as Thomas Hardy expressed in his devastating poem, "Hap": "If but some vengeful god would call to me / From up the sky, and laugh: 'Thou suffering thing, / Know that thy sorrow is my ecstasy', / ... /But not so ... / ... / Crass Casualty obstructs the sun and rain, / And dicing Time for gladness casts a moan ... / These purblind Doomsters had as readily strown / Blisses bout my pilgrimage as pain."

34 For a discussion of paradox in Burton, his indebtedness to Montaigne, and the tension between Democritus and Heraclitus in *The Anatomy of Melancholy*, see Colie, *Paradoxia Epidemica* 430–60.

35 For an account of how medieval thinkers like Avicenna and Melanchthon anticipate romantic valuations of the marginal melancholic, see Klibansky, Panofsky and Saxl, 86–90.

36 Of Montaigne and Erasmus, Hugo Friedrich wrote the following: "They both have in common the fact that they replace ethical unconditionalness with a humanity of modest averageness, and they shelter man in a wisdom that lies beyond the inconsequential contrast of reason and irrationality. Both also have in common the fact that they praise illusion as the mover of the human soul which brings happiness, regardless of whether the illusion manifests itself in the simplicity of fools or in the vision of believers, or in the poets' process of getting outside of themselves" (309). Friedrich also discusses the common sources in *Ecclesiastes* and Horace.

37 Chevalier points out how this retort forms part of the agonistic culture of word-play and insults: "don Quijote apoda al Barbero – 'señor rapista,'

'señor Bacía' (II, 1) – , lo cual demuestra sin dejar lugar a dudas que el cuentecillo picante de éste le ha herido en lo más vivo" ("don Quijote nick-names the Barber 'mister shaver,' 'mister Basin' – which demonstrates without doubt that the mischievous little story by the latter has stung him" [161, note 7]).

38 Wood judiciously refrains from seeing in Cervantes a full-blown relativism, although he does not dismiss the possibility: "the most ordinary truths can be made to look unsafe. Whether they are unsafe because they can be made to look so, is one of Cervantes's great questions" (34). Martínez Mata rejects the idea that *Don Quijote* contains epistemological quandaries, although his analysis at times borders on such a view: "En el *Quijote* … la realidad no se muestra ambigua (y así lo señalaba Parker en 1948), son los personajes los que falsean la realidad cuando les conviene" ("In the *Quijote* … reality is not shown to be ambiguous (and Parker pointed this out in 1948), it is the characters who falsify reality when it suits them" [107]). Martínez Mata also maintains that, given the "contexto burlesco" and fantastical nature of his narrative, don Quijote's response to the Canon's neo-Aristotelian aesthetic cannot be taken seriously. I offer a partial refutation of this position in my review of his book.

39 "[L]os religiosos que salen en Cervantes son casi siempre cómicos" (Bataillon *Erasmo y España* 416).

40 It is tempting to connect such a view of the plasticity of language and Sancho's physical orientation with the atomistic materialism of Lucretius: "And how these atoms are arranged makes all the difference – / Their position and formations, and what moves they give and take / From one another, for the selfsame atoms go to make / The heavens and the sea, the land, the rivers and the sun, / The same make crops, trees, animals – but by their combination / In different ways with different elements move differently. / Furthermore, all through these very lines of mine, you see / Many letters that are shared by many words – and yet / You must confess that words and lines from this one alphabet / Have sundry sounds and meanings. Letters only have to change / Their order to accomplish all of this – and still the range / Of possibilities of atoms is greater. That is why / They can create the universe's rich variety" (bk. I, l. 817–29). Redondo discusses how Cervantes's linguistic play endows words with a sort of autonomy, liberating them from their conventional signification (*Otra manera de leer* 479–84). When Borges cites Burton's "By this art you may contemplate the variation of the 23 letters …" to open his *La Biblioteca de Babel*, he takes Lucretius's insight to an extreme, conflating the combinational randomness of the universe with what we use to explain it (the alphabet).

Nabokov's "game of words" / "game of worlds," in *Pale Fire*, entertains a similar concept.

41 Not much later Sancho will claim, in his own particular idiom, that he also knows something about "la esfera celeste y terrestre" when he gives his account of the cosmos seen from Clavileño (II, 41). In contrast to the pedantic and bookish terms deployed by don Quijote, Sancho's vocabulary, as we will see, draws upon his own life experience (goats), and a rejuvenating impulse to play.

42 During the Clavileño episode, Sancho removes his blindfold in similar manner: "bonitamente y sin que nadie lo viese, por junto a las narices aparté tanto cuanto el pañizuelo que me tapaba los ojos" ("on the sly and so no one would see me I pulled the blindfold aside next to my nose" [II, 41, p. 353]). Martínez Mata comments on the use of the term, which he interprets as "disimuladamente" (64), in the description of the *bálsamo de Fierabrás* (I, 10).

43 Naturally, Rocinante opts for the comfort of his own "domestic" space: "En esto, llegó a un camino que en cuatro se dividía, y luego se le vino a la imaginación las encrucejadas donde los caballeros andantes se ponían a pensar cuál camino de aquéllos tomarían, y, por imitarlos, estuvo un rato quedo; y al cabo de haberlo muy bien pensado, soltó la rienda a Rocinante, dejando a la voluntad del rocín la suya, el cual siguió su primer intento, que fue el irse camino de su caballeriza" ("As he was saying this he came to a crossroads, and this brought to his mind those other crossroads where knights errant would pause to consider which way to go; and, to imitate them, he remained motionless for a while; but after careful thought he let go of the reins, surrendering his will to that of his nag, which followed its original inclination – to head for its stable" [I, 4, p. 99]).

44 Given the cosmological focus of the *barco encantado* episode, we might compare Cervantes's sceptical mode of narration with that of Lucretius: "But which of these is the true cause, it's hard to ascertain. / Rather, it is the *possibilities* that I explain – / What things can and do come about in all the universe / In the many worlds created different ways. I give divers / Rationales which can explain the motion of the stars / In *all* the worlds – and *one* of these has to hold true for ours, / Empowering stars with motion. Which is right? We cannot say, / When we are only blindly, step by step, feeling our way" (V, l. 526–33).

45 For a good recent study of *Don Quijote* and some of the key figures of modernity (Schlegel, Lukács, Cohen, Unamuno, Ortega, Bakhtin), see Schmidt.

46 See, e.g., Redondo, *Otra manera de leer* 430–43.

47 If this act of naming corresponds to what Barber describes as the "ceremonial view," critics have been far from concordant with regard to what the name signifies. For a discussion of the subtle dialectic formed by don Diego and don Quijote, see Presberg (ch. 5).
48 "[R]ecalca el aire festivo y primaveral de esta serie de aventuras" (*Don Quijote* II, 16, p. 150, note 7).
49 For a discussion of Kierkegaard's perspective on don Quijote, see Welsh.
50 Molho accounts for the richness of Sancho's character – what he calls Sancho's "reversibilidad" – by exploring his carnivalesque and folkloric origins, including the ambivalent figure of the simpleton ("tonto") and the trickster ("hacerse el tonto"): "Su movilidad no es sino la manifestación multiple de las virtualidades contradictorias inscritas en el personaje" ("His mobility is but the multiple manifestation of the contradictory virtualities inscribed in the character," 234).
51 See Redondo, *Otra manera de leer* 395–9. For a summary of the absence of religious observance in *Don Quijote*, see Iffland, *De fiestas* (546, note 108).
52 "[E]s de notar cómo Cervantes introduce una temática social muy seria en medio de este episodio erigido sobre directrices festivas. Subrayado aquí es el conflicto de clase muy real que existe entre los Camachos y los Basilios del mundo. Don Quijote termina como adalid de los segundos, como sería de esperar" (*De fiestas* 526).
53 This is another sense in which the ducal pair is not so different from don Quijote. If the Duke and Duchess's state of play is decadent, don Quijote's, as Iffland suggests, could be seen as subversive: "Tarde o temprano, el hecho que don Quijote lleve un carnaval permanente en la cabeza tiene que provocar un conflicto grave con las autoridades" ("Sooner or later, the fact that don Quijote carries a permanent carnival in his head has to provoke a serious conflict with the authorities" [*De fiestas* 110]).
54 In a study that came to my attention late in the process of finishing this manuscript, Anthony Cascardi notes that governor Sancho makes "allusions to pressing economic issues and to contemporary trade regulations" (*Cervantes, Literature, and the Discourse of Politics* 159). Cascardi also discusses the importance of Castiglione's *The Courtier* to don Quijote's counseling of Sancho as he takes the governorship: "The book [*The Courtier*] takes the form of an extended moral and social inquiry cloaked as a fictional dialogue whose basis lies in a commitment to serious results of various forms of 'play,' including verbal play. In *Don Quijote*, by contrast, the Duke and the Duchess sponsor an exaggerated and distorted sense of 'play,' one that is bereft of moral purpose and that turns malicious: *serio ludere* in their hands becomes *ludere* with intent to sting" (150).

55 For a reading of the episodes as a satire of an unproductive nobility, see Quint (*Cervantes's Novel* 131–50). Forcione notes the importance of Spain's addiction to gambling for Sancho's opinions as governor, and points out a similar reference in *Persiles y Sigismunda* (*Cervantes and the Humanist Vision* 208–15). With regard to the scene in the *Persiles*, Forcione observes: "The husband is driven to his desperate action not by madness or vice but rather by poverty. The agents encouraging and profiting from the victims' willingness to gamble their freedom away are the ministers of the king. Even at its most 'exemplary,' Cervantes's fiction resists reduction according to the conventional moralizing literature with which he was familiar" (212–13, note 210).

56 As Benjamín González Alonso notes in the introduction to his edition, Bobadilla's endorsement of work should not be taken for a "mercantilist" mind-set, along with the social mobility such a view entails. He was interested in maintaining existing hierarchy, and generally against interest, accumulation of wealth, *conversos* and *novedades*. He bases his promotion of work, as we saw with other *tratadistas*, on the Bible's injunction to win one's bread by the sweat of one's brow, as an essential condition of fallen man.

57 "Eso, en cuanto al enunciado. Pero, por otra parte, en cuanto a la enunciación, todos los juegos son de tahúres, no hay entretenimiento sin fullería" (Étienvre *Márgenes* 43).

58 We might contrast the "closing off" of Sancho's "no digo más" in this instance with the implicit acknowledgment of nuance in his concluding remarks during the discussion of gambling houses, "sé que hay mucho que decir en eso" ("I can see that there are lots of ins and outs to this question," 408).

59 Commenting on the festivities surrounding Saints Ignatius, Theresa and Francis Xavier, Defourneaux notes the broad appeal of such entertainments: "The triple canonization in 1622 was not only an occasion for *Te Deums* and magnificent pageantry; there were also poetry contests, the presentation of plays, jousting on horseback, and bull-fights. The latter, with dancing and masquerades, were the pleasures most enjoyed by the public, and the most important festivals frequently featured them, thus responding to the various tastes of every social class" (129).

60 Another example, in *Rinconete y Cortadillo*, is when Maniferro describes the local boy who converted the broom into sonorous instrument as "un Héctor en la música" (231).

61 "En una España corroída por la crisis, en que triunfan el cohecho, la prevaricación y la injusticia, el campesino, en el marco de una estructura

carnavalesca, la de un transitorio mundo al revés, el que corresponde a un reinado de burla, y entre destellos de comicidad, hace posible que se exprese ese afán de rectitud y de justicia que podrían provocar la restauración de España. El discurso festivo viene a ser, de tal modo, discurso político" (Redondo, "En torno a dos personajes festivos" 176).

62 See Maravall, *La cultura del Barroco*, ch. 1 (92–6).

63 Of the Clavileño scene, Forcione writes: "The point I would make is that, in this little meta-fictional scene of literary parody and farce, Sancho, rather than exemplifying the antithesis of the artist, stands very close to his creator and that his determination to play with the cosmos and to rewrite, so to speak, the Book of the World is exactly what we have seen in Periandro's determination to roam through the heavens, in Don Quixote's underworld discovery of a sun that shines with an unearthly and new radiance, and in Critilio's explanation of man's responsibility to reconnect the stars with his own imaginative powers" ("Cervantes' Night-Errantry" 471). See also Forcione's "At the Threshold of Modernity."

64 Martínez Mata notes the word's shadings in different contexts, from "knowing" ("curioso lector") to "careful," "diligent" (the "curiosos" "ingenios de la Mancha" 19, 23).

65 "[E]l escudero indica a las claras que está jugando, divirtiendo a sus interlocutores y divirtiéndose, que sabe muy bien lo que está haciendo" (Redondo *Otra manera de leer* 443).

66 See Redondo, *Otra manera de leer* 439–52. Redondo also suggests some mischievously satirical elements in Sancho's "cuernos de la luna" remark, and erotic overtones in his playing with the goats.

67 While Finello acknowledges that the pastoral "Renaissance ideal breathes" in this scene, he maintains that it is shot through with *desengaño*: "But Cervantes tailors his precarious Arcadia to fit the design of a hero in the throes of decline. Arcadia becomes for him the golden land tainted with deceit, ultimately emerging as a strangely discordant setting where he and Sancho are later trampled upon by bulls" (170).

68 Of the Ricote episode Thomas Mann remarked that "Cervantes's allegiance as Christian and loyal subject enhances the spiritual value of his freedom, the worth of his criticism" ("Voyage With Don Quixote" 361). Iffland calls it the most transgressive and dangerous dialogue of *Don Quijote* (*De fiestas* 464). A fascinating parallel to Ricote's encounter of an alternative and more tolerant society in early modern Germany is found in Stephen Greenblatt's account of the Italian Humanist Poggio Bracciolini as he visited the medicinal baths at Baden. Poggio witnesses men and women bathing together in unselfconscious community, with "many drinking heavily … and yet

there is no quarrelling, bickering, or cursing," and in which the platonic ideal seems to reign, "where all property was held in common" (175). As Greenblatt summarizes: "With his contrasting visions of anxious, work-obsessed, overly disciplined Italians and happy-go-lucky, carefree Germans, Poggio believed he glimpsed for a moment the Epicurean pursuit of pleasure as the highest good. He knew perfectly well that this pursuit ran counter to Christian orthodoxy. But in Baden it was as if he found himself on the threshold of a mental world in which Christian rules no longer applied" (176).

69 "Cervantes ha pasado del eros al ágape, de la pasión que se sume a sí misma a la *amicitia*, del solipsismo a la comunión, del ser a la comunidad o, digamos, a la condición esencial de pureza en que ser y comunidad son uno, en que el hombre sólo puede existir como amigo, compañero y vecino" (Forcione, "Cervantes en busca" 1042).

3. The *Novelas ejemplares: Ocio,* Exemplarity, and Community

1 For a discussion of the Augustinian and Erasmian attitudes toward the correct use of memory and knowledge, the pilgrimage of curiosity, the incorporation of apothegms, and the relationship of these elements to sceptic and humanist currents in sixteenth and seventeenth-century Spain, see Forcione, *Cervantes and the Humanist Vision* 225–316.

2 "En cuanto a Vidriera, su crítica moralizadora, irónica y clarividente en nada iguala las sombrías y amargas diatribas que contra el universo lanzan los típicos héroes de la novela picaresca" (*El pensamiento* 239). Castro's line of argument is echoed in Blanco Aguinaga, who also describes a polar opposition between picaresque literature and that of Cervantes. Dunn gives a more nuanced account of both the picaresque and Cervantes's relationship to it ("Cervantes De/Re-Constructs the Picaresque"; also, *Spanish Picaresque Fiction*). For a discussion of the licentiate, Cervantes's canine critics, and the spectrum of the cynics, see Riley, "Cervantes and the Cynics." Gerli distinguishes Cervantes's work from the picaresque formally, while asserting a similarity in function: "Sin beneficio de las complicaciones tramáticas, el obligatorio formato autobiográfico, la ironía velada y la relación pormenorizadora de los movimientos del protagonista por el tiempo y el espacio, Cervantes realiza la misma subversión de la realidad social que encontramos en las novelas del hampa" ("Without recourse to intricacies of plot, the obligatory autobiographical format, veiled irony and detailed account of the movements of the protagonist through time and space, Cervantes carries out the same subversion of social reality that

we find in the novels of the criminal underworld" [587]). An authoritative study on genre awareness and creation in the period is Colie's *Resources of Kind*.

3 Green, who examined the Galenic, "humour" basis for don Quijote's madness, also discusses Vidriera's pathology in similar terms ("El *Licenciado Vidriera* …").

4 El Saffar characterizes the licentiate's evasiveness in psychological terms, as a manifestation of an underlying anxiety over death: "His refusal to give his family's name or his place of origin, the fear and repugnance contact with soldiers and a sea voyage inspired in him, his solitary and restless travels, and his avoidance of love and marriage trace a pattern of escape" (*Novel to Romance* 56).

5 Discussing his shift from an anxiety-ridden stoicism to a curious form of melancholy epicureanism, Unamuno proposes a theory of humour which is in many ways consistent with Folly's description of liberation from the confining preoccupations of life: "Porque ¿qué otra cosa es el sentimiento de lo cómico sino el de la emancipación de la lógica, y qué otra cosa sino lo ilógico nos provoca la risa? Y esa risa ¿qué es sino la expresión corpórea del placer que sentimos al vernos libres, siquiera sea por un breve momento, de esa feroz tirana, de ese *fatum* lúgubre, de esa potencia incoercible y sorda a las voces del corazón" ("Because what else is the feeling of the comic than the emancipation from logic, and what other than illogic causes us laughter? And that laughter, what is it but the corporeal expression of the pleasure we feel upon seeing ourselves free, even for just a brief moment, from that ferocious tyranny, of that lugubrious *fatum*, of that power that is unaffected and deaf to the voices of the heart" [*Amor y pedagogía*, "Epílogo,"165]). In spite of the somewhat mystical character of his notion of cathartic purification, some of the most affirmative functions of humour are contained in Unamuno's association of the humorous outlook with distance and understanding, as well as his recognition of the value of being able to laugh at oneself: "Pues tal es la miserable condición humana, que no queda otra salida que o reírse o dar que reír como no tome uno la de reírse y dar que reír a la vez, riéndose de lo que da que reír y dando que reír de lo que se ríe" ("Such is the miserable human condition, that there is no other escape than to laugh at oneself or be laughed at, unless one takes the course of simultaneously laughing at oneself and being laughed at, laughing at what is laughable in oneself, and being laughable while laughing at oneself" [168]). Here we recall Montaigne's assertion that "Our own peculiar condition is that we are as fit to be laughed at as able to laugh" (I, 50).

6 "Su ser precisa holgura; su dignidad le distancia del prójimo. Tal vez por esta razón el licenciado no se atreve a adular, porque la adulación suprime la distancia, la dignidad moral que establece un respeto distanciador entre los hombres. Si el licenciado incuriera en cualquier clase de adulación se rompería" (Rosales 112).

7 Casalduero offers a somewhat mystifying example of the tendency to imbue this figure with an abstract profundity: "Al incorporarse vitalmente a Vidriera, sus palabras cesan de ser lugares comunes inocuos; son flechas penetrantes. Ni la sabiduría literaria renacentista (convertida ya en lugar común), ni la sabiduría del hombre de sociedad con la cansada luz de ocaso del último barroco. Cervantes da a sus ingeniosidades, respuestas y aforismos todo el misterio de la vida, al hacer que fluyan de un antes a un después. Muchos han sentido la atracción de ese marco – Rodaja, Rueda – ; si intuimos su esencia penetramos en la tragedia del licenciado Vidriera" ("When one engages vitally with Vidriera, his words cease being innocuous commonplaces; they are penetrating darts. Neither the literary wisdom of the Renaissance (converted already into cliché), nor the wisdom of society man with the tired sunset light of the late Baroque. Cervantes gives to his witticisms, retorts and aphorisms all the mystery of life, by making them flow from a before to an after. Many have felt the attraction of this frame – Rodaja, Rueda – if we intuit its essence we enter into the tragedy of the Glass licentiate" [112–13]).

8 "El motejar no va encaminado a enmendar conductas; el motejar pica, muerde y zahiere. Pertenece a la categoria del ingenio agresivo definido por Frued, ingenio que tan frecuentemente se manifestó y se manifiesta en círculos reducidos, cualesquiera que sean, y en especial los círculos cortesanos del Siglo de Oro" (Chevalier 60–1).

9 Joachim Ritter's account of the particular type of "laughing at" that occurs in the violence of puppet theatre illuminates both the gratification experienced by the aggressive boys in the scene above, as well as the social import of Vidriera's satirical barbs: "Im Puppentheater wird viel und gern geprügelt, und auf diesen Prügeln beruht hier der Witz. Aber diese Prügel treffen nicht beliebige Leute, sie werden nicht blind nach allen Seiten ausgeteilt, sondern gelten bestimmten Figuren: dem Räuber, dem Drachen, der alten Frau, dem Schutzmann, dem Teufel usw., und der Spaß ergibt sich offenbar eindeutig daraus, daß diese getroffen werden" ("In puppet theatre there is a good deal of gleeful beating, and it is upon these beatings the joke is based. Such beatings, however, do not befall those who are dear; they are not distributed blindly to all sides but are rather reserved

for particular figures: the thief, the dragon, the old lady, the policeman, the devil, and so on. In fact, the whole fun of the matter derives quite clearly and unambiguously from the fact that these are the characters who are struck" [73]).

10 "La comprensión no siempre es generosa. Pero la comprensión cervantina lo era; esta actitud ante la vida en modo alguno es la característica de Cervantes" (Rosales 114). Forcione, noting the assessment of Rosales, offers the following explanation: "I would suggest that the author knew quite well that his character was not speaking with his own authentic voice and that Cervantes was in fact presenting in his fool what he considered a diseased form of humour, a heartless humour of the mind of the type that was to flourish in Spain's literature of *desengaño*" (*Cervantes and the Humanist Vision* 269). Concerning Vidriera's "pathology," many critics have pointed out consistencies between his condition and case studies in Huarte's *Examen de ingenios* (see especially ch. IV).

11 Feigenbaum analyses the intricate orchestrations of illusion in this painting, as well as the related fortune-telling scenes, in which the deceiving gypsies are also being fleeced. For the notion of a "picaresque reader," see Clamurro.

12 Sieber's note in his edition contains Sebastián de Covarrubias's definition of the phrase.

13 *Cervantes and the Humanist Vision* 208–14.

14 In her essay, "Cheats, Gamblers, and Fortune-Tellers," Feigenbaum discusses the relationship between depictions of gypsies and players of cards and dice, how they emerge from biblical and moralizing *topoi*, the *Commedia dell'Arte* tradition, and contemporary social reality. Referring to La Tour's familiarity with *La Gitanilla*, Feigenbaum affirms that at the centre of his "Fortune-Teller" is an immortalizing image of Cervantes's Preciosa: "Her sidelong glance set in a milk-white perfect oval has become one of the most celebrated passages in the history of French painting" (Feigenbaum 174).

15 Forcione observes that the tale "enfolds its picaresque novel and its Lucianic satire within the containing frame of a Christian miracle" (*Cervantes and the Mystery of Lawlessness* 141).

16 See, for example, Wicks's outline of what he calls "The Total Picaresque Fictional Situation," which extensively corresponds with the narrative of Berganza's life ("The Nature of Picaresque Narrative: A Modal Approach"). For some other useful working definitions of picaresque narrative, see Guillén (ch. 3), and Wicks, *Picaresque Narrative, Picaresque Fictions*, Part I.

17 Lazarillo refers to these fishermen as "codiciosos titereros" ("greedy puppeteers") – a profession condemned by Berganza (and, as we observed, Vidriera); and their justification of displaying Lazarillo-tuna recalls some important elements of *El coloquio de los perros*: "Los señores inquisidores han mandado … lo llevemos por las villas y lugares de España, a enseñarlo a todos *como portento* y monstruo de natura" ("The inquisitors have ordered … that we take him through the towns and places of Spain, to exhibit him to all *as a portent* and monster of nature" [ch. 4, my italics]).

18 It is tempting to consider Cañizares's lack of a sense of humour, as well as Berganza's eventual manifestations of one, in light of Freud's ideas about the function of humour (which he calls "one of the highest psychic functions") in relation to defense mechanisms. He argues that true humour demonstrates an unusual strength of ego which allows one to derive pleasure in the act of confronting – rather than avoiding – that which causes pain: "It disdains to withdraw from conscious attention the ideas which are connected with the painful affect, as repression does, and thus it overcomes the defense automatism" (*Wit and its Relation to the Unconscious* 380).

19 Forcione comments on the festive character of this scene, which should be contrasted to the spatial and semantic disorder of the demonic revelry of Cañizares: "In its depiction of spontaneous acts of friendship and charity and its sharp dissociation of the pure communication of children and beasts from official discourse, it recalls the carnivalesque treatment of language in the 'Colloquy of the Squires' in the *Quixote*. As if to reverse the implications of the satanic impulses informing man's first words, Cervantes here gives expression to the humanists' utopian belief that there existed a pure, transparent language prior to the fall, that vestiges of it are perceptible in the language of children and animals, and that in the restoration of his good nature through spiritual renovation man can restore his contact with this speech" (*Cervantes and the Mystery of Lawlessness* 224). For the centrality of friendship in Cervantes, see Dunn, "Shaping Experience," 200–3.

20 Nerlich, who quotes from this essay (I,10), discusses the similarities in the discourse of the dogs and of Montaigne (see especially 268–71).

21 "Of experience" contains some of the best passages relating to Montaigne's critique of exemplarity and Stoic rigidity: "no future event will be found to correspond so exactly to any one of all the many, many thousands of selected and recorded events that there will not remain some circumstance, some difference, that will require separate consideration in forming a judgment. There is little relation between our actions, which are in perpetual mutation, and fixed and immutable laws" (III, 13, p. 816).

22 Of such cognitive pursuits in pre-modern cultures, Huizinga observes: "For him all particular knowledge is sacred knowledge – esoteric and wonder-working wisdom, because any knowing is directly related to the cosmic order itself" (105).

23 The game image in Pleberio's complaint against the world is also interesting for its desecration of the *locus amoenus* conventionally associated with benefical play, and for its frustration of productive work: "[M]e pareçes un laberinto de errores, un desierto spantable, una morada de fieras, juego de hombres que andan en corro, laguna llena de cieno, región llena de spinas, monte alto, campo pedregoso, prado lleno de serpientes, huerto florido y sin fruto, fuente de cuydados, río de lágrimas, mar de miserias, trabajo sin provecho, dulce ponçoña, vana esperança, falsa alegría, verdadero dolor" ("[Y]ou seem to me a labyrinth of errors, a frightful desert, an abode of fierce beasts, game of men who go in circles, lagoon full of mud, region full of thorns, high mountain, stony field, meadow full of snakes, blossoming but barren orchard, spring of cares, river of tears, sea of miseries, labour without profit, sweet poison, vain hope, false happiness, true pain" [Rojas 338]). As Dorothy Severin observes in the note of her edition, this passage, like many others in the *La Celestina*, has a source in Petrarch.

24 See Quint, especially his discussion of Montaigne's critique of stoicism, the inflexible principals of which were in many ways similar to aristocratic and religious zealotry: "His notion of self-mastery, the acknowledgment of one's human weakness, is almost the opposite of the Stoic sage's superhuman self-control; he rejects the Stoics' treatment of the body, their condemnation of pity, above all those moments in Seneca where intransigent virtue appears to be aligned not with yielding but with resistance to power. But his thought retains enough Stoic elements, especially the trade-off he proposes of outward compliance for inner sovereignty, to have affinities with the contemporary neostoicism of Lipsius that, Gerhard Ostreich has argued, was designed for the subject of the new absolutist state" (*Montaigne and the Quality of Mercy* 119–20).

25 Ife cites Quevedo's sonnet in his discussion of the inner voice all readers generate when making sense of the written word (*Reading and Fiction* 64–83). Cortázar, who insists on the active, complicit role of the ideal reader, includes a reference to the dialogue of reading that, in its resigned withdrawal from contemporary affairs, may have appealed to Montaigne in his later years: "Es triste llegar a un momento de la vida en que es más fácil abrir un libro en la página 96 y dialogar con su autor, de café a tumba, de aburrido a suicida, mientras en las mesas de al lado se habla de Argelia, de Adenauer, de Mijanou Bardot, de Guy Trébet, de Sidney Bechet, de

Michel Butor, de Nabokov, de Zao-Wu-Ki, de Louison Bobet, y en mi país los muchachos hablan, ¿de qué hablan los muchachos en mi páis?" ("It is sad to reach a point in life when it is easier to open a book to page 96 and have a dialogue with its author, from café to tomb, from boredom to suicide, while at the adjoining tables they speak of Algiers, of Adenauer, of Mijanou Bardot, of Guy Trébet, of Sidney Bechet, of Michel Butor, of Nabokov, of Zao-Wu-Ki, of Louison Bobet, and in my country the kids talk, What do the kids talk about in my country?" [*Rayuela* ch. 21]).

26 For a brief typology of picaresque narratives, see Weber.

27 Suggestively deploying the deconstructivist notions of "supplement" and "parergon," Baena discusses Rinconete's worn playing cards ("naipes ovados") as an emblem for the social existence of the boys. The cut-away corners, according to such a reading, are the essence of the cards even as they are discarded, just as Rinconete and Cortadillo define the very society from which they are marginalized: "son las esquinas que han sido cortadas a unos naipes hasta que éstos han quedado ovalados: Rincón y Cortado son, literalmente, lo que sobra, la hez, lo que el uso y abuso ha desgastado del cuerpo social" ("it is the corners that have been cut from some cards until they have become oval: Rincón and Cortado are, literally, what is left over, the dregs, what use and abuse have worn away from the social body" [117]). Baena then extends this principle to the entire story collection: "¿No son las *Novelas ejemplares* sin 'marco' otra baraja de naipes ovales, a los que toda esquina, todo margen, les ha sido cercenado?" ("Are not the *Novelas ejemplares* without 'frame' another deck of oval cards, from which any corner, and margin, has been cut?" [122]).

28 Noting the lack of *historia*, the formative life story that propels the narrative logic of picaresque novels, Clamurro comments on the peculiar narrative space of *Rinconete y Cortadillo*: "The prominence of jargon, the verbal distortions, the use of language as a tool of evasion, and the almost theatrical structure – along with the curious disappearance of the putative protagonists – render the question of social order the primary issue. To put it another way, the lack of novelistic conflict and the absence of dominant, well-developed characters prompt the reader to approach the text as both representation and metaphor" (73). For a discussion of theatrical elements in Cervantes's prose works, as well as the *entremés* quality of the above scenes in *Rinconete y Cortadillo*, see Close, "Characterization and Dialogue."

29 For a discussion of personification and play, see Huizinga: "As soon as the effect of a metaphor consists in describing things or events in terms of life and movement, we are on the road to personification" (136). It is also

worth recalling Bergson's description of the inverse process, of a sentient being reduced to an object, as a basic comic principle. A favourite example is Sancho's body tossed in the courtyard inn.

30 "A pesar del porte y la faz de Monipodio, a pesar de los bravos, tenemos la sensación de hallarnos en un mundo infantil, en un juego, en que la puerilidad de los jugadores les impide ver el engaño. Tan inocente es ese mundo, que Rincón y Cortado lo dominan por completo" (Casalduero 89).

31 For the "Lord of Misrule" as an inversion of inaccessible royal majesty, see Barber 24–30. A sinister aspect of the tradition, and the focus of Goethe's poem, is the Erlking's predilection for luring away young children: "Du liebes Kind, komm, geh mit mir! / Gar schöne Spiele spiel ich mit dir" ("My dear child, come, go with me! / Such pretty games I'll play with you," "Erlkönig"). Cervantes's picaresque underworlds in both *Rinconete y Cortadillo* and *La ilustre fregona* include comic variations of this motif.

32 "[P]or lo menos, suena mal a los buenos oídos; y así, torno a decir que es provechoso documento callar la patria, encubrir los padres y mudar los propios nombres" ("[F]or it sounds bad to sensitive ears. And so I repeat that it is a good idea to keep quiet about where you come from, to conceal your parentage, and to change your own name" [212]). Casalduero argued that Monipodio's respect for decorum endows him with an almost moral dignity (88–9). An example of this can be seen in his insistence on secrecy in the cuckolding work that comprises one of the many services of his thieves: "Tampoco se lea … la casa ni adónde: que basta que se les haga el agravio, sin que se diga en público: que es un gran cargo de conciencia. A lo menos, más querría yo clavar cien cuernos y otros tantos sambenitos, como se me pagase mi trabajo, que decillo sola una vez, aunque fuese a la madre que me parió" ("Don't read the name of the house nor where it is … it's bad enough that the injury should be done, without its being published abroad, for it is a great load on one's conscience. At least, I'd rather fix a hundred horns and as many *sambenitos*, provided I'm paid for my work, than mention it once, even to the mother who bore me" [237]). Such sensibilities on the part of Monipodio further suggest a non-subversive aspect of this underworld, which acknowledges the values of the official one.

33 For the traditional demarcations of holiday in Renaissance culture, and the concept of "festive abuse," see Barber, especially 73–8.

34 The final assurance in *La ilustre fregona* that Carriazo's children will not follow *their* father ("sin tomar el estilo de su padre"), underlines the sense of generational connection and atonement. For a discussion of this link, see El Saffar, *Novel to Romance*, ch. 4. It is interesting to consider Carriazo's eventual marriage and creation of a family in light of Anthony Burgess's prefatory comments to his unexpurgated American version of *A Clockwork*

Orange: "Senseless violence is a prerogative of youth, which has much energy but little talent for the constructive. Its dynamism has to find an outlet in smashing telephone kiosks, derailing trains, stealing cars and smashing them and, of course, in the much more satisfactory activity of destroying human beings. There comes a time, however, when violence is seen as juvenile and boring. It is the repartee of the stupid and ignorant. My young hoodlum comes to the revelation of the need to get something done in life – to marry, to beget children ..." (vii).

35 Recalling the "pertinence" I have been stressing with regard to the relationship between the play world and the player's real life, we might also consider Monipodio's ordered play community in light of what Geertz says about a form of Balinese play: "What sets the cockfight apart from the ordinary course of life, lifts it from the realm of everyday practical affairs, and surrounds it with an aura of enlarged performance is not, as functionalist sociology would have it, that it reinforces status discriminations ... but that it provides a metasocial commentary upon the whole matter of assorting human beings into fixed hierarchical ranks and then organizing the major part of collective existence around that assortment. Its function, if you want to call it that, is interpretive: it is a Balinese reading of Balinese experience; a story they tell about themselves" (26).

36 As Wicks points out, the two representational modes are not diametrically opposed: "Romance visions of order are integrated into the picaresque in a way that makes the concept of fictional antitype false. For Guzmán and Simplicissimus, in fact, the narrative vehicle is in tone, stance, and temporal vantage point distinctly romance-like" (*Picaresque Narrative* 50).

37 "En cada una no se limita el arte de ilusionista a los protagonistas y a los sucesos principales. Se extiende a la mayoría de los personajes y a sus actos. Los cuentos forman un tejido de ilusiones juguetones e inocentes. La tropelía resulta ser el modo artístico escogido por Cervantes para expresar novelísticamente la eutrapelia" (Wardropper 165).

38 Adding to the above list Marcela and the "escaped" girl from Sancho's *ronda* (*Don Quijote*), it seems that Cervantes regarded female *mimesis* as a more serious and socially fraught prospect.

39 "[L]a recreación es buena, por lo menos en parte, ya que purifica los humores dañinos engendrados por el ocio. Y, lo que es más importante, Cervantes aplicó esa doctrina como una justificación de la literatura imaginativa sin un obvio contenido doctrinal, incluyendo la prosa de ficción" (Jones 28).

40 "[J]usto porque las prevaricaciones de Barrabás y su vocabulario sustitutivo *degradan* un lenguaje prestigioso y hasta cierto punto elitista, contribuyen también a poner en evidencia la raíz arbitraria de ese lenguaje

culto, es decir, su asentamiento igualmente convencional. Así se dramatiza una pugna (o un cuestionamiento mutuo) de códigos artísticos que reproduce, en pequeña escala, la de todo el texto" (Checa 40).

41 "Asegura el mismo escritor que hubo quien, después de haber perdido su carroza y su tiro de mulas, se jugó al cochero, engañando al que se le ganó, pues le hizo creer falsamente que era esclavo" (Deleito y Piñuela 210).

42 For contemporary objections to women reading imaginative literature, and the understanding that private reading intensified the effects, see Ife 13–23.

43 "La conclusión no es … que mediante la evocación de las almadrabas, el texto postule la mayor 'sinceridad' o 'autenticidad' de las ansias transgresoras latentes en cada individuo; intenta, más bien, reconocer su existencia y mostrar cómo la modalidad del *romance,* en cuanto generalmente las encauza o reprime, suele basar su mensaje tranquilizador en la sublimación de nuestras pasiones más disruptivas" (Checa 36).

Conclusion

1 It is hard to resist citing here Kafka's parable "The Truth about Sancho Panza": "Without making any boast of it Sancho Panza succeeded in the course of years, by feeding him a great number of romances of chivalry and adventure in the evening and night hours, in so diverting from himself his demon, whom he later called Don Quixote, that this demon *thereupon set out*, uninhibited, on the maddest exploits, which, however, for the lack of a preordained object, which should have been Sancho Panza himself, harmed nobody. A free man, Sancho Panza philosophically followed Don Quixote on his crusades, perhaps out of a sense of responsibility, and had of them *a great and edifying entertainment* to the end of his days" (my italics). This is of course an extravagantly modern take on the autonomy of the imagination, and of the sanctuary of play (it "harmed nobody"). But Montaigne's observation – like Cervantes's novel – provides the seeds for such flourishes.

Bibliography

Alcoçer, Francisco de. *Tratado del juego*. Salamanca: 1558 (Biblioteca Nacional, Madrid R/6636).

Alemán, Mateo. *Guzmán de Alfarache*. Edited by Francisco Rico. Barcelona: Planeta, 1980.

Alfonso X. *Antología*. Edited by Antonio G. Solalinde. Madrid: Espasa-Calpe, 1960.

Anonymous. *Cantar de mío Cid*. Translated by Alfonso Reyes. Madrid: Espasa-Calpe, 1976.

– *Poem of the Cid*. Translated by Paul Blackburn. Norman: University of Oklahoma Press, 1998.

Anonymous. *Carmina Burana: Medieval Songs from the Benediktbeuren Manuscript (ca.* 1230*)*. The Boston Camerata. Dir. Joel Cohen. Erato Disques, S.A., 1996.

Anonymous. *Lazarillo de Tormes*. Edited by Francisco Rico. Barcelona: Planeta, 1980.

Anonymous. *Libro de las suertes* (Valencia 1529). Edited by Rosa Navarro Durán. Madrid: CSIC, 1987.

Ansón Calvo, M. Carmen, Nuria González Alonso, and Fernando Manzano Ledesma. "'Un golpe de suerte': las mesas de trucos en el Siglo de las luces." In Núñez Roldán, 713–24.

Apuleius. *The Golden Ass*. Translated by P.G. Walsh. Oxford: Oxford University Press, 1995.

Aquinas, St. Thomas. *Commentary on Aristotle's* Niomachean Ethics. Translated by C.I. Litzinger, O.P. Notre Dame: Dumb Ox Books, 1964.

– *Summa Theologiæ*. Translated and edited by Thomas Gilby, O.P. Cambridge: Blackfriars, 1970.

Ariès, Philippe, and Jean-Claude Margolin, eds. *Les Jeux à la Renaissance*. Paris: Vrin, 1982.

Aristotle. *Poetics*. Translated and edited by Stephen Halliwell. University of North Carolina Press, 1987.

– *Nicomachean Ethics*. Translated and edited by Joe Sachs. Newburyport, MA: Focus Publishing, 2002.

Arlt, Roberto. *El juguete rabioso*. REYSA Ediciones, Argentina.

Atkinson, William. "Cervantes, El Pinciano, and the *Novelas ejemplares*." *Hispanic Review* 16.3 (1948): 189–208.

Auerbach, Erich. *Mimesis*. Translated by Willard R. Trask. Princeton: Princeton University Press, 1953.

Avalle-Arce, J.B., ed. La Galatea *de Cervantes – cuatrocientos años después*. Newark, DE: Juan de la Cuesta, 1985.

Avalle-Arce, J.B., and E.C. Riley, eds. *Suma Cervantina*. London: Tamesis, 1973.

Azorín. *Clásicos y Modernos*. Madrid: Rafael Caro Raggio, 1919.

Baena, Julio, ed. Novelas ejemplares: *las grietas de la ejemplaridad*. Newark, DE: Juan de la Cuesta, 2008.

– "Los naipes de rincone(te)s cortad(ill)os: hacia una lectura marginal de las *Novelas ejemplares*." In Baena, 111–26.

Bakhtin, Mikhail. *Rabelais and His World*. Translated by Hélene Iswolsky. Bloomington: Indiana University Press, 1984.

– *The Dialogic Imagination*. Austin: University of Texas Press, 1986.

Barber, C.L. *Shakespeare's Festive Comedy*. Princeton: Princeton University Press, 1959.

Barnes, Julian. *Flaubert's Parrot*. New York: Vintage, 1990.

– *Nothing to Be Frightened Of*. New York: Vintage, 2008.

Bataillon, Marcel. *Erasmo y España*. Translated by Antonio Alatorre. Ciudad Mexico: Fondo de Cultura Económica, 1950.

– "Relaciones literarias." In Avalle-Arce and Riley, 215–32.

Bergson, Henri. *Laughter: An Essay on the Meaning of the Comic*. Translated by Cloudesley Brereton and Fred Rothwell. New York: MacMillan, 1911.

The Big Lebowski. Directed by Ethan Coen and Joel Coen. Universal City, CA: Universal Studios Home Entertainment, 2008.

Blanco Aguinaga, Carlos. "Cervantes and the Picaresque Mode: Notes on Two Kinds of Realism." In *Cervantes: A Collection of Critical Essays*, edited by Lowry Nelson, Jr., 137–51. New Jersey: Prentice-Hall, 1969.

Boccaccio, Giovanni. *The Decameron*. Translated and edited by Mark Musa and Peter Bondanella. New York: Norton, 1977.

Bloom, Harold. "Cervantes: The Play of the World." In *The Western Canon*, 127–45. New York: Harcourt Brace, 1994.

– *Shakespeare and the Invention of the Human*. New York: Riverhead, 1998.

Borges, Jorge Luis. *Ficciones*. Buenos Aires: Emecé, 1956.

– *Otras Inquisiciones*. 4th ed. Buenos Aires: Emecé, 1989.
– *Evaristo Carriego*. Madrid: Alianza, 1990.
Boyd, Stephen, ed. *A Companion to Cervantes's* Novelas ejemplares. Woodbridge: Tamesis, 2005.
Brée, Germaine, ed. *Camus: A Collection of Critical Essays*. Prentice-Hall, 1962.
Brownlee, Marina S., and Hans Ulrich Gumbrecht, eds. *Cultural Authority in Golden Age Spain*. Baltimore: Johns Hopkins University Press, 1995.
Burgess, Anthony. *A Clockwork Orange*. New York: Norton, 1986.
Burke, Peter. "The Invention of Leisure in Early Modern Europe." *Past & Present* 146 (1995): 136–50.
Burton, Robert. *The Anatomy of Melancholy*. Edited by Holbrook Jackson. New York: NYRB, 2001.
Byrne, Susan. *Law and History in Cervantes'* Don Quixote. Toronto: University of Toronto Press, 2012.
Caillois, Roger. *Man, Play, and Games*. Translated by Meyer Barash. New York: The Free Press of Glencoe, 1961.
Camos, Fr. Marco Antonio de. *Microcosmia y govierno universal del hombre christiano*. Madrid: 1595 (Biblioteca Nacional, Madrid R/26218).
Campo, Agustín del. "Ocios literarios y vida retirada en Rodrigo Caro." In *Studia philologica: Homenaje ofrecido a Dámaso Alonso por sus amigos y discípulos con ocasión de su 60 aniversario*, Vol. 1, 269–75. Madrid: Gredos, 1962.
Camus, Albert. *The Plague*. Translated by Stuart Gilbert. New York: Vintage, 1948.
– *The Myth of Sysiphus and OtherEssays*. New York: Vintage, 1991.
Canavaggio, Jean-François. "Alonso Pinciano y la estética literaria de Cervantes en el *Quijote*." *Anales Cervantinos* 7 (1958): 13–107.
Caro, Rodrigo. *Días geniales o lúdricos*. 2 vols. Madrid: Espasa-Calpe, 1978.
"Carta del virrey conde de Monterrey." Archivo General de Indias, México 23, N.73, 1 (1597).
Casalduero, Joaquín. *Sentido y forma de las "Novelas ejemplares."* Buenos Aires, 1943.
Cascardi, Anthony J., ed. *The Cambridge Companion to Cervantes*. Cambridge: Cambridge University Press, 2002.
– *Cervantes, Literature, and the Discourse of Politics*. Toronto: University of Toronto Press, 2012.
Cassian, John. *The Conferences*. Translated by Boniface Ramsey. New York: Paulist Press, 1997.
Cassirer, Ernst, Paul Oskar Kristeller, and John Herman Randall, Jr, eds. *The Renaissance Philosophy of Man*. Chicago: University of Chicago Press, 1948.
Castiglione, Baldesar. *The Book of the Courtier*. Translated by George Bull. Penguin, 1967.

Castillo, Diego del. *Tratado muy útil y provechoso en reprobación de los juegos*. Valladolid: 1528 (Biblioteca Nacional, Madrid R/3202).

Castillo de Bobadilla, Jerónimo. 1597. *Política de corregidores*. Madrid: Instituto de Estudios de Administración Local, 1978 (Biblioteca Nacional, Madrid).

Castro, Adrian de. *Libro de los daños que resultan del juego*. Granada: 1599 (Biblioteca Nacional, Madrid R/12418).

Castro, Américo. *El pensamiento de Cervantes*. Madrid: Imprenta de la librería y casa editorial Hernando, 1925.

– *Hacia Cervantes*. Madrid: Taurus, 1957.

Castro, Diego de. "Consulta." Archivo General de Simancas, Gracia y justicia, 993–2 (1598).

Catlow, Ruth, Marc Garrett, and Corrado Morgana, eds. *Artists Re:thinking Games*. Liverpool: Liverpool University Press, 2010.

Cavillac, Michel. *Pícaros y mercaderes en el* Guzmán de Alfarache. Granada: Universidad de Granada, 1994.

Cervantes Saavedra, Miguel de. *Exemplary Stories*. Translated by C.A. Jones. Penguin, 1972.

– *El ingenioso hidalgo don Quijote de la Mancha*. Edited by Luis A. Murillo. 5th ed. 2 vols. Madrid: Castalia, 1978.

– *El rufián dichoso* and *Pedro de Urdemalas*. Edited by Nicholas Spadaccini and Jenaro Talens. Madrid: Cátedra, 1986.

– *Entremeses*. Edited by Eugenio Asensio. Madrid: Castalia, 1987.

– *Los baños de Argel*. In *Teatro Completo*. Edited by Florencio Sevilla Arroyo y Antonio Rey Hazas. Barcelona: Planeta, 1987.

– *Novelas ejemplares*. Edited by Harry Sieber. 2 vols. Madrid: Cátedra, 1989.

– *Don Quixote*. Translated by John Rutherford. Penguin, 2003.

– *The Bagnios of Argel* and *The Great Sultana*. Translated by Barbara Fuchs and Aaron Ilika. Philadelphia: University of Pennsylvania Press, 2010.

Checa, Jorge. "El romance y su sombra: hibridación genérica en 'La ilustre fregona'." *Revista de Estudios Hispánicos* 25.1 (1991): 29–48.

Chevalier, Maxime. *Quevedo y su tiempo: la agudeza verbal*. Barcelona: Editorial Crítica, 1992.

Clamurro, William H. *Beneath the Fiction: The Contrary Worlds of Cervantes's* Novelas ejemplares. New York: Peter Lang, 1997.

Close, Anthony. "Characterization and Dialogue in Cervantes's 'Comedias en Prosa.'" *Modern Language Review* 76 (1981): 338–56.

– *Cervantes and the Comic Mind of His Age*. Oxford: Oxford University Press, 2000.

– *A Companion to* Don Quixote. Woodbridge: Tamesis, 2008.

Coleman, Alexander. "The Playful Atoms of Jorge Luis Borges." In Guinness and Hurley, 75–90.

Colie, Rosalie. *Paradoxica Epidemica: The Renaissance Tradition of Paradox.* Princeton: Princeton University Press, 1966.

– *The Resources of Kind: Genre-Theory in the Renaissance.* Edited by Barbara K. Lewalski. Berkeley: University of California Press, 1973.

"Confirmación de provisión sobre juego." Archivo General de Indias, Patronato 276, N.4, R.147, 1 (1530).

Cortázar, Julio. *Rayuela.* Madrid: Alianza, 1987.

Cotarelo y Mori, Emilio, and José Luis Suárez García. *Bibliografía de las controversias sobre la licitud del teatro en España.* Granada: Universidad de Granada, 1997.

Covarrubias, Pedro de. *Remedio de jugadores.* Salamanca: 1543 (Biblioteca Nacional, Madrid R/4033).

Covarrubias Orozco, Sebastián de. 1611. *Tesoro de la Lengua Castellana o Española.* Barcelona: Editorial Alta Fulla, 1989.

Criado de Val, Manuel, ed. *Congreso Internacional sobre la Picaresca.* Madrid: Fundación Universitaria Española, 1979.

De Grazia, Sebastian. *Of Time, Work, and Leisure.* New York: Twentieth Century Fund, 1962.

Defourneaux, Marcelin. *Daily Life in Spain in the Golden Age.* Translated by Newton Branch. Stanford University Press, 1979.

Deleito y Piñuela, José. *La mala vida en España.* Madrid: Alianza, 2008.

Dickens, Charles. *The Pickwick Papers.* London: Vintage, 2009.

"Don Martín de Basurto Alguacil Mayor de la Real Audiencia y Chancillería de la ciudad de Valladolid contra Ambrosio Diez Gascón [...]." Archivo de la Real Chancillería de Valladolid, Pleitos criminales, Caja 281.0005 (1691).

Dostoevsky, Fyodor. *The Gambler.* Translated by Andrew R. MacAndrew. New York: Norton, 1981.

– *The Brothers Karamozov.* Translated by Richard Pevear and Larissa Volokhonsky. New York: Farrar, Strauss and Giroux, 1990.

– *Notes from the Underground.* Translated by Richard Pevear and Larissa Volokhonsky. New York: Vintage, 1994.

Dunn, Peter. "Cervantes De / Re-Constructs the Picaresque." *Cervantes* 2.2 (1982): 109–31.

– *Spanish Picaresque Fiction: A New Literary History.* Ithaca: Cornell University Press, 1993.

– "Shaping Experience: Narrative Strategies in Cervantes." *Modern Language Notes*, 109.2 (1994): 186–203.

Ehrmann, Jacques. "Homo Ludens Revisited." *Yale French Studies* 41 (1968): 31–57.

Eisenberg, Daniel. *A Study of* Don Quixote. Newark, DE: Juan de la Cuesta, 1987.

"Ejecutoria del pleito litigado por Pedro Cobeta, Marcelo Merchante y consortes, vecinos de Auñón (Guadalajara), con Benito Sáenz y los suyos, de la misma vecindad, y el fiscal de Su Majestad, sobre juegos a deshoras." Archivo de la Real Chancillería de Valladolid, Registro de ejecutorias 638.0017 (1794).

"Ejecutoria del pleito litigado por Pedro Díaz de Gurbizta, Juan Ibáñez de Nierga, Diego de Oalasarre y consortes, vecinos de Lezama (Álava), con Juan de Otazu, alguacil de la dicha villa y Gaspar de la Vega." Archivo de la Real Chancillería de Valladolid, Registro de ejecutorias 2217.0022 (1617).

El Saffar, Ruth. *Novel to Romance*. Baltimore: Johns Hopkins University Press, 1974.

Elias, Norbert, and Eric Dunning. *Quest for Excitement: Sport and Leisure in the Civilizing Process*. Oxford: Blackwell, 1986.

Epictetus. *All the Works of Epictetus, which are now extant*. Translated and edited by Elizabeth Carter. London: J. and F. Rivington, 1768.

Erasmus, Desiderius. *The Colloquies*. Translated by Craig R. Thompson. Chicago: University of Chicago Press, 1965.

– *The Praise of Folly and Other Writings*. Edited and translated by Robert M. Adams. New York: Norton, 1989.

Ercilla y Zúñiga, Alonso de. *La Araucana*. Madrid: Castalia, 1978.

Espina, Diego de. "Memorial de Diego de Espina y propuesta sobre juegos." Archivo General de Indias, Filipinas 41, N.53 (1638).

Étienvre, Jean-Pierre. "Paciencia y barajar: Cervantes, los naipes y la burla." In *Actas del Coloquio Cervantino*, edited by Theodor Berchem and Hugo Laitenberger. Würzburg, 1983.

– *Márgenes literarios del juego: una poética del naipe de los siglos XVI–XVII*. London: Tamesis, 1990.

"Expediente sobre los baratos de los juegos de los sangleyes." Archivo General de Indias, Filipinas 22, R.6, N.10, 1 (1654): 1.

Feigenbaum, Gail. "Gamblers, Cheats, and Fortune-Tellers." In *George de La Tour and His World*, edited by Philip Conisbee. Exhibition Catalog and Essays. Washington: National Gallery of Art, 1996.

Finello, Dominick. *Pastoral Themes and Forms in Cervantes's Fiction*. Lewisburg, PA: Bucknell University Press, 1994.

Forcione, Alban K. *Cervantes and the Humanist Vision*. Princeton: Princeton University Press, 1982.

– *Cervantes and the Mystery of Lawlessness*. Princeton: Princeton University Press, 1984.

– "El desposeimiento del ser en la literatura renacentista: Cervantes, Gracián y los desafíos de *Nemo*," *NRFH* 34 (1986): 654–90.

– "Cervantes en busca de una pastoral auténtica." *NRFH* 36 (1988) 2: 1011–43.
– "Exemplarity, Modernity, and the Discriminating Games of Reading." In Nerlich and Spadaccini, 331–52.
– "Cervantes' Night-Errantry: The Deliverance of the Imagination." *BSS* 81.4–5 (2004): 451–73.
– *Majesty and Humanity: Kings and Their Doubles in the Political Drama of the Spanish Golden Age*. New Haven: Yale University Press, 2009.
Freud, Sigmund. *Civilization and Its Discontents*. Edited and translated by James Strachey. New York: Norton, 1961.
– *Wit and Its Relation to the Unconscious*. Translated by A.A. Brill. New York: Dover, 1993.
Friedrich, Hugo. *Montaigne*. Edited by Philippe Desan. Translated by Dawn Eng. Berkeley: University of California Press, 1991.
Frye, Northrop. *Anatomy of Criticism*. Princeton: Princeton University Press, 1957.
– *The Secular Scripture*. Cambrigde: Harvard University Press, 1976.
Fuchs, Barbara. *Passing for Spain*. Urbana: University of Illinois Press, 2003.
Gabrielle, John P. "Competing Narrative Discourses: (FE)Male Fabulation in the Episode of Grisóstomo and Marcela." *Hispanic Review* 71 (2003): 507–23.
Gadamer, Hans-Georg. *Truth and Method*. Translated by Joel Weinsheimer and Donald G. Marshall. 2nd rev. ed. New York: Continuum, 1995.
Gage, Frances. "Exercise for Mind and Body: Giulo Mancini, Collecting, and the Beholding of Landscape Painting in the Seventeenth Century." *Renaissance Quarterly* 61 (2008): 1167–207.
García Canalejas, Juan. *Libro del juego de las damas*. 1650 (Biblioteca Nacional, Madrid/R462).
García Santo-Tomás, Enrique. "Outside Bets: Disciplining Gamblers in Early Modern Spain." *Hispanic Review* 77.1 (2009): 147–64.
Gaylord, Mary Malcolm. "Cervantes' Other Fiction." In Cascardi, *Cambridge Companion to Cervantes*, 100–30.
Geertz, Clifford. "Deep Play: Notes on the Balinese Cockfight." *Daedalus* 101.1 (1972): 1–37.
Gerli, Michael E. "La picaresca y *El licenciado vidriera*: género y contragénero en Cervantes." In Criado de Val, 577–87.
Giginta, Miguel. *Remedio de pobres*. Madrid: 1579 (Biblioteca Nacional, Madrid R/11590).
Giamatti, A. Bartlett. *Take Time for Paradise: Americans and Their Games*. New York: Summit, 1989.
Gill, R.B. "Why Comedy Laughs: The Shape of Laughter and Comedy." *Literary Imagination* 8.2 (2006): 233–50.

Gilman, Stephen. *Cervantes y Avellaneda: estudio de una imitación*. México: Colegio de México, 1951.

Girard, René. *Violence and the Sacred*. Translated by Patrick Gregory. Baltimore: Johns Hopkins University Press, 1977.

Goethe, Johann Wolfgang von. *Gesammelte Gedichte*. Geneva: Lechner Verlag, 1993.

Gómez Canseco, Luis, and Zenón Luis-Martínez, eds. *Entre Cervantes y Shakespeare: sendas del renacimiento*. Newark, DE: Juan de la Cuesta, 2006.

Goncharov, Ivan. *Oblomov*. Translated by Stephen Pearl. New York: Bunim & Bannigan, 2006.

Góngora, Luis de. *Sonetos completes*. Madrid: Castalia, 1985.

Gracián, Baltasar. *Agudeza y Arte de ingenio*. Ed. Evaristo Correa Calderón. Madrid: Castalia, 1987.

– *El Criticón*. Ed. Santos Alonso. Madrid: Cátedra, 1990.

– *El Héroe. El Discreto. Oráculo manual y arte de prudencia*. Ed. Luys Santa Marina. Barcelona: Planeta, 1990.

Grandbois, Peter. "Lost in the Details: Translating Master Peter's Puppet Show." *Cervantes* 27.2 (2007 [2008]): 59–79.

Green, Otis. "*El Licenciado Vidriera*: Its Relation to the *Viaje del Parnaso* and the *Examen de ingenios* of Huarte." In *Linguistic and Literary Studies in Honor of Helmut A. Hatzfeld*. Washington: Catholic U of America Press, 1964.

– *Spain and the Western Tradition*. Vol. II. Madison: University of Wisconsin Press, 1968.

Greenblatt, Stephen. *Renaissance Self-Fashioning: From More to Shakespeare*. Chicago: University of Chicago Press, 1980.

– *The Swerve: How the World Became Modern*. New York: Norton, 2011.

Greer, Margaret R. "Diana, Venus and Borrowed Dogs: On Hunting in *Don Quixote*." In *Cervantes y su mundo* (III), edited by Robert A. Lauer and Kurt Reichenberger, 201–22. Kassel, Germany: Reichenberger, 2005.

Guillén, Claudio. *Literature as System*. Princeton: Princeton University Press, 1971.

Guinness, Gerald, and Andrew Hurley, eds. *Auctor Ludens: Essays on Play and Literature*. Philadelphia: John Benjamins, 1986.

Guzmán, Pedro de. *Bienes del honesto trabajo y daños de la ociosidad*. Madrid: 1614 (Biblioteca Nacional, Madrid R/7707).

Haley, George. "The Narrator in *Don Quijote*: Maese Pedro's Puppet Show." *Modern Language Notes* 80.2 (1965): 145–65.

Hampton, Timothy. *Writing from History: The Rhetoric of Exemplarity in Renaissance Literature*. Ithaca: Cornell University Press, 1990.

Hardy, Thomas. *Selected Poems*. Edited by Robert Mezey. New York: Penguin, 1998.

Hart, Thomas R. "Versions of Pastoral in Three *Novelas ejemplares*." *Bulletin of Hispanic Studies* 58 (1981): 283–91.
Hawthorne, Nathaniel. *Hawthorne's Short Stories*. New York: Vintage, 1946.
Hildebrand, William H. "Bartleby and the Black Conceit." *Studies in Romanticism* 27. 2 (1988): 289–313.
Homer. *The Odyssey*. Translated by Robert Fagles. New York: Penguin, 1996.
Horace. *Satires, Epistles and Ars Poetica*. Translated by H. Rushton Fairclough. Cambridge: Harvard University Press, 1926.
Huarte de San Juan, Juan. *Examen de ingenios para las ciencias*. Madrid: Cátedra, 1989.
Huizinga, Johan. *Homo Ludens*. Boston: Beacon, 1950.
Humanist Educational Treatises. Translated by Craig. W. Kallendorf. Cambridge: Harvard University Press, 2008.
Ife, B.W. *Reading and Fiction in Golden-Age Spain: A Platonist Critique and Some Picaresque Replies*. Cambridge: Cambridge University Press, 1985.
Iffland, James. *De fiestas y aguafiestas: risa, locura e ideología en Cervantes y Avellaneda*. Madrid: Iberoamericana, 1999.
– "Laughter Tamed." Rev. of *Cervantes and the Comic Mind of His Age*, by Anthony Close. *Cervantes* 23.2 (2003): 395–435.
Ihrie, Maureen. *Skepticism in Cervantes*. London: Tamesis, 1982.
Ireson, Nancy, and Barnaby Wright, eds. *Cézanne's Card Players* (Exhibition Catalog and Essays). London: Paul Holberton Publishing, 2010. (The Courtauld Gallery, 2010).
Irureta-Goyena, Pilar, ed. *El juego en el libro antiguo: Exposición bibliográfica*. Madrid: Universidad Politécnica de Madrid, 2000.
Jolles, André. "Die literarischen Travestien: Ritter-Hirt-Schelm." In *Pikarische Welt: Schriften zum europäischen Schelmroman*, edited by Helmut Heidenreich, 101–18. Darmstadt: Wissenschaftliche Buchgesellschaft, 1969.
Jones, Joseph R. "Cervantes y la virtud de la *Eutrapelia*: la moralidad de la literatura de esparcimiento." *Anales Cervantinos* 23 (1985): 19–30.
Joubert, Laurent. *Treatise on Laughter*. Translated by Gregory David de Rocher. University of Alabama Press, 1980.
Jovellanos, Gaspar Melchor de. "Elogio a Carlos III." In *Obras en prosa*. Madrid: Castalia, 1969.
– *Espectáculos y diversiones públicas*. Madrid: Cátedra, 1998.
Jung, C.G. *The Archetypes and the Collective Unconscious*. Translated by R.F.C. Hull. Bollingen Series 20. Princeton: Princeton University Press, 1969.
Kafka, Franz. *The Complete Stories*. New York: Schocken, 1971.
Kaiser, Matthew. *The World in Play: Portraits of a Victorian Concept*. Redwood City, CA: Stanford University Press, 2012.
Karrer, Wolfgang. *Parodie, Travestie, Pastiche*. Munich: W. Fink, 1977.

Karshan, Thomas. *Vladimir Nabokov and the Art of Play*. Oxford: Oxford University Press, 2011.

Klibansky, Raymond, Erwin Panofsky, and Fritz Saxl. *Saturn and Melancholy*. London: Thomas Nelson and Sons, 1964.

Kristeller, Paul Oskar. *Renaissance Thought*. New York: Harper & Row, 1961.

Kundera, Milan. *The Curtain*. Translated by Linda Asher. New York: Harper Collins, 2005.

Ledesma, Alonso de. *Juegos de Noche Buena*. Madrid: 1611 (Biblioteca Nacional, Madrid R/31282).

Levitt, Steven D., Thomas J. Miles, and Andrew M. Rosenfield. "Is Texas Hold 'Em a Game of Chance? A Legal and Economic Analysis." *Georgetown Law Journal* 101 (2012–2013): 581–636.

López de Sosoaga López de Robles, Alfredo. *El juego: análisis y revisión bibliográfica*. Universidad del País Vasco, 2004.

López de Ubeda, Francisco. *La pícara Justina*. Edited by Antonio Rey Hazas. Madrid: Editora Nacional, 1977.

López Pinciano, Alonso. *Philosophía antigua poética*. *Obras completas*, I. Edited by José Rico Verdú. Madrid: Biblioteca Castro, 1998.

"Lorenzo Aguayo, licenciado, Corregidor de la villa de Villalpando y su tierra por el Condestable de Castilla contra Diego Flórez, Alguacil carcelero […]." Archivo de la Real Chancillería de Valladolid, Pleitos Criminales. Caja 0246.0002, 1564.

Lucian. *Six Dialogues*. Translated by Sidney T. Irwin. London: Methuen & Co., 1894.

– *Dialogues of the Dead*. Translated by M.D. Macleod. Cambridge: Harvard University Press, 1961.

Lucretius, *The Nature of the Universe*. Translated by Ronald Latham. Middlesex: Penguin, 1951.

Luna, Juan de. *Segunda Parte de la Vida de Lazarillo de Tormes*. In Anónimo y Juan de Luna, *Segunda Parte del Lazarillo*, edited by Pedro M. Piñero. Madrid: Cátedra, 1988.

Luque Faxardo, Francisco de. 1603. *Fiel desengaño contra la ociosidad y el juego*. Edited by M. de Riquer. Madrid: Real Academia Española, 1955.

Lyons, John D. *Exemplum: The Rhetoric of Exemplarity in Early Modern France and Italy*. Princeton: Princeton University Press, 1989.

Machiavelli, Niccolò. *The Letters of Machiavelli*. Translated and edited by Allan Gilbert. Chicago: University of Chicago Press, 1961.

– *Discourses on Livy*. Translated by Harvey C. Mansfield and Nathan Tarcov. Chicago: University of Chicago Press, 1996.

Mann, Thomas. "Voyage With Don Quixote." 1934. In *Essays by Thomas Mann*, 325–69, trans. H.T. Lowe-Porter. New York: Vintage, 1957.
– *Confessions of Felix Krull*. Translated by Denver Lindley. New York: Vintage, 1969.
– *Death in Venice and Seven Other Stories*. New York: Vintage, 1989.
Manuel, Juan. *El conde Lucanor*. Madrid: Castalia, 1969.
Marantz Henig, Robin. "Taking Play Seriously." *The New York Times Magazine*, 17 February 2008: 38+.
Maravall, José Antonio. *La cultura del Barroco*. Barcelona: Ariel, 1975.
– *Utopia y contrautopia en el* Quijote. Santiago de Compostela: Pico Sacro, 1976.
– *Culture of the Baroque*. Translated by Terry Cochran. Minneapolis: University of MN Press, 1986.
Mariana, Padre Juan de. *Tratado contra los juegos públicos*. *BAE* 31.2 (1854): 413–62.
Martín, Adrienne. "Humor and Violence in Cervantes." In Cascardi, *Cambridge Companion to Cervantes*, 160–85.
Martínez-Bonati, Félix. Don Quixote *and the Poetics of the Novel*. Ithaca: Cornell University Press, 1992.
Martínez Mata, Emilio. *Cervantes comenta el* Quijote. Madrid: Cátedra, 2008.
Mazzotta, Giuseppe. *The World at Play in Boccaccio's* Decameron. Princeton: Princeton University Press, 1986.
McClure, George W. "Women and the Politics of Play in Sixteenth-Century Italy: Torquato Tasso's Theory of Games." *Renaissance Quarterly* 61 (2008): 750–91.
Melville, Herman. *Billy Budd, Sailor and Other Stories*. New York: Bantam, 1984.
Méndez, Cristóbal. *Libro del ejercicio corporal y de sus provechos*. 1553. Madrid: Consejería de educación, 2002.
Mendoza, Antonio de, virrey de México. "Pohibición juego de naipes." Archivo General de Indias, Patronato 180, R.76 (1539).
Mexía, Luis. *Apólogo de la ociosidad y del trabajo*. Alcalá: 1546 (Biblioteca Nacional, Madrid R/3970).
Milton, John. *Paradise Lost*. New York: Macmillan, 1985.
Molho, Mauricio. *Cervantes: raíces folklóricas*. Madrid: Gredos, 1976.
Montaigne, Michel de. *The Complete Essays*. Translated by Donald Frame. Stanford University Press, 1958.
Nabokov, Vladimir. *The Annotated Lolita*. Edited by Alfred Appel, Jr. New York: Vintage, 1991.
– *Pnin*. New York: Vintage, 1989.
– *Lectures on* Don Quixote. Edited Fredson Bowers. New York: Harvest, 1983.
Nerlich, Michael, and Nicholas Spadaccini, eds. *Cervantes's "Exemplary Novels" and the Adventure of Writing*. Minneapolis: Prisma Institute, 1989.

Núñez Roldán, Francisco, ed. *Ocio y vida cotidiana en el mundo hispánico en la edad moderna*. Seville: Secretariado de publicaciones de la Universidad de Sevilla, 2007.

Olson, Glending. *Literature as Recreation in the Later Middle Ages*. Ithaca: Cornell University Press, 1982.

Ortega y Gasset, José. "El origen deportivo del estado." *Obras*. Madrid: Espasa Calpe, 1932.

Papargyriou, Eleni. *Reading Games in the Greek Novel*. Oxford: Legenda, 2011.

Parr, James. *Don Quixote, Don Juan, and Related Subjects*. Selinsgrove: Susquehanna University Press, 2004.

Pascal, Blaise. *Pensées and Other Writings*. Translated by Honor Levi. Oxford World's Classics, 2008.

Pérez de Herrera, Cristóbal. "Discurso a Felipe II para Reforma de los Toros." (Biblioteca Nacional, Madrid R/100950/9).

"Petición del procurador Villatoro sobre prohibir los juegos." Archivo General de Indias, Filipinas 28, N.122 (1678).

Peyre, Henri. "Camus the Pagan." In Brée, 65–70.

Pieper, Josef. *Leisure, the Basis of Culture*. Translated by Gerald Malsbary. St Augustine's Press, 1998.

Pinedo, Luis de. *Libro de chistes*. Edited by Antonio Paz y Melia and Ramon Paz. *BAE* 176 (1964): 97–118.

Pirandello, Luigi. *On Humor*. Chapell Hill: University of North Carolina Press, 1974.

Plato. *The Collected Dialogues*. Edited by Edith Hamilton and Huntington Cairns. Princeton: Princeton University Press, 1989.

– *The Republic*. Translated by Benjamin Jowett. New York: Vintage Classics, 1991.

"Pleito de Alfonso María Brasa, abogado de los reales consejos, vecino de Frómista (Palencia), contra Antonio Herrera y Velarde, abogado de la Real Chancillería de Valladolid y alcalde mayor de Frómista (Palencia), por permitir juegos prohibidos en la plaza pública de dicha villa durante las fiestas." Archivo de la Real Chancillería de Valladolid, Pleitos criminales 1887.00133 (1752).

Poggioli, Renato. *The Oaten Flute: Essays on Pastoral Poetry and the Pastoral Ideal*. Cambridge: Harvard University Press, 1975.

Poppi, Antonino. "Fate, fortune, providence and human freedom." In *The Cambridge History of Renaissance Philosophy*, edited by Charles B. Schmitt, Quentin Skinner, Eckhard Kessler, and Jill Kraye. Cambridge: Cambridge University Press, 1988.

Presberg, Charles D. *Adventures in Paradox:* Don Quixote *and the Western Tradition*. University Park: Pennsylvania State University Press, 2001.

"Prohibición juego de naipes y dardos a las mujeres: México." Archivo General de Indias, Patronato 183, N.1, R.7, 1 (1583).

Quevedo, Francisco de. *La vida del buscón*. Barcelona: Planeta, 1982.

– *Poesía original complete*. Edited by José Manuel Blecua. Barcelona: Planeta, 1999.

Quint, David. *Montaigne and the Quality of Mercy*. Princeton, NJ: Princeton University Press, 1998.

– *Cervantes's Novel of Modern Times*. Princeton, NJ: Princeton University Press, 2003.

Rahner, Hugo. *Man at Play*. Translated by Brian Battershaw and Edward Quinn. New York: Herder and Herder, 1967.

"Real Cédula a la Audiencia de Guadalajara para que provea lo que convenga acerda de la pretensión del hospital de la ciudad de Zacatecas que pide se le dé confirmación de la merced que le hizo audiencia del juego de argolla o barras." Archivo General de Indias, Indiferente 450, L.A7, 1 (1622): 48–9.

"Real Cédula a los generales de las flotas no apremien a los dueños de naos que van a su cargo para que en los puertos donde desembarcan hagan fiestas, de juegos de cañas y otros bajo las penas aquí contenidos." Archivo General de Indias, Indiferente 1953, L.5 (1607): 336–336V.

"Real Cédula a los oficiales de la Casa de Contratación." Archivo General de Indias, Indiferente 1962, L.5, 1 (1538): 665–6.

Rebhorn, Wayne A. *Courtly Performances*. Detroit: Wayne State University Press, 1978.

Redondo, Augustin. *Otra manera de leer el Quijote*. Madrid: Castalia, 1997.

– "En torno a dos personajes festivos: el shakesperiano Falstaff y el cervantino Sancho Panza." In Gómez Canseco and Luis-Martínez, 161–82.

Reed, Corey. "Ludic Revelations in the Enchanted Head Episode in *Don Quijote* (II, 62)." *Cervantes* 14.1 (2004): 189–216.

Remon, Alonso. *Entretenimientos y juegos honestos, y recreaciones christianas*. 1623 (Biblioteca Nacional, Madrid R/1028).

Renson, Roland. "Le Jeu chez Juan Luis Vivès." In Ariès and Margolin, 469–87.

"Respuesta al governador de Filipinas con Razon de los juegos de los chinos." Archivo General de Indias, Filipinas 21, R.12, 1 (1638).

Reyes, Gaspar de los. *Tesoro de concetos divinos compuesto en todo género de verso*. Sevilla: 1613 (Biblioteca Nacional, Madrid R/11542).

Rico García, José Manuel. "Los romances del 'Tesoro de concetos divinos' (Sevilla, 1613) de Fray Gaspar de los Reyes." *Edad de Oro* 32 (2013): 351–78.

Rigolot, François. "Les Jeux de Montaigne." In Ariès and Margolin.

– "Problematizing Renaissance Exemplarity: The Inward Turn of Dialogue from Petrarch to Montaigne." In Vallée and Heitsch, 3–24.

Riley, E.C. "Cervantes and the Cynics (*El licenciado Vidriera* and *El coloquio de los perros*)." *Bulletin of Hispanic Studies* 53 (1976): 189–99.

Ritter, Joachim. "Über das Lachen." In *Subjektivität: Sechs Aufsätze*. Frankfurt am Main: Suhrkamp, 1974.

Rivers, Elias. "Pastoral, Feminism and Dialogue in Cervantes." In Avalle-Arce, *La Galatea*, 7–15.

Rojas, Fernando de. *La Celestina*. Madrid: Alianza, 1993.

Rosales, Luis. *Cervantes y la libertad*. 2nd ed. 2 vols. Madrid: Ediciones cultura hispánica, 1985.

Rufo, Juan. 1596. *Las seiscientas apotegmas y otras obras en verso*. Edited by Alberto Blecua. Madrid: Espasa Calpe, 1972.

San Pedro, Diego de. *Cárcel de amor*. Edited by Keith Whinnom. Madrid: Castalia, 1985.

Sánchez de la Plata, Juan. *Historia general del hombre en que se trata del hombre en común*. Madrid: 1598 (Biblioteca Nacional, Madrid R/6442).

Sánchez Herrero, José. *La Diócesis del Reino de León*: Siglos XIV y XV. León: Centro de Estudios e Investigación "San Isidoro," 1978.

Sanz Hermida, Jacobo. "Entretenimiento en la corte de Isabel de Castilla: el *Juego trobado* de Gerónimo de Pinar." In *Nunca fue pena mayor (Estudios de literatura española en homenaje a Brian Dutton)*, edited by Ana Méndez Collera and Victorino Romero López, 605–14. Cuenca: Ed. De la Universidad de Castilla-La Mancha, 1996.

Scham, Michael. "Concepts of Play in Literature of Golden Age Spain." *Hispanófila* 135 (2002): 41–59.

– "*Don Quijote* and *Lolita* Revisited." *Cervantes* 26.1–2 (2006 [2008]): 79–101.

– "*Don Quijote* and the Art of Laughing at Oneself." *Cervantes* 29.1 (2009): 31–55.

– "Dialogue and Exemplarity in Montaigne and Cervantes." *Transitions: Journal of Franco-Iberian Studies* 5 (Fall 2009): 57–78.

Schiller, Friedrich. *Letters on the Aesthetic Education of Man*. Translated by Elizabeth M. Wilkinson and L.A. Willoughby. Hinderer and Dahlstrom, 86–178.

Schmidt, Rachel. *Forms of Modernity*. Don Quixote *and Modern Theories of the Novel*. Toronto: University of Toronto Press, 2011.

Seneca. *Dialogues and Essays*. Oxford World's Classics, 2008.

Shakespeare, William. *King Lear*. New York: Signet, 1987.

– *The Merchant of Venice*. The Folger Shakespeare Library, 1992.

– *Measure for Measure*. The Folger Shakespeare Library, 1997.

– *The Merry Wives of Windsor*. Cambridge: Cambridge University Press, 2009.
Sieber, Harry. "Literary Continuity, Social Order, and the Invention of the Picaresque." In Brownlee and Gumbrecht, 143–64.
Sidney, Philip. *An Apology for Poetry*. 1595. New York: Macmillan, 1970.
Simmel, Georg. "The Adventure." In *Essays on Sociology, Philosophy and Aesthetics*, edited by K.H. Wolff. New York: Harper and Row, 1965.
Spadaccini, Nicholas. "Writing for Reading: Cervantes's Aesthetics of Reception in the *Entremeses*." In *Critical Essays on Cervantes*, edited by Ruth El Saffar, 162–75. Boston: Hall, 1986.
Spariosu, Mihai. *Literature, Mimesis, and Play*. Tübingen: G. Narr, 1982.
– *Dionysus Reborn*. Ithaca: Cornell University Press, 1989.
– *The Wreath of Wild Olive*. Albany: SUNY, 1997.
Spinoza, Benedict de. *Writings on Political Philosophy*. Edited by A.G.A. Balz. New York: D. Appleton Century Company, 1937.
Spitzer, Leo. "Linguistic Perspectivism in the Don Quijote." In *Representative Essays*, edited by A. Forcione, H. Lindberger, and M. Sutherland. Stanford: Stanford University Press, 1988.
Suárez de Figueroa, Cristóbal. *Plaza universal de todas ciencias y artes*. Madrid: 1615 (Biblioteca Nacional, Madrid R/3581).
Surman, David. "Everyday Hacks: Why Cheating Matters." In Catlow et al., 74–7.
Teja, Ángela. "El juego cortés en un diálogo de Tasso (1582)." In Irureta-Goyena, 67–76.
Tetel, Marcel. "The Humanistic Situation: Montaigne and Castiglione." *Sixteenth Century Journal* 10.3 (Autumn 1979): 69–84.
Thompson, Colin. "*Eutrapelia* and Exemplarity in the *Novelas ejemplares*." In Boyd, 261–82.
Tolstoy, Leo. *Anna Karenina*. Translated by Richard Pevear and Larissa Volokhonsky. New York: Penguin, 2002.
Torrente Ballester, Gonzalo. *El* Quijote *como juego y otros trabajos críticos*. Barcelona: Destino, 1984.
Tovar, Antonio, and Miguel de la Pinta Llorente, eds. *Procesos inquisitoriales contra Francisco Sánchez de las Brozas*. Madrid: CSIC, 1941.
Trueblood, Alan. "La risa en el *Quijote* y la risa de don Quijote." *Cervantes* 4 (1984): 3–23.
Turner, Victor. *From Ritual to Theare: The Human Seriousness of Play*. New York: PAG Publications, 1982.
Unamuno, Miguel de. *Amor y pedagogía*. Madrid: Alianza, 1989.
Valdés, Juan de. *Diálogo de la lengua* . Ed. Cristina Barbolani. Madrid: Cátedra, 2006.

Valle-Inclán, Ramón del. *Luces de Bohemia*. Madrid: Espasa Calpe, 2007.

Vallée, Jean-François, and Dorotea Heitsch. *Printed Voices: The Renaissance Culture of Dialogue*. Toronto: University of Toronto Press, 2004.

Vega de Carpio, Lope de. *El Villano en su rincón*. Madrid: Espasa Calpe, 1967.

Vives, Juan Luis. *Diálogos*. Buenos Aires: Espasa-Calpe, 1940.

– *Obras completas*. Translated by Lorenzo Riber. 2 vols. Madrid: Aguilar, 1948.

– *A Fable about Man*. In Cassirer et al., 387–93.

Voltaire. *Candide*. New York: Penguin, 2005.

Wardropper, Bruce. "La eutrapelia en las *Novelas ejemplares* de Cervantes." *Actas del Séptimo Congreso de la Asociación Internacional de Hispanistas* (1980): 153–69.

Weber, Alison. "Cuatro clases de narrativa picaresca." In Criado de Val, 13–18.

Welsh, Alexander. "The Influence of Cervantes." In Cascardi, *Cambridge Companion to Cervantes*, 80–99.

Whicher, George F., trans. and ed. *The Goliard Poets*. Norfolk, Conn.: New Directions, 1949.

Wicks, Ulrich. "The Nature of Picaresque Narrative: A Modal Approach." *PMLA* 89 (1974): 240–9.

– *Picaresque Narrative, Picaresque Fictions*. Westport, CT: Greenwood Press, 1989.

Wilson, Andrew R. *Ambition and Identity: Chinese Merchant Elites in Colonial Manila*, 1880–1916. Honolulu: University of Hawaii Press, 2004.

Wind, Edgar. *Pagan Mysteries in the Renaissance*. New York: Norton, 1968.

Wood, James. *The Irresponsible Self: On Laughter and the Novel*. New York: Picador, 2005.

– "Why? The Fictions of Life and Death." *The New Yorker*, 9 December 2013, 34–9.

Wood, Michael. "Invisible Works: Cervantes Reads Borges and Nabokov." In *Cervantes and the Modernists*, edited by Edwin Williamson. London: Tamesis, 1994.

Yovanovich, Gordana. *Play and the Picaresque: Lazarillo De Tormes, Libro De Manuel, and Match Ball*. Toronto: University of Toronto Press, 1999.

Zabaleta, Juan de. 1654. *El día de la fiesta por la mañana y por la tarde*. Edited by C. Cuevas García. Madrid: Castalia, 1983.

Zola, Émile. *The Earth*. Translated by Ann Lindsay. London: Elek Books, 1954.

Index

TORONTO IBERIC

Co-editors: Robert Davidson (Toronto) and Frederick A. de Armas (Chicago)
Editorial board: Josiah Blackmore (Toronto); Marina Brownlee (Princeton); Anthony J. Cascardi (Berkeley); Emily Francomano (Georgetown); Justin Crumbaugh (Mt Holyoke); Jordana Mendelson (NYU); Joan Ramon Resina (Stanford); Kathleen Vernon (SUNY Stony Brook)

1 Anthony J. Cascardi, *Cervantes, Literature, and the Discourse of Politics*
2 Jessica A. Boon, *The Mystical Science of the Soul: Medieval Cognition in Bernardino de Laredo's Recollection Method*
3 Susan Byrne, *Law and History in Cervantes' Don Quixote*
4 Mary E. Barnard and Frederick A. de Armas (eds), *Objects of Culture in the Literature of Imperial Spain*
5 Nil Santiáñez, *Topographies of Fascism: Habitus, Space, and Writing in Twentieth-Century Spain*
6 Nelson Orringer, *Lorca in Tune with Falla: Literary and Musical Interludes*
7 Ana M. Gómez-Bravo, *Textual Agency: Writing Culture and Social Networks in Fifteenth-Century Spain*
8 Javier Irigoyen-García, *The Spanish Arcadia: Sheep Herding, Pastoral Discourse, and Ethnicity in Early Modern Spain*
9 Stephanie Sieburth, *Survival Songs: Conchita Piquer's* Coplas *and Franco's Regime of Terror*
10 Christine Arkinstall, *Spanish Female Writers and the Freethinking Press, 1879–1926*
11 Margaret Boyle, *Unruly Women: Performance, Penitence, and Punishment in Early Modern Spain*
12 Evelina Gužauskytė, *Christopher Columbus's Naming in the* diarios *of the Four Voyages (1492–1504): A Discourse of Negotiation*

www.ingramcontent.com/pod-product-compliance
Lightning Source LLC
LaVergne TN
LVHW090147080826
844660LV00013B/700/J

* 9 7 8 1 4 4 2 6 4 8 6 4 7 *